A
HISTORY
OF
MODERN
SERBIA
1804-1918

II

Michael Boro Petrovich

A
HISTORY
OF
MODERN
SERBIA
1804-1918

Volume II

HARCOURT BRACE JOVANOVICH

NEW YORK AND LONDON

Library of Congress Cataloging in Publication Data

Petrovich, Michael Boro.
A history of modern Serbia, 1804–1918.

Bibliography: v. 2, p.
Includes index.
1. Serbia—History—1804–1918.   I. Title.
DR341.P44   949.7′1′01   76–13227
ISBN 0–15–140950–1

First edition

B C D E

Contents

II

Illustrations

A
HISTORY
OF
MODERN
SERBIA
1804-1918

II

VII

From Vassalage
to Independence,
1868-1878

Following Prince Michael's assassination in Topčider Park, Serbia was ruled for the next two decades by another Obrenović, Milan, the grandson of Prince Miloš's brother Jevrem. Looking at the beginning and the end of those two decades and eight months, the observer has a sense of *déjà vu*. In 1868 and again in 1889 a thirteen-year-old boy, an Obrenović, comes to the throne, a schoolboy in the hands of regents. One of the regents is even the same in both cases. The two decades begin with a new constitution, that of 1869, and end with another constitution, that of 1888. Milan's reign echoes Michael's before him by offering another crisis over a royal divorce, just as Milan's successor will cause a similar crisis over his marriage. Meanwhile, internal political developments revolve about many of the same issues, and foreign policy continues to depend on the Great Powers. It is all too easy to gain the impression that the more things changed, the more they were the same.

Yet the two decades saw enormous changes. Politically, a considerably enlarged Serbian principality gained its complete independence from the Ottoman Empire and, in 1882, proclaimed itself a kingdom. Economically, Serbia definitely emerged as a modern capitalist state, because of the rapid development of its trade. In the world of ideas, Serbian society abandoned its Romantic nationalism to fall more into step with the realism and positivism of the rest of Europe. Even the idea of socialism came to this small agrarian country which, though still largely peasant, had long since lost the homogeneity of a patriarchal folk society and assumed the sharper conflicts of a modern class society.

The Regency, 1868–1872

Immediately after Michael's murder, there was organized, by law, a provisional regency. It consisted of three persons: the president of the State Council, Jovan Marinović; the minister of justice, Rajko Lešjanin; and the presiding judge of the court of appeals, Djordje Petrović. They did not take it upon themselves to proclaim Michael's successor, for the law of succession, promulgated in 1859, specified that the succession was to go to the direct male heirs of Prince Miloš and, failing any, to the male heirs in the lateral line, that is, the heirs of Miloš's brothers Jevrem and Jovan. According to this law, Milan was next in line. Yet there was confusion over the whole matter. One source of the confusion was that the "Turkish" Constitution of 1838 referred only to Miloš's direct heirs and not to his brothers. Thus the sultan, as suzerain, could claim a right to intervene once Miloš's direct male descendants had died out. Another source of confusion was the role of the Great Assembly; after all, such assemblies had elected both Alexander Karadjordjević and Michael Obrenović. Was it not the right of the Assembly to elect anyone whom it chose, under the circumstances, and to present that candidate for the sultan's approval?

Milivoje Petrović Blaznavac, the minister of war, ended the confusion and advanced his own political fortunes by carrying out a military coup on the night of June 9–10, 1868, and getting the army to accept young Milan as prince. Blaznavac's political rival, Ilija Garašanin, and his cohorts, as well as the Provisional Regency and the future Assembly, not to speak of the Porte itself, were all presented with a *fait accompli* which no one had any great reason or force to oppose. Blaznavac became the strong man of the hour. When the Assembly met in Topčider on July 2, 1868, surrounded by his troops, it dutifully acclaimed Milan Obrenović IV (that is, the fourth Obrenović to rule Serbia) as prince. The new prince had already arrived in Belgrade from Paris on June 23 to await his election.

Milan Obrenović was born in Walachia in 1854. His father was Miloš Obrenović, the son of Prince Miloš's brother Jevrem. His mother was of the Romanian nobility, the great beauty Maria Catargiu. She left her husband soon after Milan's birth, unable to tolerate his dissipa-

tion. He had even pawned her jewels to be able to afford his paramours. He died young, in 1860, leaving behind debts which his son
would some day have to pay. Meanwhile Maria openly became the
mistress of Prince Alexander Cuza, the first ruler of the United Prin-
cipalities of Walachia and Moldavia, who, in turn, treated his own
wife, the popular "Domnea Elena," with scandalous disregard. Maria
Obrenović also had to endure rivals, but she found the liaison to her
advantage. Thus young Milan, who was taken by his mother after his
father's death, grew up in the shadow of one of the most corrupt courts
of Europe. Quite rightly assuming that Maria was incapable of giving
her son a decent upbringing, Prince Michael had the boy taken from
his willing mother at the age of nine and sent to Paris for an education.
His French tutor, Huet, a former professor at the University of Ghent,
gave this neglected, spoiled, ignorant, and nervous child a chance to
develop whatever good there was in him. Milan even became a fairly
successful pupil at the Lycée Louis le Grand, but his education was
interrupted by Prince Michael's assassination when the boy was thirteen. When he came to Belgrade, it was in the company of Huet, perhaps the only person he ever respected.

Because Milan was a minor, the Great Assembly named a regency
of three to take over until he reached his maturity, that is, the age of
eighteen. The triumvirate consisted of Blaznavac, Jovan Ristić, and
Jovan Gavrilović. Blaznavac represented the conservative views of the
most prosperous merchants and landowners, high officialdom, and the
military, while Ristić represented the liberal views of the majority of
merchants, the professional classes, some of the intelligentsia, and most
of the civil servants. Though Blaznavac was close to the military, he
espoused a far more cautious foreign policy than Ristić and the more
bellicose Liberals. As for Gavrilović, though a member of the State
Council, he was by then a politically harmless old man, a relic of Prince
Miloš's time, who had greater ambitions for Serbia's progress than for
himself.

The Great Assembly of 1868 made know its desires in a document
of seventeen points which was clearly the work of the coalition between the Obrenović party of the countryside and the urban Liberal
intelligentsia. The popular Obrenović faction was most interested in
the demand that the Karadjordjevići, both former Prince Alexander
and his son Peter, be held responsible for Prince Michael's assassination, and that all participants in the plot be mercilessly punished. The

Liberals were most eager to put forward their desires for political reforms, most of which were hopeful echoes of the past; they called for annual sessions of an assembly with broader powers, for freedom of the press, for trial by jury, and for ministerial responsibility to the Assembly. The Assembly's requests provided the new regime with a challenge and a program. It is in relation to these wishes of the Assembly that the four-year rule by the Regency can best be evaluated.

The government responded energetically to the demand that Michael's murderers be brought to justice. Five separate trials were held. A court-martial sentenced to death the two officers who were to have carried out a revolt in the army. The Belgrade municipal court sentenced to death fourteen civilian conspirators and handed out lesser sentences to their accomplices—including twenty years each for ex-Prince Alexander Karadjordjević and his secretary Pavle Tripković, *in absentia,* since both were abroad. A third trial was conducted by the same court in which various other accomplices were given minor sentences or released for want of evidence. The notable exception was Antonije Majstorović, the leader of the conspiracy in 1863 against Michael's life. He was now brought to trial for his part in the conspiracy of 1868 and sentenced to be shot in his own village, near Smederevo, which was held to be a lair of Karadjordjević supporters. The remaining two trials were both held in Budapest, at the request of the Serbian government. A Hungarian court dismissed all charges against the Liberal leader in exile Vladimir Jovanović and the Bulgarian revolutionary leader Liuben Karavelov. As for ex-Prince Alexander Karadjordjević and his secretary Tripković, their trial dragged on for three years, in which a lower court exonerated them, a court of appeals sentenced them to eight years and four years respectively, and the supreme court sustained the original exoneration. All these trials were supposed to lead to the conclusion that the plot against Michael had been concocted by Prince Alexander Karadjordjević, who gave the money, and carried out by various agents in Serbia, notably the Radovanović brothers.

However, there was something far too simple about this version. It left too many questions unanswered. Just what was the extent of Alexander Karadjordjević's role, and was he the leader or the instrument of the plot? To what degree were the Liberals involved, and why were their leaders in Serbia not being tried? Were Austria and the Porte implicated? While the whole story may never be known, subsequent information has led to conclusions that differ, at least in emphasis, from the official interpretation.

To begin with, a plot against Michael's life was no dark secret of a few unknown conspirators but a matter of common knowledge, both to the government and to Belgrade society. The ringleader Pavle Radovanović had openly boasted in a coffeehouse of his intention to murder Michael, and the prince was aware of this. That a plot was in the making was so well known that foreign consuls reported it in their dispatches. It was also known to the visiting Russian publicist and historian Pavel A. Rovinskii, who was staying in the very hotel where the conspirators were meeting. In retrospect, Michael's assassination was something so expected by everyone that people either passively accepted it as inevitable or actively sought ways to benefit by it. In such circumstances it was rather difficult and embarrassing later to try to define responsibility and complicity, especially where the government itself could be charged with negligence. Thus it was to the advantage of the new regime to make everything as clean-cut as possible by restricting the blame to Alexander Karadjordjević and a few conspirators. It was also to their advantage, in view of their momentary shakiness, not to implicate the Liberals but, on the contrary, to win their cooperation by granting them various government posts. The regents were eager to bring quiet to the country as soon as possible.

Today it may be concluded that ex-Prince Alexander Karadjordjević, a man of sixty-three, was less the leader than the instrument of the conspiracy. Indeed, his ambitious wife Persida and his secretary and kinsman Tripković were more actively concerned than he. It may also be concluded that the real moving spirit of the plot to kill Michael was not Karadjordjević but Pavle Radovanović, a man who combined exalted political ambitions with a personal vendetta against Michael for the latter's refusal to pardon his brother, who had been jailed for forgery. That the entire affair was far more complicated and messy than the government was prepared to allow is quite clear. It was the aim of the Regency to accede to the public demand for retribution as quickly and as efficiently as possible, while assuring to itself the least political embarrassment and the maximum benefits. In this the Regency succeeded.

The question remains as to the complicity of Austria and the Porte. The first possibility may be discounted for a variety of reasons, the chief being that Michael's relations with Austria were quite good just before his death. As for the Porte, which certainly had reason to regard Michael as a threat, there are several signs of possible involvement. There was contact between the conspirators and Ömer Paşa, the governor of Bosnia, which the Porte half admitted after the assassination by removing and degrading him. There was also a report that Blaznavac himself offered the Porte Michael's overthrow. Even if the report was untrue, it is known that Blaznavac opposed Michael's desire for war with the Turks and that he had high political ambitions for himself which the Porte may have been willing to encourage. In any event, the extent of foreign involvement in Michael's assassination remains a moot question.

Insofar as the Great Assembly's desires for reforms were concerned, the Regency hoped to give the appearance of generosity without relinquishing the substance of power. It eased the censorship and allowed public discussion of reform. The Liberals' organ, *Srbija*, edited by Ljubomir Kaljević, spoke for most of the intelligentsia when it argued that thirty-five years of repression and centralism had not borne fruit, and that it was time to try a system of free discussion and popular participation in government. The Regency seemingly responded favorably to such wishes by convening an advisory committee of seventy-six citizens on St. Nicholas Day, December 18, 1868, to discuss a new constitution for Serbia. This "St. Nicholas Committee" met for two weeks. It represented not only Conservative views but also those of the Liberals as well as those of a rising group of young Conservatives who were by no means totally behind the government. Despite their differences, they generally agreed that it was time for Serbia to free itself of the 1838 "Turkish" Constitution, which symbolized its vassalage to the sultan, and to establish for itself a more modern constitution which took into account internal developments and needs since 1838. The result of these deliberations came six months later, when a constitutional assembly of over five hundred deputies, consisting largely of peasants, a few priests and merchants, two or three lawyers, and, by law, no government employees, promulgated the Constitution of 1869.

This constitution is also called the Trinity Constitution, because it was proclaimed on Trinity Sunday, and the Regency Constitution. The latter name is especially fitting since the government generally got its way while seeming to grant reforms.

The first section of the constitution preserved all the powers of the prince, including the right to initiate, to proclaim, and to veto laws.

It also gave the right of succession not only to the direct male progeny of Prince Miloš but also, failing these, to the male progeny of Miloš's daughters. If none such existed, the Serbian people could elect any Serb it chose except a Karadjordjević. Thus the Obrenović dynasty was more secure than ever in its rights to the throne.

The second section dealt with civil rights. It guaranteed the equality of all citizens; personal freedom and property rights; the inviolability of every citizen's home; his protection under due process of the law; freedom of religion, speech, and press; and the right to petition. Yet this bill of rights was in fact virtually annulled by making these rights subject to laws instead of having the laws subject to constitutional rights. The government could still impose censorship, define qualification for editors, require newspapers to post a bond, and conduct searches. There was not a word about freedom of assembly and association. Citizens could not sue government officials in court for malfeasance. There was no right of habeas corpus. There was nothing to protect citizens from administrative deportation or banishment. Even freedom of religion was restricted by making illegal all proselytism at the expense of the established Orthodox Church. Article 38 proclaimed that "in the event of dire danger to public security the government may for a time suspend the provisions of Article 27 regarding personal freedom, of Article 28 regarding the inviolability of the domicile, of Article 32 regarding freedom of speech and press, and of Article 3 regarding the competence of the courts." It was left to the government to decide when such danger existed.

The third section dealt with the National Assembly. On the one hand it gave the Assembly the right to initiate legislation, though the Assembly shared that power with the prince. "No law," article 55 read, "can be issued, annulled, amended or reviewed without the consent of the National Assembly." Yet this legislative power was effectively curtailed by several provisions. First, the Assembly could initiate only *drafts* of laws, which it then had to submit to the prince for promulgation, subject to his acceptance. Moreover, the prince could proclaim laws, except those dealing with taxation, without the Assembly in times of emergency when the Assembly was not in session, such laws to be subsequently submitted to the next Assembly. Even the power of the purse was denied to the Assembly in that the government could dismiss a recalcitrant assembly and operate on the previous budget for the coming year. In an emergency, which was never defined, the government could also incur a debt of up to 200,000 ducats, an enormous sum for Serbia at that time, and take up to 30,000 ducats from the state treasury without the Assembly's authorization.

Other provisions further emasculated the Assembly's power. Instead of establishing a bicameral body in which a senate could act as a check on the lower house, the government resorted to a novelty: the prince acquired the constitutional right to appoint to the Assembly one of his own men for every three elected deputies. Supposedly this was to ensure the inclusion of educated men in the Assembly who might not otherwise be elected, for they were to be chosen "from among those men who are distinguished by their learning or their experience in public affairs." However, no one could doubt how they would vote since they would presumably consist of state employees. All that the government had to do to get rid of a recalcitrant appointee to the Assembly was to transfer him to another position, thus making him lose his mandate. While packing the Assembly with its own picked intelligentsia, the government could protect itself from its Liberal intellectual critics, as before, by making all civil servants as well as lawyers and persons receiving state pensions ineligible for election. Soldiers in the regular army were not only barred from standing for election but were disfranchised altogether, along with all who paid no property tax, which, in peasant Serbia, meant a relatively small number of the landless poor and servants. It is true that the constitution made cabinet ministers responsible to the Assembly as well as to the prince. However, this responsibility was limited in that the Assembly could reecommend that a minister be dismissed only if two-thirds agreed that he was guilty specifically of treason, violation of the constitution, or financial corruption, and then his case had to be tried within an unspecified time by an unspecified court. Thus the Assembly could not ask for the dismissal of ministers over policy matters or even over their abuse of civil rights, let alone incompetence or favoritism.

On the other hand, deputies were not immune from arrest if the majority of the Assembly voted to hand them over to the police for any crime, including slander of the government as broadly defined by law. The Assembly as a whole was at the mercy of the government, which had the right to convene it and dismiss it when it chose or to operate a whole year without convening it. Thus, all in all, the government had little reason to fear the Assembly.

The State Council continued to consist of civil servants. As for the courts, while they were declared "independent . . . of any authority save the law," this was an empty provision since the judges could be dismissed, transferred, or pensioned by the government. Nevertheless the constitution did guarantee public trials by jury, which was a great step forward. As for local government, the 1869 constitution made it entirely dependent on the central administration. In sum, the Constitution of 1869, while giving the appearance of acceding to Liberal demands, in fact gave the government all the advantage it needed to keep a firm grip. Serbia had a parliament, but not a parliamentary government. Whereas in countries with a true parliamentary regime it was understood that the government had to enjoy the confidence of the parliament, in Serbia it seemed as though the parliament had to enjoy the confidence of the government.

Nevertheless, the Constitution of 1869 held important improvements over the Constitution of 1838. For one thing, unlike the earlier "Turkish" Constitution, the new one was promulgated by the Serbs themselves, regardless of Ottoman sovereignty, and thus symbolized another step toward complete independence. Moreover, whereas the Constitution of 1838 divided the power between the ruler and a state council of oligarchs, with the latter being dominant, the Constitution of 1869 restored the National Assembly as the voice of the people. The Constitution of 1869 was at best a compromise between the absolutism of the prince and the democratic tendencies of the popular masses. It was also a compromise between the Conservatives and the Liberals, in which liberal reforms were proclaimed, but always giving the government the upper hand in any conflict.

As usual with such a compromise, almost no one was wholly pleased with it—that is, except the regents and the masses of the people! The regents had all the power they needed. The people were pleased that an annual assembly with greater participation than before in government affairs had been established. They were not sensitive to the limitations on the Assembly's rights. Patriarchal in their thinking, they were far more prepared to accept the need for a strong central authority than were the urban intellectuals or provincial oligarchy, whom they distrusted anyway. Besides, the crisis caused by Michael's assassination seemed to them to require a strong hand. The Liberals, of course, felt utterly cheated. A rising young group of socialists, notably Svetozar Marković, denounced the constitution as a fraud. The old Conservatives, of the political school of Prince Miloš, grumbled that it was too liberal. And when the Constitution of 1869 was overthrown twenty years later, no one was more eager to abandon it than Milan himself, who claimed that it had been foisted on him during his childhood. Thus, for two decades, much of Serbia's politics centered on the issue of changing the constitution.

Throughout the four years of the Regency the tone was one of controlled moderation, "freedom with order," as Regent Ristić liked to say, with considerably more emphasis on order than on freedom. There was practically no organized political activity in that period. The Regency maintained that parties were an unnecessary evil in a country where such harmony of interests prevailed between the people and their government. The Assembly dutifully did whatever the government asked, owing not only to the government-appointed claque among the deputies but also to the fact that local elections were generally controlled by the police. Given the new constitutional guarantee of freedom of the press, a spate of new newspapers appeared, but because of legal limitations and financial problems, they disappeared almost as quickly. Those that survived had to endure greater problems over censorship than before, when they had had to submit their copy to professional and presumably literate censors for approval. Now already printed copy was subject to the surveillance of the far less literate or tolerant police for possible violations of various laws. Thus the serious press was effectively shackled, and it was largely the satirical literary sheets with their covert allusions in the "Aesopian language" of fables, allegories, and plays on words too sophisticated for the police that got away with any political commentary at all.

Generally the repression of the Regency's police system was even greater than under Michael, for now not only the Liberals but also other groups, notably the Karadjordjević supporters and a new generation of socialists, were made to suffer. At least under Michael all that was asked was that people mind their own business and not meddle in government affairs. Under the Regency, even lack of interest came to be suspect in the eyes of a government that required everyone's active support of the dynasty and the state. Never before in Serbia's history had the police been as willing and free to impose corporal punishment, not just on ordinary peasants, as in times past, but even on young intellectuals. It was possible, with no legally acceptable evidence, for the police to give a student suspected of writing political lampoons twenty-five lashes with a switch and to banish him into the interior. One student accused of being a socialist died of such a beating. While such cases were very rare, it did not take many to embitter the intelligentsia. Many people at first sought to justify the police terror by the crisis created by Michael's assassination and attempted *coup,* but it became increasingly apparent that the Regency regarded police terror as a necessary permanent feature.

Perhaps all of this would have been more acceptable if the only victims of the regents' regime had been a few "troublemakers." However, that regime had faults that affected a great number of people. One was shameless favoritism in awarding the best positions, regardless of qualifications. Another was nepotism. For example, the large Babadudić family held many of the highest posts, including the ministry of war and the finance ministry. Another family, the Hadžitomić, a rich Belgrade merchant family, enjoyed the privilege of having among its sons-in-law Regent Jovan Ristić, the minister of the interior, Serbia's representative in Istanbul, and the prince's adjutant. The lesser members of both families held corresponding positions, so that both seemed more like political corporations than mere families. At the same time, financial corruption was becoming a feature of Serbian political life, and the period of the Regency saw several notorious scandals, involving both families.

Nevertheless, Serbia made several advances under the Regency. For a change, the government spent relatively less on military preparedness and more on education. Teachers' salaries were raised, instruction was improved by less emphasis on rote learning, regular professional workshop meetings for teachers were instituted, more books were published, the activities of the Serbian Learned Society were enlarged, and a new emphasis was given to adult education, though with discouraging results. There was a similar advance in the economy. Many companies were formed in this period. The first Serbian bank was founded in 1869. In 1871 the Belgrade Credit Union was formed. The period even saw a modest attempt to build factories. However, most of the economic progress was visible only in the towns; the countryside continued to suffer from indebtedness. One beneficial result of the increased police activity under the Regency was the suppression of a long-lasting scourge, banditry in the provinces. By public demand, a law of 1870 made it easier to open village shops, as a result of which there was a phenomenal increase in their number. A society for the advancement of agriculture was founded in 1869 by private persons; its newspaper, *Težak* (The Laborer), outlived the Serbian Kingdom. In 1870 the government founded a school for agriculture and forestry. Generally the national economy went forward after Michael's death, once it became clear that a war with the Turks was not in the offing. The Constitution of 1869 also lent a certain political stability to the economic climate. If the law and order of the Regency stifled political opposition, it had the opposite effect on economic activity.

In foreign affairs, the Regency's most notable policy was to permit Michael's whole Balkan alliance system to dissolve. It did not have to make any effort to do this; the allies were already divided by various interests. In its relations with the Great Powers, the greatest achievement of the Regency was to strike a balance, albeit a precarious one, between Austria and Russia. As a result, the Regency got away with proclaiming the new Serbian constitution without having it granted by the Porte, as the "Turkish" Constitution of 1838 had been.

The First Years of Milan's Reign, 1872–1876

On August 22 (August 10 O.S.), 1872, Prince Milan Obrenović celebrated his eighteenth birthday and thus, according to the Constitution of 1869, became legally of age. With this the Regency ceased formally. However, this did not mean that the power of Ristić and Blaznavac came to an end. The young ruler recognized his continued dependence on them when, in naming his first cabinet, he made Blaznavac premier and minister of war, and Ristić foreign minister. The third regent, old Jovan Gavrilović, was pensioned at his own request. Blaznavac was further made a general, the first to be given the rank in Serbia; till then the young Serbian army had no officer higher than a colonel. Despite the new state of affairs, Blaznavac and Ristić still needed each other too much for either to strike out on his own. Thus the partnership between the military and the bureaucracy was preserved.

Nevertheless, it was generally believed that the regime established by the Regency had had its day, and that it was time for a change. Prince Milan was assiduously encouraged in this idea by an entourage of Conservatives who kept whispering to him that the regents had usurped and misused their authority, that they had taken advantage of his minority and had allowed a dilution of the prince's powers by acceding to the Constitution of 1869. Outwardly the young prince seemed like an overplump, fainéant princeling whose main fault was a certain childish wantonness that could be controlled with proper guidance. Yet beneath this exterior Milan was a sharp-witted lad, quick to gauge the situation and quite willing to take whatever advantage of it he could. As he later admitted, he chafed under the tutelage of his regents, especially Ristić, whose cold and overbearing manner infuriated the adolescent ruler, who longed to assert his own authority.

Death intervened in 1873 to strike down Blaznavac quite unexpectedly, the victim of an angina. Milan made Ristić premier. Unable to win the cooperation of either Jovan Marinović and his Conservatives or Jevrem Grujić and his Liberals, Ristić was forced to put together a cabinet of officials, including such rising young men as Stojan Novaković and Čedomilj Mijatović, both future distinguished historians and men of letters, who became minister of education and finance minister respectively. Meanwhile, Milan, then a youth of nineteen, indicated his desire to manage military affairs himself, through his own choice of a war minister. This arrangement became the rule for the rest of the century.

From August to October of 1873, Milan made the rounds of European capitals as though to announce to the world his coming of age as a ruler. Soon after his return, he dismissed Ristić. There were several reasons for Ristić's fall: a scandal involving former War Minister Jovan Belimarković and the misappropriation of military funds, the failure of the first Serbian bank because of a financial crisis in Vienna in 1873 and its own mismanagement, and the intrigues of his rivals. But most of all, everyone was tired of the haughty Ristić and his power.

Ristić's fall brought back the Conservatives, no longer under the retired Garašanin but under Jovan Marinović, the new premier and foreign minister. Marinović was a Bosnian by birth and a European gentleman by inclination. He even spoke Serbian with a foreign accent, thanks to his Parisian education and years abroad as a diplomat. As a Conservative and a bureaucrat, he had little liking for such democratic institutions as a peasant assembly, yet he believed in enlightenment and culture in the best European style.

This led him to a series of rapid reforms, between November 1873 and January 1874. The most astounding was the immediate establishment, by administrative fiat, of freedom of speech and the press. It was as though the Conservatives were as tired of Ristić's censorship as the Liberals. A law of December 23, 1873, abolished corporal punishment. Twenty days later another law instituted a much-needed prison reform. Two more laws that same December introduced educational reforms in the gymnasia and the Great School. The latter was given greater autonomy. On December 12, 1873, the government brought Serbia an important step forward in the modern European world of commerce by introducing the metric system and a native silver currency. One month later came a Law on the Subsidization of Industrial Enterprises, which authorized the government to grant various privileges and concessions to new industries. Most of these laws were presented by the government to the Assembly, which had been convened on November 27, 1873.

The Assembly initiated one of the most far-reaching reform laws, the Law on Six Days of Land. The "day" (*dan*) was a Serbian land measurement, equal to 5,760 square meters, presumably the amount of land that one man could plow in a day. This law was the same in intent as Prince Miloš's law of 1836 which protected the peasant from impoverishment by making it illegal for him to forfeit his house, his field, two oxen, and a cow in order to pay a debt. In 1865 the amount of land thus protected by law was two "days." The Marinović Assembly, as the Assembly of 1873 was often called, extended the amount of land a peasant could not forfeit or encumber with debt to six "days," that is, about 8.6 acres. This was hardly enough, in fact, to support a family, but it was something. However much such a law benefited and protected the peasant, of course, it assumed that he was unable to manage his own affairs. The peasant supporters of the bill did not mind the paternalism as long as they were protected in what they could easily see as an unequal struggle between themselves and the ever rising forces of a capitalism with which they did not know how to cope. However, Prince Milan, who gladly signed the law, was always ready to use it as an argument against the Constitution of 1869, which he believed gave too many rights to a still immature people.

Two more laws, in January 1874, also benefited the poor peasant. The first made available small government loans—a minimum of 5 ducats instead of the previous 500 ducats—thus making it unnecessary for needy persons to go to private moneylenders who charged usurious rates of interest. The second law was intended to help already heavily indebted peasants extricate themselves from debt through a special fund, but this failed when the administration could not get sufficient capital.

It was during the Regency, with the Constitution of 1869, that political party life in Serbia really began. Up to that point, the activities of the Conservatives and the Liberals were restricted to a rather small circle of men at the top. Among the masses, politics expressed itself more within the dynastic feud between the Obrenović party and the Karadjordjević party. Once an annual National Assembly was established, the political parties, which had consisted of more or less isolated coteries, now had reason to go to the people. The Liberals constantly sought every opportunity to amend the constitution so as to make it more truly an instrument of liberal democracy. This confrontation between Conservatives and Liberals created constant political turmoil during the early years of Milan's reign.

The next year saw a quick succession of ministries. Marinović resigned in late 1874 to be succeeded by his minister of the interior, Aćim Čumić, who fell in turn in early 1875 to be succeeded by Danilo Stevanović, brother of the more famous Tenka. All of these ministries were plagued by the continuing struggle between Conservatives and Liberals, which flared into the open in the more tolerant spirit of the day. However, there were limits to the tolerance. During Stevanović's "government of reconciliation and goodwill," as it was called, Prince Milan was forced, for the first time ever, to dissolve the Assembly. By August 1875 Ristić was back, not as premier, for that title was given to Stevča Mihailović, the seventy-one-year-old patriarch of the Liberal party, whose name was needed to bring hostile factions together; however, it was Ristić who, as his representative and foreign minister, manned the helm.

The Beginnings of a Serbian Socialist Movement

One of the fruits of Serbia's increasing exposure to Western ideas in the middle of the nineteenth century was the introduction of the idea of socialism, which came to Serbia from Russia.

The first Serbian to introduce socialist ideas was Živojin Žujović (1838–1870). Sent to Russia to study at the theological academy in

Kiev, Žujović later studied philosophy in St. Petersburg and in Munich. He fell under the influence of the Russian radical thinkers Chernyshevskii, Belinskii, and Pisarev, as well as the French philosopher Proudhon, and wrote two articles in Chernyshevskii's journal *Sovremennik* (Contemporary), in 1863 and 1865. However, his utopian socialism was of the armchair variety, and his theoretical interests produced no results in Serbia.

At the time of Žujović's death, in 1870, another young Serbian, Svetozar Marković (1846–1875), became the real standard-bearer of socialism in Serbia, especially between the time of his article "To the Serbian Youth" in 1868 and his death in 1875. Marković's encounter with socialism was very similar to Žujovic's. While a student at the newly established faculty of technology of the Great School in Belgrade, Marković espoused the democratic liberalism so popular among the United Serbian Youth, and Vladimir Jovanović was one of his mentors. In 1866 the government sent him to St. Petersburg on a scholarship to study in the Institute of Roads and Communications. There Marković became imbued with the teachings of Chernyshevskii. Even the title of one of his early articles, "What Must We Do?" was an echo of Chernyshevskii's popular socialist novel *What Is to Be Done?*

Marković's break with liberalism was clearly indicated when he wrote to Vladimir Jovanović that *"the greatest misfortune for the Serbian people would be to be liberated under the Obrenović dynasty. I want liberation through popular revolt—through revolution."* From Pisarev and Tkachëv, who had taken it from Blanqui, Marković got the idea that it was the role of an enlightened and well-organized intelligentsia to lead the masses to the establishment of a new social order. Just as the Russian utopian socialists held that the peasant commune was the nucleus of that new order in Russia, so Marković looked to the South Slavic *zadruga*. By the winter of 1868–1869, Marković's interest in the Russian revolutionary movement had turned to participation in underground activity, and he was barely able to escape arrest by leaving Russia for Switzerland.

Continuing his technical studies in Zurich, Marković immersed himself in the socialist movement. He became affiliated with Karl Marx's International Working Men's Association, better known as the First International—via the Russian section, which joined the International in 1870. Despite his contact with Marxism, Marković remained a rather confused theoretician whose eclecticism led him into problems he could never quite resolve. In his search for a program that would be directly applicable to the Serbia of his day, Marković created his own construct, which combined Marx's philosophy of history with Chernyshevskii's ethics and agrarian socialism and borrowed revolutionary ideas from Bakunin, Tkachëv, and Nechaev. A fundamental problem in applying these ideas to Serbia was, of course, that one could hardly have a proletarian movement in a country where there was as yet no industry and therefore no working class. This is what led Marković to identify peasant with worker.

Nevertheless, what makes Marković important in Serbian history is neither his unoriginal theoretical thought nor his attempt to organize a revolutionary movement, but rather his incisive critique of Serbia's society and its development. He began, in 1868, with an appraisal of Serbian literature. He lashed out against an already outdated romanticism that refused to deal with reality critically but either fled into an idealized past or artificially copied the forms and traditions of a bygone folk literature. His view of Serbia's economic development was that the country was entering into capitalism late, at a time when the capitalist system of more advanced countries was clearly showing its inability to solve the problems it had raised. Marković hoped, like the utopian agrarian socialists of Russia, that Serbia might even skip capitalism and pass into socialism directly via the *zadruga* or cooperative communal system. He opposed not only what he regarded as the injustice of capitalist economic exploitation but also the oppression of the bourgeois state. No Serb before him had criticized as sharply the abuses of the centralized bureaucratic monarchy in Serbia or the system itself. A system that was fundamentally so bad, he believed, was not worth reforming. As for Serbia's peasant society, while he was painfully aware of its backwardness, he took a populist's pride in the ethical traditions of an egalitarian folk democracy which brought into a natural and moral harmony the dignity and worth of the individual with the needs of the community.

To win a following, Marković found it necessary first to get other Serbs to break with liberalism, as he had done. In his article *"Srpske obmane"* (Serbian Deceptions), published in 1870 in the *Zastava* (Banner) of Novi Sad, he crossed swords with his erstwhile Liberal mentors and friends. In a penetrating critique of the Constitution of 1869, Marković argued that civil liberties were not the end but only the means to something, namely, the transformation of the socioeconomic system and the political regime that rested on it. He charged the Liberals with having compromised themselves in a "fusion," as he put it, with the regime and called on them to stop deceiving themselves and others. The immediate effect of the article was to confront the United Serbian Youth with a challenge and to make the long-tolerant Serbian government withdraw its scholarship support from the young author, thus forcing him to come home, in 1870.

There he wrote tracts and, in 1871, published the first socialist newspaper in Serbia, the *Radenik* (Worker), which soon had a circulation of 1,500, an unprecedented figure in a country where 600 to 800 copies of each issue was considered a good average for any journal. The *Radenik* proclaimed a 21-point socialist program for Serbia and carried translations of Marx's writings in serial form, notably *The Civil War in France* and the tenth chapter ("The Working Day") of *Das Kapital*. Soon Marković gathered around him a brilliant group of angry young men, including such avant-garde litterateurs as Djura Jakšić and Milovan Glišić; the liberal democrat Jovan Jovanović-Zmaj, the most renowned and beloved Serbian writer of his time; and the poets Danilo Medić and Sima Popović. One of Marković's most colorful cohorts was a Bosnian Orthdox priest, Vaso Pelagić, who had also studied in Russia.

By 1872 the government's tolerance wore thin and exposed the limits of its espousal of freedom of the press. Marković barely escaped his impending arrest by crossing into Hungary in a rowboat. Soon after, the *Radenik* was banned. Marković spent the next two years abroad, mostly in Novi Sad, but also in Zurich where he met Bakunin, but he refused to work with the dynamic anarchist leader. In 1872 he published one of his most significant works, *Srbija na Istoku* (Serbia in the East). In it he extolled the effort of the Balkan peoples to free themselves from the Turks; at the same time, he was the first Serb clearly to point out the contradiction between Serbian nationalism and South Slavic unity. He rejected the idea that was central to Prince Michael's whole foreign policy and clear to Conservatives and Liberals alike, namely, that Serbia had somehow earned the right to be the leader of the South Slavs. Let Serbia free itself, Marković cried. "Serbia," he argued, "is not the prince, nor the ministers, nor the chiefs and captains, judges and mayors, government bureaus and offices. Serbia is the Serbian people who live in Serbia. . . . The Serbian people cannot more profitably employ their strength than by carrying out a complete revolution in Turkey and, with the help of the revolution, by bringing about their own complete liberation as well as that of their other oppressed brethren."

In 1873 Marković returned to Serbia and was predictably arrested. However, Premier Ristić had him freed, not wishing to alienate any more groups than he had to in his quest to organize a new cabinet. Now more than ever Marković gravitated closer to Chernyshevskii and the Russian Populists and away from Marx, whose program, he wrote, was *"one-sided and inapplicable* to almost all nations except England." Meanwhile Serbia's socialists were picking up electoral strength. In 1874 the first socialists got elected to the National Assembly. In late 1873, Marković became the editor of another newspaper, *Javnost* (The Public), in Kragujevac, the seat of the National Assembly. Unlike *Radenik,* which had devoted itself greatly to socialist theory, *Javnost* emphasized the practical political, economic, and social problems of the day. Free of the bombastic, demagogic tone of the *Radenik,* the cold analysis in *Javnost* showed a more mature Marković. No newspaper ever criticized a Serbian government as relentlessly as this one.

Finally, constitutional freedom of the press notwithstanding, Marković was arrested in early 1874 and tried for "press crimes" in a well-attended public trial. Marković was sentenced to eighteen months in prison, which amounted to a death sentence in view of his poor health. He suffered from advanced tuberculosis. On the strength of a medical examination, he was freed pending appeal of his case, and was near collapse by the time the appeal was rejected and he was imprisoned.

Upon his release, in late 1874, he founded another newspaper, *Oslobodjenje* (Liberation), which began to appear in January 1875. This paper attacked the government even more sharply than his last. Again the police charged that he was planning a treasonable undertaking and "spreading hatred against the Prince." Unable to face the ordeal of another trial, Marković gave up the paper. He traveled to Vienna to seek a cure, but the doctors pronounced his case hopeless. Seeking a sunnier clime, he went to Trieste, from which he intended to proceed south to the Bay of Kotor by ship. He died in a Trieste hospital on February 26, 1875, at the age of twenty-eight. He did not live to see the long-awaited revolt in Bosnia and Hercegovina which erupted in July.

Serbia and the Balkan Crisis of 1875–1878

Jovan Ristić was the undisputed master of Serbia's foreign policy from 1868 to 1878. In his later writings he always maintained that, contrary to the opinion of his critics, he did not depart from Prince Michael's program. He was right to the extent that the Regency continued to cultivate relations with the other Balkan nations and to encourage revolutionary activity in the Ottoman lands of Europe. But after 1868 international conditions were less favorable for the realization of Michael's ambitions. The France of Napoleon III was no more after the Franco-Prussian War of 1870 and the Paris Commune. Russia, disappointed in Blaznavac, was veering toward the Bulgars, especially in enabling them to gain their church autonomy from the Greeks. The Christian states of southeastern Europe were going their own way, even Montenegro. The Regency had neither the moral nor the physical force to accomplish much more than a holding action. Probably Ristić never really believed in the possibility of a Balkan federation or a South Slavic state. An experienced diplomat, he doubted the ability of the Balkan peoples to decide their own destinies without the Great Powers, and for the moment the Great Powers were disposed to preserve the integrity of the Ottoman Empire. As a further guaranty of peace in eastern Europe, there was the meeting of the emperors of Germany, Austria-Hungary, and Russia in Berlin in September 1872. While no political agreements were made at the meeting, the Austro-Hungarian and Russian foreign ministers Andrássy and Gorchakov agreed to work for the status quo in the Eastern Question. Thus the Serbian government, whether led by Conservatives or Liberals, had reason to curtail its efforts to fan revolution in the Ottoman lands. The government of Prince Nicholas in Montenegro followed suit.

By this time even the United Serbian Youth, which was no longer either united or youthful, had also lost its enthusiasm for an aggressive program of national liberation. Its more militant members, led by Svetozar Miletić of Hungary and inspired by Svetozar Marković, organized the Fellowship for Serbian Unification and Liberation (*Družina za ujedinjenje i Oslobodjenje srpsko*), the aim of which was to raise a rebellion in Bosnia and Hercegovina. The socialists were eager to combine a revolution for national liberation with a general social and political revolution. They even carried on negotiations with Blaznavac, but when the latter died, Ristić refused to deal with them. Instead, his government cracked down on the fellowship.

In Bosnia and Hercegovina, there was great turmoil. Local leaders sent appeals to Austria in 1872 and to the Russian tsar in 1873, during Alexander II's visit to Vienna. The memorandum to the tsar explained that they were forced to rebel, and it begged the powers not to abandon them. In 1874 some leaders from the Hercegovina district of Nevesinje met and decided to take up arms the following spring. They communicated their decision to both Serbia and Montenegro. The Turks discovered the plot and arrested all the leaders who did not flee. A general wave of terror ensued. Though Serbia and Montenegro had long planned, abetted, and hoped for an uprising in Bosnia and Hercegovina, neither government was eager for it now. Rather, it was the exasperated Christian populace of the Ottoman provinces who precipitated the crisis, led by members of the former United Serbian Youth and various socialists and local nationalists. In mid-1875, when the Turkish authorities began to use force to collect excessive taxes, the revolt flared up, in July, with the outbreak of the so-called "Nevesinje Rifles." It soon spread among the Orthodox and the Roman Catholics of Hercegovina and Bosnia.

Serbia had been nurtured for so long on a bellicose romantic nationalism that not much was needed to arouse the nation. A wave of sympathy for the insurgents swept over the entire country. Protest meetings everywhere began with the recitation of the lines by the patriotic poet Milan Kujundžić:

> Standard-bearer, raise the standard!
> Venture forward, go!
> There whence comes the deepest moaning
> Of the slave in woe.

Everyone felt it his duty to do something for the rebels. Within days 2,000 volunteers formed in Belgrade. The streets were full of them, armed to the teeth. Danilo Stevanović's government was certainly unable, and probably not willing, to stem the tide. Young Prince Milan, who was visiting in Vienna, was assured by Andrássy that it was all just a local flare-up that would soon pass. However, when Milan hurried home, he was met at the Sava station not only by the usual dignitaries, troops, and public, but also by a contingent of volunteers in full battle dress, who escorted him with cries of "Long live the Serbian King! To battle! At the Turks! Give us war!"

A few days later elections to the National Assembly gave the more belligerent Liberals a majority, and the Conservative regime was at an end. Old Stevča Mihailović, who had been a regent in 1859, was made premier, at least in name, while the two key portfolios were given to Ristić as foreign minister and Jevrem Grujić as minister of the interior. Ljubomir Kaljević, leader of the younger Liberals, became president of the Assembly. The Liberal victory was complete, much to Milan's chagrin. He was forced to accept a "government of action" that was diametrically opposed to his views. He wished a strong monarchy, the Liberals wished a liberal democracy. The Liberals and the people were ready for a war to achieve a united Serbdom, but Milan had no such interest. A half-Romanian born abroad and educated by a Frenchman, Milan had never been imbued with Serbian patriotism. He also knew the disposition of the Austro-Hungarian and Russian governments and feared that an indiscretion might cost him his throne. But the Serbian people were caught up in an ecstasy of patriotism. The heads of both other Serbian dynasties, the reigning Prince Nicholas of Montenegro and the nonreigning, but willing, Peter Karadjordjević, had declared themselves for a war of liberation, and the latter actually went to Bosnia-Hercegovina to fight as a volunteer. Milan could not afford to lag behind. "Whatever course events take," the Austro-Hungarian consul in Belgrade wrote home, "it is very probable that the result will be fatal to the House of Obrenović."

The National Assembly met in Kragujevac and decided to help the insurgents of Bosnia and Hercegovina: the vote was 77 for, 30 against, and 5 abstaining. It also gave the government the right to a loan of three million ducats and certain emergency powers in case of war. Both decisions were kept secret. However, there was nothing secret about the warlike mood of Serbia's people. It was natural, under the circumstances, for the apprehensive Turks to station troops along the Bosnian-Serbian border. It was also natural for such an act to inflame Serbian passions even more. Ristić was caught between a prince who openly opposed war and a people who were eager for one, even though Serbia was physically not prepared for one. Meanwhile the powers counseled restraint, and an Ottoman army was poised at the border.

Prince Milan took the initiative by bringing about the fall of the Ristić-Grujić government. The best substitute he could come up with was a coalition of younger Liberals and younger Conservatives, under the premiership of the thirty-five-year-old Ljubomir Kaljević. The new premier, educated in Heidelberg and Paris, was a politically ambitious man who was able to get along with all sides. Similarly the new foreign minister, Djordje Pavlović, was a young Conservative who could not have been more peace-loving by nature. The Kaljević cabinet lasted about six months, dutifully devoting itself to internal reforms, all designed to lessen the power of the police. Prince Milan, too, was pretending that nothing was happening west of the Drina River. He even brought to Serbia his fiancée, Natalia Petrovna Keshko, whose father was a Russian colonel and Bessarabian landowner and whose mother was, like Milan's, of the Romanian gentry. Seemingly oblivious to the crisis around him, Milan married Natalia in October 1875.

While Milan was trying to keep Serbia calm, the uprising in Bosnia and Hercegovina grew from a local affair into an international crisis. Andrássy's Note of December 30, 1875, called for reforms in Bosnia and Hercegovina; Bismarck was much more to the point when he proposed that Austria-Hungary annex the two Ottoman provinces. As compensation, he suggested that Russia regain Bessarabia, that Britain take Egypt, and that France and Italy seek compensation in North Africa. Meanwhile the insurgents raised demands of their own that went beyond the Andrássy Note.

Worst of all, for Milan, was the lack of a clear signal of any sort from Russia. In this period Milan was still dependent on Russian, rather than Austrian, advice. The trouble was that Russia had not one, but two, policies toward the Balkan crisis, which were opposed to each other. The official view, that of Tsar Alexander II and his foreign minister, Prince Gorchakov, was for Russian cooperation with Austria and Germany regarding the Balkan crisis, which meant, in effect, keeping Serbia and Montenegro from warring on the Turks. The opposite view was held by the Russian Panslavists, led by Ivan Aksakov and many important figures in Russian society, in the government, and in the foreign ministry. Chief among this last group was Count Nikolai P. Ignatiev, the powerful Russian envoy to Istanbul, and his staff of consuls throughout the Balkans. A whole network of Slavic Benevolent Committees sprang up in cities of the Russian Empire. It became almost fashionable for a long-repressed Russian public opinion to find expression in as unimpeachably respectable and patriotic a concern as sympathy for one's Slavic "little brothers" suffering in the Balkans. This sympathy was all the greater in that it expressed a traditional Russian theme of Orthodoxy versus Islam. By early January 1876, the Slavic Benevolent Committees, the Russian Red Cross, various newspapers, and other unofficial institutions had collected and sent almost 360,000 rubles to needy refugees in Bosnia and Hercegovina. For a benefit concert to raise money for this cause, Tchaikovsky composed his musical rhapsody to Slavic solidarity, the *Marche Slave*, based on Serbian folk tunes. Never before had Russian public opinion expressed itself so openly and forcefully, including all segments of the population. For the first time in the century, the Russian government found it necessary to take public opinion seriously into account. This was not difficult, because Tsar Alexander II and Gorchakov also personally sympathized with the cause of the Balkan Christians.

Prince Milan was in a remarkably similar situation. As the reports of the sufferings of the Christians of Bosnia and Hercegovina poured in, an aroused Serbian society became increasingly difficult to control. The Liberals, who undoubtedly expressed the feelings of most Serbs on the subject, kept up a steady barrage of arguments in the press in favor of intervention. If several thousand Hercegovinian guerrillas could withstand the waning might of a decadent Ottoman Empire, they argued, could not the Serbian army do even more? And would not Serbia's intervention be the long-awaited signal for a general uprising of Balkan Christians? Austria would not dare war on Turkey's side, because Russia would not allow it. Come what may, the question of Bosnia and Hercegovina had been raised, and the only way Serbia could ensure its own participation in the eventual fate of the provinces was to join the fray. There were arguments dealing with the domestic situation as well. Serbia's economy required expansion beyond its present borders. The Serbian people had paid dearly in taxes for military preparedness; either fight now or stop spending more on armaments and make peace with the Turks forever. Meanwhile, the "communist" menace had already come to Serbia; war would counter it and restore national unity.

Serbia's socialists also favored war. They saw a general Balkan uprising as a popular revolution whose consequences could bring about radical socioeconomic and political changes. A war could do much to curtail the power of the hated bureaucracy in Serbia and to put guns into the hands of the peasantry.

❧ The Conservatives were for peace, but they were a minority. Moreover, they were continually assailed by pangs of patriotism and sympathy for their suffering kinsmen as well as by the thought that, as the people became increasingly bellicose, they themselves might be trampled by the rush when it came. Besides, the views of leaders such as Marinović were greatly determined by their view of the international situation, and to the degree that Russia wavered, so did they.

While Prince Milan anguished, so much so that he even threatened to abdicate during fits of anxiety, several events took place in April and May of 1876 that affected his final decision to go to war. A general insurrection exploded in the heart of Bulgaria, bringing down on the Bulgarians the full wrath of the Ottoman might. The ensuing massacre, enshrined in William Gladstone's famous pamphlet "The Bulgarian Horrors and the Question of the East," was to bring even British opinion against the Turks. At the end of May, a *coup d'état* forced Sultan Abdülaziz to abdicate in favor of his nephew Murad V. This was merely the first in a series of crises in the Ottoman government.

At this moment there arrived in Serbia a Russian retired general, Mikhail G. Cherniaev, a hero of the Central Asian campaign and editor of the nationalistic newspaper *Russkii Mir* (The Russian World). He did not come officially, but as an emissary of the Moscow Slav Committee. Yet it seemed clear to Serbs that he would not have come to offer his services to Serbia without the tacit approval of his government. Actually, Alexander II was furious and threatened to strip Cherniaev of his military decorations, but Gorchakov counseled caution. Alexander's failure to renounce Cherniaev openly only confirmed the Serbs in their mistaken belief that the tsar's government secretly supported the general.

The whole situation, external and domestic, resulted in the fall of Kaljević's already moribund cabinet in early May, just a week after Cherniaev's arrival. Prince Milan reluctantly restored the Ristić-Grujić "action ministry," headed nominally by Stevča Mihailović again. By May 24 Cherniaev was proclaimed a Serbian citizen and commander of the eastern armies. On June 16 a treaty of alliance was concluded by Serbia and Montenegro. After that Gorchakov could no longer prevent the inevitable conflict. On June 22 the Serbian cabinet decided on war.

On June 29 Prince Milan proceeded to army headquarters. The next day his proclamation of war was made public. On July 2, 1876, the forces of Serbia and Montenegro crossed into Ottoman territory.

The same day General Cherniaev issued a manifesto calling for a general Balkan uprising in the name of "the holy cause of Slavdom," for freedom, for "the Orthodox cross," and for the unity of the Balkan peoples. While most Serbs looked west to their fellow Serbs in Bosnia and Hercegovina, their Russian military commander was looking beyond the Serbian world. Knowing that little Serbia could not withstand the Ottoman might long, his Panslavic patrons in Russia hoped that Serbia might keep up the fight long enough—two months, they believed—to allow Russian public opinion to push Russia into the war. Cherniaev, Grujić, General Zach, and others in Serbia agreed that Serbia's military thrust should be not in Bosnia and Hercegovina, despite Serbian ambitions and sympathies there, nor against Niš, which was too well protected; rather, they looked east to Bulgaria. By joining with the Bulgars, Serbia would show that its cause was a general Balkan one, not just a national one. Moreover, when Russia entered the war, help would come from the east. Nevertheless, the other fronts could not be abandoned, and it was decided to try to cut Ottoman communications between Niš and Vidin in the east, and to send a force to Bosnia, toward Sjenica, in the southwest, where not much resistance was expected.

The Serbian forces were divided into four armies, named after the rivers in whose valleys they were stationed: the central army of the Morava, 68,000 strong, under Cherniaev; the army of the Timok, to the east, with 25,000 soldiers under Colonel Lešjanin; the army of the Drina, in the west, with 20,000 soldiers under General Alimpić; and the army of the Ibar, 11,500 soldiers under General Zach. This last was to proceed across the border with Bosnia into Sjenica. All four armies suffered disastrous defeats, despite numerical superiority in most of the encounters. Just two weeks of fighting revealed how ill prepared Serbia was. The Turks were far better in the field and had the most modern weapons. While they were using the latest Krupp cannon, the Serbs were dragging around homemade cannon, smelted in Kragujevac, which were still of the kind loaded from the front. A Serbian eyewitness described the Serbian people's army as a motley force of peasants, many still dressed in sheepskins and fur caps, who looked more like some primitive tribe on the move during the medieval Great

Migration of Peoples than like a modern army. The peasant soldiers were undisciplined and inexperienced men whose ragged advances were accompanied by scattered shooting from a distance and whose withdrawals quickly turned into panic-stricken flights. The few professional officers were quickly decimated, because peasant soldiers would not march unless they saw an officer leading them. The local militia commanders were on the whole incompetent to replace the professional officers. Even at the top, except for Cherniaev, not a single Serbian officer had had any battle experience. Cherniaev himself, though battle-hardened and brave, lacked the ability to direct large and complicated operations.

The first two weeks shattered another illusion besides faith in the fighting qualities of the Serbian army; there was no general Balkan uprising. Even the revolts that had been in progress in Bosnia and Bulgaria grew weaker. Once Serbia entered the war, the Austro-Hungarian government strictly forbade its South Slavic subjects to send help or volunteers to Bosnia. As for the Bulgars, many Serbian leaders felt mortified at the repeated failure of the Bulgarian insurgents to undertake even those offensive actions that they could have, notably the cutting of railway communications. Many Serbs regarded the Bulgarian failures as sheer betrayal of the common cause. The Serbs of Vojvodina were full of enthusiasm, but did practically nothing to help. For political reasons, the Montenegrin army avoided joining with the Serbian and concentrated its efforts in western Hercegovina, where there were relatively few Turks, so that it could not contribute to the Serbian operations at all. There was no hope in involving the Greeks and Romanians in a war that was going so badly, especially as Russia made no move to intervene. Although Ivan Aksakov and the Moscow Slavic Committee, later aided by other Slavic committees in the empire, recruited hundreds of Russian volunteers for service in Serbia, these volunteers—not all heroic idealists by any means, but adventurers and ne'er-do-wells of all kinds as well—proved to be more of an embarrassment than a help, once they arrived. Of the roughly 5,000 that were recruited, about 2,000 never reached the Serbian front, but either remained in Russia or enjoyed life in Romanian and Serbian cafés. The Panslavists also arranged for a private Russian loan to Serbia to replenish its empty treasury, but the loan was woefully inadequate and did not reach Serbia until after the campaign. There was no doubt that the Panslavic campaign in Russia had succeeded in winning the support of unofficial Russia, but even the Panslavists understood that all was in vain as long as official Russia stood by passively.

Finally, on August 23, 1876, Cherniaev sent a telegram to Belgrade from the Aleksinac front advising a truce. Prince Milan and his government agreed. So did Prince Nicholas of Montenegro. But Cherniaev had his own plans. He hoped to take advantage of an armistice to gain time and to force Russia's entry into the war. To accomplish this, he had his subordinates organize a "spontaneous" movement in the army to proclaim Serbia an independent kingdom. This would make a Serbian-Ottoman peace impossible. It would also put Cherniaev and his entourage in control of Serbia. Milan was greatly tempted, but Andrássy made quite clear to him that Austria-Hungary would not stand for it. Thus he refused the offer and frustrated Cherniaev's attempt. By late September the truce was at an end, and the fighting resumed.

The steady friction between Cherniaev and many Serbian military and government leaders now burst into flame. To the Serbs Cherniaev seemed to be a megalomaniac who was quite prepared to sacrifice Serbian lives to accomplish his ends. His interference in Serbian internal affairs caused much bitterness. A Serbian major violently denounced him before Ristić and warned the minister against this "Russian madman." Cherniaev also surrounded himself with only Russian officers, especially since there were more Russian than Serbian officers in Serbia at the time. Serbian resentment was exacerbated by the bad behavior of many Russian volunteers. A crisis arose when the Serbian war minister, Colonel Tihomilj Nikolić, formally wrote to Cherniaev, "From all sides, both from the city of Belgrade and the provinces, there come to me complaints against the Russian volunteers, who overindulge in spirits and in drunken state commit scandalous acts in hotels, cafés, and the streets." Cherniaev was infuriated and threatened to leave Serbia along with all the Russian volunteers. To avoid this, the Serbian government expressed its regrets. The war minister, however, stuck to his guns and accused Cherniaev of usurping his powers and misusing funds. The behavior of the Russian volunteers became such a problem that the Slavic committees in Russia sent an agent, General V. D. Dandevil', to Serbia and instructed him to expel all who "have conducted themselves in a manner unworthy of a Russian soldier." Matters came to such a pass that the Serbs refused to believe there were any decent men among the Russian volunteers. On the other hand, many Russian officers had nothing but contempt for their raw troops, who often fled the battlefield, or inflicted wounds on themselves to avoid action, or even fired on their Russian officers who sought to keep order.

The catastrophe came at Djunis, on the left bank of the Morava in central Serbia, when, on October 29, 1875, the Serbs fled pell-mell before the Turks while the Russian volunteers suffered great losses. With a key to the Morava Valley in Ottoman hands, and the road to Belgrade wide open as a demoralized Serbian army scattered, Cherniaev asked Prince Milan to telegraph Tsar Alexander that only an immediate armistice could save Serbia. The tsar reacted promptly. Without consulting the other powers, his government sent an ultimatum to the Turks to cease fighting within forty-eight hours and to accept an armistice of six to eight weeks. The Porte complied at once. With the war at an end, Serbia looked no longer to the Panslavists but to official Russia to protect its interests at the international conference that followed in Istanbul.

The war had cost Serbia a great deal, in lives and money. There were about 15,000 casualties: 5,000 dead, 9,500 wounded, and the rest missing. This was a severe loss for a country that numbered only 1,300,000 inhabitants. Most of the war had been fought on Serbia's soil. Eastern Serbia was devastated. About 200,000 people were left homeless. Psychologically, too, the war was a shock to a nation that had believed so long that Serbia would lead a general uprising of Balkan peoples to their triumph and liberation. There was also a general disappointment in Serbia's leaders as it became apparent that Prince Milan and Ristić generally left everything up to Cherniaev. In short, in November 1876, Serbia was weakened, demoralized, and utterly dependent on Russia. Ironically, it was precisely at that point, as Serbia was suing for peace, that official Russia began to act belligerently.

On November 4 the Serbian government decided to send an emissary to Russia to acquaint the tsar with Serbia's plight. Their preference was Ristić, but ten days later Gorchakov replied that he would receive only Jovan Marinović, the leader of the Conservatives. Ristić immediately offered his government's resignation, but Milan wanted no such crisis. The only change he made was to replace Nikolić with Sava Grujić as war minister. The Serbian government hoped for Russian assurance that the war would bring about the liberation of the

South Slavs, that Serbia would receive Bosnia and Old Serbia (while Montenegro would receive Hercegovina) and would thus become a kingdom under the Obrenović dynasty, and that the Russians would give Serbia a loan of 12,000,000 rubles and 100,000 breech-loading rifles. Short of these conditions, Serbia would have to conclude immediate peace. Very pleased that St. Petersburg had picked Marinović instead of Ristić, Milan instructed the Conservative leader to assure the tsar that he would follow Russia's advice in the future, and to tell the Russian leaders that he considered the present political organization of Serbia to be the main cause of its misfortune. "For my part," Milan's secret instructions to Marinović read, "I would be happy if the Imperial Government judged it expedient to contribute to a political reorganization of Serbia."

Marinović reported from St. Petersburg that the Russians were somewhat taken aback by Serbia's territorial requirements, but that in any case these would have to await the outcome of the international conference in Istanbul. The tsar told Marinović that he could give no definite reply to the Serbs since he did not know whether or not there would be a war, nor what the aims of such a war would be—merely to improve the condition of the Christians or to partition Turkey. In the latter case he was disposed to grant Serbia some increase in Old Serbia. As for a loan, the Russian government dispatched General A. P. Nikitin to Serbia as head of a military mission and gave him a million rubles to finance Serbia's rearmament.

Nikitin reached Belgrade on December 24, 1876. He was aghast at Serbia's failure to carry out any serious military preparations. Worse yet, he discovered that Serbia had only about 9,000 men under arms. Prince Milan actually admitted that the Serbs wished to use the Russian money just to keep the government machinery going, and that no one could rely on the Serbian army not to flee or surrender if forced to fight again. Nikitin left Belgrade on January 10, 1877, taking back with him all but 150,000 of the million rubles he had brought. All that Serbia got out of the mission was 10,000 rifles, 50,000 rounds of ammunition, 8,000 pairs of boots, and 10,000 pairs of overshoes.

Meanwhile Russian-Austrian parleys regarding their role in the Balkans resulted in the Budapest Convention of January 15, 1877. Austria exacted as its price for Russian military intervention in the Balkan crisis the right to occupy Bosnia and Hercegovina. It also insisted that Russia stay out of the western Balkans, though it could cooperate militarily with Serbia and Montenegro outside their borders. This agreement thus placed Serbia, unlike Bulgaria, outside the zone of a Russian military occupation, and made Serbia a secondary question for Russia.

This was evident at the Istanbul Conference (December 23, 1876, to January 20, 1877), at which Ignatiev did little more for Serbia than ask for the *status quo ante bellum,* except for a slight rectification of the border involving two villages, although he asked more for Montenegro—some border regions of Hercegovina and three Adriatic seaports. In private, he spoke as though he were willing to have Serbia learn a lesson for its presumptuous disregard of Russia's counsel in the past. He shocked the Serbs by his efforts to award Niš, Skopje, and even Prizren to the Bulgars. The failure of this conference hardly displeased the Serbs.

When, on January 25, 1877, the Turks offered to negotiate peace directly, the Serbian government quickly agreed, with the full support of Russia and Austria. Though the terms, *status quo ante bellum,* were no better than Ignatiev's, and did not even include the two border villages, the Serbian government was eager to accept. An inevitable consequence of this act was that it worsened Serbian-Montenegrin relations. Prince Nicholas let it be known that he no longer felt bound by any alliance with Serbia. Moreover, Serbia lost much of its former influence in Bosnia. Russian Panslavists, by this time, were ready to ignore Serbia and concentrate their good intentions on their other little brothers, the Bulgarians.

On February 26, two days before the expiration of the armistice, a Great Assembly met in the National Theater of Belgrade and approved the treaty by acclamation. No sooner was this done than the Assembly was told to go home. The government dissolved it in order to prevent being censured. The deputies were completely taken aback. Only about a quarter of the 420 signed a petition asking the prince to reconvene the Assembly. When the president of the Assembly saw Minister of the Interior Radivoje Milojković, the latter told him coldly that the Assembly had been called for one purpose only, to ratify the treaty, and that any other business would have to be taken up by a regularly convened National Assembly. The minister advised the president of the Great Assembly to go back home, to Šabac, and to be careful what he said on the way or his neck would be wrung like a sparrow's! When the president got home, he fell ill from the shock of this experience.

When the regular Assembly did meet, in June 1877 in Kragujevac, it was not a newly elected one but the same one that had been elected in 1875 before the war. It sat for less than a month, but Ristić's government could not escape criticism. The Conservative opposition argued quite plausibly that the war had been premature and in vain, since Russia would have gone to war, if so disposed, even without Serbia. Now that it had already shot its wad, Serbia was forced to see the Eastern Question settled without being able to influence the outcome. The opposition also chided the government concerning internal matters, especially the government's restrictions on freedom of the press and on local self-government during the war. There were complaints over abuses of the requisitioning system by which the moneyless government had been forced to acquire provisions for the army. However, in the end the Assembly confirmed the government's wartime measures, extended the government's emergency powers, and approved some additional sources of revenue. Thus the Assembly of 1877 turned out rather better for the Liberal government than was expected.

On April 24, 1877, the Russian government finally yielded to the pressure of the Panslavists and public opinion and declared war on the Ottoman Empire. Russian troops crossed into Romania at Iași and Galati and moved slowly to the Danube. Far from rejoicing over the long-hoped-for event, the Liberal government of Serbia found itself torn between those who urged war (Premier Stevča Mihailović, Jevrem Grujić, and a minority in the army) and those who counseled neutrality (Ristić and Milojković). The latter group saw no point in fighting if Bosnia was to be relegated to the Austrian sphere, and if the Russians were disposed to award not only Vidin but Niš and even Old Serbia to Bulgaria. Meanwhile Vienna moved quickly to warn Serbia against any involvement. Gorchakov similarly informed the Serbian government, in a telegram sent on May 8, 1877, "The will of His Majesty the Emperor is that Serbia remain on the defensive and abstain from any aggressive or provocative act. It will be up to the Prince to judge what measures he should adopt in conformity with his resources and on his own responsibility." Prince Milan was dismayed, but there was nothing to do but to comply. Apparently the Russians acted with an eye to Vienna, for Tsar Alexander II wrote to his brother, "The advice we gave to Serbia created the very best impression in Vienna." The Russians were eager to avert an Anglo-Austrian-Turkish coalition. The Serbian government also feared Austria. It all seemed rather reminiscent of Serbia's situation at the time of the Crimean War.

Yet beneath these appearances there was quite another reality. As Milan's special emissary to the tsar, Colonel Catargiu, discovered in Kishinev in late April, and as Prince Milan and Ristić were informed by the tsar in Ploești in June, the Russians did not wish to keep Serbia out of the war indefinitely. They were merely afraid that Serbia was so weak that the Turks would swiftly overrun the country and endanger the Russian advance. The Serbs were advised not to do anything until the Russian army had crossed the Danube, and even then, Gorchakov cautioned Ristić, the Serbs were to give the impression that Russia was pushing them into the war. According to the Austro-Russian Convention of January 15, 1877, the Austrian government was prepared to accept Serbian-Russian military cooperation *outside* of Serbia, that is, on Ottoman territory, but there were to be no Russian troops in Serbia itself. All in all, the Russians looked upon the Serbs as being more trouble and cost than they were worth militarily, and Gorchakov referred to Prince Milan, in a talk with Romanian Prince Charles, as *"un embarras."* Bulgaria was more important to Russia, because of the Straits.

Left without any financial assistance from Russia, Milan's government did not even attempt to prepare for war. When Russian troops crossed the Danube into Bulgaria on June 23, 1878, and their commander, Grand Duke Nicholas, called on the Serbs to declare war, the Serbian government was caught by surprise. It replied that the Serbs required five to six weeks of preparation. However, the Russian forces in Bulgaria found themselves so hard pressed by the Turks that an immediate diversion would have been most welcome. Thus, on July 26, Colonel Catargiu, Milan's emissary to the tsar (and maternal uncle), telegraphed, "The Tsar has told me that Serbia should move. Ignatiev tells me to telegraph you that Serbia's future will be compromised if it remains another 12 days without moving." The next day Catargiu informed Milan that the tsar had authorized the sending of a million silver rubles to Serbia and had told him that he would regard it as a "considerable personal service," which would not be forgotten, if Serbia entered the war within twenty days. The Russians sent similar plans to Greece and Romania. Though promised Thessaly and Epirus, the Greeks were too discouraged by the Russian military setback in northern Bulgaria to commit themselves. The Romanians, who had declared their independence of the sultan on May 13, and whose help the Russians had previously spurned, agreed to join the Russians. In fact, Prince Charles was given command over the troops at Pleven (Plevna), but the costly failure of several attempts to take the Bulgarian fortress by storm meant that a siege was necessary. It proved to be a long one—143 days, until December 10, 1877.

During this period the Serbian government had neither the means nor the will to join the war within the time set by Tsar Alexander. Apart from their unpreparedness, the Serbs were troubled by the Russian lack of progress in northern Bulgaria. If Serbia joined the war, and the Russians had to withdraw back across the Danube, then Serbia would surely be overrun by the Turks. In any event, the Serbian government took the half-million rubles that the tsar's government sent as a first installment and made preparations, but it did not make a move throughout the crucial siege of Pleven, despite Russian urging. Rather, it used its desperate financial plight to enter into long negotiations with the Russians over money. Finally on December 12, 1877, the Serbian government received an unsigned telegram from the Russians assuring it of 150 silver rubles a day for each thousand soldiers that crossed Serbia's border, on condition that at least 25,000 troops be involved. Later this was expanded to include border guards as well. Meanwhile the Russians refused to accept any obligations concerning Serbia's political demands; they made it quite clear that, because of Austrian opposition, Serbia's annexation of Bosnia was out of the question.

Pleven fell to the Russians and their Romanian allies on December 10, 1877. Serbia declared war on the Turks three days later. This timing embittered the tsar. Compared with the fighting Romanians, the Serbs looked like cheap opportunists. Also, the fact that Serbia had just fought a war against the Turks without the support of Russia was treated by the Russians, with some justice, as a foolhardy indiscretion. Moreover, Russia chose to forget its own tardiness in helping the Serbs to prepare immediately after the Serbo-Turkish war. Even so, the capture of Pleven by no means meant that the Russians would no longer need the Serbs. The question was: How much help were the Serbs capable of giving?

Just three days before the fall of Pleven and less than a week before Serbia's entry into the war, there erupted a mutiny in the army and a local uprising known as the Topola Rebellion. One of five battalions refused to take an oath to Prince Milan during a ceremony on a field near Kragujevac. The mutineers made their way to Topola, a center of pro-Karadjordjević sentiment, and attempted to raise a rebellion. They failed. A subsequent investigation revealed that the aim of the ringleaders had been to restore a Karadjordjević to the throne, presumably Alexander's son Peter. How much any Karadjordjević was personally involved in the plot remains a moot question. As for the ringleaders, four were shot and two were pardoned after a period of imprisonment. The whole affair was no more than an ill-prepared local coup. However, it did much to raise political passions in Serbia at a time when unity was essential.

The second Serbo-Turkish war lasted only six weeks. The first battle took place on December 19, 1877, and the last on February 3, 1878. The war was fought exclusively in southeastern Serbia, because of coordination with Russian troop movements and because Austrian opposition to Serbian entry into Bosnia made a campaign there politically impossible. Once the Russians took Sofia, on January 3, 1878, the Serbian army in fact fought on its own. Its greatest success was the taking of Niš, Pirot, and Vranje, the key points to Old Serbia. Its greatest setback was in Samokovo, where its army of 25,000 was still caught in a stalemate when the Russians, forced by the European Powers, offered the defeated Turks an armistice after the capture of Edirne (Adrianople) on January 20, 1878. The armistice was signed on January 31.

The war had cost Serbia 5,400 casualties: 708 dead, 2,999 wounded, 159 missing, and 1,534 dead in hospitals. It had been fought in winter, in cold rains and mud, over rough terrain. The soldiers fought surprisingly well, this time under their own Serbian officers, though their inexperience showed badly. With the end of the war, it was for Russia and the other powers to determine what Serbia would get for its pains.

Serbia and the Peace Settlement of 1878

When the time came for peace negotiations, the Russian authorities did not support Serbia's territorial aspirations. Knowing that they could not touch Bosnia, because of Austria, the Serbs asked for the *paşalıks* of Niš, Prizren, Skopje, and Novi Pazar, plus Vidin and its environs as far east as Lom. This meant South Serbia, Old Serbia, northern Macedonia, and the northwestern territory of Bulgaria. Grand Duke Nicholas refused even to deal with the Serbs but referred them to St. Petersburg. There the Serbian emissary Milosav Protić was bluntly told by Nikolai Giers, assistant minister of foreign affairs, that "the interests of Russia came first, then came those of Bulgaria, and only after them came Serbia's; but that there were occasions on which Bulgarian interests stood on equal footing with the Russian." Count Ignatiev, the chief Russian negotiator of peace terms with the Turks, sought for Bulgaria not only Vidin, to which the Serbs had some aspirations, but even Niš, which was ethnically Serbian and for which the Serbian army had shed much blood. Although Ignatiev hoped to gain Novi Pazar for the Serbs as compensation, it was very doubtful whether Austria would stand for that. It was so unthinkable for the Serbs to lose Niš that Prince Milan warned Grand Duke Nicholas that the Serbian army would not surrender the town even to the Russians. Apparently the threat was taken seriously.

On March 3, 1878, the Russians and the Turks signed the Treaty of San Stefano. It was ratified on March 20. The Russians made no attempt to include Serbia or any other Balkan ally in the negotiations. As at Bucharest in 1812, or Akkerman in 1826, or Adrianople in 1829, so at San Stefano Russia was to settle the fate of the Balkan peoples without their participation, and they were to be grateful for whatever they received. All of them got something. The treaty proclaimed Serbia, Montenegro, and Romania independent. Montenegro was considerably enlarged and given the Adriatic port of Bar (Antivari). Romania lost Bessarabia to the Russians, but it was given Dobrudja (Dobrogea) as compensation.

Serbia received only 150 square miles of territory, which was less than the 200 square miles awarded to Montenegro. It was deprived of northern Macedonia, Pirot, and Vranje, all of which were awarded to the new autonomous Bulgaria. In compensation, Serbia was given territory to the southwest toward Novi Pazar and Mitrovica, but not the towns. Thus, in effect, Serbia's only prizes at San Stefano were the recognition of its independence and the town and district of Niš.

It was a rude shock to the Serbs. They were not permitted to keep even the territory they had succeeded in occupying during the war, but had to give it up to a new "Great Bulgaria." As Ristić described the Bulgarian case in his history of the events, "A people who had contributed nothing for their freedom, suddenly saw itself not only free, but the master of its own state of four million inhabitants, a state larger than any other of the little national states in the Balkan Peninsula." This was incomprehensible to Serbs who had fought one war with the encouragement of unofficial Russia and a second war with the encouragement of official Russia, and who now had to remain content with a little Serbia while their erstwhile protégés the Bulgars acquired for themselves a Great Bulgaria that was larger than Serbia or any of the other Balkan states. If Russia favored Bulgaria, it was not for sentimental but strategic reasons involving Russia's own aspirations.

The bitterness of Serbia's people at their treatment by Russia was profound. Prince Milan's bitterness was even greater in that with him Russophilism had been an article of faith. Yet there was more to come. No one was satisfied with the Treaty of San Stefano except the Russians and the Bulgars. Austria and Britain were especially distressed, not to speak of the Turks. The Austro-Hungarian Foreign Minister Andrássy invited the Great Powers to a conference "to establish the accord of Europe with regard to the modifications which it would be necessary to make" in the treaty. All the powers agreed, though Gorchakov objected to Vienna as the meeting place. Bismarck became involved as an "honest broker," and the proposed conference turned into a congress to be held in Berlin.

Almost immediately Ignatiev began to make the rounds of the European capitals to buttress Russia's case. To pacify Austria, the Russians were quite prepared to sacrifice the Serbs in order to keep their gains in the eastern half of the Balkan Peninsula. After some discussion, the Russians were disposed to concede to Austria the right not just to occupy, but to annex, Bosnia and Hercegovina; to secure Serbia's economic as well as political dependence; and to take over the whole western part of the Balkan Peninsula as a protectorate except for the Sancak of Novi Pazar and Montenegro's gains. When Austria asked even for these lands, the Russians balked, and so the discussion ended until Berlin.

Meanwhile the Serbian government hoped at least to avert the consequences of San Stefano by temporizing. It argued that it would not evacuate Serbian troops from Vranje, Pirot, and Trŭn until the Turks evacuated the territory around Novi Pazar and Mitrovica. The Serbs were quite determined to stand their ground, and fortunately the Russians chose not to press them, since the Treaty of San Stefano had been placed in a diplomatic limbo by the forthcoming Congress of Berlin.

While the Russians were arguing their case in Vienna, so were the Serbs. Prince Milan had by now been thoroughly shaken in his reliance on Russia. A new pro-Austrian policy was in the making in Belgrade. Milan instructed Ristić to stop in Vienna on his way to Berlin and to see Andrássy. He also gave him a personal letter to Andrássy in which he referred to the growing awareness in Serbia of a "community of interests" with Austria-Hungary. While Ristić generally hoped to avoid having Serbia in either Russia's or Austria's sphere, he was only too glad at that moment to parley with the Austrians in exchange for clearly defined gains, in this case Pirot, Vranje, and Trŭn. During their talk, Andrássy told Ristić that Austria-Hungary would support Serbia's claim to Pirot and Vranje and to the general area in the southeast. However, Andrássy insisted that Serbia renounce its promised gains in the direction of Novi Pazar and Mitrovica inasmuch as Austria regarded the Sancak of Novi Pazar as being in its sphere. Moreover, he required commercial and railway connections with Austria-Hungary, which would place Serbia in Austria's economic sphere. Finally, he warned that if the Serbs did not agree, they could not expect his support even for Niš itself.

Neither of Andrássy's conditions troubled Ristić much. The territory in the Sancak was a lost cause anyway, since it was a foregone conclusion that Russia would not risk opposing Austria on Serbia's behalf. As for being in the Austro-Hungarian economic sphere, Serbia had little to lose from better trade relations or from a much needed railroad. On July 7, 1878, Andrássy and Ristić signed an economic agreement. One provision called for a railway in Serbia connecting Belgrade with Niš, Pirot, and Vranje, with eventual connections between Vienna and Belgrade and between Niš and Istanbul. Another provision dealt with the eventual conclusion, after the final peace, of either a trade treaty or a customs union between Austria-Hungary and Serbia. A third provision gave Austria-Hungary the right to regulate the Danube River at the Iron Gate and permission to use temporarily the Serbian side of the Danube as an operational base. There was nothing objectionable or dangerous to Serbia about the agreement except, possibly, a customs union, and there Ristić saw to it that the agreement specified that the prior agreement of both parties would be necessary. On the whole, the agreement offered Serbia real benefits.

The Congress of Berlin met from June 13 to July 13, 1878. In general, its greatest effect was to modify the Treaty of San Stefano by creating more of a balance in the settlement. Great Bulgaria was divided into three: a northern autonomous state, a southern half with a special administration under the Turkish government, and Macedonia, which was to remain entirely Ottoman but with certain reforms. On the other hand, Austria-Hungary was given a mandate to occupy Bosnia and Hercegovina and to garrison the Sancak of Novi Pazar, thus providing a wedge between Serbia and Montenegro. Austria-Hungary would not even consider awarding Serbia the territory near Novi Pazar and Mitrovica, and Russia did not intervene in the matter. Thus Serbia got nothing to the west and southwest, except for a couple of villages on the Bosnian border, Mali Zvornik and Sakar, which Ristić had tried for years to bring into Serbia, where they belonged in the first place. As for the southern border, the Turks, supported by the British, demanded the return of Vranje as well as Grdelica Canyon, which formed a strategic pass. However, Austria stood on Serbia's side in the matter, and the territory went to Serbia. As for Pirot and Trŭn in the east, Russia wanted them to go to Bulgaria. Ristić frankly told the Russians that Serbia was so eager to get this territory that, if the Russians proved difficult, Serbia would turn to Austria for help at whatever cost. Eventually a compromise was reached: both Pirot and Trŭn were given to Serbia, though a good part of the Pirot district went to Bulgaria. Later in the proceedings, however, Serbia lost Trŭn when it was awarded to Bulgaria as compensation for some alteration in the Bulgarian border in favor of the Turks.

The net gains for Serbia at the Congress of Berlin were the following: Serbia's independence was confirmed by the powers; it was able to preserve Niš, Pirot, and Vranje; and it received 200 square miles of territory instead of the 150 square miles it got at San Stefano. That

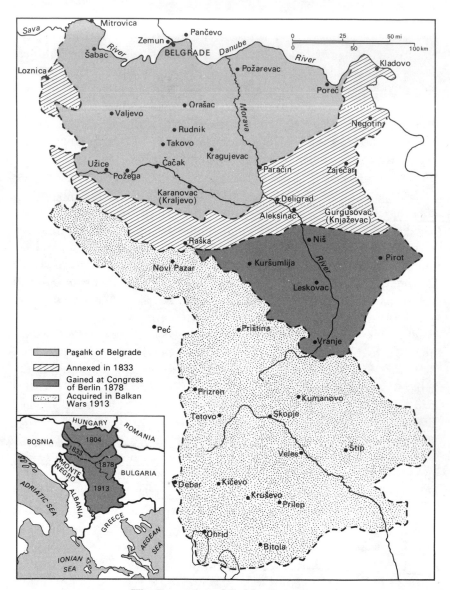

The Expansion of Serbia 1804–1913

Serbia got so little of what it wanted was blamed on the Russians. That it got as much as it did was attributed to Austria-Hungary's support. Russia's diplomats had made quite clear to the Serbs that Serbia was in the sphere of Austria-Hungary. Serbia's problem now was how

[400]

to benefit from Austria-Hungary's support without becoming a satellite and without entirely losing contact with Russia. This quest for a balance between East and West was difficult in that it involved domestic politics as well; the Liberals were still of the opinion that Austria was the chief threat to Serbia. They showed this by the great reluctance of their cabinet ministers to approve the Andrássy-Ristić economic agreement.

The Congress of Berlin was a turning point in Serbia's history. Instead of bringing about Prince Michael's program of the liberation of the Balkan peoples by themselves and the creation of a large South Slavic state, the Balkan Crisis of 1875–1878 resulted in a quite different solution. The Balkan peoples did not decide their own fate; the Great Powers did. The Balkan peoples were made the pawns of Great Power rivalries. Instead of a Balkan confederation or a South Slavic state, the peninsula was more than ever divided into national states, now independent of Turkey but not free of their dependence on other powers. Instead of being brought together, as their leaders had once hoped, an enlarged and now independent Serbia and a partitioned Bulgaria found themselves separated by two spheres of influence, those of Austria-Hungary and Russia, and by conflicting aspirations for the future. Centered in the Morava Valley and unable to expand to the east, west, or north, Serbia's only hope for future expansion was to the south, into the Vardar extension of the Morava route, into Macedonia. This was also Bulgaria's hope. A collision was inevitable. Finally, Serbia's experience during the Balkan Crisis made it far more receptive to the idea of a Greater Serbia than to the ideal of Yugoslavism, which had once enjoyed warm support, at least among young liberal romantics. In an age of *Realpolitik*, political romanticism was no longer fashionable or profitable.

VIII

From Independence
to Satellite Kingdom,
1878-1889

The First Years of Independence, 1878–1880,
and the Economy

Independence swelled Serbian pride, but it did not solve Serbia's problems. After the Congress of Berlin, the fiction of old Stevča Mihailović's premiership was dropped, and on September 30, 1878, Jovan Ristić was made premier as well as foreign minister. The immediate tasks that the now independent government faced were to integrate the newly annexed territories into the state, to revive Serbia's finances, and to fulfill the obligations incurred by the Andrássy-Ristić economic agreement.

In the new territories, the most pressing need, from an administrative viewpoint, was the establishment of law and order. The problem was complicated by the political backwardness of these Ottoman regions. Though a network of judges and local police was quickly created, Serbia's laws could not yet be applied to a primitive region in which feudalism still existed. Judges were instructed to judge not on the basis of Serbia's legal code but "according to conscience and conviction and with a regard for popular justice and customs." Lawyers were not recognized in the area until 1881, on the assumption that the simple populace could be fleeced by shysters. Serbia was bound by the Congress of Berlin to respect the property rights of the local Muslims, many of whom owned large estates with Christian tenants. The government could not simply dispossess these landowners, nor could it buy them off, because it lacked funds. It could only force the tenants themselves to buy the land within five years. The Ottoman government complained that this was plain plunder in a legal form, inasmuch as the tenants paid very irregularly or not at all, on the assumption that they would pay a lump sum at the end of five years. Meanwhile the landlord was left without anything. In 1882, the government was able to establish a loan fund that enabled peasants to pay off the landlord and to repay the government over a period of from fifteen to twenty years.

The Ristić government was faced with an empty treasury, at a time when the state needed more money than ever, in view of the expenditures necessitated by expanded frontiers and independence. The administration of newly annexed areas and the establishment of foreign missions, as befitted a newly independent country, required money. The budget for the fiscal year 1878–1879 was bigger by 3,000,000 dinars than the budget for the previous year. The government hoped to cover much of the deficit through the sale of certain obsolete army supplies and food. However, the only sure way out of the difficulty was to raise taxes.

An unpopular new tax, passed on January 31, 1879, was called into being by a law loftily entitled "The Law on the Settlement of the State Debt Incurred in the War for the Liberation and Independence of the People." It was meant to spare peasants, who had suffered enough from requisitioning during the war, and civil servants, whose income was low, so the burden was placed on tradesmen and professional men. The resulting howl of protest was a sign of Serbia's modernization, for it demonstrated how many Serbs belonged to this rising middle class. The tax struck hard even in the villages, where there were taverns and grocery stores. It was levied according to the annual income of the taxpayer, but this was problematical in two ways: first, it was inevitably passed on to the consumer anyway; and second, it was rarely paid in full, owing to the fact that local tax boards generally consisted of neighbors, friends, and relatives. So out of an expected revenue of 1,500,000 dinars, the government actually collected about a third of that sum.

The central government got its money, and its revenge, by annulling the assessments made by local boards and by sending its own assessors around the country. These civil servants spared no one, and often the new assessment was as much as ten times higher than the first. This raised an even louder hue and cry. The Assembly of 1879 was so opposed to the tax that the minister of finance—none other than the great Liberal Vladimir Jovanović—had to resign and the tax was repealed. After that the only way out for the state was to impose a surtax, which was fair in that the poor paid nothing, citizens with a middling income paid little (about four dinars), and the prosperous paid on a graduated scale. In reality, of course, the greater part of the tax was paid, as always, by the peasantry.

During the Ristić regime, by a law of December 22, 1878, Serbia took another step forward by establishing its own currency. The new unit was the silver dinar, and six million of them were minted. The law authorized the minting of gold coins of twenty dinars and ten dinars, and silver coins in denominations of five, two, one, and one-half dinars. There were also copper coins ranging from ten paras to one para. The government was authorized to mint 10,000,000 dinars in gold, 3,600,000 in silver, and 1,200,000 in copper. The adoption of the gold standard was a sign of Serbia's coming of age in the modern world of commerce.

The building of a railroad was another such sign. According to the Andrássy-Ristić agreement of 1878, Serbia was to build a cross-country railroad within three years. The Serbs were reluctant to proceed without simultaneous agreements with Bulgaria and the Ottoman Empire, for unless the railroad were an international link, there would be little use for it in Serbia. However, the Austrians insisted that the Serbs go ahead with all three lines—Belgrade-Niš, Niš-Vranje, and Niš-Pirot—regardless of Bulgarian or Ottoman plans for linking lines. As the Austrian demand was tied to the successful conclusion of an advantageous trade agreement, the Serbian government was forced to agree, yet Ristić refused to commit himself to build the Niš-Pirot line within the three years. When he threatened to resign over the matter, Austria-Hungary relented. By the Railroad Convention of April 8, 1880, Serbia obligated itself to Austria-Hungary to build a railroad from Belgrade to Vranje, via Niš, but not to Pirot, within three years.

The Assembly of 1880, which was convened in extraordinary session just to ratify the Railroad Convention, objected to it strenuously on the grounds that a trade agreement with Austria should come first, and that as long as Bulgaria and the Ottoman Empire were not linked to the railroad, Serbia was doomed to become an economic colony of Austria-Hungary. Ristić replied that he, too, was aware of the latter danger, and that that was why he wanted the railroad—as Serbia's only sure outlet to the sea. The Ottoman railroad from Salonika to Skopje was already a fact, and there was no obstacle to extending the line to Vranje, especially with Austro-Hungarian help. Ristić ended his speech to the Assembly with a kind of battle cry: "Salonika, to Salonika!" The Railroad Convention was ratified by a vote of 122 to 40, with 3 abstentions.

The next step was a trade agreement with Austria-Hungary. Serbia needed it far more than Austria-Hungary, since according to the decisions of the Congress of Berlin, Serbia's previous customs duties remained in force until new agreements were made. This meant that Austria-Hungary could raise its tariffs at will while Serbia had to maintain its tariff at the old rate of 3 percent. Thus, far from hurrying Serbia, as with the railroad, Austria-Hungary temporized and even worked against Serbian imports by banning Serbian cattle, in November 1878, ostensibly because some were diseased. In January 1879 Austria-Hungary raised its tariff on Serbian pigs, which accounted for 41 percent of Serbia's total exports, from 1.05 florins in silver to 2 florins in gold. Since Austria-Hungary would not conclude a trade agreement with Serbia until it ratified the Railroad Convention, Serbia turned to other countries for trade agreements. In 1879 it concluded preliminary trade treaties with Britain, Italy, Russia, Switzerland, and Belgium; all included the most-favored-nation clause. Since Serbia sent no exports to these countries, the treaties were of political rather than economic significance; Serbia was asserting its new rights as an independent nation. A permanent trade treaty with Great Britain in early 1880 was also of greater political than economic importance in that Britain was thus the first nation formally to renounce the previous right of its citizens in Serbia to immunity from Serbia's laws and courts as well as from taxes and guild regulations.

Negotiations for a trade treaty with Austria-Hungary began in mid-1880 and went badly. Austria-Hungary insisted that it already enjoyed most-favored-nation treatment as a result of a treaty of 1862 with the Ottoman Empire, which included Serbia. The Serbian government took the view that the Berlin Treaty did not bind Serbia to Ottoman commercial agreements but merely to existing tariffs, based on Serbia's rights as an autonomous part of the Ottoman Empire. Despite the whole complicated legal hassle that ensued, the point was of great importance to Serbia, because it would not permit itself to be bound by an Ottoman treaty of 1862. When the Serbian government offered Austria-Hungary most-favored-nation treatment on a reciprocal basis, the latter refused, insisting on the validity of its treaties with the

Ottoman Empire. In September 1880 Austria-Hungary sent Serbia what amounted to an ultimatum on the question. What hurt the Serbian government most was Austria-Hungary's apparent refusal to deal with Serbia on an equal basis. If Serbia gave in, Austria-Hungary would enjoy maximum economic privileges in Serbia, simply on the basis of an old treaty with the Ottoman Empire, without the necessity of concluding a trade treaty with Serbia, while Serbia would enjoy no corresponding privileges in Austria-Hungary in the absence of a trade treaty. The Austro-Hungarian government was not avoiding a trade treaty with Serbia, but by insisting on its rights under the Ottoman treaty of 1862, it was in a position to put pressure on Serbia in the negotiations.

The whole matter was of serious significance in Serbian internal politics as well, since the Ristić government was sensitive to opposition charges of selling out to Austria. On the other hand, nobody, including Prince Milan, and least of all the merchant class, liked the idea of Ristić's ultimate weapon—a tariff war, for this would be ruinous for Serbia. Finally, on October 21, 1880, the Ristić government presented the prince with the reasons for its inability to give in to Austria-Hungary in the matter. Milan could not accept these reasons, and five days later the Ristić government resigned. Thus ended the regime of a man who had directed the country for twelve years, almost without interruption. Ristić was a scholarly pedant and a meticulous diplomat who never even tried to win popularity and who enraged his young prince with his air of an aloof schoolmaster. It was by sheer personal ability that he wielded his authority. He was undoubtedly one of modern Serbia's few great statesmen.

The Development of Political Parties

After Ristić's fall, two new parties came to the forefront of Serbia's political life, the Progressives and the Radicals. Milan entrusted the new government to the Progressives, on two conditions: that they sign the commercial treaty with Austria and that his friend and secretary Čedomilj Mijatović be made foreign minister and minister of finance. The Progressives readily agreed, and their leader Milan Piroćanac was made premier.

The Progressive party emerged from the young Conservative group. After Prince Michael's death in 1868, the older leaders of the Conservative party retired from the scene—notably Ilija Garašanin and Nikola Hristić. Many of their lieutenants found it expedient to collaborate with the dominant Liberals, even to the point of joining their governments. After all, Ristić's "Liberal" policies were hardly distinguishable from those of the Conservative Garašanin. Some young Conservatives resented this and opposed the alliance of old Liberals and old Conservatives in the name of essentially liberal ideas. In fact, they objected to the 1869 constitution as not being liberal enough.

Their leader, Aćim Čumić, who had studied law and political science in Heidelberg and Paris, even had dealings with the democratic and socialist left, at the time the newspaper *Radenik* (The Worker) was founded in 1871 as the first socialist newspaper in the Balkans; he and six other young progressive intellectuals signed a political program published in *Radenik* that called for local autonomy for communes and districts, freedom of the press, assembly and association, an end to the standing army, and similar measures. In 1873, with the fall of the Liberal government, Čumić was taken into Marinović's cabinet of "Young Conservatives" as minister of the interior. At first he tried to carry out some of his progressive ideas, at least by proclamation, but he soon perceived that he lacked mass support. Politics drove him to a more neutral position and, finally, to adopting repressive measures himself, against the radical left in general and Svetozar Marković in particular. Čumić himself later went all the way from being premier for a brief three months in 1874–1875 to being sentenced to death for his part in the Topola Rebellion of 1877. His sentence was reduced to ten years, and he was eventually amnestied, in 1880. After this he disappeared from public life.

However, other Young Conservative leaders carred on: Milan Piroćanac, Ljubomir Kaljević, and Djordje Pavlović, to whose number were added Čedomilj Mijatović and Stojan Novaković. They were all educated and highly respected men. Piroćanac had studied law in Paris and was a distinguished jurist. Kaljević had studied political science in Heidelberg and Paris and was the editor and owner of several newspapers. Pavlović also had studied law in Paris and was for seven years a professor of civil law at the Great School before becoming director of the Credit Bank of Smederevo. In 1875–1876 he was foreign minister under Kaljević's premiership. Mijatović had studied law in Munich, Leipzig, and Zurich, was a professor in the Great School, and finance minister in several cabinets after 1873. He was also a popular writer and a historian of note. Novaković's education was restricted to Serbia, yet he was to become greater than all of his peers as a scholar, first in literature and philology and then as the dean of Serbian historians. In the 1870s he served alternately as gymnasium professor, head of the National Library and Museum, professor in the Great School, and, on two occasions, minister of education. There was also Milutin Garašanin, who studied the technical sciences in Paris and the military sciences in Metz as a lieutenant for two years, and whose political career, beginning as a deputy in 1874, was certainly enhanced by the name of his distinguished father, Ilija Garašanin. These men and others like them gained a large following and became the dominant political party in Serbia from 1880 to 1886.

The reasons for their rapid rise to power were mostly economic. Austria-Hungary's measures against Serbian imports hurt the livestock merchants and wealthy peasants a great deal, and when Ristić threatened a ruinous tariff war as well, they would endure no more. The Liberals' attempt to lay an income tax on the commercial and professional classes also earned their hostility. The peasants, too, who had suffered enough during the war, thanks to requisitioning, now again bore the brunt of the war debt. There were political reasons as well for the Liberals' fall. At the top, Prince Milan hated Ristić so much that he forgot his own duty to be politically neutral and actually intrigued with the opposition to topple his own government. Further down, radicalism was making rapid headway among the masses. The same rising middle class that opposed Ristić and the Liberals also felt that sterner measures had to be taken to suppress the spread of socialist and other radical ideas among the lower classes. And so on October 31, 1880, the Progressives came to power, under the premiership of Milan Piroćanac.

In addition to the Liberals, the Progressives had against them the Radicals, another new and rapidly growing party. The remote ideological beginnings of Serbian radicalism in general may be traced to those Serbian student groups in St. Petersburg and Zurich in the 1870s that gravitated in their ideas between Russian populism and anarchism on the one hand and Marxism on the other, and whose best-known member was Svetozar Marković. The Zurich group even procured a Serbian printing press and began to publish the works of Chernyshevskii, Marx, and Robert Owen, as well as books of their own. One by one these students, who were largely in technical fields such as engineering, began to return to Serbia on completing their studies. Svetozar Marković was among the first, and the best known, but there were others, most notably, in view of his later career, Nikola Pašić.

From the start there was a rather broad spectrum to Serbian radicalism, ranging from the socialism of Svetozar Marković to the ideas of bourgeois revolutionary democracy. A bridge between the two was Adam Bogosavljević, an educated man who returned to the village life of his native eastern Serbia, where he organized the peasants. His main ideas, which reflected those of Marković, were his radical opposition to the bourgeois system and his insistence on local communal autonomy. Because he was a frequent deputy in the Assembly, he was also committed to parliamentary democracy, and in time he came closer to bourgeois liberalism than to revolutionary socialism.

The Radical party itself was even more to the center. Its leader Nikola Pašić had, in 1875, actively participated in Svetozar Marković's newspaper *Oslobodjenje* (Liberation). In the same year he had taken money collected in Serbia to the rebels in Hercegovina. During the Serbo-Turkish wars he served as an engineer. In 1878 he was elected a deputy to the Assembly by his native Zaječar, in eastern Serbia. From that time on he became the leader of the radical opposition in the National Assembly.

Another important leader of the Radicals was Pera Todorović, who was more important than Pašić as a political organizer in the countryside and as a journalist. Todorović's stormy political life began as a schoolboy, when he was expelled from the Belgrade gymnasium for a student rebellion. He studied in Budapest and Zurich, where he became acquainted with Bakunin. He returned to Serbia in 1871, a disciple of Chernyshevskii and one of Svetozar Marković's first supporters. He wrote reports of the Assembly's doings in Marković's newspaper *Javnost* (The Public). In 1874–1875, he was editor of the first socialist literary journal in Serbia, *Rad* (Labor), which carried articles by Svetozar Marković and others as well as translations of Chernyshevskii and Pisarev. In 1876, when a socialist candidate won in local elections in Kragujevac, Todorović created quite a stir by unfurling a large red banner with the word *Samouprava* (Self-Government) inscribed on it. The government chose to regard this as a revolutionary act and jailed him for treason. His trial was postponed because of the war with the Turks, which he was allowed to join as a volunteer. He served in General Cherniaev's headquarters and received a medal for bravery. When the war ended, he fled to Hungary to avoid arrest. In Novi Sad, he published a socialist journal, *Straža* (The Guard), for which he was deported. He went to Paris, but returned to Serbia in 1880 after Ristić's fall.

Despite their ideological origins and name, many Radicals were far from being socialists and revolutionaries. On the contrary, they perceived that their theoretical socialism was hardly applicable to a Serbia that was so underdeveloped economically and socially. Moreover, these so-called Radicals, as they were popularly known, were not averse to making political compromises to achieve their ends. In the 1880 elections to the Assembly this meant a virtual coalition with the Progressives, though it lasted only through the elections. Their victory was a crushing defeat for the Liberals, who received 7 out of 128 seats. This was the price the Liberals paid for their unpopular economic measures and for becoming bureaucrats alienated from the electorate. In the new Assembly, the presidency went to the man who received the most votes, a Conservative, Aleksa Popović; the vice-presidency went to Nikola Pašić, a Radical, who got the next highest number of votes. However, Prince Milan vetoed the second choice and another Conservative became vice-president. The Radicals replied on January 20, 1881, by coming out with a new newspaper, *Samouprava* (Self-Government). The first page of the first issue bore the Radicals' Program, signed by thirty-eight deputies, with the note that another thirty-eight deputies joined them but preferred not to give their names. If this was so, then the Radicals and their supporters held a majority in the Assembly.

The Radical Program of 1881 was, in effect, the formal beginning of the Radical party as such. It called for the following: amendments to the 1869 constitution to ensure universal manhood suffrage and abolition of the State Council; a simplified and cheaper administration by abolishing all intermediary offices and giving local districts and communes self-government; elective judges for civil cases and juries for all criminal cases; direct graduated taxes, and a national bank with regional banks to be controlled by the citizens, to provide credits for agriculture, trade, and industry; free public education with an emphasis on civic training and applied arts; a more popular army, with military drill in secondary and high schools; close ties with Montenegro and Bulgaria, and aid to still unliberated regions; and complete freedom of press, assembly, association, local autonomy, and security of person and property. It also proclaimed *Samouprava* as the official organ of the Radical party. All deputies of the 1881 Assembly were invited to sign the program, which was in the keeping of Nikola Pašić.

Obviously there was nothing "socialistic," "republican," "pro-Karadjordjević," or even "radical" about the program. What frightened the Progressives was that the Radicals might well hold a majority in the Assembly. Just as Serbian politics had revolved for a generation around the struggle between Conservatives and Liberals, now the political arena would be occupied for another generation by the struggle between Progressives and Radicals.

Serbia Becomes Austria-Hungary's Satellite and a Kingdom

The Progressive government headed by Pirocánac was Austrophile in outlook. It bound Serbia to Austria-Hungary through two instruments, the Trade Treaty of 1881 and the so-called "Secret Convention" of June 28, 1881.

The first was no usual trade treaty. It was based on the mutual recognition of both neighbors that they had reason, by virtue of the volume and complementary nature of their trade, to give each other privileges they would not grant others. Austria-Hungary found a way to do this by extending to all of Serbia the tariff privileges usually accorded to narrow border zones, at least for the most important articles of trade, notably Serbia's pigs, cattle, hides, and agricultural products such as plums and jam. Serbia allowed manufactured goods from Austria-Hungary similar privileges. Such an agreement, however immediately advantageous to both sides, meant in effect that Austria-Hungary was encouraging Serbia to be an agrarian colony while discouraging the development of Serbian industry. Thus the trade agreement served to lock Serbia into Austria-Hungary's economy with all of the disadvantages that an agrarian economy has in dealing with an industrial economy. One sign of this disparity was the fact that Austria-Hungary received most-favored-nation treatment with no reciprocal rights for Serbia. Moreover, Austria-Hungary reserved for itself a certain freedom of action that could have a crippling effect on Serbia; for example, it could stop the importation of pigs any time it chose, or it could ban Serbian livestock if there was even a suspicion of disease. Austria also carefully protected its own goods in Serbia by insisting that no discriminatory internal taxes be placed on them to make their price higher than native products. It also limited Serbia's right to declare a monopoly on only tobacco, salt, and gunpowder, assuring Austria-Hungary's sugar, matches, paper, and other articles of a safe market in Serbia. Thus the Serbian government signed away several important rights in exchange for a trade which in fact could only make it increasingly dependent on Austria-Hungary. How much economic power Austria-Hungary already wielded over Serbia, even without such a trade treaty, is apparent from the fact that 77 percent of Serbia's imports came from Austria-Hungary and 82 percent of its exports went to it at the time the treaty was being negotiated. On the other hand, what Austria-Hungary got from Serbia amounted to only 1½ percent of its total imports.

When this trade treaty was brought to the Assembly for ratification, Nikola Pašić proposed its rejection, largely because the Radicals feared that with it Serbia's infant industry would not survive, and thus Serbia would be doomed to remain an undeveloped agrarian country. The progressives argued that if Serbia's industry was weak, it was for lack of capital and a ready labor force; the only way Serbia could accumulate enough capital, they maintained, was by assuring its agricultural products the best terms possible in foreign markets, and Austria-Hungary was offering Serbia advantages the latter could not expect to get from any other state. In this conflict between two truths, immediate profit won out over future considerations, that is, the benefits to present Serbian agriculture outweighed the disadvantages to a still future Serbian industrial development. The Assembly ratified the treaty in June 1881.

It did not have the opportunity to ratify the second binding tie with Austria-Hungary, the Austro-Serbian Convention of June 28, 1881. Besides Prince Milan, only three political leaders—Mijatović, Piroćanac, and Milutin Garašanin—knew about it until 1893, when it became public knowledge in Serbia. Its entire text was not published until 1920, by A. F. Pribram in Vienna.

The Secret Convention was signed just ten days after the Alliance of the Three Emperors (Dreikaiserbund): William I of Germany, Francis Joseph of Austria-Hungary, and Alexander III of Russia. The terms of that alliance that concerned Serbia most were that Russia would not oppose the annexation of Bosnia and Hercegovina by

Austria-Hungary at some opportune time, and that Austria-Hungary would similarly not oppose the eventual union of Bulgaria and Eastern Rumelia. It is in the light of this agreement that the Secret Convention between Austria-Hungary and Serbia must be seen. The Austro-Hungarian government needed to consolidate its regime in Bosnia and Hercegovina in order to carry out their annexation. This meant that Serbia had to be kept from fomenting national revolution among the Serbian population there, who were more numerous than any other single group.

Prince Milan, on the other hand, deeply resented his abandonment by Russia in 1878, especially at a time when Serbia's desperate financial plight necessitated foreign aid. Moreover, he had certain ambitions both for himself and for his country. He did not forget the attempt, during the war, to make him king. More importantly, he knew that, given the postwar settlement, Serbia's only avenue of expansion was Macedonia, and there his greatest obstacle was Bulgaria and its patron, Russia.

There is some difference of opinion as to who approached whom first concerning the agreement. Premier Pirocanac suspected that it was Prince Milan, while Foreign Minister Mijatović thought it was Baron Benjamin (Béni) von Kállay, the Hungarian diplomat and the leading Balkan specialist in Austria-Hungary's foreign ministry. At any rate, it is clear from the ease with which the negotiations went that both parties to the agreement wanted it very much. It is also clear from the precautions taken by both sides that each was eager to keep the agreement a secret. Though its terms had been discussed in Vienna, especially at the time of Milan's visit in June 1881 during a trip that had taken him to Berlin and St. Petersburg as well, the Secret Convention was signed in Belgrade, that same month, by the Austro-Hungarian minister in Belgrade, Baron Herbert, and Serbia's Foreign Minister Čedomilj Mijatović. Prince Milan revealed its contents to his premier and war minister, Pirocanac and Milutin Garašanin, only after it had been signed and he had sworn them to secrecy. The prince even pretended to them at first that the treaty had not yet been signed, but they found out about its ratification by chance from the Austro-Hungarian minister. They were so aghast at what had been done that they immediately tendered their resignations. The prince refused to accept them for fear of revealing the treaty. Finally, after a covert crisis of several weeks, Pirocanac and Garašanin agreed to remain in their posts, but only after the foreign ministry was taken from Mijato-vić and given to the premier, as a guarantee that nothing would be done behind their backs again. Mijatović remained in the cabinet, however, as minister of commerce.

The shock Piroćanac and Garašanin experienced is quite under-standable. By the Secret Convention of 1881, Prince Milan in fact signed away Serbia's right as an independent nation to determine its own foreign policy. Milan's gains from the agreement were spelled out in articles 3 and 4. The former gave Austria-Hungary's promise to recognize his title as king whenever he chose to assume it. The latter stipulated that Austria-Hungary would support Serbia's southward expansion, except in the Sancak of Novi Pazar. This was a dubious gain at best, since Serbia's eventual expansion into Macedonia hardly depended on Austria-Hungary alone. To pay for these gains, Prince Milan promised, in article 2, that Serbia would not tolerate any "polit-ical, religious or other intrigues" against the Dual Monarchy, includ-ing Bosnia and Hercegovina as well as the Sancak of Novi Pazar. This meant the abandonment of Serbia's traditional support of Serbian na-tionalism in those provinces as well as of the idea of a union with Montenegro. Even more crucial was article 4, in which it was agreed that "without a previous understanding with Austria-Hungary, Serbia will neither negotiate nor conclude any political treaty with another government, and will not admit to her territory a foreign armed force, regular or irregular, even as volunteers." Article 5 bound Serbia to maintain benevolent neutrality in case Austria-Hungary found itself at war with one or more powers; this article again specifically included Bosnia-Hercegovina and the Sancak of Novi Pazar under the term "Austro-Hungarian Monarchy."

Apart from these provisions, article 1 was a declaration of mutual amity, article 6 called for an eventual agreement on military coopera-tion, article 8 fixed the term of the treaty at ten years with possibility of renewal and amendment, article 9 obliged both sides to secrecy, and the last article called for ratification of the treaty in Belgrade within fifteen days.

It was apparent that Prince Milan had simply agreed to everything Vienna proposed to him. Hoping to undo some of the effects of the Secret Convention, Piroćanac went to Vienna in an effort to get a new interpretation of article 4. On October 30, 1881, the Habsburg gov-ernment agreed to a declaration that article 4 did not "impair the right of Serbia to negotiate and conclude treaties, even of a political nature with another government." This was interpreted to mean that Serbia would not conclude any treaty contrary to the spirit and intent of the Secret Convention. Moreover, it was not required that the Serbian government submit any such treaties to the Austro-Hungarian government for previous approval. As a result, Piroćanac was pleased to have obtained a satisfactory reinterpretation of the Secret Convention. What he did not know was why it was so easy for the Austro-Hungarian government to make such a seeming concession. Unknown to Piroćanac, Prince Milan had sent a personal declaration one week earlier to Kállay which stated that "of my own free will . . . I hereby . . . assume the formal engagement on my honor and in my quality as prince of Serbia, not to enter into any negotiations whatsoever relative to any kind of a political treaty without communication with and the previous consent of Austria-Hungary."

It was not the motive or the goal of the Secret Convention that was so bad for Serbia, since Serbia had no choice at the time but to make close ties with Austria and nowhere to expand except into Macedonia. What hurt was the nature of the agreement itself. For the sake of an uncertain future gain, Prince Milan gave Austria-Hungary a certain present gain, and at the price of a serious limitation on Serbia's independence. Yet, from a long-range point of view, the arrangement with Austria-Hungary had some salutary effect. It bought Serbia many years of peace with a powerful neighbor who, instead of being hostile, even contributed to the economic advancement and modernization of Serbia.

Soon after the Secret Convention was signed, Serbia was proclaimed a kingdom, on February 22 (March 6 N.S.), 1882. It was hardly a proud and happy occasion. Serbia was so caught up in internal troubles that most people, not even suspecting what the declaration of the kingdom had cost, quite simply regarded it as a political diversion. Indeed, the new king was on the verge of abdication at the time of his elevation to the royal title.

The Regime of the Progressives, 1880–1886

Serbia's first years as a kingdom, and Milan's last years as a ruler, were filled with turmoil and scandals, both public and private. These troubles were all the more lamentable because Serbia was making excellent progress in becoming a modern and rapidly developing nation. Both the troubles and the progress may be attributed in large part to the Progressive party.

The Progressives, who ran the government, deserved their name insofar as they were admirers of Western enlightenment and technical achievements who truly wished to transform their country. Politically they were even more advanced than the old Liberals in their desire for civil rights and individual freedoms. Yet precisely because the Progressives saw everything through Western eyes, they were, in fact, less democratic in their attitude toward the masses of the people. They saw little similarity between Western parliaments and Serbia's annual Assembly composed largely of peasants who hardly comprehended the needs of a modern cultured state. What the Progressives wanted was a system in which the enlightened and the progressive forces of Serbia, however few, could lead the many unenlightened and backward to a better life. In political terms, they hoped for an elitist oligarchy, which could be achieved by having a senate of intellectuals and prosperous men of affairs and an electorate divided into voting classes, as in Romania, according to the amount of taxes they paid. Pirećanac once observed that "the main thing is to assure the preponderance of intellect over sheer numbers." These Serbian Whigs were, historically, a more modern, more cultured version of the Constitutionalists. And like the Constitutionalists of the 1830s, the Progressives wished to have a constitution to their liking. They began to work toward this end almost as soon as they came to power. King Milan was not happy about the liberal aspects of the Progressives' program, but he, too, did not like the Constitution of 1869 for reasons of his own. And so he supported this goal.

To prove their good faith and high principles, the Progressives proposed a series of laws in the spring of 1881 which the National Assembly passed with enthusiasm. The Law on the Press abolished virtually all remaining restrictions on freedom of the press, except one—issues of newspapers could be confiscated or banned for inciting to rebellion or for *lèse majesté*. Not only was the press taken out of the hands of the police, but it was even shielded from the courts in libel cases by all kinds of provisions, which any skillful editor could use to keep his case out of court altogether. In effect, then, Serbia enjoyed an almost complete freedom of the press, but not for long; the government was soon to repent and, in July 1882, amended the law. A newspaper could thereafter be banned also for spreading nihilism and communism, of which the Radicals were often accused by their opponents. Rules involving violations of laws on libel and other offenses were tightened to permit more effective prosecution. The police were also given more discretion in deciding what was criminally inflammatory writing.

A Law on Meetings and Associations, the first of its kind in Serbia, was not quite so generous. While meetings were declared free and not subject to previous permission by the police, as were nonpolitical associations, political associations were subject to police regulation. However, the police could not deny a permit to political organizations unless their bylaws were contrary to law, and the authorities reserved the right to examine the minutes of their meetings and to send observers to them. Still the law was a great step forward in a country in which political meetings were never permitted and political associations were banned in principle. Political parties had not existed as formal organizations at all but merely as unorganized persons who shared the same views or interests. When, in Ristić's time, the Conservatives reserved some rooms in a Belgrade coffeehouse for their gatherings, this was regarded with great suspicion. Thus it was with the law of 1881 that political parties with a formal organization, meetings, dues, and so on became possible and a party was not held to be tantamount to a conspiracy. Whereas before politics was discussed only by assemblymen and journalists, and only whispered by others, now politics became a public affair.

The Law on Judges established a judiciary that was, for the first time, independent of the executive. In the future the government could not dismiss, pension, or transfer judges at will but only according to strict regulations and with the consent of the judiciary. While it continued to appoint whatever judges it wished in the lowest courts, it had to pick judges for all higher courts from a list of candidates compiled by the judges themselves. Salaries of judges were raised to give them greater financial security. In all these matters, the French and Belgian models were generally followed.

In other reforms, a law of 1883 abolished the national militia or home guard and made military service in the regular standing army a general obligation. It was hoped to gain thereby a standing army of 100,000 men. At the same time, to attract more men into becoming officers, this service was made the highest-paying in the state service.

With this Serbia began to get a caste of officers such as it had never had before.

Another law in early 1883 (December 31, 1882 O.S.) established, for the first time, universal compulsory elementary education. It came at a time when only one-sixth of the children of school age were actually in school, and when still roughly 90 percent of the population was illiterate. The law required that children who did not go on to higher schooling after completing four years of elementary school had to remain in elementary school another two years. Under Stojan Novaković's incumbency as minister of education, another teachers' preparatory school was also established, and teachers' salaries were substantially raised.

Naturally these and other new state needs, for example, the establishment of a diplomatic corps and foreign missions, all made the budget of the newly independent Serbian state greater than ever before. During the Progressive regime, from 1880 to 1886, state expenditures rose from 19 million dinars to 46 million dinars. A good part of this increase was due to the war debt, especially the loan from Russia. The Progressive government also incurred foreign debts in order to build the railroad it had promised Austria-Hungary and to establish a fund for agricultural credit.

Fortunately state revenues also increased in the same period from around 20 million dinars to a high of 39 million dinars in 1885. Various new taxes were devised to accomplish this: a stamp tax, a tax on alcoholic beverages, a tax on tobacco, a tax on a salt monopoly granted to the Anglo-Austrian Bank, a tax on places of business and artisans' shops, and customs duties, which doubled in the three years after 1879 owing to increased trade. Despite the increase in revenue, the Progressives' government had a deficit every year, which reached 14 million dinars by 1886. Instead of blaming this on the extraordinarily rapid increase of state needs, critics generally blamed the slipshod administration of Commerce Minister Čedomilj Mijatović.

A major advance was the law of January 18, 1883, establishing the National Bank. An attempt to create such a bank had been made in 1869 by the Regency after Prince Michael's assassination, but it had failed because of bad investments and the European crash of 1873. It never had the right to issue currency. After the Congress of Berlin in 1878, despite the fact that Serbia began to mint its own silver and gold coins, traders felt the need for a more flexible money supply and greater access to credit. Currency speculation and deficits in the state budget and in the balance of payments caused by import surpluses and repayment of foreign debts combined to put pressure on the supply of loanable funds. To help meet the situation, a Serbian Credit Bank (*Srpska Kreditna Banka*) was created in Belgrade in 1881 by the Länderbank of Vienna with help from the Comptoir d'Escompte of Paris. When this bank failed to accumulate more than a million dinars in paid-in capital, the Serbian government resolved to found a purely domestic bank of issue.

Though organized as a private joint-stock institution, the new National Bank (*Narodna Banka*) was granted powers of lending to other banks and the exclusive right to issue currency. The notes were only in large denominations of 50, 100, 500, and 1,000 dinars, payable in gold. To accommodate a traditional distrust in paper money, the law made clear that private persons, unlike state institutions, did not have to accept paper currency. And indeed, private recipients of the paper currency generally rushed to the bank to exchange it for gold. This severely limited the bank's supply of gold, which in turn limited its capacity to issue currency. This problem lasted until 1885, when the National Bank was authorized to issue silver notes of 10 dinars. People were not as quick to convert these to silver, and so the problem of supply was gradually solved and confidence in paper money rose. Nevertheless, the traditional distrust of paper money never quite vanished, and many Serbs found comfort in whatever hoards of gold coins they could stash away for hard times.

While the National Bank served a much needed function, one of its greatest failings lay in not promoting branches in the interior. However, this failure encouraged the growth of new banks, largely savings and credit institutions. Over fifty banks sprang up in the interior in the first decade following the founding of the National Bank. Prior to that time there had been only three such institutions.

The first great scandal of King Milan's last years occurred over the building of Serbia's first railroad. When the Ristić government obligated itself to Austria-Hungary to build the railroad within three years, that is, by 1883, no one considered who was to build it or with what means. Eventually it was decided that the state would pay the costs and that the railroad would be national property. However, it was obvious that a foreign concern would have to construct it and operate it for lack of native experience and personnel.

From the companies that submitted bids, the Progressive government chose the Paris firm of Eugène Bontoux. He had been director of the Südbahn firm in Vienna when he was called to Paris to become director of the Union Générale, established in 1878. Bontoux's proposal was that Serbia pay 198,000 francs per kilometer of rail line. The whole matter had a political aspect from the start; Bontoux had Austrian connections whereas his chief rivals, the Poliakov firm and a Russo-Belgian firm, both had Russian connections, which pleased the Panslavic-minded Radicals. The Radicals severely criticized the granting of the concession to Bontoux, on several counts: that the price was excessive, that the negotiations were conducted secretly, that there was no open bidding, and that Bontoux was too closely associated with Austria, which had more than enough influence in Serbia already. On this last score the Radicals were more right than they knew, for there was actually a secret agreement between Bontoux's Union Générale and the Länderbank of Austria which gave the latter a 30 percent interest in the Serbian railroad.

There was a keen public discussion of the railroad question, not only in the National Assembly but in the opposition newspapers, which took advantage of the new tolerance of freedom of the press to hint at bribery. It was during a long speech by the Radical peasant tribune Ranko Tajsić in the Assembly that Serbia probably first heard of the state of Wisconsin in the United States. Tajsić referred to a railroad scandal that had occurred in Wisconsin a generation before in which all the assemblymen but four, the governor, the lieutenant-governor, the secretary of the treasury, his assistant, thirteen other state officials, and many clerks were bribed. He read from a book how many "dinars" each received.

Despite various protests, the Assembly approved the Bontoux contract on March 22, 1881, by a vote of 97 to 57, with 5 abstentions. Nevertheless, the affair left a decidedly bitter aftertaste among the people. Rumors of bribery and corruption in high places continued to sweep across the land. An Austrian report observed that there was not a village in Serbia that had not heard the rumor that Prince Milan himself had received anywhere from one to three million dinars from Bontoux. The rumors were readily believed because of the unpopularity of the railroad project. Most of Serbia's peasant population could see no benefit to themselves from a railroad, and it was painfully apparent to them, thanks to the increase in taxes, what it was going to cost them, for the railroad alone accounted for a 30 percent increase in the national budget.

Having weathered one crisis over the Bontoux contract, the Progressive government soon found itself in another. In early 1882 the Union Générale collapsed, and Bontoux and his principal associates were arrested for irregularities in their operation. In France this crash triggered one of the worst financial crises since the fall of John Law's Banque Royale in 1720. Émile Zola made it the subject of his novel *L'Argent*. The fall of the Union Générale was no less a blow for the Progressive government in Serbia, especially after it had convinced the National Assembly that the French firm was worthy of confidence. The Union Générale owed Serbia 34,485,331 dinars at the time of its collapse. This was 8 million dinars more than the whole normal annual budget of Serbia. Much of this money was gained as a result of a bond issue which the Union Générale floated for the Serbian government and which the government chose to keep in the Union Générale. Finance Minister Mijatović was condemned for bad judgment in depositing the money with the Union Générale instead of with the French Bank, despite the favorable rate of interest the former institution had offered.

With the help of the governments of France and Austria-Hungary, the reputable Comptoir National d'Escompte formed a new company in 1885 to take over, and a way was found to lessen Serbia's losses from over 34 million dinars to 12.8 million dinars. This was done simply by having the new firm renounce the excess profit of 15 to 16 million dinars that the Union Générale was going to take. Even so, the new firm could expect a profit of 3 to 4 million dinars. All this showed what a bad deal the Progressive government had made in the first place, so bad that it was natural for many to ask whether it was mere stupidity or corruption that had led it to such an arrangement. The fact that Milan, whose personal finances were in desperate straits, had made use of Bontoux's firm for speculating on the French market gave fuel to the rumors that he had been bribed.

The reverberations among the populace were unprecedented in Serbia's history. It seemed as though the state had suddenly gone bankrupt. Public trust in the government was at a dangerously low ebb. Though no one has ever offered documentary proof that either Milan or any minister had received bribes, many people believed the opposite, and with reason. That Bontoux's agents had offered bribes to lesser figures, especially deputies in the Assembly, was a matter of public knowledge. There is also evidence of a later date that Bontoux offered sums to the prince and his ministers, though whether any of them accepted the bribes is a moot point. Mijatović, in his memoirs, attested to the fact that the bribes were offered. The verdict of history seems to be that Prince Milan and his Romanian uncle, General Catargiu, received bribes from Bontoux as did various underlings, but that the ministers did not. Whatever may be the true facts in the case, the Progressives were undoubtedly open to charges of high-handedness and imprudence.

The cabinet was ready to resign in the face of the storm, but Milan would not let them, nor would Austria-Hungary, which needed the Progressive cabinet. Their condition for remaining was the immediate proclamation of Serbia as a kingdom, with which to parry the attacks of the opposition in the Assembly. Milan accepted, not only to enhance the prestige of his dynasty, but also to gain a larger civil list to repair his own financial situation. Under these sorry circumstances, the Kingdom of Serbia was proclaimed on February 22 (March 6 N.S.), 1882.

Instead of resigning the Progressives put through a series of laws aimed at the Radical opposition. One of these, in July 1882, amended the Law on the Press. It authorized the banning of newspapers for spreading nihilism and communism, of which the Radicals were often accused by their opponents. Rules involving court procedures in cases involving libel and other press offenses were tightened to permit more effective prosecution. A law in June 1882 imposed a fine of 1,000 dinars on deputies whose absence caused the Assembly to be without a quorum. This was aimed at a favorite tactic of the Radicals to obstruct the business of the Assembly. A week later a law was promulgated to establish a mounted police force able to go wherever needed to preserve public order. The government explained that such a force was needed to suppress banditry, but the Radicals feared otherwise. The Radical leader Pera Todorović promptly dubbed this police cavalry *sejmeni* (from the Turkish *seğmen*), to evoke the memory of the dread mounted gendarmerie of Ottoman times, and the name stuck in popular parlance.

The Progressives lost much support by the zeal with which they got rid of their political opponents—not the Radicals, who were too new and inexperienced to be considered a present danger, but the

Liberals, whose possible return to power worried the Progressives. Probably no Serbian government more mercilessly purged the civil service of its political opponents than the Progressives. In their first year in office they pensioned sixty-five civil servants and dismissed twenty-six, whereas throughout its whole four years the previous Liberal government had pensioned only eight and dismissed only one.

It was when the Progressives dared even to replace the head of the Orthodox Church of Serbia, Metropolitan Michael (Jovanović), that they shocked many people. Both the Progressives and Prince Milan regarded Metropolitan Michael as a pillar of the Liberal regime. This energetic prelate was also a staunch Panslavist and Russophile who had worked closely with the Slavic Benevolent Societies in Russia in the late 1870s. Vienna was particularly wary of him because of his influence among the Orthodox priests of Bosnia and Hercegovina. All this was reason enough for the Progressives and Prince Milan to seek his downfall. Metropolitan Michael himself provided the needed excuse by opposing as uncanonical the application of the tax on professional men to the clergy. Michael and his Council of Bishops held that the priesthood was not a business venture but a vocation granted "by the grace of the Holy Ghost," and thus nontaxable. Until the state law was reconciled with canon law, Michael refused to comply. For this rebellious act he was relieved of his post, on October 30, 1881, like any government clerk, except that he did not even get a pension. The government did not consult the Council of Bishops or ask it to confirm the deed, as canon law required.

The Radicals, who were anticlerical, remained neutral, but the Liberals raised a hue and cry. They called on the clergy to refuse to baptize, marry, or bury until the government relented. However, the bishops, who were fearful for their own positions, were cowed into obedience by Prince Milan. Public opinion sympathized with the metropolitan.

Even more serious for Serbia was the unfavorable reaction in Russia. The Russian minister in Belgrade was instructed by the tsar to convey his displeasure to Milan. The prince replied that this was an internal matter and that he intended Serbia to be a modern state in which the civil law took precedence over canon law.

Milan had neither the power nor the popularity to effect such a policy. The people understood that what was really involved in the whole conflict was politics, both domestic and foreign. Milan's Russophobia had all of the intensity of the jilted lover. When Tsar Alexander II was assassinated, in March 1881, Milan even forbade Metropolitan Michael to deliver a eulogy and would not permit the government to send the new tsar, Alexander III, the usual condolences. Both in Serbia and in Russia the affair of Metropolitan Michael's dismissal took on the aspect of a religious conflict between Orthodoxy and Roman Catholic Austria-Hungary. The issue was seized upon by such Russian public leaders and statesmen as the nationalist editor of the *Moskovskie Vedomosti* (Moscow News), Katkov, Ignatiev, and Pobedonostsev, then procurator (*Ober-Prokuror*) of the Russian Orthodox Synod and former tutor of the new tsar. As a result of such pressures, the Russian government informed Milan that Russian-Serbian relations would not be "tolerable" until the metropolitan was restored to his post.

To give his dismissal of Michael a semblance of validity, Milan, now king, promulgated a new law on the composition of the Synod, the ruling body of the Church, which permitted the government to pack it with its own lay representatives, including the premier, the minister of education and church affairs, the president of the State Council, the presiding judge of the supreme court, and five deputies of the National Assembly. The Council of Bishops resolutely rejected this uncanonical act. Even the government's temporary replacement for Michael, Bishop Moses, deserted it. The government thereupon ignored the Council of Bishops and had its reformed Synod elect a new metropolitan, Archimandrite Theodosius Mraović, a retired professor of theology, even though no bishop attended the session. However, no Serbian bishop would consecrate him. The Serbian government then turned to Austria-Hungary for help. Vienna applied the necessary pressure until the Serbian patriarch in Austria-Hungary, German (Andjelić), agreed to perform the rite, in Sremski Karlovci. When the Serbian bishops still refused to recognize the new metropolitan, they were all dismissed, without pensions. Three new bishops were consecrated, again with the help of the Serbian hierarchy in Austria-Hungary.

The scandal rocked all of Serbia and echoed even in Russia. The Russian Orthodox Church refused to recognize the new metropolitan of Belgrade and closed the Serbian church in Moscow for daring to mention the man's name in the Liturgy. It also welcomed Michael in Russia, where he spent several years in genteel exile, till his return in 1888. In Serbia people were scandalized at the treatment accorded to their bishops and were very much against the new hierarchy. Metropolitan Theodosius had the reputation of being too worldly, in the Western style of the Austrian Serbian clergy, and too attracted by wine, women, and song, as well as cards, while Michael was an ascetic churchman of the old type whose very faults were somehow popular in that they were reminiscent of the rough-and-ready way of the heroic warrior-priests of national epic poetry. Eventually the Serbian government won, especially after the patriarch of Constantinople and the Orthodox churches of Greece and Romania recognized Theodosius. But, again, it was a costly victory which lost the government much support.

All of these crises must be seen in the light of the active political struggles of the day. Thanks to the laws of the Progressives themselves, the new freedom for political organization and expression resulted in more widely spread political activity than ever before in Serbia.

The Liberals were the first to take advantage of the law permitting the organization of political parties. How unused everyone was to the new freedom may be judged by the cautious manner in which they went about it. On September 29, 1881, seventy-four Liberal leaders, including Ristić, met in the Belgrade Library, a Liberal center since 1848, and organized a "Society for the Advancement of Literature"! It was more a gathering of old cronies than a public meeting. Out of it came a new newspaper, *Srpska Nezavisnost* (Serbian Independence). Its first issue, on October 1, 1881 (O.S.), contained the program of the Liberal party. In foreign affairs it stressed the unification of all the Serbian lands in the Balkan Peninsula and a customs union with neighboring peoples leading to a confederation. In domestic affairs the Liberal program called for a defense of constitutional rights and progress in the spirit of modern times.

Now it was the turn of the Radicals to organize. However, they did not begin with a literary society of a few leaders in Belgrade. As their call for organization, in the November 7, 1881 (O.S.), issue of their organ *Samouprava* (Self-Government) declared, "We have no special standard-bearers, we have no leaders or chiefs. We are all equal fighters for our convictions. . . . Our command is our brotherly consultation and agreement. And our army? It is all those who have endured and suffered, who still endure and suffer, under this fatal bureaucratic order in Serbia."

The Radicals instituted something quite new in Serbian life—a network of local party associations throughout the countryside. Until then the popular masses were not regarded as active participants in partisan politics. This was supposed to be the exclusive preoccupation of a relatively few city intellectuals. The peasants and artisans had their own political preferences, but these were on quite another level, often within the framework of traditional local dynastic loyalties. It was as though while the few at the top were playing political chess, the rest of the people could at best play only checkers. The peasantry was an elemental force whose likes and dislikes were either negligible or to be controlled and manipulated from above. When Pera Todorović and other Radicals went straight "to the people," to borrow the famous phrase from the history of Russian populism (*Narodnichestvo*), they politically activized the peasantry and organized a party apparatus at the grass roots level with a success whose rapidity startled the government and the other political parties, especially the Progressives.

Not everyone was disposed to play the game of politics, however. On October 23, 1882, on his return from Vienna, King Milan was almost assassinated at the door of the cathedral by Jelena Ilka Marković, the widow of Colonel Jevrem Marković, who had been executed, it was said by Milan's personal wish, for his part in the Topola Rebellion of 1877. While the motive of revenge was clear, Milan chose to see his would-be assassin as the instrument of a Radical plot. Her husband, the brother of the socialist Svetozar Marković, had been a Radical deputy in his day. Jelena Ilka Marković numbered the Radical leaders, notably Pera Todorović, among her friends. The Radical satirical journal *Ćosa* (Hairless) had just recently run a poem about an unpopular oriental despot which ended with the rebellious people shouting:

> You lived and you reigned
> Just as you liked;
> And now you must die
> Just as we like.

Moreover, why had the aggrieved widow waited over four years to revenge her husband? The subsequent investigation could find no link between the Radicals and the crime. Nevertheless, Milan was eager to seize the excuse to declare a royal dictatorship, but the Progressives were not the men for such a *coup d'état*.

A week after the attempt on his life, Milan decided to bolster his government by inviting the battle-hardened Liberals back and enticing them to join in a coalition government with the Progressives, as long as they left foreign affairs to him (with his man Mijatović as foreign minister) and did not bring Metropolitan Michael back. The Liberals refused.

The investigation of Jelena Ilka Marković dragged on for months. Only one accomplice was found, Jelena Lena Knićanin, also the widow of a colonel. As the investigation continued, the latter woman was found hanging by her neck in her prison cell, under circumstances that seemed all the more suspicious because the government would not make public a report of the autopsy. Soon after that, the guard who had been outside her cell also lost his life, at the hands of a colleague whose gun accidentally went off. The public inevitably connected the two deaths. Finally Ilka Marković was sentenced to death but had her sentence commuted to imprisonment, though she asked for no pardon. Soon after, she, too, was found dead in her jail cell, hanging by a towel around her neck. It was clear to those who knew her that she no longer had a will to live after the trial, but again the public suspected the government of foul play.

In the wake of these disturbing events, the election of September 1883 took place, the first in Serbia's history involving electioneering by organized political parties. It was largely a contest between Progressives and Radicals, in which the party in power even resorted to a methodical purge of the civil service, especially the police and teachers, to get rid of old Liberals and new Radicals. In various places, particularly in eastern Serbia, there were incidents in which peasants offered physical resistance to the police when the authorities attempted to brand their cattle and assess their property for tax purposes. On election day, September 19, 1883, the populace swarmed to the polls as never before, determined to vote as they pleased and not, as so often in the past, as the local police chief wanted. The Radicals won, by a two-to-one majority, thanks not only to popular support and excellent local organization but also, it was said, to Russian rubles.

Milan was not unprepared. Accepting the resignation of the Progressive ministers, he dismayed everyone by refusing to appoint the victorious Radicals in their place. Instead, he entrusted the government to an old Conservative out of the past, Nikola Hristić. When the new Assembly met, Hristić's first act was to read the king's decree opening the parliament, and his second act was immediately to adjourn the parliament. To stave off trouble, the Hristić government issued a decree calling for the confiscation of all private weapons. In an unsigned article in the Radical newspaper *Samouprava* (Self-Government), Pašić wrote that every Serb knew that without a rifle there was no freedom. When the authorities began to collect the arms, in October, most people complied, except eastern Serbia, especially in Pašić's electoral district. On November 6, 1883, Pašić slipped across the Sava into Austria-Hungary and his less fortunate colleagues were arrested, a mass local uprising, the so-called Timok Rebellion, erupted. Pašić hoped to go to Bulgaria and from there to reenter Serbia and join the rebellion, but the government forces won before he could carry out his plan. With its superior rifles and artillery, the army crushed the uprising within a week. By November 13, 1883, the revolt was over. Ninety-four of the leading participants were sentenced to death, though only twenty-one ringleaders were actually executed. Some 734 others were sentenced to prison or hard labor, including Pera Todorović, against whom the government had no evidence whatever except two newspaper articles, one of which was not even his but Pašić's. The Timok Rebellion was no mere spontaneous uprising, but an organized event, incited and led by the Radicals. This is not to deny the economic origins of the Timok Rebellion as the most serious peasant uprising in Serbia's modern history. Economic conditions were very bad in this recently Ottoman region in which there had been so much destructive warfare in the recent Serbo-Turkish wars. Economic discontent merged with the political desire for local self-government, so assiduously propagated by the Radicals, and hostility toward the bureaucracy and a standing army. In this conflict of the peasantry with the bureaucracy and army, the latter easily won the day.

Milan could not stand Hristić for long. He could not deal with this old-fashioned, stiff bureaucrat who had never ridden on a train and who had not stepped foot outside Serbia since 1847. Despite the advice of Vienna, which felt safe with Hristić, Milan called back the Progressives. This time Milutin Garašanin was made premier and Stojan Novaković minister of the interior. The other ministers were largely known as administrators.

That their main thoughts were of law and order is evident from two laws that they promulgated in 1884. One consolidated small local government units into larger ones, which would be more economical to administer and easier to control. A second law abolished the hated mounted police but established a full-fledged nationwide gendarmerie organized like the army, with a cavalry and an infantry.

Another law of 1884 represented a milestone in Serbia's modernization. It ended the poll tax, which had lasted for about a half-century, since the time of Prince Miloš. However suitable it might have been to a primitive, homogeneous peasant society, the poll tax did not correspond to a modern differentiated society in which there were far more diverse groups and variations in income. The law of 1884 replaced the poll tax with: a land tax, a tax on buildings, a tax on capital income, a tax on income from personal work, and a personal tax, which was a remnant of the old poll tax, but based on a division into five categories.

In general, the government of Milutin Garašanin and Stojan Novaković had no domestic trouble; the Radicals were dispersed or cowed after the Timok Rebellion, while the Liberals were restrained as usual. It was in the realm of foreign relations that the new government experienced its most difficult problems, and behind these problems there was always Russia, which had every reason to want a friendlier ruler on the throne of Serbia. King Milan lived in the constant knowledge that there was another candidate for his crown—Peter Karadjordjević, Alexander's son. Peter had already gained great popularity as a guerrilla fighter in Bosnia in 1875. In 1883 he improved his position by marrying Zorka, the daughter of Prince Nicholas of Montenegro, thus uniting two Serbian dynasties. It was generally believed that this marriage was made not in heaven but in St. Petersburg. Coming as it did at the same time as an attempt on his life, Milan began to fear that the Russian government was capable of anything to get rid of him.

His fears were heightened by the fact that Bulgaria had become a haven for about fifty Serbian rebels after the Timok Rebellion. These men went in and out of Serbia with alarming ease and engaged in various provocative acts. The Bulgarian press openly supported them, despite the Serbian government's protests. On top of everything, a border incident took place at Bregovo, where the Obrenović family had an estate. A change in the course of the Timok River had joined this estate to Bulgaria, and Milan insisted on keeping a guard of Serbian soldiers there. A Bulgarian guard drove the Serbian soldiers back, on June 3, 1884. Two days later the Serbian government sent an ultimatum demanding the withdrawal of the Bulgarian soldiers from Bregovo and of the Serbian refugees from the border area. The Serbian demands even included the expulsion of Metropolitan Michael from Bulgaria, even though he was visiting Sofia on a valid passport and had no connection with the Timok Rebellion. Sofia rejected the ultimatum, and on June 9, 1884, Serbia broke off diplomatic relations with Bulgaria. The Russian government encouraged the Bulgars to stand firm and not make any concessions, even though Prince Alexander Battenberg of Bulgaria was disposed to pacify his Serbian colleague and personal friend. Since the Liberal government of Dragan Tsankov in Bulgaria enjoyed the full backing of Russia in the affair, Tsankov declared to his cabinet that he was willing to go to war against Serbia if necessary. Though Milan and Prince Alexander came to a personal resolution of the quarrel, the Bulgarian cabinet refused to accept the terms. When Tsankov was replaced by Petko Karavelov as premier, it made no difference, though Karavelov was a Russophobe.

Just then Milan encountered still another threat to his position in the person of his wife, Natalia. Relations between them were severely strained when Natalia discovered that Milan was having an affair with one of her closest friends. Their quarrel became a public scandal. The public was on the queen's side; she was well liked and known for her charitable works. Of Russian origin on her father's side, Natalia was very pro-Russian and anti-Austrian. She objected strenuously to Milan's plan to have their son Alexander schooled in Austria. Seeing himself threatened on all sides by Russian-backed foes—the Radicals, Peter Karadjordjević, Prince Nicholas of Montenegro, Metropolitan Michael, the Bulgarian government—Milan became convinced that his wife was also a tool of the Russian conspiracy against him. When, in the spring of 1885, even Ristić was given almost royal treatment by the tsar during his visit there, this only enraged Milan more.

The final and worst affront came on September 18, 1885, when Bulgaria declared its union with Eastern Rumelia. Milan saw this as the first step in the restoration of San Stefano Bulgaria. Macedonia would be next. Serbia could never allow this. Equilibrium in the Balkans would be lost if a Greater Bulgaria were allowed to overshadow Serbia. The Treaty of Berlin had been violated. Serbia required compensation and would get it even if it had to fight. Such were Milan's views. The Serbian people did not see it this way at all. To fight Austria for Bosnia or to fight the Turks for Macedonia was perfectly understandable to them, but to oppose Bulgarian fellow South Slavs for annexing their own land was hardly reasonable. When Milan ordered military preparations and a call to the colors, the people responded with little enthusiasm.

Like all Serbs, King Milan would have preferred to get his "compensation" in Ottoman territory, but his memories of Ottoman military power were still too vivid and he had no foreign support. On the other hand, it seemed good to him to weaken Bulgaria sufficiently to keep it from effecting its claims in Macedonia. Behind Milan's strategy there was always the hope of provoking a war between Russia and Austria-Hungary, for he believed that Austria-Hungary's victory would provide the quickest way to Serbia's southward expansion.

The Austro-Hungarian Foreign Minister Count Gustav Kálnoky did everything to dissuade Milan from war with Bulgaria but tell him that Austria-Hungary would abandon him if he tried. After all, despite its somewhat vague wording about support for Serbia's expansion to the south, the Austro-Serbian Secret Convention did not envisage a war with Bulgaria. However, Milan preferred to listen to the encouraging assurances of the war party in Vienna and to the aggressive Austro-Hungarian minister in Belgrade, Count Khevenhüller. After ensuring the Porte's neutrality, Milan declared war on Bulgaria on November 14, 1885, and the Serbs attacked.

Few Serbs really understood what the war was about, but whether they did or did not, they were against it. The Radicals were definitely opposed to a war against a neighboring Slavic people whom they regarded as Serbia's most natural partners in a future Balkan confederation. Besides, the Bulgarian government of both Tsankov and Karavelov had resolutely stood by the Radical refugees. As for the Liberals, Ristić and his followers generally subscribed to the justice of King Milan's desire for compensation to restore Balkan equilibrium after the unification of Bulgaria; however, they too opposed fighting the Bulgars for this instead of seeking Ottoman territory in Old Serbia and Macedonia. The Progressives were committed to follow Milan's lead, but except for Milutin Garašanin, few did so with much enthusiasm. As for the Serbian people at large, they knew that the Bulgars had never hurt the Serbs, and that the two neighbors were closely akin in race, speech, religion, and way of life. Instead of resenting the unification of the Bulgars, the Serbs believed it would be far better to emulate their neighbors. From the standpoint of pure power politics, there is no doubt that King Milan saw more clearly than any other Serb the historic necessity of a test of strength between Serbia and Bulgaria, both in the light of the larger configuration of the Great Powers and of the local quest for hegemony in the Balkans. However, even if the high-handed monarch had been able to communicate all that he knew and saw to his subjects, it is doubtful whether they would have accepted his reasoning.

The war was a disaster for the Serbs. Their military strategy was very simply to take that part of western Bulgaria, including the districts of Vidin and Sofia, that Milan wished to keep as compensation. It seemed as if, in Serbian minds, this was to be more an occupation than a war, especially since the Serbian popular image of Bulgars was that of peaceful folk who made good gardeners. The reality was quite different. Thanks to Russian training and money, the Bulgarian army outclassed the Serbian in numbers, training, and artillery. Had Milan attacked a few weeks earlier, when most of the Bulgarian army was in Eastern Rumelia, he might have been able to take Sofia easily with his 28,000 rifles. However, the Bulgars had brought their troops back and were ready for him, with an army twice as large as the Serbian, owing to the fact that the Rumelian army joined forces with that of northern Bulgaria. The Serbs were woefully ill prepared. They did not even have good maps of the terrain they hoped to take. Though Milan had no talent along military lines, he insisted on taking personal command and assured himself of a free hand by keeping his most experienced commanders away. The decisive encounter of the war took place at Slivnitsa on November 17, roughly halfway between the border and Sofia. While the losses on both sides were heavy, the Serbs got the worst of it. After three bloody days, the Serbian defeat was complete. The Bulgars then chased after the retreating Serbs into Serbia itself. On November 27 the Bulgars took Pirot after another resounding victory. Their goal was Niš, a town they had coveted in the past. There was even talk of taking Belgrade.

Austria-Hungary could not allow Serbia's defeat. On November 28 Count Khevenhüller made his way to Prince Alexander's headquarters and advised the Bulgarian ruler to stop. When Alexander refused, Khevenhüller on his own initiative delivered what amounted to an ultimatum: if the Bulgarian armies continued to advance into Serbia,

Austro-Hungarian troops would defend Serbia. He also warned the prince of a possible occupation of Bulgaria by Russia. Later, as the result of criticisms from the tsar and Bismarck, Kálnoky repudiated Khevenhüller's action as having gone beyond his instructions. Nevertheless, Khevenhüller was successful in stopping the war. The final peace was signed on March 3, 1886. It was probably the shortest peace treaty ever concluded. It consisted of a single article stating that peace was restored between Serbia and Bulgaria.

For Bulgaria the great gain of the war was an indirect one: it won the approval of the Great Powers for the unification of Bulgaria and Eastern Rumelia. If the powers were not disposed to give Bulgaria any of the advantages of a victor in Serbia, the least they could do was to recognize Bulgaria's unification.

For Serbia the war was a serious blow to its international reputation and its national pride. Milan's own loss of confidence seemed to extend to his whole nation. However, Bulgaria's success had made Serbs realize, as never before, that Bulgaria was indeed the main obstacle to Serbia's expansion into Macedonia, and this realization inspired the public organization of the Society of St. Sava to carry out Serbian cultural propaganda in Macedonia soon after the war. More immediately the war brought about the fall of the Progressive government and the eventual abdication of King Milan.

The Progressives' Downfall and King Milan's Abdication, 1886–1889

The Bulgarian war determined King Milan to abandon his crown and country. The records of those who were with him after Slivnitsa agree that the young monarch was a broken man who had lost all capacity and will to function. As he informed Queen Natalia in a letter sent from Niš to Belgrade, he was resolved to take her and their son and leave Serbia. He wrote out his abdication and handed it to Garašanin, who flung it aside angrily and, with the frankness of a soldier, rebuked his king the way a sergeant would dress down a malingering private. Because no one would accept his abdication, Milan even thought of a half-abdication, by which he would turn over the government to his wife as regent while he took over the army. His ministers did the opposite: they took away his command of the army but made him remain as king.

The king's attempt to abdicate had several consequences which, thanks to his suspicious nature, poisoned the air for the rest of his reign. For one thing, it worsened the already strained relations between him and his wife. Queen Natalia was not personally ambitious or politically inclined. But neither was she willing to see her son's right to the throne jeopardized. Therefore, she let it be known that she would act as regent if necessary. Though he himself had suggested it, the king then suspected his wife more than ever of working against him. He also came to believe that Piroćanac and Ristić had joined her in a Progressive-Liberal plot to dethrone him. Again, though he himself had suggested abdication, he was made sickly bitter by the suspicion that anyone should think it a good thing.

Such fears and doubts led him to seek his friends among their foes. Because Milutin Garašanin and Piroćanac were personal enemies, Milan sought out Garašanin, despite their own past differences. Thus, himself discredited by the war, Milan made the error of keeping in office his discredited premier. The king was so desperate for support, even from the Radicals, that as soon as he returned to Belgrade, he had Pera Todorović, a man recently imprisoned for high treason, brought out of his cell and offered him and his colleagues amnesty in exchange for a working agreement between Garašanin and the Radicals. Deeply disappointed in the people he hoped to lead, broken by imprisonment and beclouded by morphine, a drug he took for a liver ailment, Todorović was only too glad to accept. On January 13, 1886, King Milan amnestied all the participants in the Timok Rebellion except those who were still abroad.

It looked as though two political camps were in the making: King Milan, Garašanin, and Todorović's Radicals on the one side, and Queen Natalia, Piroćanac's Progressives, and Ristić's Liberals on the other. However, the dividing line between them was not at all clear-cut. While the Progressives sided with the policies of Piroćanac, they looked to Premier Garašanin as their leader, a contradiction that apparently was not clear to them at the time. The situation was no clearer among the Radicals. When King Milan permitted forty of their leaders to meet in Niš on February 18, 1886, in the expectation that they would decide to collaborate with Garašanin, all but Todorović and one other voted against any such collaboration. On the contrary, they called for constitutional changes aimed at ending the king's personal regime. In this they were closer to Piroćanac and Ristić. The king had obviously erred in ascribing too much to Todorović's ability to influence his party.

Soon after, the King himself confused the issue by two extraordinary acts. He urged on Natalia a temporary regency while he would go away on a long but temporary leave of absence. Whether he wished merely to test her reaction, or whether he hoped that the Radicals would be more amenable if they had the popular queen to deal with, can only be conjectured. Secondly, in March Milan offered the government to Ristić, after Garašanin threatened to resign over the failure to win Radical support. Perhaps this too was a maneuver, for Ristić had his ministers all lined up and ready to present to the king when Garašanin, who hated Ristić, changed his mind and stayed on, as the king had hoped he would. Meanwhile, the fact that Ristić had not included Piroćanac in his proposed cabinet did not bring the two of them closer together. Yet Ristić demonstrated what many had not believed possible, that he was willing to accept a mandate from the king. Garašanin made some changes in his cabinet, largely to accommodate the king's desire to extend his own personal rule. Of the seven ministers, three were active army officers and two were reserve officers, men who knew how to take orders and give them. A politically undistinguished colonel was made foreign minister, which only signified King Milan's desire to manage foreign affairs himself. The king's loyal servant Mijatović, who had concluded an honorable peace with Bulgaria, was returned as finance minister. Milan had reason to feel secure at least in his cabinet.

He did not enjoy the support of the nation, as the elections of 1886 showed. Despite pressures of all kinds, which shocked even the Austro-Hungarian minister in Belgrade, the government could come up with only the barest majority. Unable to win a safe margin in the elections, the government resorted to assuring one by police terror. As the deputies arrived in Niš, where the Assembly met, the police took advantage of every possible excuse to arrest or send back home representatives of the opposition. The usual charges were "irregular" traveling papers or mandates. Thus, at the first vote taken in the Assembly, the government accounted for 80 votes and the thinned out opposition for only 68 votes. Still not satisfied, the government-controlled committee for the verification of deputies' mandates annulled the mandates of 24 opposition deputies. Garašanin then addressed the Assembly and blamed Serbia's defeat on the Radicals and the Timok Rebellion. However, the country was hardly convinced.

King Milan no longer felt secure in his relations with Austria-Hungary either. He had a gnawing fear that after his defeat at the hands of the Bulgars, Vienna had no more use for him. His fears increased in August 1866, when a group of Bulgarian army officers overthrew Prince Alexander Battenberg, with Russian encouragement. Milan became suspicious that Austria-Hungary might be preparing the same fate for him. Austrian Foreign Minister Kálnoky tried to reassure Milan, during the latter's visit to Vienna, but it seemed clear that Kálnoky was more intent on weakening Russian influence in Bulgaria than on strengthening Austro-Hungarian influence in Serbia.

Milan felt least secure of all with his own wife. His suspicion of her supposed political ambitions became an obsession. She, however, hardly suspected the depths of his anxieties and assumed that the real cause of their quarrel was his extra-marital affairs. Secure in her own virtue, she treated him with the scorn of a spurned wife. How much politics and personal differences were intertwined became clear on April 17, 1887; Queen Natalia publicly snubbed a foreign diplomat's wife at a service in the court chapel, because she suspected the woman of being one of her husband's paramours. Milan was so enraged that he wrote Natalia a letter informing her that they could no longer live together and that she was to leave the country. At the same time, Garašanin tendered his resignation as premier. Still he served as intermediary between the king and queen, and the next day got them to sign an agreement to have their son Alexander educated abroad. This was used as an excuse to explain the queen's departure from the country. She and Alexander left for the Crimea on May 12, 1887, with full honors, and a public scandal was averted.

Garašanin again withdrew his resignation, but the king no longer trusted him; Garašanin appeared to him to have been too sympathetic with the queen. The political implications of the royal quarrel became considerably enlarged when Milan got it into his head that he needed proof of Austria-Hungary's support in his intention to divorce the queen. When Vienna decided to remain correctly aloof in what it considered a private affair, Milan decided to seek solace from the Russian minister in Belgrade, Persiani.

The comic-opera aspect of the crisis received full play owing to a telegram from Queen Natalia that was badly written and carelessly read. On June 7, 1887, she wired from Yalta that she was leaving for Sevastopol and that she would be back in two or three days. She meant back in Yalta, but Milan feared that she meant back in Belgrade. He immediately summoned Garašanin and insisted that the queen's return to Serbia be prevented, by force if necessary. Intent on avoiding a scandal, Garašanin refused in a stormy scene. The next day he and his government again resigned, all over a misunderstood telegram; but the break between Milan and Garašanin was in the offing anyway. Seven years of Progressive administration had come to an end.

To please the Austrians, Milan turned to Nikola Hristić to replace Garašanin, but only as a sheer formality, so this attempt to create a new cabinet failed. Thereupon Milan gave Ristić the mandate, on June 13, which resulted in a Liberal-Radical coalition government. All Milan asked was that Ristić not include any "jailbirds," that is, Radicals who had been imprisoned after the Timok Rebellion. Ristić asked for three changes of policy: a rapprochement with Russia, though continuing to maintain good relations with Austria-Hungary; the return of Metropolitan Michael; and an amended constitution that would put an end to the king's personal regime. Milan agreed to everything, though he asked that the question of the metropolitan's return be postponed three months.

For a while Milan's one thought was to gain the most favorable conditions possible for his abdication. This included making certain that Natalia would not replace him as regent. He was so adamant in this that he even devised the plan of making Ristić the regent. To prepare the way for this, Milan made a trip abroad. However, in Vienna, Emperor Francis Joseph persuaded him not to abdicate.

Meanwhile the Serbian public was well aware that a fundamental change had taken place in their country's political life. For the first time in many years, crowds in the streets of Belgrade shouted "Long live Russia" and "Down with Austria." A wave of public reprisals against various Progressives swept the countryside. There were fifty homes destroyed and seventy cases of arson. When a mob appeared outside Garašanin's house and began to pelt it with stones, that professional artillery officer came to the window and shot five bullets into the crowd, though he succeeded only in wounding one man. Progressives were murdered in some villages, and there were lynchings with all degrees of cruelty.

One result was that when the elections for a new assembly took place, in late September of 1887, the Progressives did not dare take part. Nor did the party in power win. Of 146 elected deputies (ten elections were annulled), the Liberals got only 59 seats to the Radicals' 87. Ristić made up for the disparity in the appointment of the government's deputies by allocating 40 to the Liberals and 12 to the Radicals. The coalition between Liberals and Radicals could not last long under the circumstances, nor did King Milan wish it to. He even let the Radicals know, discreetly, that they could have the government all by themselves if they wished. On December 29, 1887, the Ristić cabinet resigned because of inner tensions.

If Ristić was not asked to form a Liberal government of his own, it was because he had made clear to the king that in the event of a war between Russia and Austria-Hungary (which seemed a likely prospect in 1887 over the Bulgarian question), the Liberals would support Russia. On Austrian advice, the king turned over the cabinet, except for the foreign ministry, which was his own preserve, to Sava Grujić. The idea was to let the Radicals lock horns with the Liberals and spend their popularity in tussling with the government's serious financial problems. The king did all he could in the meantime to cultivate the Radicals. As a New Year gesture (January 1 O.S., 1888) he amnestied all the Radical refugees abroad, with the exception of Nikola Pašić. He also made Sava Grujić, a professional soldier, a general. On January 23 he permitted the Radicals to dismiss the Assembly and call for a new one. The elections in February brought an almost complete victory for the Radicals; only fifteen Liberals and no Progressives were elected.

The king believed that the Radical government would heed him and that the Radical Assembly would heed their government. It did not work out that way. The Radicals took advantage of their strength to undo as much as possible of what the Progressives had done and to put into practice their own program. A series of new laws ensued to bolster the local autonomy of the communes and to restore, in part at least, a popular militia together with the standing army. The Radicals had been in power only four months when the king forced Sava Grujić's resignation. The chief reason was not the domestic politics of Serbia but the domestic problem of the king—the queen.

Natalia wrote to Milan from abroad in March that she was coming to Belgrade for a few weeks. It was understood that her purpose was to settle an important question still outstanding from the royal couple's agreement of the year before, namely, where the heir to the throne was to receive his education. She favored Russia. Milan favored Austria. Grujić preferred Serbia. It was, of course, not entirely a personal matter for the parents to settle. The government had a prime interest in the manner of the crown prince's education. In view of Grujić's view, it was clear to Milan that he had better get himself a new government before Natalia arrived.

The time had come to resort to that last political reserve—old Nikola Hristić and a cabinet of bureaucrats. He had already quelled one Radical uprising, in 1883, and now, it was rumored, he was prepared to strike again. However, there were two more important things on King Milan's mind—the queen and his abdication. For one brief moment in Serbia's history everything, even a new constitution, was either connected with the king's personal affairs or subordinated to them. The king desired his freedom from his wife, especially since he had hopelessly and very publicly fallen in love with Artemis Hristić, the Greek wife of a foreign ministry official whom he made his personal secretary in order to be nearer his paramour. The king was not yet thirty-five and was eager to enjoy life after his nerve-wracking troubles. He was willing to abdicate and settle down in some civilized country with the woman he loved. To do this, he needed a divorce. But he could not leave until he had arranged for his future (particularly regarding his debts) and his son's future. The latter would depend in large measure on the goodwill of the Radicals, whose strength in the electorate was overwhelming. Milan sought to ensure their support by granting a new and liberal constitution. Moreover, young Prince Alexander had to be educated where Milan wished, even if it meant taking the boy away from his mother. All of these problems were of one piece in Milan's strategy, even though he acted in most irrational and contradictory ways to resolve them.

King Milan's quarrel with his wife was the scandal of Europe. He even involved Bismarck in the unsavory affair by getting him to place the Serbian queen under police surveillance in Wiesbaden, where she and her son were staying, in order to keep her from going to Belgrade or, worse yet, to Russia. The king sent War Minister General Kosta Protić to Wiesbaden to persuade the queen to accept an official separation and to surrender her son temporarily, with the understanding that he would be returned to continue his education in Wiesbaden. Natalia stubbornly refused to make any accommodation.

The king then decided on sterner measures. Through Bismarck's direct intervention, Alexander was forcibly taken from his mother by the German police, in the sight of a scandalized Europe. Milan also formally asked the Serbian Orthodox Church for a divorce. No Orthodox ecclesiastical court could possibly accept as sufficient grounds for divorce mere personal and political incompatibility. But the king could hardly present his own adultery as a cause. He felt he should be granted a divorce simply because he was the king. The embarrassed church officials could not decide whether the case should be brought before the regular ecclesiastical court or before the whole Council of Bishops, neither of which wished to touch it. Finally, Metropolitan Theodosius, who was Milan's creature anyway, signed the divorce decree that Milan submitted to him, even though the legality of this act was more than dubious from the standpoint of canon law. The divorce increased public sympathy for Natalia. Serbian society, which frowned on any divorce, found this one especially despicable. However, Milan soon gave his subjects something else to think about.

The divorce decree was published in the official newspaper *Srbske novine* (Serbian News) on October 12 O.S., 1888. Two days later the paper printed King Milan's personal proclamation, unsigned by any of his ministers, calling for a Great Assembly to meet on December 2 to amend the Constitution of 1869. The next day Milan appointed a committee including the leaders of the Liberals, Progressives, and Radicals to work out the draft of a new constitution, and made the respective leaders of the three parties—Ristić, Garašanin, and Grujić—vice-presidents of the committee. This group worked for over a month, under the surprisingly able chairmanship of King Milan himself. The king took the position that, regardless of the varying strength of the three parties at the time, all should be involved in the drafting of the constitution and committed to it, as a guarantee for the future. Thus the draft reflected a compromise rather than the actual predominant strength of the Radical party. That strength showed itself at the Great Assembly, which met on December 23, 1888. Five-sixths of the delegates were Radicals, and one-sixth were Liberals; the Progressives again could not muster a single man. If the Radicals thought they could effect any changes in the draft through the Assembly, they were mistaken. The king used his legal prerogative to inform the Assembly that they had the right either to accept the draft "from cover to cover," as he put it, or to reject it, but they could not tamper with it. Of 600 delegates, only 73 voted against the draft and 3 abstained—all Radicals.

The Constitution of 1888 (actually promulgated in early 1889 by the new calendar) was more democratic than the Constitution of 1869 in many significant ways. While the Constitution of 1869 included civil liberties, it generally left their definition and scope to legislation; the Constitution of 1888 spelled out these civil liberties in greater detail and made them less liable to legislative limitations. For example, the section on freedom of the press specifically listed measures that could not be taken against the press, such as censorship, previous approval by the authorities, the payment of previous bail, and administrative reprimands. The new constitution, unlike the old, did not permit the king or the Assembly to suspend constitutional rights, even in an emergency such as a rebellion or a war; only a specially convened Constitutional Assembly could do this. The new constitution permitted citizens to sue officials, without the previous approval of the responsible minister. It made ministers more responsible to the Assembly. It proclaimed the independence of the judiciary and specifically forbade special star-chamber courts. It gave the State Council the right of review over ministerial decisions and all laws to determine their constitutionality.

The new constitution substantially increased the powers of the Assembly. Before, only the ruler could initiate legislation, and he could legislate even when the Assembly was not in session. Now king and assembly could initiate legislation equally, and the king could not make even temporary laws on his own. The Assembly was also given greater power over the purse. Previously, if the Assembly did not vote in a new budget, the government could operate on the old budget. The new constitution made this impossible except in cases in which the king dissolved the Assembly, and then for no longer than four months. Moreover, the government was now obliged to present for the Assembly's review an annual account for the previous year. The new constitution gave the Assembly the right of interpellation, investigation, and reception of petitions. It made it possible for deputies to become ministers, thus underscoring the principle that the ministers were not just the king's men. According to the new constitution, the government no longer had a right to appoint a third of the Assembly. Deputies would be chosen by completely direct elections; up to then elections in the districts, as distinct from the towns, had been indirect.

Also, Serbia at last got the right of *secret* elections, thus curtailing the traditional power of the police to influence the outcome. Only the democratic-minded Radicals were against the secret ballot. Influenced by their populist conceptualization of the ideal commune, they had the idea that public voting was somehow more moral. They also had every reason to suppose at the time that the pressure of public voting would work to their benefit, in view of their recent success at the polls. Thus, paradoxically, it was the king and the elitist Liberals who insisted on the secret ballot.

In two respects there was still a lack of equality in the elections. Universal manhood suffrage continued to be restricted to taxpayers, and the voter had to pay at least fifteen dinars per year in direct taxes. While the sum was not large, it was sufficient to deter those poor who were not sufficiently interested to vote in any case. Another provision obliged each circuit (*okrug*) to elect, among its total delegates, at least two "qualified" men, that is, persons with a higher education. Both of these provisions reflected a desire to keep the masses from having complete control.

But they did not reflect simply the selfishness of the privileged. Indeed, the people at large were given so much freedom under the Constitution of 1888 that there was some danger that the political life of the country would be entirely in the hands of the peasant masses, together with a sprinkling of small town merchants and a few priests. The vast majority of these people had little or no education. Their needs were simple. Their view of the central government was largely negative. Their horizons were limited to the borders of their commune or district. Their loyalties were regional rather than national when it came to anything but war. If Serbia was ever to achieve the status of a modern national state, it would have to rely on educated men with broad horizons and with ambitions for their country as a whole. Modernization required an intellectual and scientific elite to provide impetus and direction until the whole populace could be lifted. As for democracy, the important thing was to make it possible for all to have an equal opportunity to an education, and this was not easy, especially since many peasants themselves tended to resist education for their children. Moreover, the whole process became increasingly complicated as social differentiation became more and more determined by differences in wealth rather than in education and employment.

In the matter of local administration, the Progressives wanted to divide the country into six large regions, on the theory that the central government could thus administer the country more effectively. The Radicals wanted many small local districts, on the theory that the central government would find it harder to interfere with local government. The result was a compromise.

The constitution divided Serbia into fifteen circuits (*okrugs*), each divided into districts (*srezes*), and these into communes (*opštinas*). Each district was to have one representative for every 4,500 taxpayers. Belgrade elected four representatives, Niš and Kragujevac each elected two, and 21 towns elected one each. All male citizens 21 years of age could vote if they paid at least 15 dinars of direct taxes a year, though members of a *zadruga* could pay less. This last was a concession to the Radicals. The greatest concession made to the Radicals was in the restoration of local self-government through assemblies and boards at all three levels—circuit, district, and commune. These local governments would concern themselves with all questions dealing with the maintenance and development of cultural institutions, the economy, transportation, public health, and finances at each level. They were also given the power of taxation.

These examples show that the Constitution of 1888 was indeed a considerable step forward in the democratization of Serbia. It represented a kind of fusion between earlier concepts of folk democracy and the newer apparatus of a modern centralized state. It fell short of what the Radicals would have wished, but it gave far more than the king had previously been willing to give. Whereas the king stood for his own personal rule, with a bureaucratic system and a professional standing army, the Radicals stood for a parliamentary system, local self-government, and a people's army. The Constitution of 1888 was a compromise. The Radicals achieved a parliamentary system and a measure of local self-government. The king was forced to share power with the Assembly as never before, but the bureaucratic system and the army remained largely intact. Such was the political amalgam on which Serbia's government was based as of 1888. The question was whether it would stay together and for how long.

King Milan had no intention of staying to find out. He was convinced that the constitution was preposterous and could not last. He had granted it as a bribe to the Radicals in order to win peace until his son achieved his majority. By then, Milan was sure, everyone would see that it did not work. He was right. The Constitution of 1888 lasted only twelve years and four months. Having obtained his divorce, assured his son's future, arranged for the payment of at least some of his debts, and granted Serbia a new constitution with something for everybody, Milan was at last ready to abdicate. He picked the occasion with his usual flair for the dramatic—the day of the seventh anniversary of the proclamation of the Kingdom of Serbia, March 6, 1889. At the reception at court in honor of the anniversary, Milan had his abdication read to a stunned assemblage.

Though he had reigned twenty-one years, Milan was still only thirty-five years of age. Politically he was a spent man. In other ways, he had a whole life ahead of him, which he was determined to enjoy to the hilt. Assuming the title Count of Takovo, he went to Paris. However, he was by no means through with Serbia yet.

IX

The Reign of
King Alexander Obrenović,
1889-1903

The Ascendency of the Radical Party, 1889–1892

Forty-eight hours after Milan's abdication on March 6, 1889, Serbia found itself with a new king, Alexander Obrenović, a new regency, and a new government, organized by the still young Radical party, all under a constitution that was so new it had not yet been properly put into effect. The time seemed auspicious for a fresh start.

The Royal Regency that Milan chose for his thirteen-year-old son consisted of ex-Premier Jovan Ristić, General Kosta S. Protić, and General Jovan Belimarković. There was no doubt that Ristić, with his impressive experience and personal eminence, was the leader of this triumvirate. It seems ironic that Milan should have chosen for his son's regent the same Ristić who had served as regent over him during his minority and against whose tutelage he had chafed so much as a youth. However, Ristić was known for his loyalty to the Obrenović line and for his opposition to the Radicals. The first act of the Regency was to issue a proclamation to the people of Serbia the aim of which was obviously to set the tone for an easy transition from one reign to another. After pointing to the successes of Milan's reign as well as to "a certain lack of success," the regents promised to uphold the constitution and to carry out their charge in a nonpartisan spirit. Their statement was friendly and positive. "With the young King on the throne, with a new Constitution in our public life," the proclamation read, "let us, in God's name, begin a new life, a new period of work and austerity, giving special effort to the national economy and to the welfare of the people." Ristić made a point of formally resigning as leader of the Liberal party so as to stress his political neutrality as regent.

The thirteen-year-old king was hardly known to his people. He lived a lonely life, torn in the struggle between his parents and isolated from the world by a strict regimen supervised by an army officer. This friendless boy lived the life of a virtual prisoner. There was almost no time that he could call his own as his tutors stuffed him with knowledge and subjected him to a military training for which he was ill suited by temperament. On horseback he was so ungainly that he looked as if he were always about to fall off. Probably as a result of so much schoolwork, he became nearsighted and had to wear glasses. He was a good and diligent student, but showed no special aptitude or interest in anything. As the outer world was closed to him, he learned to close himself off from others. Under his pleasant and polite exterior was a self-contained personality that developed on its own, deprived of parental love or deep friendships. When it later broke out and revealed itself, it took his entourage by surprise. However, for the first three years of his reign, the boy king remained in the background. His people saw him only on rare, ceremonial occasions.

The most noteworthy of these was the celebration of the five-hundredth anniversary of the Battle of Kosovo (June 15, 1389 O.S.). The king, regents, court, cabinet, and Metropolitan Michael went to Kruševac, Prince Lazar's medieval capital, and from there to Žiča Monastery, where Alexander was anointed king. The entire observance was designed to evoke patriotic feelings, to link the Obrenović dynasty with the Nemanja dynasty of medieval Serbia, and to stress modern Serbia's role as the historic heartland of all Serbs, in and out of the kingdom.

Milan's abdication was a triumph for the Radical party. The premiership was given to General Sava Grujić, the ranking Radical leader in Serbia at the time. He organized a cabinet composed completely of Radicals except for the minister of war, Colonel Dimitrije Djurić, a nonparty officer who, though closest to the Liberals, was Grujić's personal friend and an obliging colleague who never made trouble. Of sixteen places on the State Council, the Radicals were awarded ten, compared with five places for the Liberals and one for the Progressives. The Radicals gained a similar preponderance in the supreme tribunal, the court of cassation, or appeals. The real head of the Radical party, Nikola Pašić, was still in political exile, as a result of his part in the Timok Rebellion of 1883. However, probably hoping that Pašić's return would lead to dissension among the Radical leaders, ex-King Milan petitioned the Regency, just four days after his abdication, to amnesty Pašić "that his voice, too, might join with the voice of the whole land: long live King Alexander I!" The Regency complied the next day. Pašić's return greatly strengthened the Radical party. Until Pašić could take his rightful place as premier, his followers made it possible for him to enter the National Assembly as a deputy for Belgrade, and he became the Assembly's president. Meanwhile the Regency extended an amnesty to all the remaining participants in the Timok Rebellion, whether in prison or abroad, and many of these were given government posts. Thus the Radical party enjoyed popular support and tremendous political power.

The party had come a long way since it had been founded, barely two decades before, by a handful of socialist-minded students, and formally organized in 1881. However, as it gained power, and the heavy responsibility that power entails, it was to become markedly less radical, until its name became an ironic misnomer.

The composition of the Radical party's representation in the National Assembly showed that, despite its predominantly peasant backing, it was hardly a peasant party. The leading Radical deputies belonged to three groups: prosperous farmers, small town merchants, and urban intellectuals. These groups were identifiable by their clothing. The farmers wore sheepskin coats, baggy pants, and peasant sandals or boots, and the others wore Western-style clothing, with the difference that the intellectuals generally wore redingotes, scarves, and shoes, while the merchants wore short coats, no scarves, and boots. Also, the farmers shaved and the others sported beards.

The farmers were generally a negative political force. Their ideology was based on a deep resentment against the state and the city, both of which grew and prospered as the countryside became poorer. Their program was largely to check the power of the centralized state through local autonomy and to keep down taxes. Despite limited successes in this effort, the rural group was not very effective. It lacked coordinated strength, political experience, and ideas. Their most noteworthy representative, Ranko Tajsić, was such a headstrong and cantankerous professional oppositionist that he eventually parted company with the party, much to its relief.

The small town merchants were rather more influential, enough to make party theoreticians worry about the party's ideological purity. Some of these men took advantage of their political power to enhance their private fortunes through such privileges as the tobacco monopoly, forest rights, and state contracts. But since this was an inevitable part of Serbian politics, it seemed right, for a change, to give the underdog a break.

The party leaders were the intelligentsia. To take the Radical cabinet of 1889 as an example, only one minister lacked a higher degree. Three were professors of the Great School: Finance Minister Mihailo Vujić, Minister of Justice Gliša Geršić, and Minister of Education Andra Nikolić. All were to become members of the Serbian Royal Academy for their scholarly and literary accomplishments. However, there was a noticeable difference between the intellectuals in the Liberal and Progressive ranks and those in the Radical party. Whereas most of the former two groups had been educated in Paris, most of the Radicals were trained in the German-speaking lands—Germany, Austria, and Switzerland. Whereas the "Parisians" were, as a rule, very Western in outlook, the Radicals gained from French, German, and Russian socialist writings a dislike for the capitalist West and its materialism. Moreover, the Radical intelligentsia included a large proportion of native-trained professional men, especially gymnasium professors and teachers, mostly in the hinterland, who found in the Radical party an outlet for their ideals and an escape from the boredom of provincial life.

In the 1880s all these intellectuals were engaged in the task of applying the ideas of social democracy to Serbian society. Their goal was a decentralized democratic state based on self-governing communes with a sovereign popular assembly at the top to control the bureaucracy, and a people's army. Whereas the peasant Radicals looked upon the state as an alien and hostile force to be avoided and checked, the intellectual Radicals saw the state as a potentially useful instrument to be taken over and transformed to serve the people. Thus it was the historic task of the intellectual Radicals to turn a hitherto politically passive peasantry into an active political element, within the state structure rather than outside of it, as the peasants would have traditionally preferred. Because of the disparity that marked the various groups within the Radical party, this process was not without its inner struggles.

Of the two opposition parties, the Liberals and the Progressives, the former were by far the more serious challenge to the Radicals, because of their electoral strength and because they had Ristić. Even though

Ristić was politically neutral as a regent, and in such matters he was punctilious, he soon reached the conclusion that he could not manage the Radicals, and that sooner or later, when they lost their popularity, they would have to go. Meanwhile the leadership of the Liberal party was assumed by Jovan Avakumović, a distinguished lawyer schooled in Germany and France and coryphaeus of a whole group of provincial lawyers. This younger generation of Liberals decided that the best way to deal with the Radicals was to fight fire with fire. They emulated the demagogy of the Radicals and attacked them on many of the same issues that the Radicals had raised when they were not in the government: high taxes, the salt and tobacco monopolies, the standing army, the power of the bureaucracy. Old Ristić did not like the style of these younger men, and they did not like his, but they realized that they needed one another.

The Progressives did not get a single assembly seat in the elections of 1889, and only one in 1890, for their leader Milutin Garašanin. He was hardly an opposition member anyway, inasmuch as he hated Ristić far more than he hated any Radical. Yet the Progressives were not a force to be ignored. They had a lively press, which constantly needled the Radicals, often with a tone of sardonic superiority and biting satire.

The chief charges against the Radical regime were that it could not maintain the security of person and property, and that it was guilty of an unprecedented partisanship in the conduct of government affairs. Both charges were true. The accession of the Radicals to power created the popular impression that the strict observance of law and order as understood by the old bureaucracy was out of fashion, and so there was a marked swing to the other extreme. A general air of lawlessness took over, with the revival of banditry in some regions. The notion grew that no one who sprang from the people would be arrested and punished by the people's government. Theft, arson, and murder were all on the increase, and were often the work of local Radical authorities eager to square accounts with their political enemies, especially the Progressives. According to Progressive statistics, about fifty of their men lost their lives in 1889 alone. The most scandalous open attack on the Progressives took place on May 26, 1889, in the middle of the day in the center of Belgrade, when an outdoor political meeting of theirs was stoned and many of their members were beaten, despite the presence of the police. Garašanin was charged with shooting a youth to death. He had to leave the country for a year, until a court decided that the charges against him were unfounded. Garašanin wrote in a newspaper article, "Today murders take place not only in byways and at crossroads, but under the roof of the state. Before, one had to fall into the hands of robbers, but today it is enough to fall into the hands of the authorities." However exaggerated such charges were, there was enough supporting evidence to tarnish the reputation of the Radicals.

The charge of extreme partisanship in government was also true. All previous governments in Serbia had taken advantage of their power to purge the civil service of their enemies and to award posts to their own followers, but none previously had done so with the zeal and thoroughness of the Radicals. The Radical party had suffered much persecution before it came to power, and now it was determined to reward the chief sufferers. King Milan had once referred to them as "jailbirds," and many of them did come to positions of power, sometimes literally, from their prison cells. With them, patronage was not simply a political matter but a religious obligation toward one's brothers. Not to be a Radical was to be an infidel unworthy of any public trust. Even at the lowest level of government, the struggle to achieve the sacred aim of local self-government became a frenzied, sometimes murderous, scramble for power.

Nevertheless, during their tenure of power—from March 7, 1889 to August 21, 1892—the Radicals put through many enlightened laws that brought Serbia closer to democracy. These laws were designed to put into effect the new Constitution of 1888. Because the Radicals had an overwhelming majority in each National Assembly during those years, it was easy for them to suit these laws to their own programs, insofar as the constitution would permit.

The new Law on the Election of National Deputies interpreted the constitution very broadly when it permitted all eligible members of a *zadruga* to vote whether each paid the necessary minimum of fifteen dinars in direct taxes or not. A supplementary law made clear that, in fixing the number of deputies each electoral district could send to the Assembly, the population of the urban centers had to be included, even though they sent deputies of their own. This increased the representation of the rural population at the expense of the urban population and offset the effect of the constitutional provision that each electoral district had to elect at least two deputies with a higher education, which inevitably meant townspeople.

The new electoral procedure was so arranged that voters could not split their ticket; thus one was compelled to vote for all the candidates that a given party proposed. Actually, there was no "ticket" in the sense of a list of candidates that the voter marked. Rather, the law established "ballots" in the original meaning of the term, namely, little balls which voters cast into the party box of their choice. The Radicals argued that such a system was best suited to a still largely illiterate nation. However, the political effect of not being able to split a ticket was to increase the hold of the dominant party over the electorate.

After 1888 the people of Serbia enjoyed the benefits of free and secret elections based on proportional representation and universal manhood suffrage, with voters' supervision over the election process and strict legal provisions to prevent government interference in elections. The trouble was, however, that enlightened laws did not in themselves prevent shady practices, made all the more possible since one party held such a preponderance of power. Now instead of police pressure, there was the pressure of party bosses, who sometimes went beyond legal limits in garnering votes. There were all kinds of irregularities at the polls; for example, local authorities distributed voting permits to their own supporters even though they were not eligible by virtue of not having paid sufficient taxes. It also became the practice for a party to gain votes by paying the minimum tax of fifteen dinars for voters. In sum, government pressure was replaced by party manipulation of the electorate.

Local self-government was the keystone of the Radicals' program. By self-government they meant that every commune should elect its own officials rather than having them appointed by the central government. They also insisted that only small communes, rather than the larger ones of at least 500 taxpayers that the Progressives had established, made self-government meaningful. The Radicals' Law on Communes went to the other extreme and more than doubled the number of communes by setting the standard of a minimum of 200 taxpayers, and even fewer for isolated settlements. This expression of grass roots populism was more democratic than it was practical, for it created a multitude of self-governing units many of which were not economically strong enough to provide their people with needed services. Thus it continued to be necessary for higher jurisdictions, especially the circuits, to provide their own personnel at the local level. The law did not end supervision of the communes; the State Council still kept watch over their legality, and the regional or circuit authorities had to approve local elections and budgets. Thus while self-government meant the right to choose one's own local officials, it did not mean complete administrative and economic independence from higher agencies of government. However, the law did end police interference in local affairs.

The Radical regime put through a series of laws designed to ensure the civil rights guaranteed by the 1888 constitution: a law on the press, a law on public meetings and associations, a law on juries. Yet however enlightened these laws were, now that the Radicals were in power, they saw to it that previous loopholes in the law which permitted various "excesses" were plugged. For example, court proceedings in libel cases were tightened up to prevent evasion; a distinction was made between public meetings in enclosed spaces, which required no permit, and outdoor meetings, which did; and controls were placed over the composition of juries to make them more willing than before to find demonstrably guilty persons guilty (there had been a disappointing reluctance on the part of local juries, out of either fear or local partiality, to find anyone guilty of anything).

In sum, the Radicals hardly lived up to their name in the legislation they enacted concerning government and civil rights. They already had a liberal constitution as their framework and saw fit to do little more than to put it into effect. Despite all shortcomings, however, Serbia at the end of the nineteenth century had a more democratic government than many far more advanced countries in Europe.

Ex-King Milan and Serbian Politics, 1889–1893

It is astonishing how much of the political energy of Serbia was spent in the quarrel between King Milan and Queen Natalia. Even after Milan's supposed divorce and abdication, his differences with his wife were far from private. They affected Serbia's domestic politics and produced international repercussions. In this bitter contest, the young king was the pawn.

If ex-King Milan preserved any role in Serbia after his abdication, it was because of his foresight in including in the 1888 constitution the provision, in article 72, that he was responsible for his son's education.

He had done this to exclude Natalia. In a special agreement signed a day after his abdication, Milan consented that the place of his son's education would be determined by himself "in agreement with the Regency," and that the queen mother could visit Alexander from time to time each year, though not in Serbia. Milan's role as guardian of his son's education gave him a weapon that he would wield with great effectiveness when the time came.

Natalia knew nothing of Milan's agreement with the Regency. She expected that after Milan's abdication she would be called back from Russia to take up her role in Belgrade as queen mother. Only through the intervention of the Russian government was she prevented from returning to Serbia as soon as her son became king. In fact, Natalia had the sympathy of the Serbian government as well as of the people. It is politically unwise to come out against motherhood in any country. Legal minds discovered that if the agreement with Milan precluded Natalia's meeting her son in Serbia, it did not prevent her from coming to Serbia without meeting him; after all, she still had the rights of a Serbian citizen.

The government negotiated with Natalia and, on August 22, 1889, with Milan's consent, even offered her the right to visit Alexander in Serbia for two or three weeks at a time once or twice during each year, with all of the honors due to the queen mother. Natalia refused the offer, preferring not to give away her legal right to reside in Serbia permanently. This time the Russian government did not intervene. The Serbian government had no recourse but to warn Natalia that if she insisted on coming to Serbia on that basis, she would not be extended any royal honors, the court would be closed to her, and she would not see her son. Natalia called their bluff. She arrived in Belgrade on September 29, 1889, and was greeted with flowers and the encouraging shouts of well-wishers, but as she rode past the royal palace to her private residence, all the gates were shut, the windows were curtained, and the guards failed to salute.

Natalia had correctly gauged the moral strength of her position as a mother. Within two weeks the Serbian government persuaded Milan to relent sufficiently to have mother and son meet, though not at court. Thus Alexander was finally able to visit his mother, though he saw her only seven times in fourteen months. She had accomplished this much of her purpose and still evoked public compassion. Meanwhile she established herself in her private residence, and her salon attracted the cream of Belgrade society, among them Progressive and Liberal worthies. Soon she had recruited a political clique and a public following. Radical ministers began to complain that they found the opposition in the Assembly easier to deal with than this obstinate woman.

Milan became so exasperated that he decided to come to Belgrade too. He would not sit in exile while his estranged wife endangered his position at home. Besides, this restless, vigorous young man found life as the "Count of Takovo" dull, even in Paris, without money and mistress. While Artemis chastely waited in Istanbul for a divorce from her husband, Milan's ardor could not be sustained by her letters. Nor could an annual appanage of 360,000 dinars sustain the habits of this reckless bon vivant and gambler. Milan needed money, and he yearned to be a political and social lion again. When he arrived in Belgrade on May 16, 1890, it looked as if he had come to stay.

He became so politically active that on July 4 the embarrassed government was forced to issue an official communiqué. "The present sojourn of H. M. the King Father in Belgrade has given rise, both in the country and abroad, to various interpretations and all kinds of rumors," it read. "These have probably been especially inspired at present by certain speeches and conversations of the King Father in public places and with news correspondents." Stressing that Milan had come to Serbia only to attend his son's end-of-year school examinations, the communiqué stated, "The statements by the King Father in said speeches are only the expression of private opinion, and are not new, so that, neither in their intent, content, or circumstance, do they have any effect on state relations or on the regular establishment and development of constitutionalism and parliamentarianism in Serbia."

This denial notwithstanding, the government was worried about the possible influence of Milan's activities, especially in the army. The minister of the interior even took to sleeping in the ministry building so as to be ready with at least his gendarmerie in case of a military putsch. Milan's cultivation of the army was especially apparent when he had his son's chief tutor, Dr. Lazar Dokić, a physician and professor of biology, replaced by an officer of the general staff, Colonel Jovan Mišković. Meanwhile the ex-king and the Radicals became locked in an open vendetta. Milan revealed the full extent of his ambitions in a talk with Ristić when he blurted out, "Give me power, in one form or another, and let me put an end to this situation." Ristić replied that the Regency would not relinquish its power to anyone but the Great National Assembly. He would soon be proven wrong.

While Milan worried the government, Natalia worried him. On June 23, 1890, she carried out a coup of her own by asking the Assembly of Bishops of the Serbian Orthdox Church to declare invalid the divorce decree signed by former Metropolitan Theodosius. The reinstated Metropolitan Michael, Milan's archenemy, was only too glad to comply and five days later solemnly declared the divorce decree to have been "contrary to existing law and without any legal foundation." In the eyes of the Church, Natalia was still Milan's wife. Milan was infuriated. He had renounced the throne to get rid of Natalia and to be able to marry Artemis. He placed such pressure on the Regency that Ristić was forced to require Metropolitan Michael to issue another decree stating that the Assembly of Bishops did not regard itself as competent to reopen the case. Metropolitan Michael complied, but tried to save face by not registering or placing his official seal on the document. However, he was forced to do so when an irate Milan stormed into his office with a lawyer. After that all Metropolitan Michael could do was to beg Ristić to persuade the ex-king not to make public this document "so as not to arouse the people, for there has been enough scandal."

Natalia decided to appeal to the National Assembly, in which she hoped to benefit from her popularity. To block this attempt, Milan negotiated with another of his enemies, Nikola Pašić, leader of the Radical party and president of the Assembly. He offered to leave Belgrade if the Regency and Radical government gave him written assurances that he would be protected from attacks by the Radical press and that the Assembly would declare itself incompetent to consider Natalia's appeal. He received these assurances and departed on October 29, 1890. The Radicals were only too glad to make such a deal, for they feared Milan far more than they pitied Natalia. On December 11, 1890, the Assembly declared itself legally unqualified to act on the queen mother's appeal. Natalia was finally defeated. To add to her bitterness, she received a letter from Ristić—a belated reply to her angry denunciation of him—in which the offended old regent gave her the most severe scolding his cultivated sangfroid would permit. "A wife either submits to her husband or leaves him," he wrote. "That holds for queens as well, even more so. You did not wish to do either. While you are imposing yourself on your husband, you have sown sparks of discord among the people and are keeping the country in a state of constant crisis and tension."

Having won this victory over Natalia, Milan returned to Belgrade, on the eve of March 6, 1891, just in time for the celebration of the ninth anniversary of Serbia's proclamation as a kingdom. He had returned to settle the problem of his finances and to complete his victory over Natalia. He demanded that he be given a lump sum instead of his monthly allowance from the civil list, and that Natalia be expelled from Serbia. In exchange, Milan promised to leave Serbia and not return until his son was of age. The ex-king asked for a huge sum, some six million dinars. Pašić was willing to buy off the troublesome king father, but not at so high a price. After considerable haggling, they agreed to a settlement of one million dinars outright, with a loan of two million dinars against the ex-king's estates as collateral; in other words, half of what Milan hoped to get. Having no reason to trust his word, the government also made Milan agree to renounce his rights both as a member of the royal family and as a citizen of Serbia. All of this was put in writing on April 11, 1891, and signed by Milan, the regents, the entire cabinet, and King Alexander's guardians. However, it was kept a secret at the time and only gradually revealed to the public through various decrees and resolutions. The first came on the very day of the agreement, when Milan's promise not to return to Serbia until the majority of King Alexander was solemnly read to the Assembly. On the following day a decree released a million dinars "for the needs of the Royal Household"; this was how Milan's payoff was managed. There now remained the question of the queen mother.

While the Assembly's resolution regarding Natalia's departure was only in the form of a suggestion to the government, Pašić decided that it provided him with sufficient authority. After unsuccessfully trying to persuade the queen mother, both orally and in writing, to quit Serbia, his government decided to use force. On May 18, 1891, an inspector of the ministry of the interior, the chief administrator of Belgrade, and the commander of the gendarmerie called on Natalia and ordered her to follow them to the waiting steamship *Deligrad*. She refused. During a give-and-take of two hours between Natalia and her would-be escort, a crowd gathered around her residence, attracted by the three coaches and guards outside. When Natalia finally emerged, the coaches were surrounded by a crowd that grew constantly as the procession made its way to the Sava embankment. As the coaches came to the cathedral and were making the turn near Kalemegdan Fortress to descend to the river, the crowd became violent. Some picked up cobblestones from piles on the street, which was being repaired, and pelted the gendarmes; others unhitched the horses of Natalia's carriage and pulled it themselves back to her residence, while she, in turn, wept and smiled. Her return to her home was a great victory for the crowd, which continued to mill about on the street. The government sent in the army cavalry. When the cocky crowd wounded their officer and several men with stones, the order was given to fire. At that point the infantry also arrived. Even though most soldiers shot into the air, as the walls of the surrounding buildings long testified, there were several dead and wounded in the crowd. The dismayed mob quickly dispersed. Never had a Serbian government shot at the people of Belgrade before, and here the Radical government was doing it. That night the middle of Belgrade looked like an occupied city as the army bivouacked in the streets.

The next day, just before dawn, the authorities returned for Natalia, not at her front door, but over the back wall, using ladders, which earned Inspector Sima Pavlović the lasting nickname of "the ladder carrier." This time Natalia left quietly, along streets lined with soldiers and gendarmes. She was put on a train for Zemun, on the Austro-Hungarian side of the river. There she boarded a Russian steamer, the *Kazan,* and went down the Danube to Turnu Serevin, in Romania, from where she proceeded to eastern Romania and to Bessarabia to join her family.

The "Sixth of May" (O.S.), as the episode of Queen Natalia's expulsion became known in the press, earned the government much censure. The nation was shocked at the sight of their queen being led away by the police like a vagrant. The affair was also one more scandal to titillate a Europe that was becoming accustomed to viewing Serbia as a kind of comic opera. The people could not easily forget that it was the Radical government that had fired on the people of Belgrade and shed their blood in the streets. While Pašić did not escape blame, the public held especially Ristić and Minister of the Interior Jovan Djaja responsible. The Progressives and the Liberals turned their press against the Radicals. Even the rank and file of the Radical party, as well as the Radical deputies to the Assembly, were angry. While they approved Pašić's desire to rid the country of Milan, even at the cost of ousting Natalia, they did not like the manner in which that ouster had been conducted.

In July 1891, Ristić and Pašić accompanied King Alexander on a trip to Russia. Both politicians felt the need to repair their damaged reputations at the tsar's court. More important, the troubles of the Obrenović family only made Peter Karadjordjević seem more attractive to the Russians, who had every reason to distrust Obrenović Austrophilism. Russian Panslavic circles saw in Peter Karadjordjević's marriage with Prince Nicholas's daughter Zorka the possibility of a future unification of Serbia and Montenegro. Ristić hoped to enhance the Obrenović position by a marriage between King Alexander and either a Russian or a Montenegrin princess. While nothing came of these hopes, there was a more immediately practical aspect to the Serbian visit to St. Petersburg. Since it was to the benefit of the Russian government to get Milan away from Serbia, Ristić and Pašić were able to get the tsar to furnish the equivalent of the additional two million dinars that Milan still had coming to him as a part of his agreement. It was handled as a "loan" to Milan by the Volga-Kama Bank. In return, on October 11, 1891, Milan gave his word of honor to Tsar Alexander III not to come to Serbia again. However, as the ex-king told his private attorney, "Whenever I shall have to, I will simply ignore this and go to Serbia. . . . These are political matters, where a word of honor does not have that strict sense."

Perhaps out of awareness of Milan's carelessness about promises, the Serbian National Assembly passed a law on March 26, 1892, officially declaring Milan no longer a member of the royal household or a citizen of Serbia and forbidding his return. However, not even that deterred the ex-king, for he still held the king in this game of chess—his son Alexander, who was devoted to him.

Several developments occurred in Serbia between June 1892 and April 1893 which strengthened Milan's hand. On June 16, one of the three regents, General Kosta Protić, died. According to the constitution, the Assembly was to pick his successor. Pašić wanted the position, and there was every reason to suppose that the Assembly would choose him. However, the regular Assembly was not in session, and Ristić delayed in convening an extraordinary session inasmuch as he wished to block Pašić's appointment. Finally Pašić and his government resigned in protest. They were replaced by a Liberal government headed by Avakumović.

Once in power, the Liberals resorted to a whole series of measures— more foul than fair—to bolster their strength. They began a campaign of intimidation at the local level, especially against the teachers, who were apt to be Radicals. They dismissed Radical authorities at the communal level, which was often not hard to do because of various financial irregularities for which the government had a right to remove guilty incumbents. The Liberal government flagrantly ignored the State Council, which was empowered to act as a watchdog but which had no bite. The Liberals also disqualified thousands of voters for their failure to pay taxes; they estimated that 150,000 out of 400,000 eligible taxpayers had defaulted on their taxes. By applying the law strictly and disfranchising these people, the Liberals seriously cut Radical support. During the election campaign, the Liberals used the police and the army in various regions to intimidate the people. An unknown assailant even took a shot at Pašić, but missed. On March 4, 1893, just five days before the election, there was bloodshed, in the village of Goračica, a Radical stronghold, when peasants armed with hoes and axes refused to let a new set of local officials take over from the old. The cavalry arrived, and in the resulting melee a dozen persons were killed and seven wounded.

On election day 236,892 voters came to the polls, more than in previous elections. The Radicals received 130,316 votes, the Liberals 91,831, and the Progressives 14,745. Despite the Radicals' victory, they in fact lost 22,619 votes from the last elections, while the Liberals gained 68,283 and the Progressives 5,850. Apparently the pressures applied by the Liberals, plus a certain popular disenchantment with the Radicals, benefited the Liberals a great deal. Nevertheless the Radicals proved that they could win an election even without being in power.

The Liberals contrived to accomplish by parliamentary maneuvers what they could not at the polls. When the Assembly met in Belgrade, on April 6, 1893, the Liberals made improper use of technicalities to revoke the mandates of enough Radical deputies to assure themselves of a bare majority of four votes. It was enough to assure the Liberals of a regent of their choice. However, they never had an opportunity to make the choice, for they were outsmarted by a mere boy—their king.

On April 13, 1893, King Alexander invited both regents, Ristić and

Belimarković, as well as the entire Avakumović cabinet to dinner in the royal palace. While he was entertaining them, units of the army took over the ministries of the interior and foreign affairs, the city administration of Belgrade, and the telegraph office. They also surrounded the homes of the regents and ministers as well as the Assembly building. Meanwhile the unsuspecting dinner guests amused themselves along with their young host, whose composed manner betrayed none of what was going on outside the room. As the main course was being served, the king's first adjutant whispered into his ear that all was ready. The boy arose and proposed a toast to his guests, who were by now puzzled. He thanked them all for their loyal service and declared that he was taking the royal authority into his own hands, before coming of age. Ristić chose to treat this as a joke. Shouting "Hear, hear!" he proceeded to lecture his charge on the gravity of such a step. However, an adjutant interrupted him with the cry "Long live the King!" As the cry was taken up by officers and guards outside the room, the king left his petrified guests. When they sought to leave, they were forced back at the point of bayonets. When they refused to sign their resignations, they were kept in the palace all night while newly appointed ministers were brought in by palace coach.

King Alexander signed a hurriedly written proclamation to his people: "Serbs! From this day I am assuming the Royal authority into my own hands. From this day the Constitution enters into full force and operation. Depending on the lucky star of the Obrenovići, and on the basis of the Constitution and the Law, I shall govern the country, and I call on all of you to serve me faithfully and with devotion." Lazar Dokić, the king's tutor and physician and a professor of anatomy, physiology, and zoology, was appointed premier and entrusted with forming a new government.

Even though Alexander was precociously able, it is obvious that a lad of sixteen could not have engineered such a coup on his own. Ristić was quite right when, in his later history of the events of "The First of April" (O.S.) he saw ex-King Milan as the originator and moving spirit behind the plot. An ambitious man who was not yet forty, who repented his renunciation of the throne, who had grown tired of the life of an exile and even of his mistress, and who wallowed in debts despite the huge sums given to him, Milan had compelling motives for trying to regain power, at least through his son. It was not for nothing that ex-King Milan had so assiduously curried the favor of the army. His efforts paid off well in the coup of the First of April.

The Royal Turnabout, 1893–1895

The immediate beneficiaries of the king's coup were the Radicals. Even though the Dokić cabinet was formed by moderates rather than hard-liners such as Pašić, the Radical party was ecstatic over the First of April and used its new position of power for all it was worth. The new government impressed the young king with its avowed desire to uphold the law, yet it began with an unconstitutional act. It prorogued the Assembly, thus depriving the Liberals of their ill-gotten majority. It also took advantage of its powers by dismissing Liberal local administrations throughout the country and substituting Radical officials. In Belgrade, after the old municipal administration was run out of office, their Radical successors were escorted to the city hall by a band of folk musicians. When a deputation of citizens came from Kragujevac to complain to the king about a similar turnabout there, Alexander replied, as his former tutor and present premier, Dokić, had assured him, "Under this government there are no illegalities, and there can be no question about it; I believe and I know that the government is opposed to all illegalities."

The elections to the new Assembly, held on May 30, 1893, took place in peace and quiet. The Liberals made no attempt to present candidates but chose to boycott the elections. As for the less timid Progressives, who had been allies of the Radicals, the latter were glad to have a token handful of them in the Assembly. The Assembly met in Belgrade, in extraordinary session, on June 13, 1893, in the National Theater, to hear King Alexander take his oath to uphold the constitution he had violated by his coup.

In his speech from the throne, the young boy manfully defended his action on the grounds that he could no longer permit the Liberal government to undermine the constitutional foundations of the state. The Radical Assembly enthusiastically expressed its agreement and acted accordingly by undertaking to have the Liberal Avakumović cabinet punished for its misdeeds. After a brief investigation, the Assembly resolved to try Avakumović and his ex-ministers before a court of sixteen members, half of them state councilors and half of

them appellate judges. The accused were charged with eleven violations of the constitution. The investigation brought out so much dirty
linen that foreign diplomats in Belgrade advised the government not
to carry the matter to extremes. However, the Assembly was eager for
revenge; after all, the Liberal government had shed Radical blood at
the Goračica riot. But after a falling out with the Radicals, King
Alexander stopped the trial on January 28, 1894, by pardoning all of
the accused, with whom he had meanwhile been plotting the downfall
of the Radicals.

In the beginning the young king's relations with the Radicals were
quite good. It seemed to many that Dokić had replaced the Ristić
Regency and that the king was as obedient to him as premier as he had
been to him as tutor. However, neither of Alexander's parents could
tolerate the situation, especially Milan, who had not encouraged his
son's coup just to be shunted aside. The law that forbade Natalia's
return to Serbia was meant to be in force only during Alexander's
minority; the law forbidding Milan's return had no limit. Milan's first
step to annul this law and to regain influence in Serbia was to
meet with his son in September in the northern Adriatic resort town of
Abbazia (Opatija). After that meeting Alexander became cool toward
the Radicals and no longer behaved as Dokić's pupil but as Milan's
son. It was obvious that Milan had to get rid of the Radicals if he was
ever to return to Serbia, for they had no desire to have him back and
lose their hold over "the Radical king," as Alexander began to be
called after his coup.

While it seemed that the Radicals were all-powerful in this struggle,
they were considerably weakened by an intraparty split between the
moderates, who dominated the cabinet, and the hard-liners, who were
more powerful in the party organization. Soon after the April coup
the press began to distinguish between the "court Radicals" and "extreme Radicals." The former included Dokić, Sava Grujić, and their
colleagues in the cabinet. The latter were identified with Nikola Pašić,
Kosta Taušanović, and Ranko Tajsić. Hoping to eliminate at least
Pašić from an active role in the party, the Dokić government packed
him off to St. Petersburg as minister to Russia. However, this did not
help them much. At the Radical party's annual convention, held in
Čačak during September 1893, Grujić and several other cabinet ministers were severely criticized, and only one member of Dokić's cabinet
was elected to the party's executive board. Moreover, when the Na-

tional Assembly met on November 13, 1893, its Radical deputies elected as leader of the party caucus Tajsić, who was so extreme that even Pašić had a hard time with him. The Dokić-Grujić group and the Taušanović-Tajsić group engaged in a duel that came out into the open in November, when Grujić succeeded the ailing Dokić as premier. The former group even campaigned against a member of the latter group, Milovan Marinković, in elections for Belgrade's mayor. When that attempt failed, they vowed to bring about the fall of Grujić's government in the Assembly. Thus, the Radical party provided its own government with an opposition. The house divided against itself soon fell.

The crisis came over Alexander's decision to invite his father to return to Serbia. Milan was already on his way when the king informed Grujić, on the evening of October 20, 1893. To make certain that nothing would prevent his father's arrival, Alexander went behind his war minister's back to give orders to the army, the Danube Division, to stand ready in case of any opposition. It was another coup. Unable to assume responsibility for an act that they held to be both illegal and politically unwise, the Grujić government had no choice but to resign.

Ex-King Milan arrived in Belgrade on January 21, 1894. That very same day, using his son's strep throat as a pretext, he began to take matters into his own hands. After presenting to the Radicals conditions they could not accept, such as an amnesty for the Liberal ex-ministers under trial and his continued stay in Serbia, Milan made a complete break between the Radicals and his son. It had long been his conviction that the Radicals were either crypto-republicans or pro-Karadjordjević, and that in either case no Obrenović could be safe on his throne as long as they held power. He would have preferred a Progressive-Liberal coalition to take their place, but the Progressives were too wary of a struggle with the mighty Radicals to join, and the Liberals were too unpalatable by themselves after the First of April coup.

Thus, on January 24 a neutral government was formed, under the premiership of Djordje Simić, a professional diplomat. The Radicals refused even the three portfolios offered to them. Of the seven members of the Simić cabinet, only two had ever been ministers before, Finance Minister Čedomilj Mijatović and Minister of Justice Andra Djordjević. However, all of them were highly qualified and respected men with professional training. From this standpoint, they were probably the best group of cabinet ministers Serbia ever had; yet they were only a transitional government insofar as their essential purpose was to quiet political passions.

Simić and his colleagues failed utterly to achieve this aim. The Radicals in the National Assembly and in the party press immediately staged an offensive. They declared the Simić government to be unparliamentary in that it had been formed from outside the majority in the Assembly. The Radical newspaper *Odjek* (Echo) further charged that Milan wished to annul the Constitution of 1888 and to bring Serbia under Austrian influence. Nothing could be more indicative of Serbia's freedom of the press at the time than the epithets that Radical writers hurled at Milan: drunkard, gambler, Parisian vagabond, drunken majesty, vampire, adventurer. However, the Radicals were leaderless for the moment. Pašić was in St. Petersburg, and Grujić had been forced to withdraw by the "extreme Radicals."

The Radicals were not the only ones to be concerned about greater Austrian influence in Serbia after Milan's return. The Russian court was also disturbed. According to Pašić, Tsar Alexander III referred to Milan as "that animal" while the empress expressed the opinion that "all human vices" were gathered in that one man. The Russian government telegraphed an official protest to the Simić government on January 25, 1894, against Milan's presence in Belgrade. Simić was reminded that the government had paid a goodly sum to Milan precisely to assure his absence from the Serbian scene. When Simić proposed to go to St. Petersburg himself to pacify the Russian government, he received the cold reply that he would be welcome in Russia after Milan quit Serbia. In actual fact, Austria-Hungary had nothing to do with Milan's return or the fall of the Radical government; on the contrary, Vienna had consistently advised a policy of good relations with all the powers. It was not foreign policy but domestic considerations that lay behind the events caused by Milan's return.

It was not long before the Simić government found its task impossible. On the one hand, it was forced by the court to effect a purge of the administration in which forty to sixty percent of the Radical incumbents were ousted. This understandably seemed far from conciliatory to the Radicals. On the other hand, the kings—father and son—kept getting angrier and angrier at Radical public attacks and urged even stronger measures. They became so sensitive that they caused

Finance Minister Mijatović to resign after the unauthorized publication in the Radical press of the latter's letter to a French banker which stated, "It would not be a good thing if King Alexander were led to the idea that Mr. Pašić took precedence over the King of Serbia in Russia." When Simić and another colleague joined Mijatović in leaving the cabinet, a new government had to be formed.

The new government was entrusted to Svetomir Nikolajević, an ex-Radical who was generally held to be Milan's agent. Under his premiership a series of remarkable acts took place. On April 29, 1894, his government decreed the annulment of the laws that forbade the return of Milan or Natalia. The queen mother had no benefit from this because the original law was valid only while King Alexander was a minor; however, the law against Milan's return had no such limitation. When the Radicals began to organize public meetings to protest against this decree, Nikolajević—in his capacity as minister of the interior—issued another decree, on May 12, forbidding such meetings as being harmful to "public tranquility and order." When, on May 17, the court of appeals, acting as a supreme court, declared the government's decree concerning Milan's return invalid, on the grounds that a mere administrative decree could not annul a law, the crown replied with a pronouncement of its own: on May 21, 1894, King Alexander abolished the Constitution of 1888 and restored in its place the Constitution of 1869. Thus one of ex-King Milan's greatest unfulfilled desires had finally been satisfied. It cannot be said that Milan liked any constitution that limited royal powers, but he certainly preferred the Constitution of 1869 to that of 1888.

Belgrade did not react at all, as though already accustomed to royal coups. The provinces sent a stream of telegrams and deputations to the capital to congratulate the king. By this time even some Radicals were willing to climb on the bandwagon. The Radical leaders in Belgrade were crushed by the seeming lack of concern their own constituents had for constitutionalism. The Liberals and Progressives exulted, for under the 1869 constitution they would have more of a chance to counter the power of the Radicals. Conservative opinion had always been against the 1888 constitution as being too liberal and the work of the Radical party. Thus the abrogation of the Constitution of 1888 cannot be attributed to Milan alone, but to that whole group of conservative academics and merchants who felt as Nikolajević did when he declared once in a speech, "A country can live a politically stable and peaceful life only when the leading word belongs to men of brains and property."

All in all, the abrogation of the Constitution of 1888 struck the country as being less a coup than a return to normalcy after a brief and rather unsuccessful experiment. As Radical officials were sent into retirement, familiar old Liberals and Progressives took their places. Not only the administration but also the judiciary was purged; in the court of appeals only those judges remained who had not voted for the decree of April 29 against Milan's return. Minister of Education Andra Djordjević, himself a professor of law, held that educators should not involve themselves in politics, and on the strength of this conviction he undertook an unparalleled purge of the many teachers throughout Serbia who were active in the Radical party. Pašić returned to Serbia in mid-summer of 1894 to try to rally the party, but he soon had to flee abroad a second time when he heard of the government's intent to implicate him in a conspiracy to foment a revolution.

The Čebinac Conspiracy, as it has been called after its leader, Mihailo Čebinac, an industrialist from Kraljevo, had as its aim to overthrow the Obrenović dynasty and to bring Peter Karadjordjević to the throne. Because Peter would not consent to murder, the conspirators hoped to incite an uprising like that of 1883. Čebinac was arrested before anything came of the plot. With him several prominent Radicals whom he implicated, and others who had had dealings with him, were arrested. Though little, if any, evidence was brought out against them at the trial, all but two of the accused received prison sentences of from one to three years. A half year later all were amnestied. The Radical press openly proclaimed Čebinac an agent provocateur who did the bidding of the police in order to justify the suppression of the Radical party. Whether or not this was true, the result, at least momentarily, was precisely that, as the Radicals were left leaderless.

Nikolajević had his own troubles as premier. On the one hand, he could not achieve a much needed working agreement with the Progressives and the Liberals because of the opposition of the latter. On the other hand, he was unsuccessful in dealing with two kings at once. He was tactless enough on one occasion to confront them both with the question Which one was really king? Finally he resigned in disgust.

His successor, seventy-six-year-old Nikola Hristić, was brought out of retirement to head a government of specialists. This third Hristić government in Serbia's history lasted less than a year, from October

1894 to July 1895. His main role was to take responsibility for the Čebinac trial and to see to it that the new National Assembly, elected on April 19, 1895, be acceptable to the crown, a task at which Hristić was a proven master. The restoration of the Constitution of 1869 made his task all the easier in that it gave him the police powers to which he was accustomed from times past. The results were predictable. The Radicals and the Liberals decided just before the elections to boycott them, so the outcome was a clean sweep for the Progressives. In the towns, only a quarter of the eligible voters went to the polls, and in the countryside, just over a third. Except for fifteen or sixteen Liberals who rejected their party's decision to boycott the elections, all the winners were Progressives. When, under the 1869 constitution, the government selected its own quota of deputies, which it chose equally from among Progressives and Liberals, the result was that the Liberals had only about 30 deputies out of 240, and the Radicals had none. Even those few Liberals were such tools of the government that they refused their party's order to quit the Assembly and were expelled en bloc from the Liberal party.

The new Assembly dutifully gave legal sanction to the royal coup of May 21 abolishing the Constitution of 1888, which it was not competent to do since this should have been the prerogative of a great assembly. It also voted a substantial allowance to Milan of 360,000 gold dinars. It was well known how badly the chronically indebted ex-king needed the money. Indeed, people began to wonder if the entire aim of the royal revolution that had been carried out under Milan's aegis had not been simply to rescue him from his financial straits. The Assembly also passed a series of laws that gave the government greater powers of repression. The right to conduct criminal investigations, which the Radicals had given to the courts, was now returned to the more controllable police. Another law gave the government the right to appoint local police commissioners, whom the local communes had to pay out of their own budgets. Hristić gave assurances that such commissioners would be appointed only in places that had demonstrated their inability to maintain law and order on their own.

Even as cooperative an assembly as this one balked, however, at what the government considered its most important assignment, to approve a loan agreement that Finance Minister Vukašin Petrović had concluded the previous December with the Ottoman Bank of Paris, the Handelsgesellschaft Bank of Berlin, and the Länderbank of Vienna.

Not only were the terms of the agreement not very favorable to Serbia, but Petrović had concluded the agreement without consulting anyone outside the government. The bill before the Assembly was doomed when Stojan Novaković, then ranking leader of the Progressives, ordered the Progressive deputies to oppose it. Its defeat caused Petrović to resign. More importantly, it moved ex-King Milan to leave Serbia in a rage.

Milan's sudden departure, on the eve of Petrović's resignation, was so obviously tied to the defeat of the loan agreement that it gave fuel to rumors that Milan had stood to gain three million dinars from the deal. Milan's abrupt removal seemed like that of a general leaving the scene of a defeat. It is not known whether Milan was financially involved in the matter; however, it is known that he supported the loan agreement to such a degree that he could regard its fate in the Assembly as a test of his political strength.

There was more to it than that. Milan's position in Serbia depended largely on two factors, his hold over his son and his hold over an assembly packed with Progressives. He found that hold over both slipping, and in both cases there loomed the unseen presence of Queen Natalia.

Milan and Natalia had political as well as personal differences. Whereas Milan was for an all-out war against the Radicals, the more cautious Natalia counseled her son to be on good terms with them for the sake of the dynasty. Even after the break with the Radicals, she was determined to act as mediator and to effect a reconciliation. To accomplish this, she resolved to go to Serbia personally. An important element in these plans was her long and continued good relations with the Progressives, who were always much more sympathetic to her than to Milan. Natalia had a good opportunity to influence her son when Alexander came to visit her in Biarritz in January 1895. Her success was made all the easier by Alexander's burgeoning disillusionment with his father's political talents. Moreover, as Alexander grew to manhood, he was less and less disposed to have his father play the leading role. This tendency was revealed in his almost eager willingness to listen to criticisms of his father's efforts. No one was better able to make such criticisms to him than his mother. Her powers to persuade were improved in that she, unlike Milan, had nothing to gain personally. Thus Alexander's whole change in attitude toward his father and his politics may be dated from his stay in Biarritz.

That vacation of over a month in Biarritz provided another fateful turning point in Alexander's young life. In Natalia's home there—to which she gave the name of Sashino, the Russian nickname for Alexander—the king fell madly in love with his mother's lady-in-waiting Draga Mašin, a young widow, considerably older than he but still fresh and attractive. Deprived of any normal association with girls of his own age, it was almost inevitable that this royal teenager should be smitten by the charms of an experienced woman ten years his senior. He insisted that Natalia come to Belgrade, with her lady-in-waiting. Natalia readily agreed, on condition that Milan leave Serbia first. Alexander was ripe, politically and personally, to accept, without much thought as to what he would do if Milan refused. As it turned out, he did not have to concern himself; the problem was solved for him when Milan left on his own after the Assembly's rejection of the loan agreement. Milan blamed his son for this disgraceful defeat and left in a huff after a quarrel. It is doubtful, under normal circumstances, whether Milan would have reacted so violently, or whether Alexander would have let his father go, over the mere defeat of a loan agreement in the Assembly. Obviously both felt that their relationship had suffered a basic change.

Queen Natalia, Progressives, and Radicals, 1895–1897

Queen Natalia returned to Belgrade on May 10, 1895, four years after she had been so shamefully hustled out of the country by the police. To wipe out that memory, the government now greeted her with four days of unbroken public ceremonies, fireworks, and entertainments. She was met at the station by thousands of cheering subjects, and not only by old friends but also by old foes. Hristić, under whose premiership her divorce had been extorted, and Pašić, under whose premiership she had been so rudely ousted from Serbia, both stood on the station platform with top hats in hand. Best of all, Milan was not there. Natalia's triumph was supreme.

Almost immediately the court began to seek a new government to replace Hristić. The king negotiated with the Radicals, but they wanted too much—a return to the Constitution of 1888. The Progressives also wanted too much—a government that was completely their own. Each side had an advantage—the Radicals their popular strength, the Progressives their unchallenged power in the Assembly. Though the latter advantage was temporary, it was of great momentary importance to the king since only the Assembly could approve a new loan agreement to save the Serbian treasury from disaster. While Alexander was negotiating, the highly offended old Hristić resigned before being asked to do so, thus forcing the king's decision. The financial problem was pressing, and so Alexander turned the government over to the Progressives. As a result of Garašanin's previous decision to remove himself from politics to become minister to France, it was Professor Stojan Novaković, eminent historian and litterateur, who led the Progressive party at the time. He became premier on July 7, 1895, to the bitter disappointment of the Radicals and the queen mother. The king tried to placate both by assuring them that as soon as a new loan agreement passed the Assembly, the Progressives would be made to give way to the Radicals.

It did not quite turn out that way, but almost; Novaković's Progressive government lasted barely a year and a half. It had to endure the hostility of the other parties and of Queen Natalia and her coterie. Natalia worked against the new loan agreement just as Milan had worked for the old one. Like Milan, she regarded the matter as a test of her political strength. Thus when the new loan agreement passed the Assembly, by a vote of 174 to 54, Natalia reacted as Milan did, by leaving the country in a rage. She had no intention of leaving permanently. Her act was designed to demonstrate to the Radicals that she bore no responsibility for the Progressive government's actions.

The Novaković government was a political anomaly in that it had no visible support, except for a packed Assembly which everyone knew did not represent the will of the majority of the people. Natalia opposed it openly, Milan was *hors de combat,* and Alexander acted as though the government had been forced upon him. Neither the Liberals nor the Radicals would collaborate with it, nor were they asked. Yet the Novaković government did serve a purpose that went much beyond the loan agreement; it provided a middle ground and a breathing spell which everyone needed to consolidate his forces. For Alexander the Novaković government was, covertly, a boon. As neither his father nor his mother supported it, this made him independent of them. At the same time, the meticulous Novaković carried on the affairs of state, especially in the field of foreign policy, with an assurance that freed the twenty-year-old monarch from many duties. This allowed him to enjoy fully his mother's many balls and the company of Draga Mašin, once Natalia returned to Serbia that December.

Meanwhile the Radicals mellowed enough to lower their conditions to two: an amended Constitution of 1869 rather than a return to that of 1888, and a Radical ministry or at least one that would be favorable to them. To counter this, the Progressives came up with an amended constitution of their own, carefully worked out largely by Novaković himself. However, the Radicals provided a most impressive sign of their popular strength when they organized a mammoth public rally in Belgrade's Topčider Park on August 9, 1895, to which over 35,000 people flocked from all over the country. In the end, it was ex-King Milan who gave the Novaković government its deathblow, by convincing Alexander, during a brief meeting on Austrian soil in December, that the Austro-Hungarian government was seriously displeased with Novaković's hostility. The immediate upshot of this was curious. As soon as Alexander reached Vienna, without consulting Novaković at all, he conferred a medal on the Austro-Hungarian Minister of Finance Benjamin Kállay, who administered the provinces of Bosnia and Hercegovina. Nothing could have served so dramatically to disassociate King Alexander from Novaković's nationalistic foreign policy than this honor to an avowed adversary of Serbian aims in Bosnia and Hercegovina. Novaković took the next step himself. Taking advantage of a disagreement between the court and the minister of justice over an allegedly unconstitutional proposal, Novaković resigned with his entire cabinet on December 26, 1895, two weeks before the king intended to get rid of him.

With the fall of the Novaković government came the dissolution of the Progressive party. Never having enjoyed the support of the people, it could no longer exist once it lost the support of the court that it had served. Unwilling to suffer again the retribution that the incoming Radicals would severely inflict on them, the Progressives simply ceased to exist as a party.

It was the "Court Radicals" led by Djordje Simić to whom Alexander handed the reins of government on December 29, 1895, though not entirely; Premier Simić had to include certain Liberals and neutrals trusted by the court. Simić himself was a polished diplomat and bureaucrat who had been educated in Germany and in Paris and who had spent most of his career, from 1867 to 1884, as Serbian minister to Sofia, St. Petersburg, and Vienna. Ideologically he was a Western liberal who had known and admired Édouard Laboulaye and who had translated Benjamin Constant's work into Serbian. He broke with the Serbian Liberals when Ristić sided with King Milan while he (Simić) was on Queen Natalia's side. As a Radical he was acceptable to the court precisely because of his moderation and willingness to serve and to mediate.

The most important task of the Simić government was to have been an amended version of the Constitution of 1869. Here the Radicals were forced to give in to King Alexander's insistence that the new constitution be proclaimed by the king rather than by a constitutional assembly. Having made their peace with the royal coup of 1894, the Radicals agreed to this as well. Soon they were also persuaded to postpone the constitutional question because of the crisis created by the Cretan Insurrection of 1896 and the resulting Greco-Turkish War, which involved Macedonia and Serbian interests there. They were forced to swallow something else—Milan's return. Milan had thrice been refused reentry into Serbia by the Novaković government, owing to Natalia's insistence. However, he now threatened to cause a public scandal by publishing certain things about Natalia. Though Natalia laughed at this threat, Alexander was frightened into inviting his father for the Christmas holidays, quite on his own. Five days later he then confronted the Simić government with this *fait accompli*. The cabinet was ready to resign, but succumbed to the entreaties of the young king, who said to them, "You can see very well that I am a sick young man. I have been brought to this by the unhappy life of my parents and the continuous struggle with the love that I owe to both of them. I feel that I no longer can endure this struggle and would rather leave the throne than hinder my parents by force from coming to Serbia. . . ." The cabinet imposed two conditions: that Milan come for only fifteen days and not come back after that until the revision of the constitution was amended, and that after Milan left, Natalia might come to Serbia and stay until the revision was completed. When Milan arrived, on January 8, 1895, he stayed almost a month and announced he was returning in March. Natalia arrived February 19. Each warned Alexander against the other.

Meanwhile the Radical party gathered its strength in the countryside. In a short time it regained 1,200 out of 1,300 communes, either legally or by local riots and lynchings. When elections were held on

July 4, 1897, for a new assembly, the results were unprecedented. The Radical party received all the votes since the Liberals preferred to boycott the elections, and the Progressives existed no more. To give at least some semblance of a politically mixed body, the king appointed among his own deputies, to which he had a constitutional right, 25 Radicals, 15 Liberals, 7 former Progressives, and 14 neutrals. Thus the crown created a parliamentary opposition to its own government. The Assembly's president was Nikola Pašić. Now a successful businessman in his fifties, with a family and a patriarchal beard, Pašić appeared to many to have evolved from a revolutionary to an opportunist. His willingness to accept from the crown the post of president of the Belgrade commune seemed to confirm this view. Yet, in fact, Pašić was only following the Russian cue, to oppose Milan by supporting Alexander.

Milan was intent on doing the Radicals harm, and they knew it. The Simić government warned Milan that if he returned to Serbia, no royal honors would be shown him. On the other hand, the Liberals found it expedient to join Milan's camp. As for Natalia, she lost her hold on Alexander when her plans to marry him off to Princess Xenia of Montenegro, Nicholas's daughter, failed, and she quarreled with Draga Mašin and provoked her resignation as lady-in-waiting. After that, Draga was no longer tied to Natalia's residence in Biarritz and could be with Alexander whether Natalia was in Belgrade or not. Once Draga became Alexander's mistress, in the spring of 1897, Natalia became the main threat to their relationship. Once again love was to influence the politics of an Obrenović ruler.

To Natalia's great chagrin, Alexander decided to visit his father in Carlsbad (Karlový Váry) in mid-1897. He promised to visit Biarritz afterward and to bring Natalia back to Serbia with him. Instead, after the quarrel between Natalia and Draga, it was Milan who returned to Serbia with Alexander. When they arrived in Belgrade on October 19 and emerged from the railroad car, the waiting cabinet was stunned. Alexander did not even wait for their resignation but dismissed Simić and his colleagues that same morning.

Once more the wheel had turned. During his whole career as king up to that point, Alexander had subjected himself to one influence after another: in 1893 he was under his tutor Dokić, from late 1893 to the spring of 1895 under Milan, from the spring of 1895 till the fall of 1897 under Natalia, and now he was under Milan's influence

[473]

again. After 1897 Natalia was never to return to Serbia. However, Milan's influence was not to last long either. King Alexander was ready to strike out on his own.

The Personal Regime of King Alexander, 1897–1901

With the inauguration of a new cabinet on October 23, 1897, under Dr. Vladan Djordjević, there began another phase, the final one, in the reign of King Alexander. Its program was delineated in a letter of October 22 which the king addressed to his new premier and which was published the next day (October 11 O.S.) in the official newspaper *Srbske novine.* Pointing to the need "to ensure the financial, economic and military might of Serbia," it called for an end to "the fruitless political partisan struggle in which already too much valuable time has been lost in achieving the progress of the people and the state." The king therefore desired an "impartial administration" that would "establish law and order." In his last sentence the king promised, "I guarantee to the new government stability of the system and all the time needed for successful work." It was a comforting promise in that the Djordjević government was the thirteenth in eight years!

The new cabinet was well suited to carry out this "Program of October 11." Vladan Djordjević's role was more that of an obedient court chamberlain than of a premier. He did not even pick his own ministers. The court selected them. Except for one Liberal, they were all politically neutral men or nominal Progressives. A successful physician, man of letters, and diplomat, Djordjević was a vain man who was ever ready to do the bidding of his royal masters.

The "Regime of October 11" was, in fact, a personal one in which King Alexander was pleased, at first, to share power with his father. Alexander felt that he needed Milan to keep the Radicals at bay. Milan was by now a graying and presumably wiser man who was ready to settle down. One of the first official acts of the Djordjević government was to make "General H. M. King Milan" commander of the Serbian army. Thus Alexander contrived to keep his father busy with military affairs, for which he had no liking anyway, and to take on the political administration himself. Moreover, while no one feared Djordjević, there was much reason to fear Milan, especially with the army in his hands. The Regime of October 11 commanded respect as few previous Serbian governments had been able to do.

Political party life was reduced to a minimum. The Progressives tried a comeback but were severely hampered when their nominal leader, Milutin Garašanin, died in early 1898, and their actual leader, Stojan Novaković, was made envoy to Istanbul. The Liberals, who were deeply disappointed that they had not been given the government, became increasingly divided as the Djordjević government enticed their members with posts, especially in the police and communal administration. The Radicals announced their intention to assume "the position of a determined but legal and loyal opposition." They, too, felt the effects of Djordjević's tactics of divide and conquer. It is instructive that the government chose to entice the more extreme Radicals, notably Jovan Djaja and Kosta Taušanović, with posts, while it sentenced Pašić to nine months in prison for slandering King Milan. The "slander" consisted of a single sentence in a published letter in which Pašić merely stated that he "had been against King Milan." Radicals in the civil service continued to be purged.

The results of the elections to the Assembly in the spring of 1897 were astounding: 112 Liberals, 62 Progressives, 19 neutrals, and only a single Radical were elected. Almost as surprising as the disastrous defeat of the Radicals was the impressive return of the Progressives, which could be explained only by the machinations of the government. Minister of the Interior Jevrem Andonović was awarded the Order of Takovo First Class on the very day of the election, June 4. In naming its own constitutional quota of deputies, the government again favored the Progressives; it also chose many Liberals, and the very few Radicals it selected were "safe" appointments of civil servants. Even a good number of the divided Liberal deputies were ready to cooperate with the government.

When this Assembly met in Niš in June 1897, it was ready to do the bidding of the government. To make sure of this, local police chiefs were brought to Niš to keep an eye on the deputies from their districts. Under the circumstances it was easy for the government to win approval for a whole series of repressive laws, notably those limiting freedom of the press, assembly, and association. A new measure strictly forbade all government employees, teachers, clergy, and anyone receiving any money from the state treasury to be members of political parties or even to attend political meetings. Political associations could hold meetings only in Belgrade or the chief town of every district, but not in the villages—where the Radicals had their main strength. They also had to submit their statutes to the government for approval. This meant that all previous political parties had to disband and organize all over again. As for the press, the oppositional wing of the Liberals were the first victims of the new policy when the government prevented the renewal of their newspaper *Zastava* (The Banner). The police "persuaded" the editor to resign. When a new editor was found, the government appointed him a civil servant against his will, thus making him ineligible. When not even this succeeded, the printer was warned that his press would be destroyed and he returned to his homeland in Austria-Hungary. Before the Liberals could respond to this challenge, they, like the other parties, were legally disbanded and had to wait on the pleasure of the government to be reformed.

Throughout all this the Liberal leader Jovan Ristić tried to remain on good terms with the court, hoping that the Liberals would again have their day once the Djordjević government went the way of its predecessors. However, it became clear after the first year of the Regime of October 11 that the Djordjević government was no mere stopgap but a permanent fixture. Ristić died in 1899 without ever regaining power. On the contrary, with the legal disbanding of all parties subject to approval of their statutes, Alexander and Milan succeeded in creating a court coalition of Liberals and Progressives whose one bond was their obedience to the Crown. Politically, by 1898 the Crown had made itself supreme by crushing the Radicals and by crippling or capturing the Liberals and Progressives. It could also count on a completely subservient Assembly. By a law of August 2, 1898, the government also got the right to appoint the heads of local communes, by royal decree in the towns and by the fiat of the ministry of the interior in the villages. These appointees were paid handsome salaries by the central government to ensure their loyalty. The triumph of King Alexander and Milan seemed complete. However, it was clear that, the election results notwithstanding, the Radical party still enjoyed a good deal of popular support. Milan was not content with beating the Radicals at the polls; he yearned to extirpate them root and branch.

The opportunity presented itself on July 6, 1899, when on the afternoon of the Feast of St. John (June 24 O.S.), King Milan was shot at but barely scratched as he was riding in an open carriage. The would-be assassin was quickly apprehended. This event—the so-called

"St. John Attempt"—turned Serbia upside down in a political crisis that involved both Russia and Austria-Hungary.

The would-be assassin, Djura S. Knežević, was a twenty-five-year-old Bosnian of humble station and even more modestly endowed intellect who lacked any personal motive for his deed. King Milan assumed, even before the investigation began, that the Radicals were behind it all and, that very evening, had Pašić and other Radical leaders arrested, without a shred of evidence against them. To give himself a free hand, Milan had Belgrade and its entire district placed under martial law and had the judicial proceedings take place in a court-martial. During the following six weeks there was a general roundup and purge of Radicals, most often without any legal procedure whatever. Men were arrested, dismissed from government posts, placed under house arrest, and even exiled by simple police order. To whip up public enthusiasm, the government "encouraged" a wave of congratulatory telegrams and deputations to be sent to the court in which loyal citizens could express their gratitude at Milan's escape. It was enough for a man not to take part in this campaign to excite the suspicion of the authorities and bring unpleasant consequences on himself. The leaders who were arrested were subjected to cruel treatment that would have been horrifying even if they had been found guilty, let alone before they were even brought to trial. This so shocked the population, especially intellectuals and the youth, that the Obrenović dynasts steadily lost much of the sympathy they had in the beginning.

The political reverberations of the trial were far-reaching. While the court openly blamed the Radicals and privately blamed the Russians along with them, the Radicals in turn charged that Milan had concocted the whole affair just to get at them. Not even today are enough facts known to warrant a definitive judgment. There are indications that lead to all these hypotheses.

The most tantalizing version was that advanced by Milan, that the plot had been engineered by the Russian secret police in the hope that the Obrenović dynasty would fall and give way to Peter Karadjordjević. No one has ever successfully linked Peter Karadjordjević to the plot, but certain facts in the case point to at least the possibility of Russian intervention. For diplomatic reasons these facts were never brought out at the trial; however, Milan spoke of them to others, including the Austro-Hungarian military attaché in Belgrade. According to Milan's version, the chief architect of the plot was Colonel

Grabov, chief of the Russian secret service in the Balkans, whose head-quarters were in Bucharest. It is beyond dispute that Grabov more than shared his government's distaste for Milan. It is also true that the Russian tsarist secret police were capable of the most nefarious undercover acts, as the history of their war on the Russian revolutionaries shows. It was brought out at the trial that the accused Knežević had been in Bucharest, quite unaccountably, before the attempt on Milan's life. During his investigation, when Knežević was shown a photograph of Grabov's residence in Bucharest, he allegedly identified the house as the one in which he had received money to carry out his deed. Premier Djordjević later wrote that a Serbian servant at the Russian legation in Belgrade had admitted to a state prosecutor that the Russian envoy Mamulov had offered him money to kill Alexander and, according to other reports, Milan.

Yet if Milan's secret file pointed to the Russians, there was nothing there to implicate the Radical party leaders, except possibly one, the maverick Ranko Tajsić, and then Tajsić's ties were not with the Russians but with Montenegro, to which he fled to avoid arrest.

The official charges against Knežević and others did not mention the Russians. The whole plot was presented as a domestic affair for which the Radicals were responsible. Milan was determined to have both Pašić and Taušanović, the chief Radicals, executed. The Russian government was equally determined not to allow this. It even sought the aid of the Austro-Hungarian government in a common démarche to the Serbian government, but Vienna preferred to influence the Serbian court independently. To avoid the open intervention of these powers, Alexander and Milan gave in. However, Milan insisted on saving face. He did this by frightening Pašić into making a public statement before the court-martial that though he was not personally guilty of the attempt on Milan's life, he was politically responsible for not preventing the crime. Pašić's statement won him universal contempt for his opportunism and cowardice; yet it must be said in his defense that he had every reason to believe at the time that his life depended on such a statement.

As for the other accused, Knežević and Tajsić were condemned to death; Knežević was immediately shot, but Tajsić enjoyed the protection of his exile in Montenegro. About a dozen Radical leaders were given sentences of from five to twenty years, though not one was proven to have been involved in the attempted assassination. Pašić was sentenced to five years, but he was immediately pardoned. His close friend Aca Stanojević was also released as innocent, apparently as part of Pašić's deal with Milan. Those sentenced to imprisonment were so inhumanly treated that their plight became a national and even international scandal. Having just been through Dreyfus's rehabilitation by a court-martial in France in 1899, the foreign press was especially sensitive at the time to political trials. There is no doubt that the reputation of Serbian justice and the already shaken reputation of the Obrenović dynasty suffered greatly, both in Serbia and abroad, as a result of the St. John Attempt.

The reputation of the Obrenović dynasty was to suffer even more dramatically over the next affair that rocked Serbia soon after—King Alexander's marriage with his mistress Draga Mašin. Queen Natalia had tried to arrange a Russian match for her son, but failed. In 1900 it was King Milan's turn to act as a matchmaker. Also led by political aims, Milan sought a German marriage for Alexander. With Alexander's consent, he had already made all the preliminary arrangements for the hand of Princess Alexandra von Schaumburg-Lippe, when on July 15 Alexander stunned his entourage with the news that he intended to marry Draga Mašin. Not until July 19, four days after he had begun to share his secret with members of the court, the cabinet, and the army, did Alexander inform his father, who was in Carlsbad with Premier Djordjević. The news produced universal consternation. Minister of the Interior Djorde Genčić even tried to spirit Draga Mašin out of the country before the engagement ceremony and to keep the king in the palace by force; however, he failed, and was to pay heavily for his failure later.

King Alexander found himself virtually abandoned by everyone in his quest to marry Draga. Utterly crushed and humiliated, King Milan sent a telegram in which he disapproved of the marriage and resigned as commanding general of the army. For once he and Natalia agreed, for she too was outraged. Vladan Djordjević's cabinet resigned. Reliable old Nikola Hristić was again called on to form a new government, but even he refused after Milan's telegram arrived. It was three days before the king could find eight men in all of Serbia who were willing to form a government that would assume responsibility for such a marriage; headed by Aleksa Jovanović, an undistinguished judge, the "Wedding Cabinet" included unknown underlings so lacking in stature and experience that they seemed to be playing at being ministers.

As for the army, the generals scolded Alexander to his face for thinking of such a marriage, while behind his back some of them even let Milan know they were prepared to do anything that he ordered. Serbian society regarded the king's intention as simply scandalous.

It was bad enough for a twenty-four-year-old youth to marry a widow of thirty-six. But it was far worse than that. Draga's father had ended in an insane asylum, and her mother was an alcoholic. Draga herself had never borne children to her first husband, a young engineer, and was suspected of being barren, an unredeemable curse in the eyes of a peasant patriarchal society and a decided disadvantage to any ruler's wife, as Michael Obrenović's wife Julia had discovered. The fact that Draga was a commoner bothered only a few critics; indeed, her Serbian origins could have made her more attractive to a nationalistic nation. However, Draga brought with her no tangible benefit such as a Russian or a German princess might—a dowry and a political advantage. Any of these reasons would have disposed people against such a marriage, but there was even more, known at first only to a few and then to everyone. Draga Mašin had a shady past as a poor young widow in need of the financial support of gentlemen friends. This was no mere hearsay, though public rumor certainly exaggerated when it made Draga out to be a streetwalker. Nor was the news kept from King Alexander. Not one, but several, men of high position, ministers and generals, told him to his face of Draga's past. One of them even told him that he had had Draga himself for a not excessive sum of money. A member of a delegation of merchants warned the king that Draga suffered from a sexual disease that made her incapable of bearing children.

There is no better indication of King Alexander's stubborn infatuation than his refusal to heed any of these reports, though he listened to them with a remarkable composure. This immature, love-starved young man who had been deprived most of his life of parental love, found in the older and stronger Draga all that he desired; and more, for she brought with her a ready-made family of three sisters and two brothers for whom he showed a love that was all the more touching in that it was used by them rather than sincerely returned.

To make his marriage more acceptable, Alexander accepted a deal with the Russians: Tsar Nicholas II agreed to be best man at the wedding, by proxy, if Alexander agreed to make peace with the Radical party. The Radicals made clear in secret talks that their conditions for such a peace were threefold: the establishment of a constitutional regime, amnesty for the imprisoned Radical leaders, and Milan's permanent alienation from Serbia. Such was the political price of Alexander's marriage with Draga. The personal price was his break with both his father and his mother. The architect of this whole agreement was the Russian chargé d'affaires in Belgrade, Pavel Mansurov, who stood in the tsar's place at the wedding, on July 21, 1900.

Alexander's marriage was fraught with political consequences. The king revealed the full extent of his infatuation with his wife and of his despotic nature by equating opposition to his marriage with treason. Not even his parents were spared. The police were ordered to prevent Milan's reentry into Serbia, by force if necessary. The same Russian Colonel Grabov whom Milan implicated in the St. John's Day attempt on his life now came to Belgrade to place his secret service at Alexander's disposal in order to spy on Milan in Vienna. The king threatened to try his own mother for treason, in absentia, if she persisted in writing insulting letters and open postcards against Draga. The members of the Djordjević cabinet were all subjected to various punishments and public vilification in the official press. Djordjević was stripped of his rank as a colonel in the military medical service. He and two other former ministers were forced to flee the country. Various members of the court were summarily dismissed or transferred. The greatest purge took place among the army officers who were loyal to Milan; many were pensioned and even forbidden to wear the uniform.

Conversely, various civil and military posts were given to a host of men simply because they declared themselves for Alexander's marriage with Draga. Alexander made pathetic efforts to win popularity for his wife. Her name was given to regiments, schools, and villages. Her court dress was made to imitate the Byzantine robes of Serbia's medieval queens as pictured in monastery frescoes; however, it only made her look like an actress playing a part in a historical play. In many ways she was an actress, and at her best when she deceived her husband with news of her pregnancy. Alexander had such a yearning to be a father and to refute the charge of Draga's barrenness that he did not hesitate to announce to an incredulous and shocked nation that Draga was pregnant, just a month after the wedding. A Parisian physician was found to attest to Draga's condition, and she began to wear maternity clothes as soon as possible to glory in the role of an

expectant royal mother. If Alexander was so sure that Draga was pregnant, it was because, even before they were married, Draga had twice
left the country ostensibly to have abortions. What he did not know
was that this was also a deception.

While the news of her pregnancy was false, the news of King Milan's
death in Vienna on January 29, 1901, was real enough. An attack of
influenza cut short the life of this desperately lonely and crushed man
at the age of forty-seven. Even in death Milan was a problem. While
Alexander naturally wished to have his father buried in Serbia, Emperor Francis Joseph insisted on fulfilling Milan's written request to
be buried in Austria-Hungary, in the Serbian Orthodox monastery of
Krušedol. Milan's funeral was less that of a Serbian king than of a
vassal of the Habsburgs. Serbia's relations with Austria-Hungary were
already strained by Alexander's marriage; now they were made worse
by what Alexander took to be Francis Joseph's insult after Milan's
death. In all this the Russian government and the Radicals could only
secretly rejoice while Draga could feel freed at last from the haunting
fear that Alexander and Milan would one day again be reconciled.

Serbia under the April Constitution of 1901

The first harbinger of a new course was the arrival, soon after Milan's
death, of the new Russian minister to Serbia, T. V. N. Charykov. The
Russians secretly sought to ensure their ascendency in Serbia by encouraging Alexander to establish a more truly constitutional regime,
knowing that the pro-Russian Radicals would then be in power.

Alexander had several reasons for acquiesing. He was angry at
Francis Joseph and eager to end Serbia's dependence on Austria-
Hungary. Internally, his enemies had been liquidated or chastened,
and the Radicals were in a compromising mood. He also wished to
secure the right of succession for his future female children, in the
event that he had no male offspring, and to ensure for his wife the role
of regent in case of his death. All this required a constitutional
change, for the old constitution did not provide for such contingencies.
Since the personal regime established in 1894 had been more Milan's
work than Alexander's, it seemed fitting that it should pass away with
its author. Alexander and Draga both felt a pressing need to gain
popularity, and a constitutional regime seemed to be an effective way
to win friends.

Alexander began to take steps to satisfy the conditions set by the Radicals. Milan's death had already settled one, with reassuring finality. In February 1901 Alexander reshuffled his "Wedding Cabinet" by ousting three ministers. Two of these who were especially obnoxious to the Radicals he replaced with Radicals Mihailo Vujić and Milovan Milovanović. In late March he replaced the Jovanović cabinet entirely with one headed by Vujić, consisting of an equal number of Radicals and Progressives. Without delay the new government presented to the king a new constitution, which he promulgated himself on April 19 by royal decree, even though the previous constitution, that of 1869, stipulated that only a Grand National Assembly could do so. At the king's suggestion, the Radicals and the Progressives merged into a single political bloc. Though not a "fusion" into one party, as many believed, the bloc even had a common newspaper, the *Dnevnik* (Daily).

The "April Constitution" was a compromise, and therefore pleased no one entirely, except perhaps the Progressives. Its main authors were Ministers Milovan Milovanović, a Radical, and Pavle Marinković, a Progressive. Milovanović hoped to duplicate the Radicals' Constitution of 1888. Marinković used for his model the aborted constitutional draft prepared by the Novaković government. King Alexander hoped to keep as much of the 1869 constitution as possible. The result was a mixture of democratic, conservative, and reactionary provisions.

Its most significant new feature was a bicameral legislature consisting of an elected assembly of 130 members, and a senate of 51 members three-fifths of whom were appointed by the king. The king felt more secure from Radical hegemony knowing that he could rely on the checks and balances inherent in a divided cabinet and a divided parliament. The legislative power was now more equally shared by king and parliament than under the Constitution of 1869.

In general, the democratic electoral system of the 1888 constitution was preserved, including the secret ballot. The houses of parliament were equal, except that the lower house had the final word on the budget. Having granted this much, the king refused to accept parliamentarianism completely; thus the April Constitution made no provision for ministerial responsibility to the parliament, though it did make ministers subject to prosecution for illegal abuse of their powers. A state council was given the right to consider complaints both against ministers and against unconstitutional laws or decrees. Moreover, the government reserved the right to operate on the previous year's budget if the Assembly was dissolved before approving a new budget. Civil rights were recognized but narrowly defined and made subject to limiting legislation. The independence of the judiciary was confirmed. Constitutional provisions could not be suspended or changed as easily as under the 1869 constitution.

In sum, the Progressives were pleased with the new constitution, the Radicals felt that half a loaf was better than none, and the completely ousted Liberals opposed it entirely. Hoping to gain popular support, the Liberals now took a more democratic stance than the Radicals, which was quite a novelty.

The April Constitution exacerbated a process of division in the Radical party that had begun earlier between the old guard and the young hopefuls. The old guard, who consisted of former ministers, councilors, and other dignitaries, all bound by the memory of persecution, looked upon their compromise with the crown as a necessary political expediency. Their junior colleagues, of whom there was an ever increasing number, suspected their seniors of selling out and of having gone soft. They saw no need to make deals with a king who lacked the support of the people and whose word could not be trusted. They were for struggle rather than compromise with the crown. Unable to go along with what they regarded as the opportunism of their elders, the young Radicals formed a party of their own, the Independent Radical party. Its platform was essentially the Radical party program of 1881 and the Constitution of 1888. Yet if their program was an old one, their lively temperament injected a fresh vigor and boldness into Serbian politics. King Alexander, whose chief tactic was one of divide and rule, shortsightedly rejoiced at this split in Radical ranks as he had at similar divisions within the Liberals and the Progressives; however, the Independent Radicals had an importance that went far beyond their numbers, for they included the vocal intelligentsia of Belgrade.

The people looked upon the April Constitution with cold indifference, as the work of political bickering at the top that had little to do with them. The peasantry never showed much interest in constitutions, not because they were illiterate and ignorant, but because they were wise with experience. Having seen constitutions come and go, they knew very well that what would decide matters in Serbia was not what constitutions said but what those in power did with the law to suit their own ends. Thus the April Constitution did not win any great popularity for Alexander and Draga among the peasantry, the vast majority of the population.

What popularity they had was severely damaged when the sham of Draga's pregnancy became clear. In mid-April a French obstetrician, Dr. Caulet, and two Russian obstetricians, Dr. V. F. Snegirëv and Dr. Gubarov, arrived in Belgrade. Caulet had been Draga's physician before and had diagnosed her supposed pregnancy in August. Snegirëv and his assistant had been invited by Russian Minister Charykov on orders from his government, which had been alerted by Queen Natalia that Draga was incapable of bearing children. Caulet admitted to his Russian colleagues that his earlier examination had been perfunctory and that he had signed the affidavit attesting to Draga's pregnancy under pressure from a Serbian colleague. A new examination by all three doctors revealed that Draga was not pregnant but had a tumor.

Alexander was furious with the doctors, refused to accept their verdict, and even suggested that Snegirëv should be beaten and thrown out of the country. Eventually wiser counsels prevailed. An official communiqué on May 18, 1901, blamed Dr. Caulet for his mistaken diagnosis. However, the public believed otherwise. Draga had a history of false pregnancies. She had not only deceived Alexander before, on at least one occasion and perhaps two, when, as his mistress, she went abroad on the pretext of getting an abortion, but she had tried, even earlier, to deceive a Frenchman who was working in Serbia into marrying her by pretending to be pregnant. Moreover, even after the examination in April 1901, Draga claimed twice that she was pregnant, but Alexander was by this time wise enough not to make any more public announcements about a pregnancy. Meanwhile there were disquieting reports from those who knew both Draga and her sister Hristina, who was truly pregnant at the time, that Draga hoped to palm off Hristina's child as her own. However, Hristina had a miscarriage, and the Russian physicians arrived before Draga could make other plans. Whatever the truth of any of these reports may be, the result was a ruinous scandal which not only affected Serbia itself but which the eager foreign press dragged from one end of Europe to the other. Family scandals of the Obrenović rulers had always provided good copy for European newspapers.

The political results were disastrous for Alexander. It was now quite apparent that the last of the legitimate Obrenović line would never have an heir as long as he was married to his beloved Draga. Never had the stock of the pretender Prince Peter Karadjordjević been higher. A personally popular figure, married to a Montenegrin princess, favored by the Russian Court, Peter Karadjordjević now seemed surer than ever of gaining the Serbian throne. To improve his own position, King Alexander sought desperately to arrange a visit for himself and Draga to Russia, but Tsar Nicholas II had had enough and put the visit off indefinitely. Instead, the royal couple made a tour of Serbia, hoping to whip up enthusiasm, but they were met with such indifference that the police had to organize "spontaneous" demonstrations of public affection.

While Alexander's popularity was waning, that of the Radicals was again on the rise, judging by the elections of August 4, 1901. Though not entirely free of the customary police pressure, the elections were freer than they had been under Alexander's personal regime. It was not so much the police as the electoral law that troubled the opposition, for it gave a tremendous advantage to the party gaining even a plurality in any district. For example, even if a victorious party received just 40 percent of the total votes, it was entitled to 90 percent of the seats allotted to that district. Thus out of 130 seats in the Assembly, the "old" Radicals won 84, the Progressives 26, the Independent Radicals—who were making their political début—14, and the Liberals of the Avakumović-Ribarac group only 6, while the Liberals of the Andonović faction won none at all. The "old" Radicals were clearly in the saddle again. Even in the Senate they had, if not such a decisive majority, at least a plurality, largely because, of 18 senators elected by the people, 17 were "old" Radicals and only one was a Progressive.

The Radicals used their victory to enact a series of laws affecting election procedures, the press, public meetings and associations, the State Council, the criminal law code, the army, local communes, and other matters. These laws showed the willingness of the "old" Radicals to compromise, both with the crown and with their old ideals, for while some of the new laws generally tended in the direction of the more democratic provisions of the 1888 constitution, they also preserved restrictions of various sorts.

Nevertheless, King Alexander was far from content with even so cautious a constitutionalism and parliamentary system. He meddled into everything, giving directions to members of Parliament, trying to change or to circumvent its laws, and even stooping to personal attacks in the semi-official newspaper *Dnevnik*. He had the police persecute his critics. His ministers had to excuse themselves in private, protesting that they knew nothing about such things, while the court gave direct orders to the police. The latter were especially zealous in putting pressure on recalcitrant newspaper editors. The king also continued his efforts to make Draga popular. Schools and hospitals were named after her. Her birthday became a national holiday celebrated with parades. A medal was struck in her honor as an award given to women who had distinguished themselves in their service "to the King, the Royal House or the State."

Draga's advancement of her own family was far more disquieting. Her brothers and sisters were conspicuously present at court, even at official functions where, contrary to protocol, they stood next to the royal couple. Draga even sought to have them proclaimed members of the Royal House. This could have been dismissed as harmless were it not for Draga's childlessness. There were strong rumors that Alexander intended to adopt Draga's younger brother, Nikodije Lunjevica, and make him his successor. Young Lunjevica, an army officer widely known for his drunken orgies, attracted a small following of sycophants who took to addressing him as Your Highness. People feared that the king was so bound to the Lunjevica family that he was willing to give them even the throne of Serbia. Feelings ran so high that the king had to make a public denial that Lunjevica was being considered as his successor.

By 1902 a mounting number of incidents revealed the ever uglier mood of the country against both the king and his government.

One of the most impressive demonstrations of popular displeasure with the reign was the funeral of the Radical leader Kosta Taušanović in early 1902, which looked more like a political mass meeting. Ljubomir Živković, a very vocal Independent Radical deputy, turned his eulogy into a harangue against King Milan's despotism, which contained many pointed allusions to Alexander as well.

The best writers of Serbia trained their sights on the king and his government, and their pens were more effective than rifles. The fables of Radoje Domanović, then a young teacher and a Radical, became a sensation, especially his *"Stradija,"* the name of a mythical country "famous for its swine and tomfooleries" in which the ministers played musical chairs while the police spared voters the trouble of choosing candidates to parliament. The equally young Milan Grol wrote a short article that aroused Alexander's ire. It read:

Imagine a bad dream,

A destitute little nation, with two million paupers, and a debt of half a billion,

A land with day laborers for a penny and officials receiving 20,000 dinars,

A dishonest government of incompetent Ministers, of drunken Ministers,

A tattered and hungry army full of generals' gold epaulets,

A Church of soiled miters,

A civil service replete with ranks and dirty linen,

A Parliament presided over by usurers and dominated by spies and forgerers,

A press in the hands of informers and provocateurs, and in which jailbirds write,

Imagine a country where this is not a dream, a nation that has experienced all of this.

The students of Belgrade were less literary and more direct in their protests. In March 1902 they had to be ejected from the galleries of the Senate because of their loud protests against the restrictive Law on Assemblies and Associations that was being considered at the time. The students were especially angry at Pašić, whom they regarded as a turncoat. When the students transferred their protests to the building of the Great School, the police violated the time-honored sanctity of academic immunity and beat the students. Twenty were arrested and nearly two hundred expelled.

The army was dangerously disaffected. On the one hand, the men were poorly clothed and ill fed. The salaries of the officers were in arrears for some months in 1902. Some of the best officers had been dismissed for their loyalty to Milan. On the other hand, the king caused much resentment by advancing a favorite adjutant to the rank of general over the heads of many senior aspirants.

Meanwhile a false general appeared on the scene in a freakish episode that set the whole country agog. In the dawn of March 5, 1902, a twenty-eight-year-old man, Rade Alavantić, accompanied by four accomplices, crossed the Sava River from the Austro-Hungarian side and attempted to carry out a putsch in Šabac, his home town. Dressed in a general's uniform, he simply ordered customs guards to follow him, as he did the firemen in Šabac, and with them tried to take over the local gendarmerie. However, he failed to convince their commander and was shot by him in a gun fight. Alavantić's last words were "Long live Karadjordjević!" The entire incident was historically reminiscent of the Obrenović-inspired "Hussar" Rebellion of 1844 against Prince Alexander Karadjordjević, when men in bogus uniforms also crossed the Sava from Austrian Srem into Šabac. What lent it special importance was the fact that the name of Karadjordjević was involved. Moreover, though unknown at the time, Grabov's Russian secret agents had been previously informed of the undertaking, which might explain how Alavantić obtained the money for his general's uniform. It was more generally believed in Serbia at the time that Austria-Hungary was behind the attempt, since Alavantić had crossed into Serbia from Austria with a uniform obtained in Zemun. King Alexander did not use the attempted coup against his political enemies, as Milan had done after the St. John's Day attempt on his life. Only the immediate protagonists were tried and punished, with exemplary severity. However, an already apprehensive Alexander could not help but be disturbed by the fact that the Alavantić affair again brought to the fore, and so sensationally, the question of the succession to the throne.

Other omens cast a shadow over the Obrenović dynasty at the time, in a manner that particularly impressed the superstitious. In mid-1901 a storm felled the tree at Takovo under which Miloš Obrenović had proclaimed the Second Insurrection against the Turks in 1815. In April 1902 the news reached Serbia that Queen Natalia had become a convert to Roman Catholicism. It seemed to many to be less an act of faith than a symbolical gesture of her repudiation of the Obrenović dynasty and a rejection of her son, who was, after all, the lay head of the Orthodox Church of Serbia.

With so many signs of disaffection around him, the king needed a strong government. In the "fusion" of Radicals and Progressives, the latter were by far the inferior partners. Besides, there was no real unity between them anyway, as became apparent in Parliament. The Vujić cabinet was very weak, even though its leading figures were Radicals; the trouble was that they enjoyed the confidence of neither the young Radicals nor of Pašić's following, both of whom attacked the Vujić government openly in Parliament and in the press. The stalemate that ensued became evident in May 1902 when, after causing the fall of

Vujić's government, Pašić received the king's mandate to form a new one. The king assumed that Pašić's continued unpopularity, stemming from his statement before the tribunal at the time of the St. John's Day affair, would force him to cooperate with the court. Yet Pašić found it impossible to recruit a suitable cabinet and had to return his mandate to Vujić. Meanwhile Alexander blamed the Radicals for everything that went wrong. He came to look upon the April Constitution of 1901 as merely an instrument for their power.

On October 17, 1902, Alexander dismissed the Vujić government, ostensibly for having failed to arrange for his much desired visit to Russia. He had General Dimitrije Cincar-Marković organize a cabinet of neutrals, but changed his mind that same night, before the new cabinet had been proclaimed. Instead, he gave the mandate to Pera Velimirović, hoping to get another, stronger version of the Radical-Progressive coalition under Vujić. The attempt failed. The last issue of *Dnevnik*, the newspaper of the coalition, appeared on November 17, 1902 O.S. Meanwhile *Odjek* (Echo), the organ of the Independent Radicals, appeared on the political scene with the following program:

We wish the fatherland to be more important to all Serbs, more important than anything else, than anyone else. . . . We desire the disappearance of a personal cult, of idol worship, but let every Serb stand erect and not hold himself in a bent position or crawl. We wish an end to a personal regime that derives its strength from moral weakness and lack of character, ignorance and empty vanity, insatiable appetites, and financial straits, and that a new generation of civic workers arise, men with morals and character who are conscious of their rights and human dignity.

Odjek branded Velimirović's government as that of the "fourth party," its name for politicians who, lacking a political base of their own, did the king's bidding. The phrase was so applicable that it caught on in the parlance of the day.

When the Radicals in the Assembly made clear that a majority of them were not behind the government, Velimirović resigned, and on November 19, 1902, General Cincar-Marković was finally allowed to organize his own cabinet, the "government of generals," as it became known, because three ministers were generals. This government was, in fact, a vehicle for the return of King Alexander's personal regime. Supported by the right-wing Liberals, right-wing Progressives, the "Court Radicals," and the "fourth party," the king began his personal rule by postponing Parliament and began war on the four opposition newspapers with his six pro-regime newspapers. Because the law forbade prosecution of editors for *lèse majesté* as in the old days, the warfare was fairly open; though the opposition had to resort at times to veiled allusions to the king and his henchmen, no one could miss the mark.

On Sunday, April 5, 1903, a demonstration of trade apprentices protesting over their legal status as servants turned into a large political rally when they were joined by several hundred students who cried "Long live the Constitution!" though there were also shouts for a republic and against both the king and the queen. The police, the gendarmerie, and the army quelled the tumult with no regard for human life. Demonstrators were killed and wounded, and over a hundred persons were jailed, though only briefly. The opposition accused the king of having provoked the bloodshed to justify suspension of the constitution. The king blamed everything on his political enemies. He suspended the Constitution of 1901 "for a short while" and "until further orders." The reason stated was that Parliament did not respect the king's constitutional rights and the press had overstepped its bounds in "taking advantage of what the Constitution allowed by demanding what the Constitution did not allow." The suspension of the constitution lasted exactly three-quarters of an hour—from 11:15 P.M. to midnight of April 6, 1903—just long enough for the king to dismiss Parliament, cancel all appointments of senators, retire the State Council, annul the laws on communes, elections, and the press, and appoint new judges to the highest court. As soon as successors were named to the vacated seats and new laws were proclaimed by royal decree, the constitution was put back in force, if, indeed, it had much force after that lightning stroke.

The Radicals boycotted the ensuing elections, held on June 1, 1903. Their participation would hardly have mattered much in view of the police terror and sense of fear throughout the country. Predictably the regime won a clean sweep, with right-wing Liberals winning 72 seats, the right-wing Progressives 34, and the "Court Radicals" 24. The government's candidates gained a total of around 180,000 votes; the opposition received only 1,500. King Alexander's personal regime seemed at last secure. Yet it was to last only ten days—thanks to that ultimate weapon of politics, assassination.

Serbia's Foreign Relations, 1889–1903

Before he abdicated, King Milan had been careful to renew his Secret Treaty with Austria-Hungary. On March 19, 1889, the regents informed Vienna in writing that they intended to adhere to the treaty. As for the party in power, the Radicals, they knew no more about it than did the rest of the country.

The first instance in which Austria-Hungary intervened, according to its treaty rights, was the return of Metropolitan Michael to Belgrade after the exile imposed on him by Milan. The metropolitan was a fiery nationalist whose dream of a united Serbdom led him to close relations with Russia, especially the Panslavists. His designs on Bosnia, Hercegovina, and the Sancak of Novi Pazar, where the clergy were in effect so many agents of Serbian nationalism, disturbed the Austro-Hungarian government. Inasmuch as an article of the Secret Treaty specifically stated that Serbia would not tolerate any political, religious, or other activity to be directed against the Dual Monarchy, particularly in those provinces, Vienna protested against Metropolitan Michael's reinstatment as head of the Orthdox Church of Serbia. In its ignorance of the Secret Treaty, the Radical government regarded this as unwarranted intervention in Serbia's internal affairs and rejected the protest. Regent Ristić knew better, however, and Austria-Hungary was content to let the matter ride on his assurance that the metropolitan would not be permitted to engage in any intrigues.

Soon after, the Austro-Hungarian government made another protest, as a result of the ultranationalist celebration in 1889 of the five-hundredth anniversay of the Battle of Kosovo. Vienna was disturbed that the Serbian government had chosen that very time to distribute weapons to its national militia in certain regions. Ristić was warned by the Austro-Hungarian envoy in Belgrade that if the Serbian government continued to disregard its obligations, the Austro-Hungarian government might well "lose any interest in the preservation of Serbian independence."

Vienna was also apprehensive over the nationalistic tone of the Serbian press. In this respect it found the Radical newspaper *Odjek* (Echo) no less aggressive than the usual chauvinist press, and this was all the more disturbing because Jovan Djaja, director of the Serbian foreign ministry, was held to be the moving spirit of the newspaper.

The regular appearance in the Serbian press of such phrases as "national aspirations," "Slavic solidarity," "subjugated brethren," and "Serbdom" troubled the Austro-Hungarian government very much.

Matters came to a head in May 1890 as the result of a state funeral accorded to the popular nationalist poet and editor of *Velika Srbija* (Greater Serbia), Stevan Kaćanski. In a church crowded with officials and officers, the writer Dragutin Ilić began his eulogy with the words "Down with Austria!" The Austro-Hungarian government lodged an energetic protest, and Belgrade was forced to make an apology. Soon after, the Hungarians decided to close their border to shipments of Serbian pigs wherever there was the slightest evidence of disease. The reason, as Hungarian Premier Wekerle admitted to the Serbian envoy in Vienna, was political. The measure was taken in midyear, before the height of the season for exporting pigs, apparently to remind Serbia of Austria-Hungary's control of their trade. Certain Radicals, notably Finance Minister Vujić and Minister of the National Economy Taušanović, welcomed an all-out tariff war with Austria-Hungary; however, the Hungarians called off their restrictions by fall.

In mid-1891 the Austro-Hungarian government gave the Serbs another reminder. Foreign Minister Count Kálnoky felt obliged to warn Belgrade that if the Serbian press continued its aggressively nationalistic tone, the press of Vienna and Budapest would reveal the truth about Serbia's financial straits. Because the Serbs were attempting to negotiate a more favorable trade agreement with Austria-Hungary at the time, Belgrade took the hint.

In general, once the Austro-Hungarian government and the Radical government took each other's measure, there was no further trouble during the latter's term of office. Kálnoky was more interested in lessening Russian influence in Bulgaria than in intervening in Serbia's domestic muddle. The important thing for him was to keep Serbia from intervening in the affairs of Bosnia and Hercegovina. This was difficult to do, in that Serbia was a sanctuary for Serbian political émigrés from those provinces.

The chief foreign policy aim of the Radicals was friendship with Russia. Here Pašić was the moving spirit. As a political exile, he had come into contact with Russian Panslavist circles, thanks to Metropolitan Michael. In February 1890, as president of the Assembly, Pašić visited Russia and was graciously received by Tsar Alexander III, who even conferred a medal on him. At a banquet of the Slavic Benevolent

Society, Count Ignatiev introduced him as "a distinguished worker for the Slavic cause and a Russian friend." During his stay, Pašić succeeded in obtaining a gift of 75,000 rifles and ammunition as well as a loan of three million dinars for military purposes. However, he failed to win a Russian trade agreement and loan to extricate Serbia from its dependency on Austria-Hungary; there was no practical basis for trade between two such predominantly agrarian countries which were physically separated from each other.

Russia was interested in Serbia at the time largely as a result of its troubles with Bulgaria under Prince Ferdinand and Premier Stambolov, both of whom desired to free Bulgaria of its dependence on Russia and to establish closer ties with Austria-Hungary. It is ironic that each of these Balkan neighbors was trying to escape the clutches of one Great Power by getting closer to the opposite Great Power, and that in so doing, each was being used against the other. The Russian government saw an advantage in being able to use Serbia as a point of constant pressure on Bulgaria. It was with this intent that Russia became embroiled in the Serbo-Bulgarian quarrel over Macedonia.

In July 1891 King Alexander, still a minor, visited St. Petersburg in the company of Regent Ristić and Premier Pašić, who was also foreign minister. Tsar Alexander III promised them that he would not permit Austria-Hungary to annex Bosnia-Hercegovina, and he promised Russian support of Serbian claims in Macedonia. At the same time he made it clear that Serbia could pursue a policy of friendship with both Russia and Austria-Hungary. Apparently the Russians wished to commit themselves to Serbia just enough to serve their purposes in Bulgaria but not enough to cause trouble with Austria-Hungary.

Serbia had tried to conclude an agreement with Bulgaria that was supposed to be the basis for another Balkan alliance. However, when Pašić went to Sofia in the fall of 1889 for this purpose, Stambolov rebuffed him. The Bulgarian premier reasoned that since his main foe was Russia, he could more surely rely on Ottoman support than on the friendship of a Serbia that was seeking a rapprochement with Russia. After this Serbo-Bulgarian relations suffered one crisis after another. There was great apprehension in Sofia that Serbia was being used as a center for a plot against Prince Ferdinand and Premier Stambolov. When an assassin almost killed the latter in the spring of 1891 and some of the conspirators fled, the Bulgarians accused the Serbs of harboring them. The whole atmosphere was reminiscent of the tension before the Serbo-Bulgarian War of 1885, except now the roles were reversed: it was Bulgaria that had Austrian backing, and Serbia that was a base for Bulgarian political émigrés. Not even the Slavic-minded Radicals, who wished an agreement with the Bulgarians, could surmount the pressures of the diplomatic situation or of Serbian national ambitions.

The chief object of rivalry between Serbia and Bulgaria was the Ottoman-held province of Macedonia. In the nineteenth and early twentieth centuries the chief ethnic group in Macedonia, especially if one excludes Salonika, was South Slavic. It was claimed by both the Serbians and the Bulgars, on the basis of a variety of arguments—historical, linguistic, ethnographic, and geographic. It occurred to practically no one on either side at the time that the Macedonian Slavs might be a separate ethnic group. Culturally, the Bulgars had several advantages over the Serbians, not the least of which was the predominance of the Bulgarian Orthodox "Exarchate" there after its establishment in 1870 with the sultan's blessing. The only religious affiliation Eastern Orthodox Macedonians could choose was either the Greek Patriarchate of Constantinople or the Bulgarian Exarchate. Most Macedonian Slavs chose the latter.

Earlier in the nineteenth century, Serbia's interest had been directed toward the unification of all Serbs. If the Serbs of the Austrian Empire were beyond reach in view of Austria's might, there was hope that at least the Serbs of the declining Ottoman Empire could be brought into the fold. In the middle of the century the chief Serbian targets for expansion and unification were Bosnia and Hercegovina. However, once Austria-Hungary ensconced its administration there in 1878, thanks to the Congress of Berlin, Serbia was forced to turn elsewhere. The chief targets became "Old Serbia," that is, the region from Serbia's southern border to the Šar Mountains, and Macedonia to the south. The Serbian government had shown an interest in this area even before this date. In 1868, under the Regency, there was formed a cultural committee in Belgrade whose chief aim was the opening of Serbian schools in Old Serbia and Macedonia. By 1873 there were over sixty such schools, in centers such as Kičevo, Kratovo, Kruševo, Gostivar, Veles, Debar, Kumanovo, Skopje, and Tetovo. A school was also founded in Prizren in 1871 for the education of teachers and priests.

Until the Serbo-Turkish war of 1876, the Ottoman authorities did not interfere with these Serbian cultural activities. However, after the war Serbian schools in Macedonia virtually disappeared, though they continued to exist in Old Serbia. The Treaty of San Stefano, which awarded almost all of Macedonia to Bulgaria, was a shock to the Serbs that was only partly relieved when the Congress of Berlin returned the province to the Ottoman Empire. When King Milan's Secret Convention of 1881 with Austria-Hungary forced him to renounce all pretensions to Bosnia and Hercegovina, his government decided to renew its Kulturkampf in Old Serbia and Macedonia. The Serbo-Bulgarian War in 1885 and Serbia's defeat only intensified this resolve. In August 1886 there was established in Belgrade the Society of St. Sava, supposedly a private organization but actually a front for the Serbian government. Its main public activity was the establishment of schools in Old Serbia and Macedonia. By 1887–1888 it had opened 37 elementary schools staffed by 54 teachers. The following year the number of schools rose to 42.

At that very time Stojan Novaković was appointed Serbian envoy to Istanbul. Among his successes there was the establishment of two Serbian consulates in Macedonia, one in Skopje and one in Salonika. Even more significantly, in 1888 work began on a railroad connecting Belgrade, Vranje, and Skopje, and a new trade agreement expanded commercial relations between Serbia and the Ottoman Empire. In March 1887 the Serbian ministry of education formed a special section for "Serbian Schools and Churches outside of Serbia." In 1887–1888 the Serbian legation in Istanbul published almanacs and primers, partly in Serbian and partly in the Macedonian Slavic tongue.

Only after King Milan's abdication in 1889 did this cultural activity in Old Serbia and Macedonia attain real momentum. In June of that year the section on Serbian schools and churches outside of Serbia was transferred to the foreign ministry and given the designation "PP" (*poverljivo prosvetno*, literally, "confidential cultural"), but usually called simply the Propaganda. This happened just as two more Serbian consulates were established in the area, in Bitola and in Priština.

Serbian cultural propaganda in Macedonia was seriously hampered by the lack of a Serbian church organization to compete with the Bulgarian exarchate or the Greek patriarchate. The Ottoman authorities took the position, in accordance with the traditional *millet* system, that nationality was determined by religious affiliation. Hence, in the absence of a Serbian church jurisdiction in Macedonia, the Serbian nationality, unlike the Bulgarian or the Greek, could receive no official recognition. In 1890 the Porte issued charters to Bulgarian bishops in Skopje and Ohrid, thus fulfilling a long-standing Bulgarian ambition. The murder of a Serbian priest in Ohrid, for which the newly arrived Bulgarian bishop was blamed, was only a portent of the struggle to come. To counter the Bulgarian advance, the Serbian government tried to get the patriarchate of Constantinople to support Serbian Schools and the Slavic liturgy in its jurisdiction, but the Greeks would not hear of the proposal. On the contrary, the Greek bishop of Skopje, where most of the flock was pro-Serbian, banned the Slavic liturgy, threw out all Slavic prayer books, and suspended a Serbian priest. This caused many to join the Bulgarian exarchate or to boycott the church altogether.

Hoping to convince the patriarchate of Constantinople of the necessity of a Serbo-Greek cultural alliance against Bulgarian advances in Macedonia, the Serbian government accepted Stojan Novaković's suggestion and in October 1891 sent an envoy, Vladan Djordjević, to Athens with a proposal of an alliance. The proposed agreement called for common action by the Serbian and Greek governments against the exarchate and against Bulgarian propaganda in Macedonia "inasmuch as this propaganda has taken hold and has spread into districts which do not belong to the Bulgarians." However, nothing came of the plan, because both sides disagreed over their respective spheres of influence in Macedonia and because the Greeks feared that any such joint action would only cause the Turks and the Bulgarians to draw closer to each other.

The Serbian government then tried to gain the favor of the Porte, which, after all, held Macedonia. However, it became apparent that Istanbul was in no mood to make any concessions it did not have to make. The Serbian government hoped that the Russians might supply the necessary pressure. It no longer placed its hopes in Russia's Panslavist circles. In 1890 the Slavic Benevolent Society published a map of Slavic peoples, done by its zealous member General Komarov, which showed not only Macedonia but also Old Serbia as Bulgarian. Even the president of the society, Count Ignatiev, the architect of the Treaty of San Stefano, agreed with the Serbian protest that this was too much. Tsar Alexander III and Foreign Minister N. K. Giers also agreed, and the latter assured Pašić, who was Serbia's envoy to Russia at the time, that "he would never favor Greater Bulgarian aspirations at the expense of Serbian rights and interests." As proof of its good faith, the Russian government disposed the patriarchate of Constantinople, whose cause it supported in its dealings with the Porte, to appoint Serbian bishops in Skopje and Ohrid, where the Porte had permitted the installation of Bulgarian bishops.

Though the Radicals had always condemned King Milan's anti-Bulgarian policy, once in power they found themselves pursuing the same policy, for the sake of Macedonia. The Radical government sought to gain its ends through the favor and cooperation of the Porte, Athens, and especially St. Petersburg. It went so far in its efforts to curry the favor of the Turks that, in 1891, it even withdrew its support from the Society of St. Sava. This was done partly for internal political reasons—the president of the society and some of its leaders were opponents of the Radicals—but largely because the Turks regarded the society as a training ground for turning Macedonians into agents of aggressive Serbian nationalism. As four-fifths of the society's budget for its school and seminary came from the government, these institutions were closed and the society almost faded away entirely. The government took the view that the introduction of pro-Serbian teachers and priests in Macedonia had to be carried out openly, legally, and with the Porte's approval. This meant the need to tone down the overt glorification of the society's work in the Serbian nationalist press and a more discreet approach by these teachers and priests. However, far from abandoning their political role, the government wished to strengthen their capacity for covert activity. All this was a transition from a rather amateurish expression of idealistic patriotism to a more professional application of Realpolitik. Even with the change in methods, however, the main thrust of Serbian activity in Macedonia and Old Serbia till 1903 was cultural rather than revolutionary. Its success may be measured by the fact that by 1901 the Serbians had established there 226 elementary schools, 4 gymnasia, a school of theology, and 3 high schools for girls.

This policy paid off in that the Porte permitted a series of concessions such as the installation of a Serbian bishop in Prizren in 1896 and the inauguration of Serbian schools in the district of Kosovo. However, it still would not grant recognition to a Serbian *millet,* or ethnic community, outside of Old Serbia. Nor would the patriarchate of Constantinople permit a Serbian bishop in Skopje, even though the local

Slavic population, in turn, would not permit the newly appointed Greek bishop, Ambrose, to enter their church.

The whole situation changed in May 1894, when Prince Ferdinand of Bulgaria replaced Stambolov with a pro-Russian government under Konstantin Stoilov. A dramatic reconciliation ensued between Bulgaria and Russia. The tsar's government advised the Balkan Slavs to cooperate. In the spring of 1896 the rulers of Bulgaria and Montenegro visited King Alexander, one after the other. Ferdinand was treated rather coolly by the Novaković government of Progressives, but Nicholas's arrival in Belgrade was the occasion for a great outpouring of Pan-Serbian solidarity, especially since he came on St. Vitus's Day, just in time for the commemoration of the Battle of Kosovo.

Meanwhile Serbia's relations with Austria-Hungary worsened. Between May and December of 1895 the Hungarians slapped embargoes on Serbian pigs three times on the grounds that the pigs were diseased, even though the Serbs claimed otherwise. The crisis inspired stricken merchants to talk openly and bitterly about decreasing Serbia's economic dependence on Austria-Hungary. Some of them hastily formed a stock company to establish a slaughterhouse and meat-packing plant in Serbia, and the Assembly voted a subsidy for the venture, but this could not alleviate the immediate crisis. The affair hurt Serbia's pride as well as its pocketbook, for the Novaković government was forced to accept mixed commissions of Hungarian and Serbian veterinarians on its own soil for the inspection of pigs before their exportation.

The Cretan Insurrection against the Turks in 1896 and Greek intervention on the island caused Serbia and Bulgaria to consider what their compensation might be in case Greece won Crete. Unprepared for war, the Serbian government decided, despite the desire of the Serbian public for action, to reach an accord with the Bulgarians. On March 3, 1897, during a visit to Sofia, King Alexander and Prince Ferdinand reached the following gentlemen's agreement: that both governments would consult with each other concerning their interests in the event that the Eastern Question were reopened; that neither would undertake on its own any action that might upset the status quo; and that until the spheres of their influence in the Ottoman Empire were defined, neither party would obstruct the cultural national activities of the other in the Ottoman lands but would help one another. They also agreed to invite Montenegro to join in the agreement. However, the Bulgarians refused to commit themselves at that time to a delineation of the two countries' spheres of influence. When King Alexander visited Cetinje a month later, Prince Nicholas not only expressed his willingness to join but also proposed a territorial definition of the Montenegrin and Serbian spheres in the Ottoman Empire. This time it was Serbia's turn to demur, just as Bulgaria had done with Serbia.

In exchange for maintaining neutrality when the Greco-Turkish War broke out on April 17, 1897, the Simić government was finally given the right by the Porte to open Serbian schools in the districts of Bitola and Salonika; moreover, the Greek bishop of Skopje, Ambrose, was withdrawn by the Turks and sent to Veles, and a Serbian archimandrite was made administrator of the diocese in his place, thanks to a compromise with the patriarchate of Constantinople. The Simić government was encouraged thereby to press for more, namely, the restoration of the Serbian patriarchate of Peć, but withdrew this plan when the Russians objected. Russian policy at the time favored the integrity of the patriarchate of Constantinople. Meanwhile the Bulgarians also placed pressure on the Porte during the Greco-Turkish War and won five bishoprics in Macedonia. Despite their gentlemen's agreement, neither the Serbians nor the Bulgarians consulted or helped one another achieve any of these gains.

On April 30, 1897, during a visit of Emperor Francis Joseph and his foreign minister, Count Agenor von Goluchowski, to St. Petersburg, Austria-Hungary and Russia signed an understanding in which they agreed to maintain the status quo in the Balkans with the hope of "eliminating the danger of a rivalry disastrous to the peace of Europe on the seething soil of the Balkan Peninsula." This did not keep either power from working undercover to enhance its influence in Serbia or Bulgaria.

The Russian government turned sharply against Serbia in 1897 after ex-King Milan returned there and King Alexander, with his father's connivance, established his personal regime on October 23. St. Petersburg regarded Milan as an instrument of Austria-Hungary, and so it acted accordingly. In December Tsar Nicholas II granted an official audience to the pretender to the throne of Serbia, Peter Karadjordjević. The Russian government also interceded on Bulgaria's behalf in getting Bulgarian bishops in western Macedonia, which it had previously looked upon as a Serbian sphere. At the same time Russia required Serbia to repay in full its debt of five million dinars incurred in loans in 1867, 1876, and 1890. When the new Russian minister to Serbia, Zhadovskii, was appointed in mid-1898, after a delay of some eight months, his manner toward ex-King Milan and Premier Djordje-vić was one of calculated rudeness. Even Emperor Francis Joseph commented on it to Russian Foreign Minister Muraviëv in November 1898. The Serbian Court retaliated by pointedly failing to invite Zhadovskii to a banquet to which all the other foreign diplomats had been invited, with the result that Zhadovskii was recalled by his government and the Russian legation was once again left to a chargé d'affaires, Pavel B. Mansurov. It was obvious that as long as Milan remained in Serbia, Russo-Serbian relations would suffer.

Bulgaria and Montenegro followed the Russian lead. In Macedonia the pro-Bulgarian element appropriated the Serbian church in Kumanovo and forced the Serbs to build a new one. Several pro-Serbs were murdered in the districts of Bitola and Salonika for their efforts in opening Serbian schools. As Serbian official protests to Sofia were to no avail, the Djordjević government considered the agreement of 1897 null and void. Crisis after crisis aggravated the hostility between the two Southern Slavic neighbors. Each side feared an attack from the other, and had reason to, in view of military preparations on both sides of the border. The Bulgarians were especially apprehensive that as long as Milan was commander of the Serbian armies, he would seek to redress his humiliation at Slivnitsa in 1885. Luckily, it was to the interest of neither Russia nor Austria-Hungary to change the status quo in the Balkans at that time, so both powers exerted a restraining influence. Nevertheless the rivalry went on. When, in late 1899, the patriarch of Constantinople finally appointed a Serbian bishop for Skopje, the Bulgarians persuaded the Porte to refuse him the necessary *berat,* or charter.

At the same time, Serbian-Montenegrin relations deteriorated to the point that Prince Nicholas was discouraged by the Serbian government from stopping in Belgrade on his way to Sofia. Diplomatic relations between the two states were virtually discontinued for a while. Various indications pointed to Cetinje as the center of an anti-Milan campaign which Milan himself feared might end in his assassination. The fact that Ranko Tajsić, the Serbian Radical leader, fled to Montenegro after the St. John's Day attempt on Milan's life in 1899 seemed to confirm this suspicion.

Serbia fared no better with the Porte. Vladan Djordjević's personal embassy to Istanbul did not move the sultan to act on any of some half-dozen Serbian requests, despite Serbia's offer of a defensive alliance. On the contrary, Serbia was forced to protect itself from the border raids of the sultan's Muslim Albanian subjects in the Kosovo district. Border clashes resulted in death and devastation for Serbs on both sides of the boundary, and in a general flight of Serbian refugees from Ottoman territory into Serbia. Because the Porte remained deaf to Serbian protests, Belgrade finally had to send troops against the Albanian raiders. Only then did the Porte agree to a joint peace-keeping operation along the border. However, in actual fact, the Porte was hardly willing to make trouble with its turbulent Albanian subjects. This convinced the Serbian government that it had little to expect from any Turkophile policy.

Worsened relations with Russia meant almost automatically closer ties with Austria-Hungary. It was thanks to a loan arranged by Finance Minister Kállay of Austria-Hungary that Serbia was saved from financial disaster and enabled to repay its debt to Russia. Under the pro-Austrian Djordjević government Serbian pigs became miraculously healthy again and could cross the border without trouble from veterinary inspections. Vienna also became Serbia's intercessor with the Porte, gave warnings to Bulgaria whenever matters seemed to be getting out of hand and kept Belgrade informed of Montenegro's dealings. In return, the Djordjević government toned down the nationalist press regarding Bosnia and Hercegovina and curtailed the activities of the political émigrés from those two provinces.

Unlike Milan, Alexander was not a confirmed Austrophile. He preferred to keep an equal and safe distance between Austria-Hungary and Russia and to have some room for maneuvering. The price for Russia's benevolence was ex-King Milan's head. That problem was solved, first, during the affair of Alexander's marriage with Draga Mašin, when Milan, who was abroad at the time, broke with his son and did not come back to Serbia, and finally in early 1901, when Milan died.

Though divided on internal matters, Mihailo Vujić's coalition cabinet (April 5, 1901–October 17, 1902) was pro-Russian. For their part, the Russians hurried to reestablish their influence in Serbia and to bring all three South Slavic countries together again. The new Russian minister to Belgrade, Charykov, arrived promptly after Milan's death; indeed, King Alexander suspended the official mourning period to give him a cheery welcome. Nothing could have pleased Alexander more than the tsar's willingness to be best man—by proxy—at his wedding. Once the Radicals came to power, in 1902, Serbia's pro-Russian policy was assured. Minister Charykov became the chief adviser to the crown and the cabinet and felt free to interfere in both foreign and domestic policy. The chief of Russian espionage, Colonel Grabov, was permitted to place his agents in strategic posts.

With Russia's help, a rapprochement between Serbia and Bulgaria was negotiated. However, Macedonia remained the stumbling block. The Bulgarians were more successful than the Serbians in Macedonia for a variety of reasons, not the least of which was Bulgaria's willingness to talk about an autonomous Macedonia whereas the Serbians spoke in terms of a partition of Macedonia. By the autumn of 1902 rivalries between various guerrilla groups in Macedonia reached such a pitch and local disturbances became so widespread that King Alexander prepared his armies for an imminent war. Russian Foreign Minister Vladimir N. Lamsdorff came personally to Serbia to keep Alexander from any rash move. Lamsdorff made it quite clear, to both Belgrade and Sofia, that Russia would not allow herself to be drawn on any pretext into armed intervention in the Balkans. Lamsdorff thereupon went to Vienna and worked out a joint program of reform for Macedonia with Austro-Hungarian Foreign Minister Count Goluchowski. Their plan called for a local gendarmerie composed of Muslims and Christians, under foreign officers, to keep the peace, and a general reorganization of the tax system. This was accepted by the other powers and by the Porte, and armed conflict was averted.

King Alexander's relations with Russia soon became cool. Draga's false pregnancy irked the royal couple's best man, Tsar Nicholas, and raised the question, more seriously than ever, of the succession to the Serbian throne. The tsar kept postponing the visit of Alexander and Draga to Russia, a visit the Serbian king desperately desired to raise his declining prestige at home. There were also disquieting rumors that Russia and Austria-Hungary were giving thought to replacing Alexander with Peter Karadjordjević. Rebuffed by Russia, Alexander tried to regain the favor of Vienna, but his overtures were taken by Vienna to be merely an insincere stratagem to frighten the Russians into supporting him. In desperation, Alexander sent a personal envoy on a secret mission to Vienna to relay his willingness to restore his father's pro-Austrian policy and to offer another secret convention to that effect. In return he asked for Austria-Hungary's support of Serbia's claims in Old Serbia and northern Macedonia as well as of his decision to appoint as his successor an adopted child from the female line of the Obrenović family, who was a resident and citizen of Austria-Hungary. Vienna rejected Alexander's offer, mainly because it involved the annexation of Ottoman territory and was a violation of the agreement of 1897 between Russia and Austria-Hungary. As for Alexander's successor, Vienna was adamantly opposed to having the prince of Montenegro become king of Serbia, because the union of Montenegro and Serbia would threaten Austria-Hungary's stake in the Sancak of Novi Pazar, which separated the two Slavic countries. However, Peter Karadjordjević seemed to be no threat to Austria-Hungary at a time when Vienna and St. Petersburg were pursuing a common policy in the Balkans.

Alexander also tried to interest Sofia in a joint Serbo-Bulgarian attack on Turkey. While the Bulgarians agreed in principle, they were still reluctant to divide Macedonia into a Serbian and a Bulgarian sphere.

Alexander even made secret overtures to the Turks—as did the Bulgarians. He offered a military alliance in case of a war between Bulgaria and the Ottoman Empire. Obviously he hoped to gain no matter who won that war. However, the Turks were not enticed.

By 1903 Alexander was completely isolated in the diplomatic arena and equally isolated at home.

The End of the Obrenović Dynasty

The conspiracy against King Alexander Obrenović and his wife originated in the army—the very quarter in which he had the greatest confidence. While his police kept a watchful eye on Karadjordjević supporters, left-wing Liberals, Independent Radicals, and government officials, the army officers initiated and consummated the plot against his life. Though the Karadjordjević party and various civilian political elements later joined the conspiracy, they were not its moving spirits. Nor was the original purpose of the plot to bring Peter Karadjordjević to the throne; that came about only as a not entirely inevitable consequence.

As early as 1901, various junior officers in the army came to the conclusion that the king and queen had to be killed. These men were led neither by any political ideology nor by the hope of personal gain. Rather, they were driven by the obsessive conviction that Alexander, their commander in chief, had brought shame upon Serbia by marrying an immoral woman whose childlessness threatened to bring one of her hated brothers to the throne. Meanwhile, these young officers were convinced, Serbia was stagnating and rendered incapable of carrying out its historic mission of freeing and uniting the Serbian race through war with the Turks. It was not simply the patriotism of these young officers that was offended, but the pride of a military caste, a pride that had been assiduously encouraged by King Milan and recklessly slighted by King Alexander. Exasperated by irregular pay, some of them faced insecurity while an increasing number were denied promotion or even pensioned because of their presumed hostility to the queen. That Alexander's increasing unpopularity in the country at large had led to the general belief that the army alone was his mainstay heightened the resolve of the disaffected officers to rid themselves of this onus by doing away with the king.

In August 1901 seven junior officers, brought together by Lieutenant Antonije Antić, agreed to murder the royal pair on September 24 at the queen's birthday ball. The plan, devised by Dragutin Dimitrijević "Apis," could not be carried out, because Alexander and Draga failed to appear at the ball. Another plan to kill Alexander in the autumn of 1901 at Ub during military maneuvers also failed. By this time the conspirators, who had no political program of their own, came to realize that the inevitable political consequences of their success required the participation of civilian leaders. This task was entrusted to Djordje Genčić, former minister in the Djordjević cabinet, who had just recently been released from prison. Eventually the civilian conspirators included two Liberals, two Progressives, and a Karadjordjević supporter. They attempted to sound out the Russians and the Austrians on their attitudes and preferences in case of a dynastic change in Serbia. They concluded that the least objectionable choice to all concerned was a native ruler rather than a Russian or a German prince. Peter Karadjordjević, grandson of the famous revolutionary leader Karadjordje Petrović and son of Prince Alexander Karadjordjević, was the obvious choice. Peter, who lived in Geneva, held aloof from the conspirators; while he hoped all his life that a revolution in Serbia would bring him to the throne, he balked at murder. However, his less restrained kinsman and agent in Vienna, Jaša Nenadović, encouraged the conspirators.

While the number of civilian conspirators remained small and stable, the number of military participants in the plot grew greatly, mainly through the efforts of Dragutin Dimitrijević. By the spring of 1903 their number had reached 120. The number of people who, though not participants, knew of the plot also grew. It was inevitable that the intended victims should also learn of it. The king took extraordinary precautionary measures. He and Draga avoided leaving the palace. Draga remained inside all the time, and Alexander was surrounded by guards on the few occasions he attended public functions. The palace guard was doubled. The irony was that Alexander was to forfeit his life to some of those very guards in the palace.

At their last meeting, on June 8, 1903, the conspirators decided to invade the palace and murder the royal couple on the night of June 10–11. It was especially ironic that the military command of the coup was entrusted to Colonel Aleksandar Mašin, brother of Queen Draga's first husband. Though forcibly retired because of his hatred for Draga, he donned his discarded uniform and reactivated himself for the occasion. Young Lieutenant Petar Živković, officer in the palace guard, was to open the great oaken gate to the palace grounds from the inside. The officers had not even told their enlisted men of their intention for fear that the peasant rank and file would support the king. However, once the king was dead, the officers were confident that the troops, and the nation, would accept a *fait accompli*.

After heavy fighting with the loyal palace guards, the conspirators entered the palace at about 2:00 A.M. and rushed into the royal bedchamber, only to find it empty. A frenzied search of the palace ensued, but without success. Finally a conspirator noticed that one side of the bedchamber, which faced the street, had no windows behind the draperies. Instead, there was a concealed door. The conspirators forced the king's adjutant, who was their prisoner, to call out to the king to come out of his hiding place. "Can I depend on the oath of my officers?" the king asked through the door. The conspirators replied that he could. Alexander opened the door and was immediately cut down by a volley of shots. Draga fell dead over him. The bodies were hacked by swords and hurled from the balcony into the courtyard. This occurred at 3:50 A.M.

Troops commanded by the conspirators arrived and invested the entire palace, while other conspirators were engaged in taking over the government. In the process several more murders occurred, mostly unplanned: Premier General Cincar-Marković, the war minister, and both of the queen's brothers. The minister of the interior was left for dead, but he managed to survive. The commandant of the Danube Division was also killed, as were the king's adjutant and various palace guards, at least one of whom was a fellow conspirator killed by mistake.

Though the coup had proven bloodier than its authors had anticipated, it by no means exacted the toll of a revolution. It was not, in fact, a revolution but a palace revolt. The people at large had nothing to do with it. Though quite capable of social and economic rebellion, the Serbian peasant was politically conservative. Yet once the deed was done, the people calmly accepted the murder of Alexander and Draga.

The bodies of the royal couple were buried the next night after an eerie moonlit funeral procession that began after midnight. They were buried at three in the morning inside St. Mark's Chapel. The only persons present at the funeral, apart from the clergy and grave diggers, were two of the conspirators who came to witness the burial. Such was the end of the Obrenović dynasty.

The Culture of Serbia, 1870–1900

In the last quarter of the nineteenth century Serbia was still a predominantly peasant country; according to the census of 1884, 87.5 percent of the population lived in villages and 12.5 percent in towns. There were 3,737 villages and 70 "towns." Of the latter, only three had a population of over 10,000—Leskovac (10,870), Niš (16,178), and Belgrade (34,864). Only 20 others had a population of over 3,000. By 1899 there was an increase in urban population, but the relative percentages of town dwellers and villagers remained fairly stable. Both in size and in way of life, Serbia's smaller towns were little removed culturally from the villages. While the ethos of the towns was made different by the still lingering traditions of their Ottoman Levantine origins, the actual level of their cultural life was still very low by European standards. Both the villages and small towns clung to a patriarchal mode of life that was self-contained and suspicious of the unknown world beyond. Life in both followed a cycle of folk customs in which religious and pagan elements were merged, with the blessings of the Orthodox Church.

The most widespread institution of cultural change was the school. In 1875 there were 534 elementary schools in Serbia with a total of 23,238 pupils. Just two years later there were 558 elementary schools with 47,044 pupils. Of these schools 20 percent were in towns and 80 percent in villages. Yet schooling in the villages was badly neglected. By a law of 1882, six years of elementary education was made obligatory for all children. The actual practice fell far short of this mark. In 1887, for example, not a single village school in Serbia had even five grades, while in the towns there were only 15 five-year schools and 6 six-year schools. The education of girls was almost universally ignored. Thus the rise of literacy in Serbia was a slow and painful process, as the following figures show:

Year	No. of literate	Per 100 townspeople	Per 100 villagers	Per 100 population
1866	50,796	26.7	1.6	4.2
1874	91,039	33.6	3.7	6.7
1884	177,865	43.7	6.4	11.0

Only 12.4 percent of the women in towns were literate, and only .3 percent in the villages, that is, only one out of every 3,000 women.

Many villages had no school building, and some that had a building had no teacher. The buildings were inadequate as well as being health hazards and breeding places of disease. Even by the 1880s most schoolteachers were not professionally trained, although there were two teacher training schools in Serbia. The level of teaching was often so low that many schoolchildren never really learned to read and write, or were taught so badly that they promptly reverted to illiteracy on leaving school. Thus from the standpoint of cultural advancement, the villages of Serbia were still in darkness in the late nineteenth century, and the towns stagnated in a rustic provincial indifference to culture that was abetted by the miserly funds that the government allotted to education.

What higher culture there was, was largely concentrated in Belgrade. In the field of publishing, for example, of the 325 books that appeared in Serbia in 1883, 321 were published in Belgrade, 3 in Niš, and 1 in Šabac. Similarly, the vast majority of Serbia's newspapers were in Belgrade. Požarevac, the fourth largest town in Serbia at the time, only got its first newspaper in 1875, as did Smederevo, the ninth largest town. In 1874 there were 17 public libraries in Serbia with the grand total of 7,939 books; of these the public library of Belgrade owned 3,843.

The pinnacle of academic life was the Royal Serbian Academy, which was founded in 1887. Unlike the Serbian Learned Society, which it replaced, the academy was strictly devoted to the advancement of scholarship rather than to social action as well. It was divided into four sections: the natural sciences, philosophy, the social sciences, and the arts. By its charter it could have only 25 members, who received a monthly honorarium until it was discontinued in 1892. In that same year the membership was raised to 32. Academicians were regarded as the leading Serbs in their respective fields. Their first president was Josip Pančić (1814–1888), a naturalist and specialist on the flora and fauna of Serbia. The academy supervised the work of two other significant institutions, the National Library and the National Museum.

Despite its grandiose name and important position, the National Library of Serbia consisted of a single reading room with 25 seats until 1897, when a second room with 8 seats was added. Many people had to read standing or seated on the windowsills. The library also permitted readers to take books home. Since the library was in the same building as the Great School, it was used largely by students. The size of its holdings and the progress made in acquisitions during the last three decades of the nineteenth century may be judged from the following statistics:

	1870	1900
Manuscripts	185	627
Incunabula and rare books	31	157
New titles	12,201	32,702
Volumes	25,840	70,706
Newspapers and periodicals	121	245
Maps, pictures, etc.	400	2,358

Much of the increase may be attributed to a law that required publishers to submit three copies of all that they printed to the National Library. However, directors complained that the law was poorly observed.

The National Museum was under the same director as the National

Library until a law of 1881 separated the two institutions. In 1871 it had a collection of 12,369 items arranged in 19 sections. In those years it had few visitors—439 in 1872, 401 in 1873, and 281 in 1874. By 1892, however, it had to be moved into two buildings near the Great School to accommodate its growing collection. It was then closed to the public until 1904. Meanwhile, separate museums of natural history and ethnography were formed from its collection. The former, the Museum of the Serbian Land, was opened in 1899, and the Ethnographic Museum in 1904.

The Great School (*Velika škola*) of Belgrade was the highest institution of learning in Serbia until 1905, when it was transformed into the University of Belgrade. In the academic year 1870–1871 it had a total of 229 students—14 in philosophy (liberal arts), 42 in the technical sciences, and 173 in law. The next few years saw a rapid rise in the liberal arts and a corresponding drop in the two other fields. The increase of interest in the liberal arts, especially the social sciences, reflected the ideological mood of the young under the impress of ideas advanced by Svetozar Marković and other socialists. Moreover, as students soon discovered, little Serbia could support only so many lawyers. As for the technical sciences, students preferred to go abroad for them. The general level of the courses was very low, about on a par with the European gymnasium, and the discipline was even worse. Attendance was lax. In the academic year 1872–1873, out of 196 candidates 146 failed to take their examinations; the following year 117 failed to show up. Under Stojan Novaković, professor of history and, on several occasions, minister of education and premier, more order was introduced. During the Serbo-Turkish Wars of 1876–1878 the regular program of the Great School was discontinued because so many students and professors were in the service.

In the eighties the Great School moved forward rapidly. In 1880 the liberal arts program was extended from three years to four, to equal the other two divisions. The school's budget was raised. The students and professors increased in number and quality, and the course offerings multiplied accordingly. The Serbo-Bulgarian War of 1885 hit the school hard; so many of the students were called to the colors that lectures had to be discontinued for the brief duration of the war.

The Great School was significantly advanced by a law of 1896 that gave it a measure of autonomy and expanded its program. By 1900 the liberal arts program offered 29 subjects in 11 groups as well as seminars.

Meanwhile, the policy of sending young scholars abroad on government scholarships paid off handsomely after some two decades. The Great School was able to recruit a distinguished staff of scholars with degrees from the greatest universities of Europe. By 1905 the conditions were finally ripe for proclaiming the Great School a university.

By the end of Prince Michael's reign, Serbia was well on the road to replacing Vojvodina as the cultural center of the Serbs. As the *Danica* (Morning Star) of Novi Sad acknowledged as early as 1865, "Serbia is not yet a completely independent principality, its social classes have just begun to emerge, and its freedom of the press is still swaddled and bound in the cradle, as stiff as some Egyptian mummy. And yet in such a little state the sciences, arts and literature proliferate and progress better than among us, and that only because, to whatever extent, the Serbs there are standing on their own two feet." The inference at which this Serbian journal in Austria-Hungary hinted was that political independence was a prerequisite of cultural development. However, from the standpoint of Serbian unification, Serbia was to become a cultural Piedmont in the latter part of the nineteenth century before it was to achieve this political goal. From the 1870s on it was no longer the Serbs of Austria-Hungary that set the tone of Serbian culture. Belgrade took over the intellectual hegemony of Novi Sad, once the "Serbian Athens."

This transformation is statistically demonstrable. Out of a total of 263 books published in Serbo-Croatian in 1868, 47 emanated from Novi Sad, 68 from Zagreb, and 126 from Belgrade. In the years 1869–1872, of the 1,174 publications in Serbo-Croatian, 168 appeared in Novi Sad, 189 in Zagreb, and 568 in Belgrade—almost as many as all the rest. In the realm of literature, before the 1870s almost all the principal Serbian authors were from Austria-Hungary; after 1870 they were chiefly natives of Serbia. As for scholarship, especially after the Serbian Learned Society was replaced in 1887 by the Serbian Academy of Sciences and Arts, Belgrade became the undisputed center of Serbian learning.

This transformation coincided with another great change in Serbian cultural life, the reaction against romanticism and the advent of realism in the arts and positivism in the sciences. The new emphasis was on truth through positive scientific knowledge, whether in the world of nature or of human relations. This outlook came to Serbia by way of Russia—the Russia of such men of the sixties as Chernyshevskii,

Dobrolyubov, and Pisarev. This was the Russia that looked to such Western teachers of positivism and evolution as Auguste Comte, Herbert Spencer, Henry Thomas Buckle, John Stuart Mill, and Charles Darwin, as well as the German materialists Ludwig Feuerbach, Ludwig Büchner, Karl Vogt, and Jacob Moleschott. This was also the Russia that attracted and converted many of the South Slavic students who went there after the middle of the century.

Among these the chief bearers of the new ideas were Svetozar Marković and Liuben Karavelov. Though the latter was a Bulgar, this outstanding revolutionary nationalist had a significant influence on Serbian thought and letters during his years of exile among the Serbs of Belgrade and Novi Sad. Karavelov's story, in Serbian, *Je li kriva sudbina?* (Is Fate to Blame?), published in 1868–1869 with interruptions (because of his arrest) by the Matica Srpska in Novi Sad, was strongly influenced by both Herzen's novel *Kto vinovat?* (Who is to Blame?) and Chernyshevskii's *Chto delat'?* (What Is to Be Done?). In 1870 the journal *Letopis Matice Srpske* published Marković's articles *"Realni pravac u nauci i životu"* (The Realistic Trend in Science and Life), and *"Realnost u poeziji"* (Realism in Poetry), both of which are landmarks in the history of Serbian culture. Still fresh from his experience in Russia, which he had left the year before, Marković proclaimed in the former article, "In all of Europe one may observe a clearly drawn struggle against the old and the antiquated. This is not only a matter of a political transformation—whether to have a republic or a monarchy, but a social transformation is brewing—a transformation of society from its very base. . . . This struggle, which is already in full swing in the West, has not yet reached us, but it must reach us as well, for this is required by the law of human progress." Through Marković and his zealous associates, the Serbian public was exposed to the thought of Darwin and Chernyshevskii, and Serbian journals began to devote space to the sciences, cultural and social history, and the new philosophy. With the same dogmatic recklessness that marked the Russian nihilists, Marković lashed out against "aestheticism" and made social utility the measure of all learning and art.

Yet Marković was by no means the creator of the new atmosphere in Serbian culture, but only its harbinger. By the 1870s the Serbian intelligentsia was ready to abandon the sentimentalism and fine phrases of romanticism in favor of more "serious" pursuits. Nothing could be more indicative of this trend than the nature of the books being translated into Serbian in that decade: Rousseau's *Émile* (1872), Renan's *Life of Jesus* (1872), Lamartine's *History of the Girondists* (1875), Haeckel's *Natural History of Creation* (1875), and Darwin's *On the Origin of Species* (1879). Among literary works translated into Serbian were Chernyshevskii's *What Is to Be Done?* (1869 and later editions); Turgenev's *Smoke, On the Eve,* and *Fathers and Sons* (all in 1869); Gogol's *Inspector General* and *Taras Bulba* (in 1870) and *Dead Souls* (1872); and Hugo's *Les Misérables* and *Quatre-vingt-treize* (1872 and later).

The effect of these trends and ideas on Serbian culture was dramatic, even revolutionary. The revolt against the homogeneity of a patriarchal society took the form of a defiant individualism and, even more shocking, feminism. The revolt against the Orthodox Church, which had taken the form of a benign deism and liberal anticlericalism among the romantic generation, now assumed the sharper cutting edge of atheism and philosophical materialism. Instead of the misty visions of Panslavism and the restoration of Tsar Dušan's medieval empire, the new generation of Serbian intellectuals demanded civil liberties and a better life for the masses. It was no Marxist revolutionary or nihilist, but a Serbian Orthodox monk in Austria-Hungary, Ilarion Ruvarac (1832–1905), and a respectable Belgrade professor, Ljubomir Kovačević (1848–1918), who declared war on the nationalistic mythology of Serbian romantic historiography and laid the foundations of a new critical school of Serbian historians. The old romanticism did not vanish without a struggle; in fact, it was to reappear as a virulent neo-romantic integral nationalism in the next generation, once realism lost its revolutionary ardor and became sedately bourgeois.

Between 1870 and 1900 literature became politicized. Poetry retreated before prose, now that beauty for its own sake was in ill repute. The younger generation generally turned to other pursuits. At least two great poets of the romantic era, Jovan Jovanović-Zmaj and Djura Jakšić, accommodated themselves to the new times by injecting a social and political element into their art. However, the most important poet of the new generation was Vojislav J. Ilić (1862–1894). Here was a classic case of the gap between fathers and sons, for this child of the romantic poet Jovan Ilić rejected the naive nationalist ardor and sentimentalism of the *Omladina* (Youth) of 1848 and even satirized it, as in the lines

> Good old days, how many mourn you
> With your liberal fights and scandals, . . .
> When not to think too much was virtue.

In his flight from the rhetoric and heady patriotism of the Serbian romantics, Vojislav Ilić turned in part to the more elevated lyricism of the Russians, especially Lermontov, Pushkin, and Zhukovskii. His patriotism was strong (he was a volunteer in the Serbo-Bulgarian War in 1885), but it was also critical. In 1887 he was haled into court for a political poem ("Masked Ball in Rudnik") and was forced to leave Serbia for a while. Yet basically he was no revolutionary fighter. As a poet, he was at his best in his reflective, melancholy, elegiac moods, or when he evoked the memories of classical antiquity. He turned Serbian poetry away from its emulation of native folk epic poetry and gave it the standards of modern European art. Dead at the age of thirty-two, Ilić wrote only a little over a decade, but in that short time he established himself as the finest Serbian poet of his generation and perhaps the best poet that Serbia ever produced.

Apart from Ilić, the outstanding figures of Serbian literature in the last third of the nineteenth century were the writers of stories and novels. For the most part they were the conscious disciples of the great Russian writers of the day—Turgenev, Tolstoy, Dostoevskii, and Chekhov. Yet they were very Serbian in the reality that they described.

No one typified these trends so well as Milovan Glišić (1847–1908). As a disciple of Marković's socialism and Gogol's realism, Glišić brought to Serbian literature the first social satires of that period; he also enriched the Serbian public with his translations of Russian and West European works. He comes closest to being the Serbian Gogol. Yet in his portrayals of Serbian types he was by no means an imitator. There is something uniquely Serbian about his wily peasants, dishonest officials, rogue priests, and grasping tradesmen. In his quest for a realistic depiction of truth, he often based his work on real people and events. His main theme was the villainy of those "legal robbers" in power and the purity of the oppressed peasant masses. His main weapon was humor. Glišić more than any other single person introduced the Russian literature of the day to the Serbian public. In 1872 he translated Gogol's *Dead Souls* with Ljubomir Miljković. He translated Gogol's *Taras Bulba* twice, in 1876 and 1902; Tolstoy's *Kreutzer Sonata* (1892) and *War and Peace* (1899–1901); and Goncharov's *Oblomov* (1876 and 1898). Glišić also did translations of the shorter works of Pushkin, Gogol, Shchedrin, Chekhov, and Garshin, as well as of the Ukrainian Shevchenko. He translated thirty-one plays by Russian, German, and French authors. He also translated West European and American authors into Serbian—Verne, Daudet, Balzac, Maeterlinck, Poe, and Mark Twain. Glišić was by no means a great artist, but he did much to acquaint Serbian intellectuals with modern European literature and with their own country.

Laza K. Lazarević (1851–1890) was one of the first to bring the art of writing stories in Serbia up to European standards. He was an excellent example of the new generation of Serbian intellectuals. Born in Šabac and educated in Belgrade, in 1872 he went to Berlin on a government scholarship to study medicine. He received his medical degree in 1879. In Serbia he served as an army doctor and as King Milan's personal physician. While yet a student in Belgrade's Great School, he studied Russian, read Russian authors, and even translated a part of Chernyshevskii's *What Is to Be Done?* as well as some of Gogol and Pisemskii. In tune with the scientism of his day, he also translated articles by Darwin and Faraday. However, somewhat like Gogol and Dostoevskii, in later years he turned his back on his materialist, "anti-aesthetic," rebellious youth, and as a writer of short stories, returned to romantic sentimentality and extolled the simple virtues of a cohesive patriarchal family life. As he drew his themes from contemporary Serbian life, he idealized that life, lending his Mačva villages an idyllic aura that only a city boy could imagine. Nevertheless, he contributed to the development of Serbian literature a refined artistry of form and style that set new standards for later writers.

Although a Dalmatian, Sima Matavulj (1852–1908) belongs to the literary history of Serbia by virtue of having made Belgrade his home from 1889 until his death. A gymnasium professor, he eventually became a member of the Serbian Academy and was president of the Serbian Literary Society. Best known for his novels and stories based on Dalmatian life, he also wrote of other South Slavic and Serbian locales in which he had lived and traveled, especially Montenegro and Belgrade.

Svetolik Ranković (1863–1899) reflected the people and problems of the Šumadija both in his stories and in his three novels: *Gorski car* (King of the Forest), *Seoska učiteljica* (Village Teacher), and *Porušeni ideali* (Shattered Ideals). Stevan Sremac (1855–1906), a Serb from Austria-Hungary, made Serbia his home and gave to literature some of the best portrayals ever written of the Serbs of his time, especially the townspeople of Niš. A professor of history, he also wrote biographical sketches of Serbia's great figures of the past. Janko M. Veselinović (1862–1905), who began as a village teacher in his native Mačva, immortalized the villagers of western Serbia with an authenticity that makes many of his artistic tales ethnographic source material. Radoje Domanović (1873–1908) was also a writer of village life. His was the Serbia of the south and east— Pirot, Vranje, and Leskovac. At first he wrote in an idyllic vein, but as the hardships of life exposed him to the seamier side of human existence, his forte became biting social and political satire. His *Stradija* (1902) —the name of a supposedly mythical land—was the best political satire ever written by a Serb. Its tremendous popularity did much to create the atmosphere of protest and revulsion in which a whole nation found it possible to accept the murder of their king and queen as just retribution.

During this period Serbia developed its first literary critics, notably Svetislav Vulović (1847–1898) and Ljubomir Nedić (1858–1902), as well as Svetozar Marković. Although all three suffered from a certain dogmatism, both of the right (Nedić) and the left (Marković), and were necessarily self-taught dilettantes as critics, they nevertheless applied to Serbian literature modern European standards and perspectives.

The leading literary journal of the late nineteenth century in Serbia was *Otadžbina* (Fatherland). It was founded in 1875 by Vladan Djordjević with a subsidy from Prince Milan and consciously modeled after the distinguished French journal *Revue des deux mondes*. For nearly two decades, until it ceased publication in 1892, *Otadžbina* held a preeminent place in Serbian cultural life, owing to the high quality of its collaborators—Djura Jakšić, Milovan Glišić, Jovan Ilić, Jovan Jovanović-Zmaj, Laza Lazarević, Vojislav Ilić, and others. At first largely literary, by the 1880s it devoted more attention to the social sciences, especially Serbian history.

Among the purely literary journals were *Delo* (Labor) and *Srpski Pregled* (Serbian Review). The former, founded in 1894, had a politically radical flavor and was banned in 1899. However, it was resurrected in 1901 and lasted till 1915. The latter journal was founded in 1895 and was conservative in outlook. Both contributed greatly to the rising level of Serbian literature and literary criticism.

The Serbian Literary Cooperative (*Srpska Književna Zadruga*) was founded in Belgrade in 1892. As its first president, Stojan Novaković, recalled, "It was an attempt to concentrate scattered forces, to pull strands together, to bring together the works of various times and different places, to loosen the political obstacles to literature, to make known everywhere all that is Serbian." The Serbian Literary Cooperative engaged in the most ambitious publishing venture in Serbia's history. The society published not only Serbian works, from the medieval Archbishop Daniel down to modern times, but foreign classics as well. The Serbian public at the turn of the century was evidently eager for an abundant and cheap supply of good literature, for in the years that followed there was scarcely a literate household in all of Serbia whose shelves did not display the familiar blue covers of the cooperative's series. The reputation of many a Serbian author was assured when the cooperative selected his work for publication.

The Society of Literature and the Arts (*Književno-umetnička zajednica*), also founded in 1892, did much during its brief existence of five years to bring together Serbia's authors, musicians, artists, and actors.

The National Theater, which was officially opened in 1869, was a tremendous cultural influence. By 1900 it had presented around 5,000 performances of both Serbian and other authors. Belgrade was able to see the plays of Shakespeare, Molière, Goethe, Schiller, Hugo, and Ibsen. The theater also provided an outlet for Serbian and Croatian playwrights; its most popular fare consisted of native patriotic dramas based on historical themes. The theater suffered two serious interruptions in its first three decades. In 1873 it had to be closed temporarily for a lack of funds. In 1876–1877 it was forced to close again because of the Serbo-Turkish War. However, it survived to become one of the most effective disseminators of culture in Serbia.

Newspapers were probably the most widespread purveyors of modern culture in Serbia. The fact that in the nineteenth century most Serbian newspapers were the organs of political parties and groups only enhanced their popularity, for if the general reading public was not particularly eager to be educated, it was passionately interested in politics. Newspapers enjoyed a special upsurge after the Constitution of 1869 guaranteed, in article 32, that "every Serb has the right to express his thinking verbally or orally, by means of the press or in the form of art. . . ." The Law on the Press of 1870 provided for censorship, but it was fairly liberal for those times. In the decade following that law, some thirty newspapers and other periodicals were founded in Belgrade. Some towns got their own newspapers for the first time—Svilajnac (1871), Požarevac (1875), and Smederevo (two in 1875). Kragujevac got three new newspapers in that period.

Through the efforts of Svetozar Marković and his associates, Serbia got its first socialist newspaper, the *Radenik* (Worker), which appeared on June 1, 1871 O.S. It was, in fact, the first socialist newspaper in the Balkan Peninsula. Its influence was described by the eminent literary historian Jovan Skerlić as follows: "It appeared at the right time, when there was not a single progressive and opposition newspaper in Serbia, and when political and social discontent was encompassing ever widening circles. The *Radenik* found readers not only among the younger generation, but also among the readers of the liberal press, on both sides of the Sava and the Danube. . . ." The newspaper did not last long; it was banned in 1872. However, upon Marković's return from exile in 1873, he and his friends founded another newspaper, in Kragujevac, called *Javnost* (The Public). This was not the doctrinaire socialist paper the *Radenik* (later *Radnik*) had been, but it was reformist in the spirit of radical democracy. It was devoted to a discussion of practical problems rather than to social theory. However, it was soon suppressed and Marković was arrested. In 1874 Marković's followers founded *Glas javnosti* (The Voice of the Public), which lasted only a few months. Upon his release from prison, Marković tried again, in Kragujevac, with the newspaper *Oslobodjenje* (Liberation). It survived his death in early 1875 by only a short time.

A somewhat more liberal press law in 1881 quickly resulted in more newspapers. In just that one year 15 new periodicals appeared in Belgrade alone—4 political, 3 humorous, 2 literary, 2 professional, 1 military, 1 children's, 1 illustrated, and 1 for entertainment. The new political grouping into Liberals, Radicals, Progressives, and Socialists brought more newspapers into the arena of Serbian public life. The Radicals had their *Samouprava* (Self-Government). The Liberals, in the guise of a "Society for the Advancement of Serbian Literature," published *Srpska Nezavisnost* (Serbian Independence) from 1880 to 1896. The Progressives published *Videlo* (Open View), also from

1880 to 1896. After *Radnik* and its ill-fated successors, the Socialists, not yet a formal party, published *Borba* (The Struggle) , from 1882 to 1886, and a new *Radnik*.

Apart from these more or less official party organs, there were all kinds of politically oriented periodicals, the most popular being humor sheets. The tone of all these periodicals was bitterly polemic and personal. What general news they brought to the public was purely of secondary importance. But they did appeal to an audience that read very little else. Moreover, they fostered the rise of a cadre of professional journalists who became increasingly aware of the higher standards of their calling. In 1881 a meeting of Belgrade journalists decided "to found a formal club of journalists on the model of similar societies in other European countries." Its first assembly was held in 1882. One of its concerns was to bring a more professional tone to Serbian newspaper writing. It soon dissolved as a result of the Timok Rebellion of 1883, which forced its president, Laza Kostić to flee Serbia, but it was revived in 1892.

The Constitution of 1888 (actually 1889 New Style) and a new Law on the Press in 1891 brought greater freedom to the Serbian press. By this time Serbian newspapers had a much broader public than in the previous generation, and this public was interested in much beyond party politics. The outstanding pioneer of modern journalism in Serbia in this period was Pera Todorović, whose *Male Novine* (Small News) appeared in Belgrade from 1878 to 1903. It was among the first to devote itself primarily to news as well as to various subjects dealing not only with politics but also with economics, literature, art, and so on. How well the public took to this approach may be judged by the newspaper's high circulation of 30,000, which far surpassed that of any other Serbian newspaper.

An important sign of cultural progress in Serbia was the rapid increase of printing presses in the 1870s and 1880s. In the 1860s, apart from the state printing press, there were only two private presses in the land, both in Belgrade. However, beginning with 1871, other presses were established in Belgrade, Kragujevac (1873) , Požarevac (1874) , Smederevo (1875) , Niš (1883) , Požarevac and Valjevo (1884) , and Užice and Kragujevac (1885) . By 1912 Belgrade had 19 presses, and there were 30 in the interior. The most technically advanced press in Serbia was the state printing press.

In the latter half of the nineteenth century, Serbia was still removed from European music. For the vast majority of Serbs, the only forms of music they heard, or probably cared to hear, were folk songs and the chants of the Serbian Orthodox Church, and the only orchestras in their experience were Gypsy ensembles and military bands. In the realm of higher music, the two important figures in Serbia after Stanković and Jenko were Marinković and Mokranjac.

Josif Marinković (1851–1931) was born and educated in Vojvodina. His teacher of music there was Dragutin Blažek, a Czech, who convinced Marinković to continue his studies in Prague. He came to Serbia in 1881 on the invitation of the First Belgrade Choral Society. After five years he became the director of another distinguished Belgrade choir, the *Obilić*. In this period he composed many patriotic songs in the spirit of the times. The most popular of these was the martial song *Hej trubaču s bujne Drine,* which was based on the lines by Vladislav Kaćanski:

> Ho, bugler from the seething Drina,
> Blow the reveille,
> Let it sound on Šar Planina,
> Lovćen, Durmitor.

He also composed a monumental cantata to Dositej Obradović as well as many choral compositions with a sophisticated piano accompaniment. However, his purely instrumental compositions were mediocre. Marinković's passion for Serbian folk music came to its highest expression in his eleven "cycles," or choral suites based on folk melodies, all in a romantic, lyrical style. As a teacher of music in the School of Theology he also composed music for the Serbian Orthodox Church. He is generally regarded as the founder of the nationalist school of Serbian music.

He was surpassed by his contemporary Stevan Mokranjac (1856–1914), choir conductor, composer, folklorist, and pioneer organizer of Serbian musical institutions. Unlike Marinković, Mokranjac was a native of Serbia. His birthplace was Negotin. As a student in Belgrade in the early 1870s he fell under the influence of Svetozar Marković's socialist ideas, as did so many of his generation, and he was almost lost to music when he decided to enroll in the science and mathematics division of the Great School. However, he became a member of the Belgrade Choral Society, which helped him financially to go to Munich in 1879 to study music. After a conflict with the director of the Munich Conservatory, Mokranjac returned to Belgrade after only three years, to become conductor of the Kornelije [Stanković] Singing Society. He spent the academic year 1884–1885 in Rome, devoting himself particularly to polyphonic music. During the next two years he completed his training at the conservatory in Leipzig. In 1887 he returned to Belgrade as the newly appointed conductor of the Belgrade Choral Society. Under Mokranjac, the society represented Serbian culture abroad in tours to Zagreb, Sarajevo, Split, Cetinje, Skopje, Budapest, Berlin, Dresden, St. Petersburg, Moscow, and Istanbul.

The greatest monuments to Mokranjac's creativity as a Serbian composer are his fifteen choral suites, or *rukoveti,* and other compositions based on the folk melodies of various Serbian and South Slavic provinces, as well as his music for the Serbian Orthodox Church, notably his Liturgy, Requiem, Te Deum, and Acathist to the Mother of God, all based on the traditional Serbian chant. No composer has surpassed Mokranjac in either genre. On the other hand, like Marinković, he was not at his best in instrumental compositions or, for that matter, as a composer of original music not based on folk songs or church chant. Another of Mokranjac's lasting contributions to the development of Serbian music was his participation in founding a variety of musical organizations. In 1889 he founded the first regular string quartet in Serbia, along with Melcher, Schramm, and Svoboda —not one of Serbian origin. It lasted till 1893. In 1899, with the pianist Cvetko Manojlović and the young composer Stanislav Binički, he established the Serbian School of Music, which he served as director and professor of theory. He remained active well into the twentieth century.

In the field of painting, the artists of Serbia in the last third of the nineteenth century were no longer drawn to the Viennese academic style as their Classical and Romantic predecessors in Vojvodina were. For the younger generation of Serbian artists, realism was the style they adopted and Munich was their center. The three outstanding Serbian painters of this period—Miloš Tenković (1849–1890), Djordje Krstić (1851–1907), and Antonije Kovačević (1848–1883)—all studied in Munich on state scholarships.

Tenković was the first native of Serbia to receive academic training as a painter, and the first painter of the realist school. His best canvases were still lifes, pastoral scenes, and genre paintings. Among his rare portraits is one of Metropolitan Michael.

Djordje Krstić was born in Vojvodina and received his early education there. He completed two years of secondary school and two years of theological seminary in Belgrade while supporting himself as a student. In 1873 Prince Milan gave him a stipend to study art in Munich. There Krstić was influenced by Wilhelm Leibl, the leading figure in a circle of German realists, and by Gabriel von Max, the historical and genre painter. He spent ten years in Munich, during which time he visited Serbia only once. His best-known work of this period was "The Anatomist," which shows the influence not only of Courbet but of the scientism of the day abetted by the popular interest in Darwin and Haeckel. Upon his return to Serbia, Krstić devoted the rest of his life to the study of Serbian historical and contemporary subjects. Paintings such as "The Field of Kosovo" and "Saint Sava Blessing Serbian Children" reflected the nationalism of Serbian society, as did his studies of medieval monasteries, folk costumes, peasant houses, and scenes from daily life. He even tried his hand at iconography for the Serbian church, but his realistic style created much opposition; his iconostasis for the Cathedral of Niš was never completed for this reason. Krstić exerted a great influence on a younger generation of rising Serbian painters, notably Nadežda Petrović, Kosta Miličević, and Milan Milovanović.

Antonije Kovačević was a native of Belgrade and the first professionally trained painter of scenery for the theater in Serbia. Upon completing his training in Munich, on a stipend granted by King Milan, in 1876 he was employed by the National Theater in Belgrade. He also did detailed sketches of Belgrade scenes that are precious documents of the rapid modernization of the city in his day.

Despite the rise of this native generation of painters, the two most renowned Serbian artists of the latter part of the nineteenth century were from Vojvodina—Uroš Predić (1857–1954) and Paja Jovanović (1859–1957). Both spent some time in Serbia and left a deep mark on Serbian artistic tastes with their genre paintings and historical scenes. Predić's exhibition in Belgrade in 1888 was a real event in Serbia's cultural history. Paja Jovanović's much reproduced historical depictions—"Saint Sava Crowning King Stephen the First-Crowned," "Tsar Dušan's Wedding," "The Migration of the Serbs," and "The

Burning of St. Sava's Relics"—have given several generations of Serbs indelibly vivid images of their own history.

In the 1870s Belgrade underwent a rapid modernization in styles and manners. The latest fashions from Vienna, Budapest, and the Paris of the Empress Eugénie changed the silhouettes of Belgrade women as they began to wear wide crinolines and bustles and of men as they forced their frames into tight pantaloons and jackets. The increasing emancipation of women also brought their eventual liberation from corsets. The interiors of homes took on a pronounced European bourgeois look as the more affluent society of Belgrade, and even of the provincial towns, copied the furniture styles of central and western Europe, often in a helter-skelter mélange. There was a notable increase in the importation of luxury items such as porcelain, small furniture, glassware, and silver. To live in "the European manner" became such a compulsion that Belgrade society in the 1870s quickly lost its once Ottoman and Serbian patriarchal way of life. As machine-made textiles and cheap manufactured articles of all kinds reached the market, even the lower classes in the towns began to take on the styles and artifacts of European urban life.

Although the rest of Serbia remained far behind the times, a great effort was made to turn Belgrade into a modern European city. Grand public buildings were erected, streets were widened and re-paved, and European-style monuments graced squares and parks. In 1882 the equestrian statue of Prince Michael by the Italian sculptor Enrico Pazzi was erected in front of the National Theater, where it is still a landmark.

Belgrade installed its first telephone wires in 1883, just seven years after Alexander Graham Bell patented his invention. However, telephones were used only by the army until 1889, when a public system was installed. The first long-distance call was made in 1886, during the Serbo-Bulgarian War, between Belgrade and Niš. In 1895, in honor of the Serbian-American pioneer of electric communication Nikola Tesla, the Postal-Telegraph Union of Serbia caused a sensation by connecting a simultaneous concert in Belgrade and Niš by telephone so that audiences in both cities could hear it.

In 1892 Belgrade installed electric lights, but only after stormy debates in the city council. An Italian company in Milan was given the contract. The city council decided that this was also a good time to install a "munipical railway," so twenty-one kilometers of tracks were built for the city's first streetcars. These had to be pulled by horses until the electrification of the city was completed in 1893. The first electrically driven streetcars began in mid-1894. Along with this novelty came another manifestation of modern times; that November the employees of the transportation system went on strike in protest over their long hours (from 4:00 A.M. to midnight in summer and 5:00 A.M. to 9:00 P.M. in winter). The workers did not get shorter hours, but they did get slightly higher pay.

By 1899 Belgrade had 69,769 inhabitants. Despite its small size, however, it had many of the attributes of an extremely modest European capital. By 1884 it was connected by railway with Central Europe and by 1888 with the interior of the Balkan Peninsula. Culturally it was the undisputed center of all Serbdom. It had come a long way from the Turkish fortress town it had been at the time of the First Serbian Insurrection in 1804.

The Economy of Serbia, 1878–1903

One of the most important factors in Serbia's economy throughout the latter half of the nineteenth century and the early twentieth century was a rapid increase in population. Though all Europe experienced a marked rise in population in this period, Serbia's especially great increase was due to certain specific circumstances.

First, in 1878, as a result of the territorial changes ratified by the Congress of Berlin, Serbia added 10,300 square kilometers to its area and 303,097 inhabitants to its population.

Second, Serbia continued to attract immigrants from the surrounding South Slavic lands. According to some estimates, over 400,000 persons settled in Serbia between 1878 and 1912, which was equal to the entire population of Serbia in 1815. After 1878, because of the ever worsening economic and political situation in the Ottoman provinces, most immigrants into Serbia came from the south and southwest.

Third, unlike most other South Slavic lands, Serbia did not lose its population to emigration. Much of Serbia's land was more fertile than that in the surrounding mountain regions. After it gained autonomy in 1830 and independence in 1878, Serbia offered a stability and relative prosperity that neighboring peoples could well envy.

Whereas Montenegro, Hercegovina, Bosnia, and western Croatia saw many of their people go to other countries, especially the Americas, in the late nineteenth century, very few Serbs of Serbia left their homesteads.

In the four decades between the gaining of autonomy and the gaining of independence, the population of Serbia grew as follows:

1834	678,192
1843	859,545
1854	998,919
1863	1,108,668
1874	1,353,890

Within these forty years the population rose by 675,698, almost doubling itself, with an average annual increment of around 15,000.

In the four decades following Serbia's independence in 1878, the population increased at an even higher rate, as the following statistics show:

1878	1,700,000 (estimate)
1884	1,901,736
1895	2,341,675
1900	2,529,196
1905	2,724,859

This increase effected a greater density of population. While in 1834 there were only 17.9 inhabitants per square kilometer, by the end of the century this number had nearly tripled: 44.5 in 1890 and 55.7 in 1900.

The vast majority of Serbia's population continued to be engaged in agriculture. In 1866, the first time a Serbian census recorded occupations, 90 percent of the population lived off the land. Even with the development of trade and industry and the rise of an urban population, by 1900 just over 84 percent of the population made its living from agriculture while the other occupations were represented as follows: industry, 6.68 percent; public service and free professions, 4.68 percent; and commerce, 4.41 percent.

Nevertheless, the urban population grew markedly, from 91,587 in 1862 (the first year such statistics were kept) to 350,682 in 1908. The town with the greatest growth in that period was Belgrade, from a population of 54,249 in 1890 to 77,816 in 1905. Other towns also grew, as the following table shows:

Year	Total Population	Population of Towns	Towns with over 20,000	10,000 to 20,000	5,000 to 10,000	2,000 to 5,000	Total
1890	2,087,835	197,313	1	3	11	6	21
1899	2,280,508	257,434	2	6	11	5	24
1905	2,688,025	260,992	2	6	13	3	24

The most important structural change in Serbia's economy during especially the latter half of the nineteenth century was the penetration of money and credit and capitalist principles into the traditional social and economic system.

In agriculture, once money and a market economy drew the Serbian countryside into the capitalist system, it meant the end of an essentially subsistence agriculture in which the peasant household had produced for its own immediate needs and for payment of taxes and dues. Once money appeared in the everyday life of the peasants as the standard measure of economic values and the way of accumulating wealth, profound changes overtook their way of life.

Socially one of the most basic changes was the disappearance of the *zadruga* as an economic unit, as well as of a whole set of mores connected with the collective management of family property. In the latter half of the nineteenth century several pressures forced the *zadrugas* to split into individual small families. The new Serbian state with its growing bureaucratic apparatus and military needs imposed a tax load in money such as the people had never before experienced in their history. Also, the peasants required money as never before to buy the products of modern manufacturing—shoes, cloth, utensils, sugar, and other items—that they either could not produce for themselves or preferred to buy rather than make in the old way. All these pressures forced many households to seek credit as it became increasingly available, though at usurious interest rates. For all these reasons the peasant households were forced to utilize the most efficient means possible to enter the market, and if they failed, to sell what land they could spare. However, with the rapid expansion of the population, the need for land increased accordingly. All this strained the cohesion of the now rather inefficient *zadruga* and caused single families within the *zadruga* to leave it, with their share of the property, in pursuit of their own individual interests. The change from a pastoral to a predominantly agricultural economy, and the new dependence on manufactured goods rather than homemade products, meant that the family as an economic unit no longer needed the workers it once did. Thus by the end of the nineteenth century peasant households of over thirty members were a rarity.

The most obvious result of this process was a decided rise in the number of farms and a corresponding decrease in the average size of farms. Moreover, the impact of capitalism on the Serbian countryside created a rural class that had been almost unknown earlier in the century—a landless peasant proletariat. At the end of the nineteenth century 11.3 percent of Serbia's rural households were without land. As for those who owned land, the distribution was as follows:

	1889		1897	
	Number of owners	*% of total*	*Number of owners*	*% of total*
Size in hectares				
Up to 1 (2.4 acres)	32,752	13.39	26,463	9.08
1–2 (2.4–4.9 acres)	47,110	19.26	36,578	12.46
2–5 (4.9–12.3 acres)	97,720	39.95	98,642	33.61
5–10 (12.3–24.7 acres)	49,679	20.31	80,822	27.55
10–20 (24.7–49.4 acres)	14,758	6.03	40,362	13.91
20–50 (49.4–123.5 acres)	2,424	1.00	10,617	3.62
Over 50 (over 123.5 acres)	148	.06	825	.27
TOTAL	244,591		294,309	

These statistics show that, despite an increase in the proportion of medium-sized farms between the years 1889 and 1897, nevertheless in 1897 some 55 percent of all landowners in Serbia owned farms of less than 5 hectares (12.35 acres). In addition, 17,417 peasant households owned no land at all. Yet famine was virtually unknown in Serbia. On the other hand, it is clear that many peasant households were hardly able to do more than subsist on their dwarf holdings. Given the fertility of Serbia's soil, the lot of Serbia's peasantry was still better than that of the peasants in Montenegro, Bosnia, Hercegovina, and other mountain regions, as the figures for emigration from these lands show. Serbia was blessed with good soil and pastures, woods, and water supply. With effort, even small plots provided a living.

How primitive much of this farming was is evident from the fact that as late as 1893, though there were 295,880 peasant households in Serbia, there were only 99,678 hitch plows and 61,002 single-handled plows. Almost every other peasant household either did not need or could not afford a plow. The plows were made of wood, and only some had an iron tip. Iron plows had to be imported and were rare, even by the end of the nineteenth century, judging by import statistics. As for large agricultural machinery, the vast majority of farms were too small to permit its efficient use. In any event such equipment had to be imported, since no one in Serbia manufactured such things. Between 1891 and 1905, a total of only 261 threshing machines, 58 sowing machines, and 42 mowing machines were imported into Serbia. Little or nothing was done to preserve the fertility of the soil. Artificial fertilizers were unknown to all but a few, and even in places where animal husbandry provided a supply of organic fertilizer, it was often not used.

Extensive farming in Serbia was devoted largely to grains. Unlike the lands of central and western Europe, Serbia raised mostly corn, and then wheat and barley. At the turn of the century, these crops were sown as follows (in hectares):

Year	Corn	Wheat	Barley
1893	531,806	317,069	92,121
1902	524,652	325,583	88,188

The yield per hectare varied considerably from year to year, depending on natural conditions, but it was very low; the statistics for 1893 and 1908 show practically no increase. Nevertheless, especially as more and more land was given to crops while animal husbandry declined, grain assumed a correspondingly larger share of Serbia's economy. Thus in 1874–1875 Serbia exported 11,472,817 okes of wheat (1 oke = 2¾ lbs.), while in 1906 it exported 91,597,841 kilograms (1 kilogram = 2.2 lbs.). On the other hand, industrial crops took up only a small share of Serbia's arable land. In 1908 hemp occupied 14,267 hectares, tobacco 1,908 hectares, and sugar beets 2,239 hectares.

The following figures show how arable land was used in Serbia in 1893:

Cropland	1,154,883 hectares
Garden plots	30,653
Fallow	29,276
Meadowland and clover	350,971
Pastures	248,756
Vineyards	60,989
Orchards	104,194
Forestland	484,647
Marshes and other	244,810
TOTAL	2,709,164

Perhaps the greatest change in Serbian agriculture between the beginning and the end of the nineteenth century was in the relative decline of animal husbandry. During the first half of the century, Serbia was predominantly an animal-raising country. Animal husbandry reached its peak in the 1850s, then declined rapidly, and was finally stabilized at the turn of the century. The decline was especially marked in the production of pigs. In 1859 Serbia had 1,774,348 pigs, while in 1890 it had just over half that number—908,603. The statistics for beef cattle, sheep, and goats show a small absolute rise between 1859 and 1890 but a steady decline in animal population relative to human population. The latter phenomenon is reflected in the following count of animals per 1,000 inhabitants in 1859, 1890, and 1900:

	1859	1890	1900
Beef cattle	739	382	386
Horses	129	75	74
Pigs	1,637	420	384
Sheep	2,202	1,370	1,228

The decline in horses is particularly noteworthy. In 1890, for every 1,000 hectares of land there were only 34 horses as compared with 170 head of cattle. Most small farms in Serbia had no horses. As for the decline of animal husbandry in general, this came about largely as the result of cutting down forests whose acorns had provided a natural fodder for pigs and converting meadows into plowland as grain agriculture became more profitable. There were also the harmful results of the Tariff War, or "Pig War," with Austria-Hungary between 1906 and 1911.

One result of the increase in landless peasants and in the number of dwarf farms unable to provide an adequate livelihood for a growing population was the marked development of an artisan class. Village youths sought a way out of poverty by turning to various crafts and trades, as blacksmiths, tailors, tinsmiths, tanners, dyers, shoemakers, carpenters, and so on. Many of these trades were still known by their Turkish names even in late nineteenth-century Serbia, a reminder of the days when the towns and their guilds were in Ottoman hands. Indeed, Serbian blacksmiths, for example, still had to compete with Gypsies, many of whom came from the Ottoman lands, Walachia, or Hungary. Village crafts and trades remained on a very primitive level. Many artisans had no shops but worked at home or in the homes of their customers. They most often worked for a mere pittance inasmuch as many were in fact farmers whose trade was a supplementary sideline. For those who owned no land at all, it was common to travel from village to village in search of work.

In late nineteenth-century Serbia the artisans, both in towns and villages, comprised the most numerous occupation after farming. Many artisans were driven into poverty and out of work as cheap manufactured items, often imported, took over the market. As in the rest of Europe, the advent of modernization caused the near disappearance of certain traditional trades. Weavers, dyers, chandlers, gunsmiths, coppersmiths, soap-makers, and such became rarities while locksmiths, clock-makers, bookbinders, furniture makers, furriers, and —in a few towns—even plumbers took over as the retainers of a modern way of life.

Meanwhile the traditional guild system underwent a contradictory development. On the one hand, the number of guilds increased as crafts and trades proliferated and as their members sought protection from competition. On the other hand, the guilds suffered a gradual loss of power and their regulations lost force as the growth of modern capitalism made them obsolete. As the market expanded far beyond the local town square, and national and even international pressures and influences affected every Serbian locality, the guilds with their local interests and strictures were bound to decline. Indeed, no one hated the guild system more than its own lower ranks, the apprentices and journeymen, who were exploited and held back to such a degree by the masters that they rebelled. The workers' movement in modern Serbia had its real beginnings in the strikes and boycotts that the artisans staged in the late nineteenth and early twentieth centuries. By 1910 the whole antiquated guild system had been virtually junked by new legislation.

The last quarter of the nineteenth century saw the continued rapid rise of the merchant class in an ever expanding Serbian economy. This class was far from homogeneous. Throughout much of the nineteenth century, for example, town merchants used their political influence to limit the competition of village general stores on the grounds that these stores were leading the peasantry into extravagance and debt. Despite the restrictive laws of 1870 and 1891, the village merchants continued to prosper, often illegally or by selling "under the counter." The growth of the domestic market greatly expanded the merchant class in both towns and villages.

An important factor in this growth was the building of railways in the interior of Serbia. Between 1884 and 1904 a whole network of railways was constructed to connect all the parts of Serbia. In those three decades 1,664 kilometers of rail were laid. In 1908 there were 38 locomotives and 2,365 freight cars in Serbia, a pitifully small number from a European standpoint but the beginnings of an economic revolution for little Serbia. Whereas in 1897 these railways carried 110,471 tons of freight, by 1908 this figure had more than doubled, to 266,216 tons. Serbia's increasing river traffic also contributed to this expansion. By 1908 Serbia had 8 ships and 46 barges on its rivers. However, this trade affected only the border regions directly for the rivers of the interior were not navigable.

With independence and modernization came a rise in foreign trade. Between 1850 and the war with Turkey in 1876, Serbia's foreign trade doubled. That growth continued after the Congress of Berlin in 1878, thanks to Serbia's increase in area and population and to the railroads. In 1882 the total value of Serbia's foreign trade was 88,785,430 dinars; by 1908 it was 153,384,495 dinars. Moreover, after 1887 exports began to exceed imports by an annual average of 10 to 15 percent.

In the last quarter of the century, with the relative decline of animal husbandry, livestock gave way to agricultural products as the main export. In the period from 1884 to 1905 the value of agricultural exports more than doubled. During the period 1896–1905 agricultural products accounted for just over 90 percent of total exports. In the same period, over 69 percent of Serbia's imports were manufactured goods and over 12 percent were raw materials. Austria-Hungary was Serbia's best customer and chief supplier, either directly or indirectly, accounting for about 80 percent of Serbia's foreign trade between 1878 and 1900. This near-monopoly position put Serbia at a disadvantage as an economic dependency of its powerful northern neighbor. There is undoubtedly truth to the charge that it stood to Austria-Hungary's advantage to keep Serbia an agricultural colony. However, given the still primitive level of Serbia's economy and peasant way of life, it is hard to imagine that Serbia would have plunged into industrialization if only it had been free of its ties with Austria-Hungary. Political independence did not automatically bring with it those structural changes that mark the transformation of an underdeveloped agrarian economy into a modern industrial society.

Despite some earlier attempts to establish factories, industry in Serbia did not really begin to develop until the 1880s. In 1898, Serbia still had only 28 industrial enterprises, which employed a total of 1,702 workers. Most of these factories were small and involved little capital. Only 14 factories employed over 20 workers. In 1898 the government issued a Law on Assistance to Domestic Industry, which offered various benefits such as exemption from import duties and taxes, the free use of public forests and streams, special freight rates on the government railroads, and the like. This law also made it mandatory for all government branches and agencies, except the army, to purchase domestic products from certain privileged Serbian enterprises, and at prices 10 percent higher than the average world market price. However, no domestic industries were granted a monopoly, in the hope that some competition would stimulate a native industry.

After 1898, small as it was, Serbia's industry did in fact develop rapidly. In just five years the number of factories increased from 28 to 105, the number of industrial workers from 1,702 to 4,066, and the value of industrial products from 3.7 million dinars to 12.8 million dinars. Various factors account for this increase, including government concessions and the attraction of both foreign and domestic capital. However, banks played the crucial role.

Once the Serbian National Bank was established in 1884, with powers of issuing a national currency, the number of domestic banks increased greatly. In 1884 there were only 7 banks in Serbia, including the National Bank; by 1898 there were 76. Most of these were still small institutions, but nevertheless between 1884 and 1898 they boosted their aggregate paid-in capital from 3.2 million to 20.4 million dinars. These banks were quite successful in attracting domestic savings and putting them to profitable use. Of course, they were not yet strong enough, at the turn of the century, to support the rise of Serbia's industry by themselves. However, they provided a domestic financial base for that expansion that left far less room for later foreign penetration of capital than one could have supposed two decades earlier. It is certain that, given the poor state of government finances in those debt-ridden years, the public sector of the Serbian economy could not have supplied the capital and enterprise for the industrial advance that occurred after 1898. It was not until after 1903 that domestic banks played much of a direct role in investment in industry. However, they did much to provide the credit and financial machinery needed by an expanding domestic industry.

Despite rapid advances, even by 1905 Serbian industry was but a minor part of the national economy. However, it brought into being, for better or worse, a new quality in the Serbian way of life.

X

The Kingdom of Serbia, 1903-1914

The New Regime Establishes Itself

Though Serbia was left without a king on June 11, 1903, the participants in the plot against Alexander Obrenović saw to it that it was not left without a government. That very morning they organized a new cabinet composed of themselves and the representatives of various political parties. The conspirators in the cabinet included Jovan Avakumović as premier, General Jovan Atanacković as war minister, Djordje Genčić as minister of the economy, and Colonel Aleksandar Mašin as minister of construction. Ljubomir Kaljević, though belonging to no party, was a long-time supporter of the Karadjordjević dynasty and was therefore made foreign minister. The new minister of the interior, Stojan Protić, was a radical. Minister of Justice Ljubomir Živković and Minister of Education Ljubomir Stojanović were Independent Radicals. Finance Minister Vojislav Veljković was a Liberal, as were Avakumović and Genčić. Only the Progressives were left out.

Still unsure of itself, the new government informed the nation of the king's assassination as gently as possible. "Last night," their proclamation of June 11 read, "King Alexander and Queen Draga lost their lives." No reference was made to the conspiracy. The next day the press justified the killing by attacking the dead king as a tyrant.

One of the first acts of the new government was to restore the Constitution of 1901, which had been suspended sixty-five days before by King Alexander. It ignored the unicameral National Assembly whose members had been elected and appointed just ten days before; instead, it convened the bicameral Parliament that had existed before the suspension of the constitution, in the days of the Radical-Progressive coalition. Meeting on June 13, in joint session, the Parliament heard

[534]

Premier Avakumović's official version of the events of June 11. In response to the government's request for approval, both houses of Parliament endorsed the new regime and even thanked it for saving the country from disaster. The cabinet was authorized to function as "The Government of the Kingdom of Serbia" until the election and arrival of the new king.

The joint session of Parliament on June 15 was even more eventful. By the unanimous vote of 119 deputies and 39 senators, with one abstention, after deliberations that lasted only forty-five minutes, the Parliament elected Peter Karadjordjević king of Serbia. The new king was informed by telegram of his election, and he accepted the same day. A deputation of 24 members of Parliament was selected to go to Switzerland and escort the new monarch from Geneva to Belgrade.

The second important act of that session was to give Serbia a new constitution. This "Constitution of 1903" was, in fact, nothing but a modified version of the Constitution of 1888 (1889 N.S.), which had been promulgated on the eve of King Milan's abdication and suspended by King Alexander in 1894. The main point in settling on the Constitution of 1888 as a model was that a unicameral parliament was restored through abolition of the Senate. The proponents of this measure, notably the Liberals, argued that a unicameral legislature was speedier and more effective. The new constitution was formally promulgated on June 18 and published in the official gazette two days later. Moreover, all laws previously passed on the basis of the Constitution of 1888 were declared in force.

The Constitution of 1903 was in several ways an admirably liberal document. It declared Serbia to be a hereditary constitutional and parliamentary monarchy in which all Serbs were equal before the law. "The press is free," its twenty-second article proclaimed. "There can be no establishment of censorship or any other preventive measure that would hinder the publication, sale or dissemination of writings and newspapers." Freedom of religion was assured. The constitution also provided for an independent judiciary. The death penalty for political offenders was abolished. While it provided for a strong executive in the person of the king, the constitution also gave the National Assembly broad powers as the representative of the sovereign will of the people. Crucial among these powers was that of the purse; the Assembly had to approve an annual budget.

It was to a Serbia pledged to such a democratic constitution that King Peter I came, on June 25, 1903. He was personally well suited to reign under a liberal regime. Born in 1844, the third son of Prince Alexander Karadjordjević (1842–1859), Peter had spent most of his life in Western Europe. He received his education largely in Geneva and Paris. He was trained as a soldier, at Saint-Cyr and Metz, and served in the French Foreign Legion. The French government conferred on him the medal of the Legion of Honor for his distinguished service during the Franco-Prussian War of 1870. Yet, with all his military training, Peter was deeply imbued with the ideas of Western liberalism and parliamentary democracy. An admirer of John Stuart Mill, he translated Mill's essay "On Liberty" into Serbo-Croatian. Unlike his two predecessors, Milan and Alexander, both of whom came to the throne as children and whose reigns ended when they were still young, Peter was almost sixty years old when he became king. He had long since passed the stage at which younger men wish to assert themselves. Tempered by years of exile, he was quite sincere in his desire to serve as a constitutional monarch and to hold himself above political strife.

King Peter was not only basically liberal in outlook, but also intensely patriotic, in a personal way that was alien to Milan and Alexander Obrenović. His patriotism transcended the borders of Serbia to include the Serbs in Montenegro, the Ottoman Empire, and Austria-Hungary. When the Balkan insurrections erupted in 1875, he went to Bosnia to fight as a volunteer, under the name of Petar Mrkonjić. In 1883, when the Austrians quelled the rebels of the Bay of Kotor, Bosnia, and Hercegovina, he moved to Montenegro, where he was given a warm welcome. That same year he married Prince Nicholas's eldest daughter, Zorka. When she died, in 1890, after less than seven years of married life, Peter left Montenegro and took his three children, Jelena (Helen), George, and Alexander, to Geneva, where they lived until his election as king.

In addition to his Pan-Serbianism, Peter was known for his loyalty to Russia, which was duly appreciated by both Tsar Alexander III and Tsar Nicholas II. His love of Slavic Russia struck a traditional chord of sentimental Panslavism that was far dearer to Serbian hearts than the more practical and opportunistic subservience to Austria-Hungary that had tainted the last two Obrenović rulers.

In all these ways King Peter's attitudes corresponded to the general political reorientation, both domestic and foreign, that the events of June 11 had brought to Serbia. Five days after taking his oath to uphold the new constitution, he announced his intention to devote himself to the establishment of justice and freedom in Serbia, to the stabilization of finances, to the improvement of the economy, and to the modernization of the army. In his first speech from the throne, he expressed his desire for "traditional relations with powerful brotherly Russia" and friendship for Serbia's Balkan neighbors, though he did not fail to mention good relations with Austria-Hungary as well. Barely a week later, in October 1903, Minister of the Interior Stojan Protić submitted to the National Assembly the government's program, including a long list of reforms touching every aspect of national life, all in the spirit of greater democratization, economic development, and cultural advancement.

There was general satisfaction in the country at large over the new king, the new constitution, and the National Assembly. However, there were grave misgivings in some quarters, at home and abroad, both over the bloody deed that made this change possible and over the role of "the Conspirators," as its perpetrators became known. These Conspirators had a strong hold over the king, who owed them his throne.

The most serious domestic reaction to the Conspirators took place in the army, where a counterconspiracy was organized among the officers of the Niš garrison. Its leader, Captain Milan Novaković, had been in Paris for military training during the events of June 11. The horror with which the European world viewed the assassination of Alexander and Draga only added to his sense of shame that Serbian army officers should have so dishonored their uniform as to violate their oath of loyalty. Captain Novaković's disgust grew to outrage when, on returning to Serbia within a month, he found that the Conspirators in the army, some eighty of them, were using their newly acquired influence to gain control over the entire officers' corps. This trend was especially evident, it seemed to Novaković and others, in the preferential manner in which appointments and promotions were being made. Novaković began to recruit fellow officers to sign a proclamation calling for the removal of the Conspirators from state service. "Either they take off their uniforms, or we take off ours!" it read.

Just as the Conspirators consistently denied that they had been led by any desire for personal gain, so the counterconspirators later denied that their movement was directed against King Peter or the government. However, the counterconspiracy was discovered and broken before it could act. Twenty-seven officers, all from the Niš garrison, were tried and condemned, though their sentences were light; Captain Novaković himself received only two years. Though abortive, the counterconspiracy called attention to certain arguments, ably defended by Novaković at his trial, with which many Serbs could agree. He accused the Conspirators of having betrayed their military honor in carrying out a bloody regicide that was unnecessary as well as unjustifiable. As long as these Conspirators remained in power, Novaković argued, the government would be tainted by bloodguilt and corruption, and Serbia would suffer ostracism by the foreign powers.

The reaction of the foreign powers to the events of June 11 lent considerable weight to Captain Novaković's argument. The assassination of Alexander and Draga had shocked the outside world. In Russia, Spain, and Romania, court mourning was ordered. The Italian government refused for a while to recognize Serbia's new regime. King Carol of Romania resigned as honorary colonel of the Serbian regiment whose officers took part in the regicide. The firmest stand was taken by Great Britain and the Netherlands, both of which recalled their ministers from Belgrade permanently on the grounds that they had been accredited only to the late king. Despite these reactions, the two foreign powers that counted most in Serbian affairs, Russia and Austria-Hungary, while condemning the regicide, hastened to recognize the new king. However, they gave merely *de facto* recognition to the new cabinet until the Avakumović government submitted its resignation to King Peter and a new cabinet was formed, also by Avakumović. In August this cabinet was reshuffled after a disagreement over the distribution of various spoils. However, the whole cabinet was changed after the parliamentary elections of September 1903, the first in Peter's reign, when no political party received a majority sufficient to form its own cabinet. Accordingly a coalition government of the two chief contenders, the Radicals and the Independent Radicals, was formed under General Sava Grujić, with each party represented by four men.

Even with all these changes, the governments of Austria-Hungary and Russia, which agreed to act in concert in the matter, were still dissatisfied with the continued presence of so many of the Conspirators in important posts. To put diplomatic pressure on King Peter to oust these men, the envoys of both powers deliberately absented themselves from Belgrade, and their staffs were instructed to avoid attending any court functions. Ministers of other nations followed suit. The absence of the entire diplomatic corps from a court ball in early February 1904 created a cabinet crisis. After Stojan Protić declined to form a new government, Sava Grujić agreed to try again. This time four portfolios were awarded to men whose influence in Serbia's affairs for the next decade and a half was to be of decisive importance. Three of them were Radicals, and one was a professional soldier. Nikola Pašić, the new foreign minister, established the foreign policy of the Kingdom of Serbia for the rest of its existence. The tangled finances of Serbia were entrusted to the skilled hands of Dr. Lazar Paču. The ministry of education went to Ljubomir Davidović, under whom basic educational reforms were carried out. The new minister of war, General Radomir Putnik, was to lead Serbia's armies in the Balkan Wars and the First World War. This second Grujić cabinet included none of the Conspirators. Moreover, a royal decree removed many compromised officers from court positions, mostly by promoting them to positions elsewhere. The mollified Austro-Hungarian envoy, Constantin Dumba, returned to Belgrade before Orthodox Easter celebrations and had an audience with the king. The new Russian minister, Konstantin Gubastov, arrived soon after and presented his credentials to King Peter.

On September 8, 1904, King Peter was solemnly crowned, not in traditional Žiča Monastery, but in the more spacious Belgrade Cathedral, in view of the now fully assembled diplomatic corps. The new regime had finally established itself.

There was much to worry the new regime in 1904. Years of mismanagement under the Obrenović rulers had left the country deep in debt and teetering on the edge of bankruptcy. The traditional political turmoil was now complicated further by the lingering influence of the Conspirators. This in turn continued to create difficulties with foreign powers, notably Great Britain. Relations with Austria-Hungary steadily grew worse as Serbia sought to extricate itself from Vienna's grip. And Russia could offer little support at a time when all its energies were engaged in a disastrous war with Japan.

The political life of Serbia was greatly troubled by party squabbles, which caused the fall of one cabinet after another and led to raucous disputation in the National Assembly. The most acrimonious polemics divided the two leading parties, the Radicals and the Independent Radicals, especially after the latter abandoned a united front with the Radical party in the Assembly and formed their own parliamentary group. Underneath the various particular issues that divided these two once united groups was a generation gap. The younger Independent Radicals accused the Radicals of having abandoned the ideals of their youth and become opportunists. The Radicals defended themselves on the grounds of political tactics. Each side fired volleys at the other in their press—Pašić's Radicals in *Samouprava* (Self-Government) and Ljubomir Stojanović's Independent Radicals in *Odjek* (Echo). By 1906 the Radicals had definitely gained the upper hand and kept control until 1918. Meanwhile the jockeying for power as well as resignations brought on by various crises, of both domestic and foreign provenance, brought great instability to the government at the cabinet level. Between late 1904 and 1906 five governments were formed, in rapid succession, by Sava Grujić (Radical), Nikola Pašić (Radical), Ljubomir Stojanović (Independent Radical), Grujić (who became an Independent Radical), and finally Pašić again, until mid-1908.

One of the most vexing problems that faced all of these governments was the embarrassing presence of the Conspirators in Serbian political life. This vexed the Radicals all the more inasmuch as they had played no part in the conspiracy against King Alexander and felt no obligation to its participants. Moreover, the power of the Conspirators was as "irresponsible," to use a term of that day, as it was insidious, for it was hidden from public view and did not depend on votes. The question of the Conspirators had both domestic and foreign consequences.

On the domestic scene, in September 1905, after two years in prison, Milan Novaković returned to public life to take up his cause against the Conspirators with renewed vigor and accumulated bitterness. Founding a Society for the Legal Settlement of the Conspiratorial Question, Novaković published a series of charges against the Conspirators that contained some powerful arguments for their removal from public life. He accused them of undermining the authority of the government by interfering in state affairs, and of damaging the morale of the army by securing promotions and awards for themselves

Jovan Ristić
(1831–1899),
statesman and
historian

Svetozar Marković
(1846–1875),
socialist leader

Milan Obrenović,
Prince and King of
Serbia, 1868–1889

Queen Natalia,
wife of King
Milan Obrenović

Alexander Obrenović, King of Serbia, 1889–1903, and Queen Draga

Serbian peasants in their national dress

Serbian National Assembly, Belgrade

Serbian family homestead

A well in rural Serbia

Peter I Karadjordjević, King of Serbia, 1903–1918

Nikola Pašić
(1845–1926),
statesman and
political leader

Signers of the Corfu Declaration, July 1917

Alexander Karadjordjević, Prince Regent of Serbia, 1914–1918;
Prince Regent of the Serbs, Croats, and Slovenes, 1918–1921

at the expense of more qualified officers. Thus, he argued, they were endangering Serbia's unity just when it was most needed, in the face of Bulgarian pretensions in Macedonia. Moreover, the continued presence of these men made a resumption of normal relations between Serbia and Great Britain impossible. Since the murder of King Alexander was not the result of a popular revolution, he argued, but the deed of a few officers, there was no need for the people to suffer its consequences.

Novaković's campaign resulted in a second counterconspiracy, this time centered in Kragujevac. It was as abortive as the first. Finally Novaković himself was imprisoned, after the government seized the press that published his newspaper *Za Otadžbinu* (For the Fatherland). He and an imprisoned gendarmerie officer were killed in their Belgrade prison under mysterious circumstances. It created a heated controversy in the Assembly.

Meanwhile the British government made it quite clear that it wished no relations with Serbia, as Foreign Secretary Sir Edward Grey told the House of Commons, "so long as the regicide officers hold official positions and influence in the Serbian Government." In a memorandum to King Edward VII, Grey identified by name seven principal Conspirators who still held important posts: Colonel Popović, commander of the Danube Division; Colonel Mašin, acting chief of staff; Colonel Solarević, head of the Military Academy; General Atanacković, head of the Bureau of Decorations; Colonel Mišić, military tutor to the crown prince; Colonel Lazarević, commandant of the Belgrade garrison; and Major Kostić, commandant of the palace guard. Later Grey was persuaded by Premier Pašić that Solarević had no connection with the actual murder of King Alexander, and he agreed to Pašić's proposal to resume relations with Serbia if the remaining six officers were retired. With a fine appreciation for historic dates, diplomatic relations between Great Britain and Serbia were renewed on June 11, 1906, the third anniversary of King Alexander's assassination. After a face-saving delay of only one day, King Peter accepted the resignation of five of the officers, General Atanacković having resigned earlier. With British recognition, Serbia became once more a member in good standing of the community of European nations.

Serbia Seeks an Independent Role

It was not enough for the new regime to achieve domestic stability and international recognition. Its leaders sought to free Serbia from a quarter century of political and economic dependence on Austria-Hungary. If the change from the Obrenović dynasty to the Karadjordjević meant anything, it meant a rejection of the Secret Treaty of 1881 and an end to Serbia's position as a satellite of the Habsburg Empire.

This was no mere matter of national pride. If Serbia's dependence on Austria-Hungary had ever had any political or economic justification, Serbia's new leaders could not see any after the turn of the century. On the contrary, the Dual Monarchy stood in the way of two of their cherished goals—the unification of all Serbs and the economic advancement of the country. With regard to ethnic unification, not only had the Habsburg Empire for centuries been the home of a major part of the Serbian nation, but it had extended its sway over the Serbs in the late nineteenth century by occupying Bosnia, Hercegovina, and the Sancak of Novi Pazar. However great Serbian aspirations in Macedonia were, they were never as compelling as Serbia's desire for unification with the Serbs of Bosnia, Hercegovina, and Old Serbia. In the economic sphere, while Serbia's agrarian economy and need for manufactured articles complemented Austria-Hungary's economy and needs in the middle of the nineteenth century, it became clear by the end of the century that Serbia would never become a developed modern nation as long as it remained an underdeveloped agricultural dependency of the Austro-Hungarian market.

To free Serbia from its dependence on Austria-Hungary was a difficult task. Serbia's leaders faced a large and powerful neighbor which, even in peace, was capable of inflicting painful pressures simply by applying economic sanctions. Serbia could hardly hope for much Russian support in 1904 and 1905, not only because St. Petersburg and Vienna were acting in concert with each other, but also because Russian energies were engaged in a ruinous war with the Japanese. What Serbia's leaders hoped to do, therefore, was to loosen Austria-Hungary's hold on Serbia gradually while establishing political and economic ties with other nations, especially its Balkan neighbors.

That Austria-Hungary would not permit any such policy became evident from the start, in connection with two issues that faced Serbia's government in the first five years of King Peter's reign—a foreign loan and the "gun question." Like the Conspiratorial Question, the loan and gun questions also had domestic and foreign reverberations.

Even before King Alexander's death, the Serbian government was confronted by the necessity of equipping the army with modern armaments and building more railways. Both projects required substantial foreign loans. Wishing to avoid going into further debt to Austria-Hungary, the Grujić government negotiated in the spring of 1904 with a group of French and German financiers for a loan of from 30 to 40 million francs. Strong parliamentary resistance to any loan led to a crisis in which Grujić was succeeded by Pašić in late 1904. Meanwhile Vienna made quite clear not only its desire to provide Serbia with the loan, but also its insistence that Serbia place all its orders for armaments with Austrian firms, specifically the Škoda works.

Even apart from the question of dependence on the Dual Monarchy, the Serbian government had reason not to buy armaments in Austria-Hungary; the guns obtained from Škoda in mid-1903 had been unsatisfactory. Moreover, in 1904 Belgrade had great hope in a Bulgarian alliance and the Bulgars had ordered their guns from the Schneider firm of France. It seemed militarily sound for the Balkan allies to have the same weapons.

When Pašić's government reopened negotiations for the loan in the autumn of 1904, the Wiener Bankverein offered Finance Minister Lazar Paču a loan of 30 million dinars on condition that all military supplies be bought from Austria. As Serbia's railways were to provide security for the loan, the Viennese bank also proposed that Serbian state railways be sold to a limited liability company whose supervisory officials would come from Austria-Hungary. The Austro-Hungarian minister in Belgrade and his military attaché made clear to the Serbian government that its decision in the matter of the loan and the Škoda guns would be taken by Vienna to be a tangible token of its attitude towards Austria-Hungary.

The loan and gun questions occupied several Serbian governments throughout 1905. Caught between Austro-Hungarian pressure and parliamentary opposition to any loan that would bring a further financial burden on the already heavily indebted nation, Pašić was forced to resign in May 1905. His successor, Stojanović, leader of the Independent Radicals, received from the Union Bank of Vienna a much smaller loan than the 110 million francs Pašić hoped to get, thus mollifying the Assembly. He also arranged to have the Austrian Bankverein participate in the international syndicate that was making the loan, thus placating Vienna. The Stojanović government was even willing to reopen the gun question.

In the midst of this conciliatory turn of events, the Austro-Hungarian government learned that Serbia was negotiating a customs union with Bulgaria, and suspended the discussion for a trade treaty with Serbia. This high-handed act united practically all Serbian politicians against the Dual Monarchy. It was also the first step in what became an economic war that Austria-Hungary waged against Serbia.

A chief reason for Vienna's action was its concern over Serbia's new active policy of collaboration with Bulgaria and Montenegro. The success of such a policy could only facilitate Serbia's efforts to counter Austro-Hungarian influence in southeastern Europe.

Serbia, Bulgaria, and Macedonia, 1903–1905

One of the chief charges the Conspirators made against King Alexander in justifying his assassination was that he had neglected the "Serbian cause" in the Balkans. Traditionally this cause had involved three goals: the unification of all Serbs in a Greater Serbia; a union of the South Slavic peoples, or Yugoslavism; and emancipation from foreign control so as to ensure "the Balkans for the Balkan peoples."

As experience had already shown, these three goals were not always mutually compatible: indeed, they clashed with one another. A Greater Serbia that united all Serbs could only be achieved at the expense both of the Habsburg and Ottoman Empires and of Serbia's Balkan and South Slavic neighbors, inasmuch as the Serbian population in the lands surrounding Serbia was interspersed with Croats, Albanians, Macedonians, and other nationalities. Moreover, Great Power interests in the Balkans, especially of Austria-Hungary and Russia, made any Balkan settlement without Great Power participation unthinkable. Nevertheless, to the degree that they symbolized the kind of myths that engage men's hearts rather than their minds and move them to daring exploits, the goals of a Greater Serbia, a Yugoslav union, and a free Balkans for the Balkan peoples were always popular ones in modern Serbia. Under King Peter Karadjordjević they were raised to the level of Serbian national policy, with a vigor that was reminiscent of the reign of Prince Michael Obrenović a half-century before.

Since the Serbs of the Austro-Hungarian lands—and that included effectively Bosnia and Hercegovina as well—were beyond practical reach at the time, Serbia continued to look southward, to the Ottoman provinces of Old Serbia and Macedonia, to achieve its goal of a Greater Serbia. From a purely ethnic standpoint, both provinces presented certain difficulties. In spite of being the cradle of Serbian history in medieval times, Old Serbia had a large and compact Albanian population, largely Muslim. And though Skopje and some of the other cities of Slavic Macedonia were associated with Tsar Dušan and the medieval Serbian state, many Macedonian Slavs did not regard themselves as Serbs, whatever their ethnic feelings were. Indeed, the success of Bulgarian cultural and political influence among the Macedonian Slavs was a source of constant worry in Belgrade.

No sooner did the reign of King Peter begin than Serbia was faced with a serious uprising in western Macedonia, the St. Elijah Day Uprising (*Ilinden*) of August 2, 1903 N.S., led by the Internal Macedonian Revolutionary Organization. The rebels presented to the sultan and the European powers a program of twelve articles that called for the autonomy of Macedonia, Albania, Old Serbia, and Thrace. Afraid that Bulgaria might monopolize the movement, the Serbian government permitted, if not encouraged, a public campaign of sympathy for the rebels in which the press openly called on Serbian volunteers to form guerrilla bands in Macedonia. (The word for such a band or troop, *četa,* provided the name *četnik* for such a guerrilla.) The St. Elijah Day Uprising was a short-lived disaster that brought savage punishment from the Turks. Many refugees fled to Bulgaria and Serbia. For its own reasons, the Serbian government wished to encourage that wing of the revolutionary organization that believed in an autonomous Macedonia rather than in a Bulgarian Macedonia.

The St. Elijah Day Uprising resulted in several changes that the Serbian government welcomed. One was the sultan's official proclamation of the Serbs of the Ottoman Empire as a recognized nationality, or *millet.* Belgrade had long sought this status for its co-nationals in Turkey, among other reasons, to shield them from the advances of the Bulgarian exarchate and to facilitate the establishment of Serbian religious and cultural institutions in Macedonia. The Porte recognized the Serbian nationality within its borders precisely to counteract the Bulgarian national movement in Macedonia.

A second change in the Macedonian situation that Belgrade welcomed, though with apprehension, was the reform program that resulted from the intervention of the European powers. In October 1903 the foreign ministers of Austria-Hungary and Russia framed the so-called Mürzsteg Program. Approved by the other powers, this program called for various reforms in Macedonia, such as the reorganization of the gendarmerie by officers chosen by all five Great Powers, reforms in the administration of justice, and certain financial measures. What interested Belgrade most directly was the decision to divide Macedonia into administrative districts along ethnic lines. While the Serbs were skeptical about the efficacy of the reforms, and worried by such direct intervention by the Great Powers, they saw an opportunity in the Mürzsteg Program's ethnic division of Macedonia. This was consonant with Serbia's long-standing position in favor of the partition of Macedonia among the interested Balkan countries—Serbia, Bulgaria, and Greece. The Serbian government even sought to have the reforms of the Mürzsteg Program extended to Old Serbia as well, where it hoped to gain Ottoman recognition of a renewed Serbian patriarchate of Peć. After 1903 Serbian activity in Macedonia went beyond the educational and religious sphere into political action and the direct financial aid of guerrilla bands.

Even as pro-Bulgarian and pro-Serbian bands were fighting each other in Macedonia, Belgrade worked for an agreement with the Bulgarian government as the first step in a general Balkan alliance. The Serbs hoped to avert two possibilities in Macedonia—either a complete takeover by Bulgaria or an extension of an Austro-Hungarian occupation. Unable to rely on Russia, which was preoccupied with its war with Japan, the Serbian government decided to deal directly with Sofia. This was directly in the tradition of the Radical party, which had long favored close friendship with the Bulgars. Despite open rivalry in Macedonia, there were several good reasons for closer Serbian-Bulgarian cooperation, which both sides recognized in 1904.

The outcome of this South Slavic rapprochement was the signing of two treaties on April 12, 1904. The first went beyond the usual treaty of friendship to include such concrete matters as the setting of common postal and telegraph rates, the use of the Cyrillic alphabet in telegraphic communications between the two countries, the abolition of passport requirements between them, the extradition of criminals, the acceptance of each other's coinage, and the encouragement of mutual trade by the reduction of freight and passenger rates on their railways. The most important part of the treaty was its first article: "To permit the free importation of their respective products (of domestic origin), at the same time attempting to conduct similar customs policies with respect to other states, aiming at an eventual customs union (*Zollverein*)." This attempt at a South Slavic *Zollverein* led Austria-Hungary to drop its own trade negotiations with Serbia and contributed to the tariff war that ensued between the two countries.

The second Serbo-Bulgarian treaty of April 12, 1904, was a political alliance. Its first article expressed approval of the Mürzsteg Program and pledged the support of both states for its attainment. The second article called for mutual military assistance against any attack, regardless of its origin, "on the present territorial integrity and independence of their respective states, or on the security and inviolability of the reigning dynasties." Article 3 called for united action in case of an unfriendly action in Macedonia or Old Serbia. A further article envisaged a possible alliance between Serbia and Montenegro concerning the Albanian question. The treaty provided that any disputes arising from it were to be submitted to the Emperor of Russia for arbitration, and, if he declined, to the Hague Tribunal. A final protocol, signed on April 13, 1904, stipulated that the proposed customs union should not affect existing commercial treaties with other countries. An important explanatory note also specified that the Sancak of Novi Pazar was a part of the *vilâyet*, or district, of Kosovo. This implied Bulgaria's pledge to oppose Austro-Hungarian annexation of a region then occupied by Austro-Hungarian forces.

Friendly relations between Serbia and Bulgaria were furthered by three meetings of King Peter and Prince Ferdinand between May and October of 1904. While Ferdinand's two visits to Belgrade were brief stops, one of them limited to a railroad station, Peter's reception in Sofia in October was a gala affair. A few months' negotiations were begun for a Serbo-Bulgarian trade treaty. A customs agreement was settled on June 22, 1905, to go into effect March 1, 1906, and expire March 1, 1917, when it would be replaced by a common tariff schedule for both countries. However, the Serbian government asked that the treaty be kept secret until possible changes were made in the text in the light of new trade treaties then being negotiated, notably between

Austria-Hungary and both Serbia and Bulgaria. Nevertheless, for reasons of its own, the Bulgarian government submitted the treaty to its assembly for ratification in December 1905. Apparently Prince Ferdinand wished to use the Serbian-Bulgarian agreement as a lever in his dealings with the Porte at the time. As soon as Vienna heard the news, on December 28, it suspended negotiations for a trade treaty with Serbia and it closed the borders of the Dual Monarchy to Serbian livestock. The result was the Tariff War of 1906–1911, more picturesquely known as the "Pig War."

The Tariff War of 1906–1911

The suspension of trade negotiations with Austria-Hungary hit the Serbian government hard. Obviously trade with the Dual Monarchy was of far more vital importance to Serbia than trade with Bulgaria. But Vienna's peremptory demand that Belgrade renounce its agreement with Bulgaria was unacceptable to the Serbian government. Premier Stojanović and Foreign Minister V. Antonić were even more apologetic and contrite toward Austrian Minister Czikann than national pride might permit. Yet there were compelling reasons why the Serbian government could not give in to the Austro-Hungarian demand. Politically, it could not afford to turn its back on Bulgaria and so proclaim to the entire world its subservience to Austria-Hungary. Economically, it saw no reason to give up an existing advantageous trade agreement with Bulgaria in exchange for a possible trade agreement with Austria-Hungary whose terms would not be favorable if the powerful Hungarian agrarian lobby in Vienna had its way. Therefore, although the Serbian government made every attempt to conciliate Vienna, it informed Austro-Hungarian Foreign Minister Count Goluchowski on January 13, 1906, that it could not accede to his conditions.

Goluchowski's reply, transmitted on January 18, was to ask the Serbian government for a written guarantee that it would not submit the Serbian-Bulgarian customs treaty to the Serbian National Assembly for ratification for the duration of renewed negotiations with Austria-Hungary. This seemed like a decided retreat from his earlier insistence. At least it offered Serbia a final choice between two treaties. Goluchowski's concession was the result of pressure by various Austrian economic interests such as the Oesterreichischer Orientverein, the Industrial Club, the Chamber of Commerce, and other groups interested in the Serbian market. However, Goluchowski framed his reply in the form of a virtual ultimatum that Serbia accede to all changes in the Bulgarian agreement that Austria-Hungary required. The Serbian reply was as accommodating as possible, but it rejected the possibility of Austro-Hungarian intervention in Serbia's dealings with another country. This was, of course, a direct renunciation of the Secret Treaty of 1881 which did, indeed, give Austria-Hungary the right to such intervention.

Finding the Serbian reply unsatisfactory, and having made a token attempt at compromise in order to placate Austrian economic interests, Goluchowski informed the Serbian minister in Vienna on January 22, 1906, that trade negotiations between their two countries were at an end, and that the Austro-Hungarian border was being closed to Serbian livestock because of the threat of communicable disease. The blockade excluded Serbia's goods not only from the Austro-Hungarian lands but also from Bosnia and Hercegovina. Serbia replied by imposing a similar blockade on goods from Austria-Hungary.

It was clear to all concerned that the reasons for Austria-Hungary's action was neither veterinary nor economic but political. Vienna could not afford a Serbo-Bulgarian rapprochement that would threaten its interests in the Balkans. Such a South Slavic union, even a purely economic one, would fortify the Yugoslav movement in the Habsburg lands and pose a danger to Austrian control in Bosnia-Hercegovina and the Sancak of Novi Pazar. Besides, a customs war with Serbia would be a welcome diversion in Hungary, where a domestic crisis was raging at the time; Hungarian agrarian interests were pleased to be rid of the competition with Serbia's products. Aggressive military circles in the Dual Monarchy were also pleased at using at least the economic might of Austria-Hungary to humble their defiant Balkan neighbor.

Serbia's reasons for defying Austria-Hungary were also more political than economic. The loss of Austro-Hungarian trade was a blow to Serbia's exporters. Also, a customs union with Bulgaria caused some apprehension among Serbia's lesser merchants and artisans, who feared Bulgarian competition. Nevertheless, practically all Serbs could unite against the Habsburg threat to their country's independence. Only a few members of King Peter's court and a handful of Liberals advised against provoking the Dual Monarchy over a Bulgarian agreement whose worth they doubted. The rest of the country was at first solidly behind their government's defiance of Austria-Hungary. As the Serbian press made clear in its indignant reaction to Austria-Hungary's pressure, to suggest any concession was tantamount to treason.

Yet patriotism was not the sole reason why certain elements in Serbia favored a customs war. They regarded it as a welcome contribution to Serbia's political liberation and economic advancement. It would, they hoped, force Serbia to redouble its efforts in the search for new markets and in the promotion of a native industry. They argued that Serbian grain was already excluded from the Austrian market by high tariffs, and as for the livestock trade, Serbia could absorb its losses by establishing its own processing plants and exporting finished meat and animal products. The prospect of a native industry supported by the government and free of Austro-Hungarian competition was a pleasant one for a small but rising class of Serbian entrepreneurs. Smaller merchants found in the customs war an opportunity to empty their shelves of old and now sought-after goods. Storekeepers were glad to make a profit by raising prices of sugar and other imported staples. The advocates of a defiant stand against Austria-Hungary looked especially to Germany as a willing and able substitute for Austria-Hungary in the Balkan market. The more naively hopeful believed that Austria-Hungary would be sufficiently hurt by the customs war that it would be forced to relent. It took some time for these proponents of emancipation from Austria-Hungary to realize how high the price would be.

Serbian opponents of a tariff war dared to say, at least in private reports, that its effects would be economically ruinous, and that Serbia's trade with Austria-Hungary was not the result of political subservience but of mutual economic advantage. To break old ties and seek new markets was not to be accomplished overnight. One class of Serbs was so hard hit by the tariff war as to complain openly and loudly—the rural exporters of livestock. They were an influential political factor, with their main strength in the National Assembly. However, the government was able to win over at least the large exporters with compensating credits. There were even those who, though they were for economic emancipation, believed that, given Russia's impotence after its defeat in the Far East and the uncertainties of a Bulgarian alliance in view of rivalries in Macedonia, it was politically inopportune for Serbia to provoke Austria-Hungary. On the contrary, as an active participant in the trade negotiations with Vienna and Serbian envoy to Rome, Milovan Milovanović, argued, instead of making political concessions to Austria-Hungary for economic gains, the time had come for Serbia to make economic concessions to win Vienna's political support.

In the beginning the forces that were for opposing Austria-Hungary were very strong and enjoyed the support of the vast majority of the Serbian people. However, as the economic pinch became increasingly painful, and as the peasant masses found themselves caught in the scissors effect of rising prices for manufactured and processed goods and decreasing prices for their own agricultural products, more and more Serbs had second thoughts. And the Serbian government felt this growing pressure in its dealings with Austria-Hungary.

It was hardly a month after the closing of the Dual Monarchy's borders to Serbian livestock that the Stojanović government gave in to the pressure on February 23, 1906, by abandoning, in effect, the customs agreement with Bulgaria. Count Goluchowski received the news with satisfaction and immediately invited the Serbian representatives back to Vienna to continue negotiations for a new trade agreement. Meanwhile, he still kept the border closed to Serbian livestock. He was unwilling to admit so openly the connection between his politics and an allegedly veterinary decision. Besides, he still had need of applying pressure on the Serbs.

Inasmuch as the previous Austro-Serbian trade agreement expired on March 1, 1906, and the Serbian government would not accept a stopgap treaty without safeguards against the constant threat of a veterinary embargo, the Stojanović cabinet resigned on March 7. It was replaced by another Grujić cabinet a week later. Meanwhile, a verbal agreement was reached by the negotiators in Vienna, on March 16, as a *modus vivendi* until a final agreement could be concluded. Its three main points were the following: inclusion of the most favored nation clause, the mutual suspension of all reprisals, and the continuation of previous veterinary regulations. This unsatisfactory agreement ended the first phase of the Tariff War of 1906.

At this crucial point Vienna insisted on linking the trade agreement with the "gun question." While a Serbian selection commission was pondering whether to recommend the cannons offered by the Schneider-Creusot firm of France or the Krupp firm of Germany, Count Goluchowski confronted the Serbian negotiators with a virtual ultimatum, on April 5, that Serbia place its order for guns with the Škoda firm of Austria-Hungary. In the face of this pressure from abroad and domestic pressure from all sides concerning the retirement of the Conspirators and the question of a foreign loan, the Grujić government resigned on April 17, 1906. Thirteen days later the Radicals under Nikola Pasić returned to power, this time to stay.

Realizing that the Austro-Hungarian ultimatum was, in fact, an assault on Serbia's freedom as a sovereign nation, Pašić's government rejected Vienna's proposal. However, by way of compensation, it offered to place orders with Austro-Hungarian firms for 26 million dinars' worth of rifles, ammunition, and railway equipment. Vienna refused. On July 7, 1906, it declared a tariff war on Serbia that was to last until 1911. Serbia, in turn, replied by imposing its general tariff rates on Austro-Hungarian goods.

In November 1906, the Pašić government settled the loan question and the gun question by turning to France. The order for new cannons was awarded to the Schneider firm at Creusot. Finance Minister Paču also concluded a loan agreement with a group of Franco-Swiss financiers in Geneva for 95 million dinars.

The Tariff War brought a severe disruption to Serbia's economy by suddenly depriving it of the central European market. There was little possibility of increasing trade with the other states of southeastern Europe, for their economies were all similar and poor. Three tasks faced Serbia: to find new markets, to secure easy and cheap transportation of its goods, and to attract orders for its goods. The first task was taken up by a greatly increased network of consulates and commercial agencies in Alexandria, Varna, Brăila, Geneva, Naples, Istanbul, London, Marseilles, Berlin, Brussels, Salonika, Antwerp, and Malta. The problem of transportation was solved by advantageous agreements with French, Italian, Russian, Romanian, and Bulgarian steamship and transportation companies, as well as by securing from Turkey railway transit rights to Salonika and a loading zone in the harbor. The third problem was resolved through a whole series of commercial treaties, in late 1906 and early 1907, with France, Italy, Britain, Russia, Belgium, Switzerland, Romania, and, later, with the Scandinavian countries, Spain, and Portugal. Trial shipments of cattle and pigs were sent to Egypt, Italy, Malta, and Greece, but only the shipments to Italy were large enough to be profitable. Meanwhile, measures were also taken to strengthen the home market by passing laws advantageous to commerce, which made credit more available through the facilities of the National Bank and other financial institutions.

While these measures could not completely offset the loss of trade with Austria-Hungary, they went far to satisfy immediate needs and to avert an economic crisis. Serbian cattle now went to new markets in Italy and Egypt, meat went to France, lard to Britain, grain and prunes to Germany and Belgium. Serbia's balance of trade for 1905 and 1906 was as follows, in dinars:

	1905	1906	Balance
Exports	71,996,274	71,604,098	−392,176
Imports	55,600,644	44,328,642	−11,272,002
Total turnover	127,596,918	115,932,740	−11,664,178

Although exports dropped in 1906, they were still considerably greater than the average between 1894 and 1905, which was 47.7 million dinars. The drop in trade was not at all disastrous. Moreover, despite the drop, there was a healthier situation in Serbia's economy. This was reflected, in part, in the fact that public revenues, except for customs duties, actually increased. Foreign capital, especially French, Belgian, and British, was attracted to Serbia's mines. The number of industrial enterprises rose from 110 in 1906 to 162 in 1908, while the value of their production increased from 14 million dinars in 1906 to 23 million dinars in 1908 (in constant 1898 prices). Thus Serbia was successful in achieving its economic independence from Austria-Hungary, whose share of Serbia's exports fell from 90 percent in 1905 to 45 percent in 1906. At the same time Germany's percentage rose from 3 to 27, Belgium's from 0 to 9, and that of all other countries from 7 to 22. By 1907 Austria-Hungary's share had fallen to 15 percent while Germany's had risen to 40 percent.

One of the political results of Serbia's defiance was that Goluchowski's failure to force Serbia's submission contributed to his downfall in 1906. He was succeeded on October 21, 1906, by Baron Alois von Aehrenthal, who opposed the Tariff War and sought less damaging ways of furthering his country's aims in the Balkans. As he put it at a meeting of the council of ministers on October 27, 1907, "Our policy, which was based on the desire to render Serbia politically and economically dependent and to consider it as a negligible quantity, has suffered a shipwreck." Hoping to restore Austria-Hungary's grip on

Serbia's economy, in 1907 Aehrenthal offered Serbia an outlet to the Adriatic Sea with transit privileges via Bosnia and a new commercial treaty. Serbia's leaders never took the first offer seriously, but they were quite interested in the second. Negotiations were begun after Premier Pašić visited Aehrenthal in Vienna in May 1907. Despite many thorny problems, the treaty was signed on March 15, 1908. However, neither side was satisfied. The Austrian industrial interests were displeased because the treaty did not do enough to restore trade with Serbia, and they accused Aehrenthal of selling out to Hungarian agrarian interests. Serbs were bitter over the humiliating provision that Austro-Hungarian veterinarians would inspect Serbian cattle on Serbian soil; they were also disappointed that the new quota for cattle and pigs was so much lower than before. As a result of the ensuing political crisis, Pašić's government was replaced, on July 20, 1908, by another Radical cabinet, headed by Pera Velimirović. This government would have an even more volatile crisis caused by Austria-Hungary—the annexation of Bosnia and Hercegovina.

The Annexation of Bosnia-Hercegovina, 1908

In 1908 the aim of Austria-Hungary in southeastern Europe was, as in the eighteenth and nineteenth centuries, to ensure its hegemony in at least the western half of the Balkan Peninsula. Roughly this included the territory west of a line from Vienna and Budapest to Salonika, then an Ottoman port. Once a compliant satellite, after 1903 Serbia became a serious obstacle to the Dual Monarchy's ambitions in the Balkans. That is why Goluchowski was so determined to force Serbia's submission through economic pressure. However, when Serbia showed its ability to withstand such pressure, Vienna had to turn to other means. Without abandoning the Tariff War, Goluchowski's successor, Aehrenthal, pursued two other lines of attack—a railway through the Sancak of Novi Pazar and the annexation of Bosnia-Hercegovina.

Taking advantage of Austria-Hungary's military occupation of the Sancak of Novi Pazar, in early 1908 Aehrenthal asked the Porte for permission to build a railway from Bosnia to Mitrovica and for economic concessions in the *vilâyets* of Kosovo and Salonika. In exchange, he promised Austria-Hungary's benevolent restraint regarding his government's attitude with respect to the Porte's internationally guaranteed obligation to carry out reforms in Macedonia. The Porte's acquiescence greatly troubled the other European Powers, not only Russia but also Italy, which had its own ambitions in that part of the Balkans, via a foothold in Albania. The Sancak railway disturbed the Serbian government even more. As Pašić said, the success of this project would inevitably lead to Serbia's encirclement by Austria-Hungary on three sides—north, west, and south—for such a railway would only be another step in extending Austria-Hungary's domination over Old Serbia and Macedonia. Knowing that Serbia could not by itself prevent such a railway, Pašić decided to do nothing until the negotiations for a trade treaty with the Dual Monarchy were completed. As soon as they were, in February 1908, he attempted to revive an earlier plan for a railway that would link Serbia with the Adriatic coast via Ottoman territory. This time Russia was willing to support such a project, as were Italy and France. Romania also expressed interest. By the middle of February Pašić was able to report that "all the Powers except England have promised their help."

By mid-March Serbia was ready to present to the Porte its request for a right-of-way, supported by the notes of France, Italy, and Russia. Taking advantage of the rivalry between those three powers and Austria-Hungary and Germany, the Porte temporized. Meanwhile French and Italian financial interests quarreled over their respective shares in the project. This problem was settled in early June 1908, when the project was divided into its two components—the railway itself and the port facilities, presumably at San Giovanni di Medua (Shëngjin), in northern Albania. The shares in the railway were to be 45 percent French, 35 percent Italian, 15 percent Russian, and 5 percent Serbian. The shares in the port facilities were to be 55 percent Italian and 45 percent French. Though two companies were formed, the French and Italian participants were the same. Thinking that the Porte might more easily grant a concession to a French company, on June 20, 1908, the Serbian government asked the Porte to transfer its request to the Jonction Salonique Constantinople. Meanwhile plans for the building of the railway progressed, and the international syndicate held its first meeting, in Paris.

At that point a series of crises forced the abandonment of the entire project. The first came on July 5, 1908, when the Young Turks rebelled in the Macedonian town of Resen (Resna). By July 13 the rebellion was joined by the Turkish officers of Salonika and by the Albanians. In the resulting chaos the Porte was in no position to conduct normal international negotiations. An even more disturbing event shook the European powers in October 1908: On October 5 Bulgaria declared its independence of the Turks, and on October 6 Austria-Hungary proclaimed the annexation of Bosnia and Hercegovina. As though to soften the blow, the Dual Monarchy simultaneously renounced its right to occupy the Sancak of Novi Pazar. However, this in no way pacified any of the countries concerned. By its act Austria-Hungary had, in fact, violated the terms of the Treaty of Berlin of 1878. The Russian government was in no position to protest inasmuch as its Foreign Minister Izvolskii had secretly agreed to the act in advance, at a meeting with Count Aehrenthal in Buchlau on September 16, in exchange for Austria-Hungary's promise not to oppose the opening of the Straits to Russian warships. Yet feelings ran so high in Russia that Izvolskii was forced to repudiate his agreement. The French and British joined Russia in calling for an international conference to consider Austria-Hungary's action.

The status quo in the Balkans was further disturbed when, on October 7, Crete proclaimed its union with Greece. Meanwhile Serbia and Montenegro were left without any recourse or compensation.

Serbia was in an extremely weak position. It had no Balkan alliances on which to rely. It was not prepared militarily for any action in any case; it had just completed negotiations for badly needed armaments. It had no support among the powers, some of which, like Great Britain, had barely agreed to give it diplomatic recognition only recently. Besides, Izvolskii's underhanded agreement to the annexation put Russia in a bad light with both the Western Powers and the South Slavs. Unable to undertake war on its own, the Serbian government was forced to rely on the European Powers to cope with the question. At the same time, it could not ignore or suppress the outpouring of bitterness and rage both among its own population and among Serbs everywhere who looked to Serbia as the chief standard-bearer of Serbdom. For Serbia the annexation of Bosnia and Hercegovina was not simply a disturbance in the European balance of power or a violation of an international treaty; it was a threat to its program of Serbian unification and perhaps to its very existence as a free nation. Despite the mixed population of Serbs, Croats, and Muslim Slavs of uncertain nationality in Bosnia and Hercegovina, the Serbian government and people had always regarded the provinces as Serbian.

While there was no disagreement in Serbia with respect to the indignation everyone felt, there was a difference among the political leaders as to what course Serbia should follow. Two divergent views were held by Milovan Milovanović, foreign minister in Pera Velimirović's cabinet, who represented the soft line, and Radical party leader Nikola Pašić, who urged the hard line.

Even before the annexation of Bosnia and Hercegovina, when Milovanović learned of its inevitability from Izvolskii during a meeting in Marienbad (Mariánské Lázně), he concluded that all Serbia could do was to secure some compensation. His hope was to gain the Sancak of Novi Pazar and thus give Montenegro and Serbia a common border. This was too much for Izvolskii before the annexation, but Milovanović clung to the idea of compensation and made it a part of Serbia's official protest against the annexation of Bosnia and Hercegovina. Without consulting anyone, he stated in the note, "Serbia cannot find complete satisfaction unless the status of Bosnia and Hercegovina created by the Treaty of Berlin is wholly restored. Should this prove not to be possible in any way, the Royal Government, appealing to the sense of justice on the part of the signatory powers of the Treaty of Berlin, asks that Serbia be granted suitable compensation, and that for the preservation of the guarantees for the independent life of its state and of the Serbian people in general, the agreements concerning its national existence be restored at least in the measure granted by the Treaty of Berlin."

To Pašić such a request was humiliating, insufficient, and ineffective. Instead of first coming out with a minimum demand, he argued, the Serbian government should have asked for the maximum, at least as a basis for negotiation. Serbia's request for compensation was, he held, a passive acceptance of Austria-Hungary's act, and such a submissive response could not win anyone's support. Pašić urged immediate secret mobilization and preparation for war. He also insisted that Serbia ask for the removal of Austria-Hungary from Bosnia and Hercegovina entirely and for the granting of autonomy to the two provinces within the Ottoman Empire. Presumably he did not really want a war, being only too aware of Serbia's weakness, but he hoped that the threat of war might bring results. He also admitted privately that autonomy for Bosnia and Hercegovina was not likely, but that Serbia's demand would strengthen its ties with the population of the provinces. Besides, Pašić believed that Serbia had to strengthen Turkey's hand, since they were joint victims of Austria-Hungary's action, and that the European Powers had more reason to support Turkey than Serbia as a barrier to Austrian expansion. Let others ask compensation for Serbia, Pašić argued, but let not Serbia damage its own image as the champion of Serbian liberation.

Both Pašić's maximalism and Milovanović's utilitarianism found expression in the note of protest that the Serbian government directed to the European Powers. "A just solution of the Bosnian-Hercegovinian question would be realized," the note read, "only with the political emancipation of Bosnia and Hercegovina, organized in a free and autonomous state." This was Pašić's declaratory stand. The note continued, "But if the Powers are not able at present to agree on such a solution of the question, the Serbian government asks that, until that question is resolved, guarantees be given for the existence of Serbia and Montenegro as independent states." Then followed Milovanović's quest for compensation: Serbia's and Montenegro's territorial expansion and linkage by means of a corridor across Bosnia-Hercegovina, the regulation of the border between Serbia and Austria-Hungary on the Sava and the Danube, and the abrogation of article 29 of the Treaty of Berlin which limited Montenegro's sovereignty by giving Austria-Hungary certain supervisory rights in the Montenegrin littoral. If Serbia's request were granted, this would mean cutting off Austria-Hungary from any territorial contact with the Ottoman Empire, for the first time since the Middle Ages. Also, it would secure for Montenegro and Serbia an outlet to the Adriatic through the port of Bar (Antivari).

The Serbian demands must be coupled with Milovanović's intention of gaining Serbian and Montenegrin hegemony in the Sancak of Novi Pazar, which Austria-Hungary had just relinquished to the Porte. The first step in this program was to gain railway rights there from the Porte as well as the right to transport troops and munitions across this territory.

The Serbian government was in an extremely awkward position. At home it faced a vociferously indignant public whose demonstrations were so violent as to require the intervention of the police. In mid-October the National Assembly in Belgrade passed a resolution of protest against the annexation of Bosnia and Hercegovina which proclaimed the Assembly's willingness to bear any sacrifice in its support of any action that the Serbian government might undertake. The belligerent tone of the deputies left no doubt that the Assembly expected that action to be resolute, even if it led to the brink of war. This was a far cry from Milovanović's cautious policy of begging for compensation. On the other hand, the European Powers were in no mood to have Serbia add to the crisis with demands that seemed as excessive to them as they seemed modest to the Serbs.

Placing its trust in diplomacy, the Velimirović government sent its most experienced envoys to the capitals of Europe: Milovanović to London, Paris, Rome, and Berlin; Pašić to St. Petersburg; and Stojan Novaković to Istanbul.

Milovanović's mission was almost scuttled in the very beginning, in Berlin, where he met Izvolskii. Completely unnerved, the Russian foreign minister was ready, as a consequence of his repudiation of the Buchlau Agreement, to renounce all support for Serbia's compensation. It was only after Milovanović's energetic protest and threat of a revolution in Serbia that Izvolskii agreed to support Serbia's demands, but only if France and Great Britain concurred. As for the Germans, Milovanović was told that Germany supported Austria-Hungary. He was not even received by Emperor William or Chancellor von Bülow. In Paris he was received cordially but got no more than the promise that France would support Russia and would not influence it against Serbia's demands. In London, though King Edward VII would not receive him, Milovanović encountered a more favorable atmosphere. Foreign Minister Sir Edward Grey was decidedly opposed to Austria-Hungary's untimely and underhanded breach of an international agreement. The British Foreign Office had neither concern nor understanding for Serbia's position as an injured party; however, the British were willing to listen, owing to the Anglo-Russian Entente of August 31, 1907. The foreign office was impressed by Milovanović's case and promised its diplomatic help as long as Russia, as the most interested power, supported Serbia.

It was apparent that everything depended on Russia. Pašić's mission to St. Petersburg was strengthened by the presence of then Crown Prince George of Serbia, who bore King Peter's personal letter to Tsar Nicholas. Pašić himself was well known and well liked in Russia, and had no trouble in gaining the sympathy of Tsar Nicholas, certain leaders of the Russian Duma, Panslavist circles, and the Russian public at large. However, the tsar's absolutism notwithstanding, neither he nor the Russian people could make foreign policy decisions. In the highly bureaucratic regime that governed Russia, it was perfectly possible for Izvolskii to say to the Serbian minister, "I will not go into what the Tsar told you, but I can tell you that it will be as I say to you." And it was. The Russian foreign minister had great personal distaste for Pašić, whom he habitually called "that old conspirator," and regarded his mission in Russia as a most unwelcome annoyance. Izvolskii's great concern at the time was to keep the peace. He advised Pašić during their meeting on October 29, 1908, "Serbia should remain calm and not do anything to provoke Austria-Hungary and make it decide to annihilate Serbia. Russia's arms are not ready; she cannot and does not wish to make war now over Bosnia-Hercegovina, come what may. Serbia cannot prevent the annexation but, if she opposes it, she will only succeed in perishing then and there." He chided Pašić for the public demonstrations in Serbia, which made his own task all the more difficult. In actual fact, Izvolskii had reason to fear that it would take very little provocation for Austria-Hungary to overrun Serbia. Aehrenthal had seriously discussed with General Conrad von Hötzendorf that the annexation of Bosnia and Hercegovina was merely the first stage toward the dismemberment of Serbia. Despite Izvolskii's advice, Pašić returned to Belgrade as aggressive in his outlook as when he had left.

Stojan Novaković's mission to Istanbul was based on the Serbian supposition that the interests of Serbia and the Porte were brought together by the annexation. He was well received and even offered a military alliance, which Montenegro would also be invited to join. However, it soon became clear that the Porte was far more perturbed by Bulgaria's declaration of independence than by the loss of Bosnia and Hercegovina, which it had already written off after 1878. Serbia absolutely refused to consider any alliance aimed against Bulgaria; this ran counter to its policy of a South Slavic rapprochement. Besides, the Ottoman proposal of dividing Bulgarian territory between Turkey and Serbia, which would involve returning Balkan Christians to Ottoman rule, was unthinkable.

Thus the Serbian government failed to get the support it required for its program. Even Montenegro, which concluded an agreement with Serbia over their common action in the Sancak of Novi Pazar, was not eager to go beyond that. Serbian-Montenegrin relations had only recently been quite bad, thanks to several incidents, and neither side trusted the other.

Serbia's only hope remained the conference of European powers that Izvolskii was trying to organize to consider not only the case of Bosnia and Hercegovina but also Bulgaria, the Sancak of Novi Pazar, reforms in European Turkey, and several other questions, including, under point 7, "compensation to Serbia to consist of the rectification of the border on Bosnian-Hercegovinian territory, in the proximity of the Sancak of Novi Pazar." The original point 7 also added, "Similar rectification can be made for Montenegro." Sir Edward Grey had any reference to territorial compensation for Serbia and Montenegro deleted; instead, point 7 was changed to read "economic advantages to be procured for Serbia and Montenegro." Austria-Hungary, backed by Germany, would consent to no such conference unless its participants accepted Austria-Hungary's annexation of Bosnia and Hercegovina as an accomplished fact.

Meanwhile, in early 1909, Austria-Hungary got the Porte to recognize the annexation of Bosnia and Hercegovina in return for 2.5 million Turkish pounds for the loss of its crown lands there. After that, the only choice that remained for Russia and Serbia was either acceptance of the situation or war, and neither was prepared to choose war. Accordingly on February 27 Izvolskii instructed Russian Minister A. I. Nelidov in Belgrade that Serbia had to abandon its territorial claims and refrain from any provocative action. Aehrenthal was not satisfied with this, however; he demanded that Serbia accept the Austro-Turkish Agreement of February 26, formally recognize the annexation of Bosnia and Hercegovina, and give Austria-Hungary guarantees of a "correct and peaceful policy." If these demands were not accepted by the end of March, Aehrenthal told the German government, Austria-Hungary would present Belgrade with an ultimatum and invade Serbia if it were rejected. To the disappointment of Conrad von Hötzendorf and the military party at Vienna, Serbia did not provoke a war. On March 13 a crown council held at Tsarskoe Selo agreed that Russia would not go to war over the Serbs (though Tsar Nicholas apparently withheld his own decision). Eight days later the German government presented Russia with a similar ultimatum, which the Russians were forced to accept. On March 31 Serbia submitted its recognition of the annexation and promised to cease all protests and opposition to it and to "change the direction of her present policy towards Austria-Hungary in order to live henceforth on terms of good neighborliness with the latter." Serbia also agreed to reduce its army and to prevent the formation on its territory of irregular units hostile to Austria-Hungary. Austria-Hungary had won a complete victory. The crisis was at an end. Serbia did not get even its minimum as compensation. However, it did acquire prestige in South Slavic eyes as the Piedmont of the Yugoslav movement. The Serbian Question was now not just a Balkan problem but a European one.

The End of the Tariff War of 1906–1911

The Tariff War and the annexation crisis had brought Serbia and Austria-Hungary to the brink of war. The end of the latter crisis resulted in a partial relaxation of tension, but the pressure of the Tariff War continued, even though Serbia had concluded a commercial treaty with Austria-Hungary on March 14, 1908. The treaty was very disappointing to Serbia. For one thing, before the Tariff War Serbia had been free to export livestock to Austria-Hungary in unlimited quantities. After the commercial treaty of 1908, it could export only a certain amount, and then only in the form of processed meat. Though this had its good side in that it forced Serbia to build up its own meat-packing industry, still such efforts were far from adequate to satisfy the market. The treaty did give Serbia one advantage in that Austria-Hungary applied to this meat the lower tariff for live animals, but this privilege was bought at the price of permitting Austro-Hungarian veterinarians to inspect the animals on Serbian territory prior to their slaughtering. Serbia still remained at the mercy of Austro-Hungarian veterinary border regulations, which were freely manipulated by Vienna for political purposes.

After Serbia's humiliating submission to the annexation of Bosnia and Hercegovina, Aehrenthal felt that it would be opportune to relieve the pressure on Serbia so as not to force it into organizing a Balkan alliance system such as Izvolskii advocated in December 1908. He was prepared to make economic concessions, but though both parties were willing, the negotiations for a new agreement were difficult. Having just suffered a political defeat, the Serbian government could not afford to endure an economic disaster as well. Milovanović was determined to have the export of live animals included in the new agreement. On the other hand, Aehrenthal faced a major obstacle at home in the stubborn opposition of Hungarian agrarian interests to any economic treaty that favored Serbia at their expense. A cabinet crisis in Hungary compelled the Hungarian delegation to a customs and trade conference in Vienna to declare its refusal to deal with the Serbs at all. The expiration of the 1908 treaty made the Serbian government eager to reach an agreement. In talks in October and November 1909, both Aehrenthal and Milovanović showed great pliancy, but both were hampered by opposition at home. Thus all of 1909 went by without a trade agreement between the two countries.

Serbia forced an end to the deadlock by energetically engaging in several simultaneous actions that stirred Vienna. Milovanović began economic talks with Bulgaria and the Porte, which brought certain results. In March 1909, at the height of Vienna's political pressure on Serbia, Bulgaria agreed to the free transit of Serbian livestock over Bulgarian territory and, soon after, to the same privilege for Serbian weapons and munitions. The Bulgarian government even proposed to Serbia a joint economic policy toward Austria-Hungary. All this caused Vienna to fear a revival of the project of a Serbian-Bulgarian customs union. Serbian-Turkish trade talks in 1910 also appeared to proceed quite well. Milovanović's visits to Istanbul in March 1910 and again a month later, this time with King Peter, promised much at the time, though they resulted in little. Rather more substantial was a loan of 150 million dinars which Serbian Finance Minister Paču concluded in Paris on November 9, 1909. Finally Serbia took another step in the Tariff War in early 1910 by approving a tariff schedule that increased duties on the goods of countries that had no trade agreement with Serbia—notably Austria-Hungary.

In the end Austria-Hungary was moved to resume trade talks with Serbia, in late March 1910. Now the tables were turned. Vienna was eager while Milovanović deliberately took his time. They offered most-favored-nation treatment with respect to Serbia's processed meat while Serbia required a tariff agreement and a fixed quota. Thanks to its exports via Salonika and other routes, Serbia was no longer as dependent on the Austrian market as before. What the Serbs wanted above all was most-favored-nation treatment and free transit for its shipments of live animals. This was too much for Austria-Hungary.

The treaty was finally concluded on July 27, 1910, after Serbia abandoned these demands. In return, after considerable haggling with the Hungarians, Vienna agreed to allow Serbia to export to Austria-Hungary a quota of processed meat amounting to 15,000 beef cattle and 50,000 pigs, which was far fewer than the Serbs wished. However,

Serbia did get the much desired right of transit for its processed pork and for its beef via Austrian territory. It also received most-favored-nation treatment for many articles, or at least a favorable minimal tariff. Of great political importance was the separation of the agreement from other Austro-Serbian conventions. The treaty did not go into effect until it was ratified in late January 1911. With that the Tariff War came formally to an end. While the trade agreement soon raised Austria-Hungary's share of Serbia's exports from its low of 18 to 19 percent at the height of the Tariff War to around 41 percent, this was still far below the 90 percent it had been before the war began.

The Tariff War had brought about certain pivotal changes in Serbia. It turned Serbia from the passive trading partner of one large and powerful country to an active trader in several markets. Serbia was forced to seek out new trade routes and customers. Serbia's economic liberation meant freedom from the Austro-Hungarian political domination of a quarter century. Finally Serbia could carry out the tasks set for it a half century before by Ilija Garašanin and Prince Michael Obrenović: Serbian unification, South Slavic solidarity, and an alliance of free Balkan nations.

Serbia's Domestic Economy, 1903–1912

In 1903, when the new regime under King Peter Karadjordjević assumed control, Serbia was almost bankrupt. The surplus in the balance of trade that had made up for the chronic deficits in the state budget could no longer, by 1903, keep pace with the state debt. Only the loan negotiated in Paris in 1902 staved off disaster. It was not clear at the time just how bad the situation was, for the simple reason that the state's financial accounts were in such disorder; in 1903 the government did not yet have a final precise accounting for the fiscal year 1901. Thus it was possible for the finance ministry to claim a surplus of 5 million dinars at the same time the Central Auditing Commission reported a deficit of 13 million dinars.

The first task of the new Radical-Progressive administration was to bring order out of chaos and to raise more money. Of the two available means to accomplish the latter—new loans or higher taxes—the government chose the second. Unfortunately for the taxpayers, instead of instituting a direct progressive income tax, as the handful of Social-

Democrats demanded, the government resorted to the time-honored surtax.

The government also sponsored four other measures, however, which resulted in improvements. The Law on the State Budget, passed in April 1903, put an end to open-ended and unrealistic budgets by imposing rigid strictures and public auditing. In 1904 a fund of up to 10 million dinars was established with the National Bank which made it possible to function until July 1 of every year, when certain incomes from annuities and state monopolies came in, without resorting to exorbitant short-term loans that all too often could be obtained only from Viennese banks. In the fall of 1903 and spring of 1904 the Assembly passed a series of bills designed to increase the state's income: higher tariffs; a higher tax on alcoholic beverages; the protection of the monopoly on tobacco, salt, and kerosene from bootleggers; a rise in various state imposts and fees; and a surtax of 40 percent. Finally, steps were taken to improve the supply of currency by minting new coins: 6 million dinars in silver coins, 400,000 dinars in nickel coins of 5 paras, and 250,000 dinars in bronze coins of 2 paras.

Even by 1904 these and other measures brought a significant improvement to Serbia's finances. The accounts for 1904 and 1905 showed surpluses by 5.3 million dinars and 8.1 million dinars respectively. By 1905 the accounting system caught up. In 1906 Serbia had a surplus of 11.4 million dinars in its coffers. This money was to be of crucial importance in buttressing Serbia from the results of the Tariff War.

As the Tariff War showed so painfully, the basic weakness of Serbia's economy lay in the fact that Serbia entered the twentieth century as an overwhelmingly agrarian country based on a primitive peasant agricultural system. The fact that the large majority of the population —87 percent in 1900—were peasants of whom almost 90 percent owned their own farms and produced most of their own food, and many other necessities as well, gave the country a certain stability, both economic and moral. While industrial workers in more developed countries lived wretchedly and even starved, most of the people of Serbia lived on their own homesteads, which were legally protected from sequestration for debt, and did not lack for shelter, food, or clothing. On the other hand, the general level of life was still primitive and poor.

Only in the latter half of the nineteenth century did Serbia pass from the transhumant raising of livestock to the cultivation of grain and plums as the chief agricultural activity. Yet despite some increase in agricultural yields after 1895, the small size of holdings and the absence of modern technology discouraged the production of a large marketable surplus. As Serbia entered the twentieth century, four-fifths of the cultivated land was divided into holdings whose six to ten scattered plots totaled less than 10 hectares (about 25 acres) per homestead. Over half of all cultivated land—55 percent—consisted of holdings of fewer than 5 hectares (just over 12 acres). While the absence of large estates was a feature of Serbian social democracy and egalitarianism in the countryside, it also contributed to economic backwardness; Serbian agriculture lacked the stimulus of large efficient farms whose advanced methods might spread to the small holdings. Two-thirds of Serbia's peasant households used wooden, rather than iron, plows. Artificial fertilizer was unknown. Ignorance of crop rotation meant that production was lost from the third and more of land that was left fallow each year. In 1900 less than one percent of the state budget was devoted to the agricultural section of the ministry of the national economy, and only the smallest fraction of that went to the improvement of agriculture. At a time when one-half to four-fifths of the agricultural output in the rest of Europe went to the marketplace, only about one-fifth of Serbia's produce was marketed. Though by 1890 the annual output of wheat, corn, and plums had each surpassed pig sales, livestock and animal products continued to be Serbia's chief export until the Tariff War.

Industry continued to be only a minor part of the national economy in the first decade of the twentieth century. Even including mines and unmechanized enterprises of the smallest size, industrial production for 1911, for example, amounted to about a quarter of the agricultural output and, very roughly, about 15 percent of the gross national product. In 1910 total industrial horsepower was less than 25,000, and the 16,000 workers employed in industry were less than 2 percent of the entire labor force of the country. Moreover, of the skilled industrial workers in Serbia, half were imported, largely from the Czech and other Habsburg lands. In 1903, when King Peter came to the throne, Serbia had 200 flour mills, 9 breweries, 3 state factories (tobacco and silk), 34 mines, and 104 miscellaneous enterprises involving meat packing, textiles, leather, lumber, cement, and bricks, whose output barely equaled that of just the flour mills in value.

Serbian industry got a significant boost from the Tariff War. Serbia had two important prerequisites for the creation of industry—raw materials and cheap labor. However, among the factors that hindered a more rapid industrial development, the ever present shadow of Austro-Hungarian competition loomed large. Added to this deterrent was the lack of sufficient domestic capital, skilled labor, convenient transportation, and established foreign markets. The Tariff War put a stop to the flood of industrial imports from Austria-Hungary. Moreover, the protective tariffs that were introduced by Serbia in its trade treaties of 1906–1907 favored the development of industry at home and increased the government's supply of capital.

At the beginning of the Tariff War, in 1906, Serbia had 215 flour mills (161 steam and 54 water), 9 breweries, and 110 industrial enterprises, with a total annual output valued at about 30 million dinars. Excluding flour mills, breweries, slaughterhouses, and jam factories, the total value produced annually by the rest of Serbian industry equaled around 15 million dinars, as opposed to the 35 million dinars of industrial imports, largely from Austria-Hungary. To make up for the loss of these imports, Serbian industry had to more than double its production. In 1906 the ministry of national economy estimated that an investment of 30 million dinars was needed to advance Serbian industry to this point. The chief fund that the government had for this purpose came from the proceeds of the state lottery. In the fifteen years since its inauguration in 1891, its total proceeds amounted to 6.2 million dinars, of which only 3.6 million was invested in industry. In the beginning of 1907 the state had only 67,000 dinars in this fund, while applications for credit from various industrial enterprises added up to 1.5 million dinars. Obviously the state had to find additional ways to meet this demand.

A traditional way in Serbia to make up for the lack of sufficient credit was the granting of government concessions in various forms: exemptions from customs duties (usually on imported machinery, semiprocessed goods, and raw materials); the free use of state land; and lower prices for goods that were government monopolies. However, apart from being insufficient, as a source of income, the system had various other drawbacks and abuses. As peasant deputies in the Assembly were quick to point out, the cost of encouraging the rise of a domestic infant industry was passed on to the consumer. If the price of imported sugar was 80 paras per kilogram, the price of the sugar produced by the subsidized Serbian factory at Čukarica was between

90 paras and 1 dinar. Despite such problems, the Tariff War with Austria-Hungary greatly increased the requests, and the need, for concessions. In 1906 the government received 50 applications, of which the Assembly passed only 9. Thus government concessions did not play a major role in the rise of Serbian industry at the time.

One of the important indirect consequences of the Tariff War was that foreign capital was attracted to Serbia as never before. Other nations saw their opportunity to enter a market that had been exclusively under Austro-Hungarian domination. In its plight Serbia was only too eager to attract such capital, though it meant the exploitation of its natural resources by more powerful capitalist foreign interests. At first these interests were cautious and tentative, seeking to invest in commercial ventures that involved small outlays and low risks. A significant exception to this was foreign investment in Serbian mining, where the size of the required outlay was necessarily large.

British capital was so interested that in December 1906 an Anglo-Balkan syndicate was established in London consisting of around twenty large British firms that were eager to explore opportunities in Serbia, in ventures such as railroads, mining, meat packing, electrification of towns, and petroleum. Similarly, in August 1906 a *Deutsch-serbische Handelsgesellschaft* was formed in Berlin, as well as a *Deutsches Orient Handelssyndikat,* which were to devote themselves to increasing commerce with Serbia. However, they postponed all actual investments until the Tariff War was settled. Of the western powers, France was the most successful in placing its capital in Serbia, by means of government loans, orders for armaments, and railway concessions. Of the smaller European nations, Belgium and Italy became especially important. In August 1906 German and Belgian capital formed the *Banque pour le commerce et l'industrie en Serbie* in Brussels. One of its major participants, the Belgian *Banque des mines,* had a special interest in mines, timber, chemicals, and cement. Italian capital was attracted largely to the building of a railway from Serbia to the Adriatic coast. This was in connection with Italy's economic penetration into Montenegro and Albania. The *Banca commerciale di Milano* was particularly interested in linking the Bar-Podgorica railroad of Montenegro with Serbia. So was the Italian government, which actively encouraged this venture.

The most immediate support to Serbian industry during the first years of the Tariff War, however, had to come from the Serbian government itself. This recognition was reflected in the decision, in late 1907, to reorganize the ministry of national economy into five sections: administration, trade and transportation, industry, technical training, and credit institutions. The greatest thrust was given to industry and credit. A special commission was established to deal with industrial development. Among its activities was the preparation of legislation on behalf of industry. The government was understandably eager to further that export industry that was most hard hit by the Tariff War, the livestock industry. To this end it gave some benefits to meat-processing enterprises, though this help generally went to the large firms. The government even instituted the payment of premiums for large shipments of meat to new markets such as Egypt, Italy, and Malta. In response to initial complaints from various foreign customers, the government also instituted severe quality controls on exports of all articles and thus made certain to attract new markets and not to lose them. These measures provoked much protest on the part of smaller entrepreneurs, but they forcibly lifted Serbian enterprise out of its Levantine carelessness and established it in the world market.

The most significant single financial factor in the rise of Serbian industry in the early twentieth century was the role of domestic banks. Chief among these was the National Bank (*Narodna Banka*), which received its charter in 1883. In view of greatly changed conditions since that date, the National Bank sought a much wider franchise. In 1904, after the advent of the new regime, the National Bank began negotiations with the government with this end in view. However, various internal and external distractions interrupted these discussions until 1907. An agreement on a new franchise became crucial for two reasons: the Tariff War made the role of the bank more important than ever, and the bank's original charter was to expire in 1908. As a result, the National Assembly granted the National Bank a new franchise on March 28,1908, just three days before the old one expired. By its terms the National Bank greatly increased its issue of silver notes, mainly in the form of short-term credit. The beneficial results were almost immediately felt on the market. The new franchise also obliged the bank to accept the promissory notes of agricultural cooperatives, which aided that sector considerably. As for industry, the National Bank's declared policy at the start of the Tariff War was to favor it. In actual fact, the bank provided scarcely 10 percent of the 30-million-dinar increase in industrial working capital that the government estimated industry would require. The main contribution the National Bank made to industry was indirect, by extending credit to the other banks of Serbia.

In 1883, when the National Bank was founded, there were only four financial institutions in the whole country, and there was practically no industrial capital. By the end of 1907 there were 147 financial institutions and an industrial capital of up to 40 million dinars. The National Bank refused to grant credit to institutions that charged an interest of over 9 percent, that is, 3 percent over the interest charged by the National Bank. At first only 44 institutions in Serbia complied and were thus qualified for credit from the National Bank. By 1910 this number rose only to 52 institutions. Those that dealt primarily with industry or exports received a 2 percent reduction in the regular interest rate. Thus the majority of short-term credit provided by the National Bank was made available to Serbian industry indirectly through other banks, especially the large banks of Belgrade.

Apart from the credit supplied by the National Bank, the assets of other large Belgrade banks rose sharply during the Tariff War. Serbian banks not only provided credit for business but also entered the market themselves, both as long-term partners of enterprises and as entrepreneurs. As early as 1904 the large Export Bank (*Izvozna Banka*) operated commission-earning trade agencies in Budapest and Berlin and dried a million dinars' worth of exported plums in its own kilns. After the Tariff War broke out, the Export Bank and another large Belgrade bank, the Belgrade Cooperative (*Beogradska Zadruga*), expedited livestock and grain exports to foreign countries, mainly via Salonika. In 1910 the latter bank began to engage in direct industrial investment when it purchased three-quarters of the shares of a struggling glass factory in Paraćin. Apart from putting the factory on its feet, the bank's action did much to free Serbia of its dependence on Austrian glass. In 1907 the Belgrade Merchant Bank (*Beogradska Trgovačka Banka*) invested around one million dinars in a new enterprise that became Serbia's fourth cement plant, with three times the capacity of any of its domestic competitors. By 1908 its annual output exceeded the value of imported cement. Similarly, in 1903 the Commercial Bank (*Prometna Banka*) of Belgrade invested in a sawmill, which profited owing to the Tariff War. By 1910 it had cut imported Austrian lumber from two-thirds to one-quarter of domestic sales.

The majority of Belgrade banks preferred to invest in already existing enterprises. By 1911 their total commitment to new direct investment was more than 14 million dinars. In that year two large investments went to meat packing for the first time. Banks in the interior were far less involved, or not at all, except in Niš, an important railway center.

The Belgrade banks also actively invested in projects directly related to industry. The National Bank provided a million-dinar loan for the building of a short railway to connect the main slaughterhouse in Belgrade with the city rail terminal. The Mortgage Bank (*Hipotekarna Banka*) provided funds for railway construction and Belgrade's water system. Several Belgrade banks engaged in the business of providing sand and gravel to construction companies. Also, increasingly during the Tariff War, banks acted as wholesale and sometimes as retail agents for the importing of modern industrial and agricultural machinery plus coal and other scarce raw materials. The Serbian Bank (*Srpska Banka*) earned 90 percent of its annual income in this way through its "technical department." All the Serbian banks facilitated in some degree the import of machinery, coal, and other goods needed by industry, in a way not equaled by any other public institution or agency. Moreover, some banks, notably the Belgrade Cooperative, performed another useful service to industry by making available insurance, including accident insurance, for industrial labor.

How successful all these measures were in advancing Serbia's industry may be judged from the following table:

Year	Number of enterprises	Horsepower	Number of workers	Value of production in dinars
1903	105	4,258	4,066	12,832,310
1904	93	3,960	4,623	8,954,190
1905	94	4,566	4,730	13,119,573
1906	110	6,583	5,624	15,898,449
1907	126	5,626	6,201	23,797,854
1908	162	10,559	10,077	52,566,612
1910	428 (?)	24,030	16,095	74,378,000

The Tariff War of 1906–1911 was the turning point in the development of an independent modern economy in Serbia. Foreign trade was emancipated from Austro-Hungarian domination, thus turning Serbia from an economically passive satellite to an active factor in the world market. The severance of accustomed commercial ties with Austria-Hungary and the establishment of high protective tariffs made both necessary and possible the rapid development of domestic industry, with the active support of the Serbian government and Serbia's banks. Still economically backward, Serbia continued to suffer the usual disadvantages of an agrarian country vis-à-vis the industrially advanced countries. Nevertheless, Serbia's remarkable ability to deflect the deleterious consequences of the Tariff War and to build up its own economy demonstrated a strength and resilience that enhanced its prestige.

The effects of this economic emancipation and development on Serbia's political position have been noted. The social effects were as great, if not greater.

The social group most affected by the Tariff War was the merchants and industrialists. The great centralization of capital necessitated by the crisis created a sharper differentiation between small and large entrepreneurs. As the *Trgovinski Glasnik* (Trade Herald) of Belgrade observed, "when dealing with Alexandria and Genoa there can be no more trading in cattle and pigs for those who were used to having five men drive a wagonload of animals to Budapest." Whereas before 1905 there were only two large domestic export firms, in the course of the Tariff War the big banks took over and exporters found it necessary to concentrate their capital in joint ventures. For example, most of the export of livestock was carried on by four groups of merchants. A consortium for the export of grain organized in 1906 exported 4,478 carloads of wheat that year, valued at 6 million dinars. Its example was soon followed by similar groups.

What obtained in the export trade also held true for imports. The severance of ties with Vienna and Budapest created a disruption of normal traffic and credit arrangements that necessitated a general change. Only large importers and groups of importers were able to establish new commercial ties with Germany and other Western countries. Foreign firms were understandably skittish about dealing with small merchants in a still unknown market. However, thanks to the role of banks as intermediaries, the concentration of trade capital inevitably resulted in industrial investment. The result was a close identity between trade and industry, both of which were frequently in the same hands.

At the same time, the petty merchant found himself progressively left out. The decrease in trade at local fairs—from a value of 32.1 million dinars in 1905 to 9.9 million dinars in 1908—shows what a shock the Tariff War was at that level. Higher taxes and duties and the scissors effect of industrial and agricultural prices caught many small traders. The result was an increasing polarization between the large and small entrepreneurs.

This differentiation was also a geographical one, with the concentrated capital in Belgrade and the petty merchants in the hinterland. In certain branches of industry such as brewing, iron, and textiles, Belgrade was the seat of virtual cartels. Moreover, the importers were generally located in cities, whereas the exporters became increasingly located in provincial river ports or railway centers such as Smederevo or Niš. A similar dichotomy took place between Belgrade wholesalers and provincial retailers.

The political consequences of this differentiation within the middle class became clearly evident during the Tariff War. The industrialists and large importers and exporters supported the government's policy of waging the war, and were in turn supported by the government. The middling and small traders varied in their stand; some profited from the rise in prices for most articles, but others—especially the small exporters—were hard hit and opposed the Tariff War. Whatever their views were, the merchants of Serbia became a political force in the early twentieth century as never before, thanks to their numbers in the National Assembly. Consistently holding from 25 to 30 percent of the seats, the merchant deputies comprised either the largest single occupational group in the Assembly, as in 1903 and 1906, or they were a close second to the well-to-do peasants, as in 1905 and 1908. About half of the merchant deputies came from the cities, and most of the rest came from towns rather than villages. Thus, even in sheer numbers, the middle class of Serbia came to exercise a political influence far beyond their share of the total population.

Economic developments of the Tariff War resulted in greater social differentiation in the villages as well. The peasantry was caught between the fall in prices of agricultural products and livestock and the rise in prices of industrial goods. This was made all the more painful by the increase in taxes. In general, the smallest landholders suffered most. Peasants with less than 5 hectares of land (just over 12 acres) spent more than they earned. Those with between 5 and 10 hectares barely managed to hold their own. The larger the landholdings over 10 hectares, the more profit they made. Hence the extremes of poverty and affluence began to be more visible than ever before in the Serbian countryside.

[573]

The reasons for the economic woes of the small landholders were many. The increasing parceling of the land, due to the increase in population and the continued disintegration of family communes, made for a patchwork of uneconomically small plots. Primitive farming methods imposed either by the inertia of tradition or by the lack of costly implements kept productivity low. Statistics for 1906 show that a hectare of Serbian farmland yielded only a third of what a comparable hectare yielded, in value, in France. A deputy from Vranje reported in 1908 to the Assembly that among some 50,000 inhabitants in his region there were only eleven iron plows. Reports of the ministry of national economy revealed that such conditions were widespread.

Government measures to alleviate the plight of agriculture generally did too little or failed entirely. For example, a decision in 1905 to establish a fund for livestock insurance had to be rescinded in 1909 because desperate peasants began to kill and maim their own livestock at an alarming rate just to get the insurance money. To make up for the severe lack of credit, especially during the Tariff War when most available money went into trade and industry, the state established an agrarian bank in 1909. However, it dealt with the wealthiest landowners, who needed the help least but who gave most promise of repaying their loans. The government added to the burdens of the peasantry by imposing new taxes and surtaxes. The number of cases involving tax arrears doubled between 1905 and 1908.

If the vast majority of peasants pulled through the Tariff War as well as they did, it was thanks, first, to their primitive self-sufficiency, and, second, to their ability to turn quickly from livestock to cereals and other crops when the prices of livestock fell badly in 1907 and 1908. While the production of corn and oats fell between 1907 and 1908 and then rose about to their former level in 1909, the production of wheat tripled and that of barley and oats doubled in the same period. The production of grapes and other fruit, clover, and industrial crops such as sugar beets also rose significantly. Serbia's agriculture took a general turn toward a more intensive farming as peasants looked increasingly to the market. Yet it was the very primitiveness of their economy, in which the need for money did not play the role it does in the agriculture of developed countries, that enabled the peasants to withstand the shock of the Tariff War. Still, as a report of the ministry of national economy pointed out in 1906, the peasants "lead the lives of martyrs, ceaselessly laboring, earning little, ill fed and ill clothed."

The Tariff War also affected the small working class of Serbia. It intensified a process of polarization already going or among the artisans to the point that, owing to a law of 1910, the guild (*esnaf*) finally became a thing of the past, and the lower ranks of artisans assumed the same position as industrial workers. As for the latter, their numbers grew steadily with the emphasis on domestic industry caused during the Tariff War, as the following table shows:

	In breweries	In flour mills	In other industries
1906	330	836	5,624
1907	344	924	6,120
1908	364	1,009	10,077

Though the total number of industrial workers in this period was miniscule, the rise in their numbers was especially great in industries other than the traditional ones of beer and flour. The number of workers in new industries nearly doubled in three years, as the process of pauperization in the countryside drove more and more peasants to seek work in urban industry. The fact that even a rapidly growing industry could not absorb this labor force quickly enough created social problems that have attended industry everywhere in its early stages. The political labor movement grew apace, though it remained as numerically weak as labor itself. In 1907–1908 the Serbian Social Democratic party numbered 780 members. In 1910–1911 the number rose to 2,889. The low wages and sometimes ghastly working conditions brought to Serbia a series of demonstrations and strikes, especially in the mines. A strike at the Majdanpek mine involved 400 workers. Another large strike, at the Čukarica sugar factory in 1907, required the intervention of the army.

Though small, Serbia's industry went through all the horrors that attended early industrialization in more developed countries: child labor, the exploitation of female labor, a working day of up to thirteen and fourteen hours, unsafe working conditions, poor sanitation, bad housing. A special feature of early Serbian industry even after 1910 was the *ajlučar* (from the Ottoman *aylıkçı*), that is, a worker paid by the month. In Serbian industry, especially in textile factories and metal plants, such workers usually slept in the factory and often worked all their waking hours without any definite schedule. In 1910, of 2,914 workers employed in the metal industry, 539 belonged to this category. In 1910 Serbia had 56 mines. The miners, a good number of them children, endured low wages and long hours and were exposed to constant mortal danger. There were no safety regulations. In 1907 there were 5,378 miners in Serbia. Their mortality rate as the result of job-related deaths was 10 for every 1,000.

Unless one counts the Mining Code of 1866, which but touched on working conditions, Serbia had little labor legislation until 1910 except for scattered laws forbidding work on Sundays and holidays and rudimentary regulations concerning hygienic conditions in factories. While the guilds existed, apprentices were placed under the tutorship of their masters, who acted as guardians. The Law on Shops in 1910 was the most significant labor law ever passed in Serbia up to that time. Though cautiously and conservatively, it did put some restrictions on the exploitation of workers. It limited the working day to ten hours, with two hours of overtime permitted when necessary. Workers under eighteen and women were not permitted to work at night. It required employers to give workers rest periods as well as free holidays and Sundays free. It also required that workers be paid in money rather than in kind, and that employers not be allowed to sell their employees goods on credit or to make them go into debt to them in any way.

However minimal these regulations were, they at least represented a serious attempt by the government to establish decent standards, even when they were not always enforced. Moreover, the law expressly permitted workers, as well as employers, to form associations for the protection of their interests. As for strikes, while the law did not forbid them, it placed limitations on the manner in which they could be carried out so as to make them less effective. Thus a trade union movement was begun in Serbia. Even before that, however, the law had recognized a chamber of labor, the first central agency Serbia's workers had to represent their interests in public life.

Serbia's Cultural Life, 1900–1914

In the early twentieth century Belgrade had a university (founded in 1905), a national museum, a national library, an ethnographic museum (founded in 1904), a national theater, and a school of music. It boasted all kinds of cultural societies. A constant stream of books flowed into the market from the Serbian Literary Cooperative and certain private publishers such as Geca Kon (founded in 1901). The interior of

Serbia was far behind Belgrade, but even so, by the beginning of the twentieth century the Serbian hinterland was by no means covered by the darkness of illiteracy as in past generations, and even the provincial towns were exposed to European culture through schools, books, newspapers, magazines, and traveling groups of artists and actors. By 1900 Vojvodina was no longer the center of Serbian culture. If Serbia was the Piedmont of Serbian unification, it was so because of its cultural, as well as its political and economic, development. That development flourished because of Serbia's receptivity to Western European culture and its ability to absorb that culture without being absorbed by it, to assimilate it while yet preserving its own national cultural identity.

In the decade before the First World War, Belgrade was rapidly gaining the air of a central European town, despite the many Turkish-style houses, coffeehouses, and cobble-stone streets that reflected its Ottoman past. In 1900 it had 69,769 inhabitants, more than double its population in 1875. By 1910 its population rose to 89,876 inhabitants. Since over 10,000 of its inhabitants were non-Serbs, the town had a cosmopolitan character. As of 1892 the streets were lighted with electricity, and in 1894 streetcars were introduced. However, between 1904 and 1914 there were scarcely a dozen automobiles in the entire city. The first motion pictures were exhibited in 1906 by a Belgrade Jew who provided a gypsy orchestra to play appropriate mood music for Western films! The theater was a large tent, but the idea caught on and a permanent movie theater was built that fall. At the Hajduk Veljko tavern, owned by an Italian, one could obtain Munich beer and French wines, eat Italian specialties, and watch "living pictures," as the Serbs called the cinema, in the summer garden. Most of the films were German and Austrian, and the newsreels came from the Pathé brothers of France.

The Belgrade of those days boasted many imposing buildings: the new palace, the Serbian National Bank, the Administration of Funds building, the National Theater, the Grand Hotel, the Officers Club. The building of the National Assembly was begun in that period but it was interrupted by the First World War. The old narrow winding streets began to give way to wide, straight avenues that had their names on signposts. In 1911 Terazije Square became the center of Belgrade with the reconstruction directed by the Frenchman Léger. The old marketplace and Miloš's fountain were moved away, along with the horse-drawn carriages, and a spacious square took their place. The whole capital underwent a general face-lifting. The operation was entrusted to the Paris architect Cambon, who tried to give Belgrade the regular streets and blocks, wide boulevards, and circles of Paris. His efforts were interrupted by the destruction of the First World War.

The first decade of the twentieth century witnessed a great leap forward in Serbian education. In 1885 there were 534 elementary schools in Serbia. In 1903–1904 there were 1,263, and by 1911, on the eve of the First Balkan War, there were 1,425. In 1899 there were in all Serbia only 19 secondary schools and vocational schools, with 386 instructors and 6,049 pupils. By 1910, there were 49 such schools, with 723 instructors and 12,892 pupils. By 1914 Belgrade had more secondary and vocational school pupils than there had been in all of Serbia at the beginning of the century.

After 1912, with the occupation and annexation of Old Serbia and Macedonia, the Serbian government made a special effort to introduce schools in those provinces. Its motive was as much nationalistic as educational. There was a desire to strengthen the Serbian element in regions separated from Serbia for five centuries and to Serbianize the Macedonian Slavs, whose sense of national identity was not yet firm. In Old Serbia, what Serbian schools there had been ceased to exist after the Serbo-Turkish War of 1876. Even with the restoration of some after 1885, there were only 33 Serbian elementary schools in the region in 1895–1896 with an enrollment of 1,800 pupils and 57 teachers. After the Serbian nationality was officially recognized by the Ottoman government, more Serbian schools were established, so that by 1912 there were 51 elementary schools with 83 teachers in Old Serbia. After the annexation of 1912, Old Serbia and Macedonia began to get more schools and teachers, but the First World War interrupted that effort almost as soon as it had begun.

A large number of Serbian students went to Austria, Belgium, Switzerland, Russia, Germany, and especially France for their higher education. It was, in part, to spare Serbs the necessity and expense of going abroad that the Great School of Belgrade was transformed in 1905 into the University of Belgrade. This was the academic counterpart of the whole movement in those years to make Serbia independent—politically, economically, and culturally—and to strengthen its role as the center of Serbian and Yugoslav unification. As the university's first rector, Sima Lozanić, declared in his inaugural address, "It is known that the German and Italian universities, by promoting the national consciousness and contributing to the national wealth, were the chief agents in preparing the way for the unification of their nations. Thus I believe that a Serbian university will perform the same service for the Serbian people."

With the establishment of a constitutional and parliamentary democracy, it became possible to establish a university with all of the rights of autonomy to which European universities were accustomed. The new university, unlike the Great School, had five instead of three colleges: theology, philosophy, law, medicine, and technical sciences. It also had two associated but separate curricula in agriculture and pharmacy. The cornerstone of the university's academic freedom was contained in the charter provision, "University instruction is free. Instructors shall be free in the presentation of their subjects. Students shall choose the lectures that they shall attend." Despite a steady rise in enrollment, the student body remained small. In 1913 the University of Belgrade had only 1,600 students and 80 instructors, but this was a great advance over the 415 students and 58 instructors in 1900. In the Balkan Wars and the First World War, over a third of the students and many professors lost their lives, and the university had to cease its operations during the enemy occupation.

Between 1905 and 1914 some of the greatest scholars of Serbia lectured in the halls of "Captain Miša's Building." Ljuba Jovanović and Stanoje Stanojević taught national history, Dragutin Anastasijević Byzantine studies, and Nikola Vulić ancient history. Jovan Cvijić offered courses in geomorphology and the geography of the Balkan Peninsula. Tihomir Djordjević lectured on Serbian ethnology and gave courses on Romanian history, literature, and language. Jovan Erdeljanović taught general and Balkan ethnography. Pavle Popović held the chair of the literature of the South Slavs, and Jovan Skerlić lectured on Serbian literary history. Bogdan Popović dealt with comparative literature in general, and French literature and language in particular. Aleksandar Belić held the chair of Slavic philology. Branislav Petronijević taught philosophy. Svetolik Radovanović taught geology and paleontology. Mihailo Petrović and Bogdan Gavrilović were the leading mathematicians. Sima Lozanić, the first rector of the university, taught organic and inorganic chemistry. Most of Serbia's leading scientists offered courses. The University of Belgrade brought together the most distinguished Serbian scholars of the day, all of them trained in the leading centers of Europe.

Although many students continued to attend the university to prepare themselves for positions in the government, this was no longer the overriding preoccupation of the school. Rather, the University of Belgrade made it possible for Serbs to get a solid training in many fields without having to go abroad and to serve their country in a variety of professions required by a rapidly developing society.

The early 1900s were an auspicious time for Serbian literature. One century had given way to another, and one generation of writers left the scene and made room for another. A whole series of Serbian authors of the late nineteenth century died in the first decade of the twentieth: Jovan Ilić in 1901, Ljubomir Nedić in 1902, Jovan Jovanović-Zmaj in 1904, Božidar Knežević and Janko Veselinović in 1905, Stevan Sremac in 1906, Pavle Marković-Adamov and Milorad Mitrović in 1907, Milovan Glišić, Simo Matavulj and Radoje Domanović in 1908, and Laza Kostić in 1910. However, there were many young writers to fill the gap and to give Serbian letters the zest and daring of youth.

The old romanticism was gone by then, though an attempt was made to create a neoromanticism. Realism continued, but in different and variegated shapes. Serbian writing of the early twentieth century was very individualistic, as though the increasing socioeconomic differentiation were reflected in cultural life as well. There was a new spirit of independence, of striking out on one's own, that was in marked contrast with the homogeneity of the preceding generation. And yet certain trends are discernible. Just as the *fin de siècle* had brought with it lethargy and even despair, so the dramatic events of 1903 and the change they brought about led to a new upsurge of national energy and optimism that the crisis of 1908 could not dampen but, rather, heightened. It was with this spirit of national destiny that Serbia plunged into the Balkan Wars only to emerge victorious and more confident than ever. It was this spirit that the armies of Austria-Hungary and its allies failed to crush even when they had the whole Serbian army on the run during the First World War.

In the early twentieth century the main goal of Serbian literature was to achieve the level of Western Europe. Whereas the models for Serbian writers during the period of realism had been Russians, by the turn of the century educated Serbs looked to France. This transformation became apparent with the foundation, in 1895, of the magazine *Srpski Pregled* (Serbian Review). It was edited by Ljubomir Nedić (1852–1902), a founder of literary criticism in Serbia. However, the most influential literary journal in Serbia in the early twentieth century was the *Srpski Književni Glasnik* (Serbian Literary Herald), founded in 1901 by Bogdan Popović (1863–1944) and edited by Jovan Skerlić (1877–1914), both educated in Paris. This first modern literary journal in Serbia was very Western in its views and very nationalist in its efforts.

Bogdan Popović was the first critic and aesthetician to introduce to Serbia the views of Western European, particularly French, literary modernism. As a professor of French, literary history, comparative literature, and aesthetics he left his mark on a whole generation of Serbian writers. When he came on the literary scene in the 1890s, Serbian literature was still regarded as an effective means for furthering Serbian nationalism. Like Nedić, though from a different perspective, Popović insisted that literature had its own values quite apart from any utilitarianism, and that while its task was to reflect nature, it was not to copy nature but to express its essence as perceived by the artists. Thus Popović proclaimed the ideal of "the adequate expression of interesting impressions," to use his favorite definition of art. For him the formal aspects of a literary work were of paramount interest, even at the expense of its content. Such a view opened the doors of Serbian literature to all those Western literary movements of the day—impressionism, expressionism, surrealism, futurism, and symbolism.

His disciple Jovan Skerlić, literary historian and critic, also left a profound impression on Serbian culture even though he died at the age of thirty-six. His most significant works were in Serbian literary history. Apart from his monumental *Istorija nove srpke književnosti* (History of Modern Serbian Literature), he left a whole series of monographs on cultural figures of the eighteenth and nineteenth centuries such as Jakov Ignjatović, Vojislav Ilić, and Svetozar Marković. He also practically resurrected the cultural history of the Serbs in the eighteenth century in *Srpska književnost u XVIII veku* (Serbian Literature in the Eighteenth Century). His *Omladina i njena književnost* (The Youth and Its Literature) is an excellent survey of Serbian cultural life in the mid-nineteenth century. Skerlić insisted that art be related to social realities. The son of a Serbian peasant who still chanted epic poetry to the strains of the *gusle* and an educated mother from Vojvodina who read books in German, Skerlić applied Western art and learning to the Serbian scene. He discouraged Serbs from fleeing from their own Serbian reality and adopting Western modes just as he opposed those who immured themselves in Serbian traditional culture without learning from the West. He inveighed equally against those who sacrificed aesthetics to social utility and those who pursued art for art's sake. The strength of the artist, he believed, lay in his ability to plumb the depths of man, through his own experience in his own environment. This could not be done by aping foreign models, nor by shunning daily life, nor by creating a romantic past that never existed, nor by simply photographing one's environment in words. While he championed artistic freedom and multiplicity of expression, he demanded both artistic form and meaningful content.

Serbia in the early twentieth century was richly endowed with a galaxy of young writers who responded to such challenges. The major poet was Milan Rakić (1876–1938), another alumnus of Parisian schools. Though a lawyer by training and a civil servant and diplomat all his adult life, Rakić was a sensitive and powerful poet who had been deeply influenced by the French Parnassians and symbolism. His love poems are among the most erotic and yet elevated and refined in Serbian letters. His thoughtful, sensitive spirit rebelled against the petty bourgeois spirit of the crudely materialistic and arriviste urban society from which he had sprung. The passionate Serb in him evoked the lost glories of the distant medieval past in such melancholy poems as *Jefimija, Simonida,* and *Napuštena Crkva* (The Abandoned Church) and expressed his hope in Serbia's future in *Na Gazi Mestanu* (At Gazi Mestan). As he wrote in his poem *Nasledje* (Heritage):

> I feel today that in me flows
> The blood of forebears brave and hardy . . .

If his was not the saber-rattling nationalism that led Serbia into the Balkan Wars, it was the patriotism of the many young Serbs who gave their lives in those holocausts and the bigger one soon to follow.

While Rakić expressed skepticism and even pessimism, he was more elevating than depressing. Not so two other Serbian poets of the day,

Sima Pandurović (1883–1960) and Vladislav Petković-Dis (1880–1917), whose verses were drenched in the despair of death and clouded minds. Milutin Bojić (1892–1917) extolled the joy of life, inner strength, and patriotism that sustained the generation that fought in the First World War. He died as a Serbian soldier in Salonika at the age of twenty-five, soon after publishing his second book of verses, *Pesme bola i ponosa* (Songs of Pain and Pride).

The outstanding story writer of the period was Borisav Stanković (1876–1927). He, too, studied in Paris. However, his contact with Western culture merely drove him deeper into a Serbian nativism that was, in fact, semi-Oriental, owing to his birth and upbringing in Vranje, a southern Serbian town that long preserved its Turkish flavor. His collection of stories *Iz starog Jevandjelija* (From the Old Gospel), published in 1899, brought him sudden success, which was heightened by a second and third collection, in 1902, *Stari dani* (Olden Days) and *Božji ljudi* (The People of God). However, he is best remembered for his *Koštana* (1902), a poorly constructed drama but one that breathes with erotic passion. His novel *Nečista Krv* (Bad Blood), published in 1911, is generally regarded as the best Serbian novel written up to that time. Stanković took all of his material from his south Serbian environment, yet the power and depth of his depiction far surpasses the local. What may have lent his works their particular popularity was his theme of the confrontation between an old half-Oriental way of life and a new Western way of life caught so faithfully in microcosm the cultural conflict through which all of Serbia was passing. Beyond this, his heroines—Koštana, Sofka, Tašana—all represent the painful struggle of the individual against cruel social conventions.

Other Serbian writers who dealt with the rising urban society of Serbia included Milutin Uskoković (1884–1915) and Branislav Nušić (1864–1938). While Uskoković's life was too short for him to develop his talents fully, his two novels, *Došljaci* (Newcomers) and *Čedomir Ilić*, and short stories, *Kad ruže cvetaju* (When Roses Bloom), showed a talent that combined a French style with a sensitive perception of Serbian life. Nušić, who lived to be seventy-four, spanned three generations of writers. His satirical plays on the mores of Serbia's *nouveaux riches* and the intrigues and ambitions of a less than intelligent or honest bureaucracy are still such popular fare that he has become a national institution. He is less remembered today for his patriotic historical plays, which nourished Serbian national consciousness on the eve of the Balkan Wars, or for his serious dramas of contemporary life. As durably funny as his social satires are, Nušić was, in fact, a sad observer of the transformation that delivered peasant Serbia into the hands of grasping businessmen and unscrupulous careerists whose lack of conscience destroyed the lives of those about them.

In the realm of academic writing, two scholars of the period deserve special mention. One is Pavle Popović (1868–1939), who, like his distinguished brother Bogdan, was educated in Paris and became a professor of Serbian literature at the University of Belgrade. Immersed in French culture, his studies of French authors were valuable contributions to Serbia's cultural Westernization. His *Pregled srpske književnosti* (Survey of Serbian Literature), still a standard work though first published in 1909, was the first to view Serbian literary development from an artistic, rather than philological and strictly historical and biographical, point of view.

The other important scholar, Slobodan Jovanović (1869–1958), was by profession a jurist and a sociologist, and a professor. Yet most Serbs know him through his many books on Western and Serbian history. Between 1903 and the First World War appeared his studies on Svetozar Marković, Machiavelli, and the leaders of the French Revolution. In 1912 he produced the first of his series on the history of Serbia in the nineteenth century after Miloš Obrenović; it dealt with the Constitutionalists and their regime. All of these works were written for the general public, without footnotes or other scholarly apparatus. Yet any historian who has ever dealt with the subjects that Jovanović treated must be impressed with his knowledge of the sources and with his competence. He was also a brilliant stylist who combined French clarity, wit, and elegance with a Serbian homespun directness, the simplicity of epic poetry, and a profound knowledge of the psyche of his people. His prose remains a model which few Serbs have equaled and none has surpassed.

One of Serbia's most vital cultural institutions was the National Library of Belgrade. In 1903 Jovan Tomić, a historian, was named its director. He remained in that post longer than any of his distinguished predecessors, until he retired in 1927. He devoted himself to the progress of the library as much as tight budgets and destructive wars would allow. How well he succeeded in the period of 1903–1914 may be seen from the following statistics:

	1903	*1913*
Manuscripts	834	1,172
Letters	1,288	2,607
Incunabula and rare books	198	219
New books: titles	38,100	49,616
" " : volumes	96,106	135,209
Titles of periodicals		782
Pictures, posters, etc.	2,422	1,256

As a scholar Tomić had conducted research in several of the great libraries in Switzerland and France, where he was a student, as well as in Italy. Thus, though not a professional librarian (there was none such in all of Serbia at the time), he had a knowledge of what a good library should be. In addition to his efforts to improve the National Library through such features as a good central catalogue, he was also concerned about the availability of books in the interior of Serbia and helped establish six branch libraries in the country. The National Library suffered severe damage from enemy bombardment during the First World War, and many of its salvaged treasures were moved to Niš, though some ended up in Germany and Bulgaria. Tomić supervised the restoration of the library after the war. He died in 1932, which spared him from seeing the library destroyed by German bombardment in 1941.

Besides the National Library in Belgrade, there were also state libraries in Niš and Kragujevac.

Serbian journalism flourished in the parliamentary democracy in Serbia after 1903. The murder of King Alexander and Queen Draga gave a spurt to Serbian newspapers in that several dailies achieved an unprecedented circulation of up to 10,000 copies in the days following the assassination. The change of regime brought an immediate increase in the number of newspapers and magazines. In 1904 there were around 90 in the whole country, of which 72 were in Belgrade and only 18 in the hinterland.

The beginning of that year saw the advent of what was to become, and still is, Serbia's outstanding daily newspaper, *Politika* (Politics). It was founded by Vladislav F. Ribnikar, who studied in Berlin and was a correspondent for a Paris newspaper before he came home to establish, with his brother Darko, a newspaper in the latest European style. *Politika* had a large format and was published on its own presses. It contained all of the features of a modern metropolitan daily: an editorial page, news from foreign correspondents and wire services, foreign and domestic political news, articles on commerce and industry, cultural items, a women's section, and literary works in serial form. It was the first Serbian newspaper to devote a special section to sports. *Politika* became a significant vehicle for the modern enlightenment of a whole nation. Despite its name, *Politika* was the first truly professional Serbian newspaper in that it was not tied to a particular political party but was politically independent. It cultivated a professional and moderate tone of writing quite different from the often crude and personal writing of the older sheets. *Politika's* example was soon followed by others.

The rise of special interest newspapers in the period also marked the coming of modern times to Serbia. The *Trgovinski Glasnik* (Commercial Herald), *Zanatlijski Savez* (Artisans' League), and *Radničke Novine* (Workers' News) all reflected the interests of certain economic groups. The last of these deserves special attention.

The *Radničke Novine* was founded in 1897 in Belgrade as a weekly socialist newspaper. Its editors included such distinguished pioneers of Serbian socialism as Vasa Pelagić, Jovan Skerlić, Živojin Baludžić, and Dragiša Lapčević. Banned in 1899, the newspaper lay dormant for three years. It was revived in 1902 by a cabinetmaker named Radovan Dragović and Dimitrije Tucović, a student. Later Dušan Popović took over as editor and sometimes as sole writer. Again banned in March 1903, the paper was resurrected again in June, just after the assassination of King Alexander. In August of that year it became the official organ of the Social Democratic party and the Main Workers League. From 1911 to 1915 it appeared as a daily—the first socialist daily in Serbia. It was banned for a while in the spring of 1914. During the First World War the newspaper moved to Niš for a year and then returned to Belgrade in 1918.

There were other socialist newspapers in Serbia. The most important were *Borba* (The Struggle), a Belgrade fortnightly that appeared between 1910 and 1914 under Dimitrije Tucović's editorship, and *Učiteljska Borba* (The Teachers' Struggle), which was also published in Belgrade, from 1911 to 1914.

In 1912 there was a total of 302 newspapers and journals published in Serbian in all the lands inhabited by Serbs. Of this number 199 were published in Serbia, 126 of them in Belgrade. These included 24 daily newspapers; 20 literary, scholarly, and political periodicals; and 82 professional publications. In 1912 these 199 newspapers and periodicals had an annual circulation of 50 million copies. This was a far cry from those six copies of the *Novine Srbske* (Serbian News) of Vienna that reached Serbia in 1816.

Like the writers, Serbian composers of the early twentieth century attempted to apply Western training and forms to the content of a Serbian national music. They had outstanding models in Josif Marinković (1851–1931) and Stevan Mokranjac (1856–1914). While both men had already made their mark in the last quarter of the nineteenth century, they did some of their best work after the turn of the century, especially in choral compositions. Though both furthered a national school of Serbian music, they stood for high Western standards. Mokranjac also continued to organize Serbian musical life. In 1903 he founded the Federation of Serbian Choirs. In 1907 he helped create the Association of Serbian Musicians. Josif Marinković was even more venturesome than Mokranjac in his Westernism. He was the first native Serb to compose original music for the Serbian Orthodox Church instead of adhering to the traditional melodies. He even composed a church hymn, "Only-Begotten Son," for choir and organ, which was an unheard-of innovation since the Serbian Church forbids the use of instrumental music.

The turn of the century brought new forms into Serbian music. Young composers were able to free themselves from their predecessors' dependence on choral music as more and more Serbs became proficient in instrumental music and committed to music as a profession. In the early twentieth century there was an upsurge of compositions for the piano and violin, orchestral music, oratorios, and even operas. The Serbian capital provided a cultural milieu and a living for a whole group of Western-trained native musicians who comprised what came to be known as the Belgrade School.

Stanislav "Staša" Binički (1872–1942), who studied in Munich, composed in 1903 the first Serbian opera to be performed. It was called *Na Uranku* (At the Rising) and was based on a text by Branislav Nušić. In 1910 Binički conducted Beethoven's Ninth Symphony and in 1911 Saint-Saëns's Christmas Oratorio. In 1912 he conducted one of the first Serbian oratorios, Stevan Hristić's *Resurrection*. In 1912, as a founder (along with Mokranjac) and director of the Stanković School of Music (founded in 1911), he organized a series of concerts in Serbia and abroad, where he brought Serbian music to the attention of the

European public. Though a prolific composer of religious and secular music, he was known to Serbs everywhere for his patriotic "March to the Drina," which he composed in 1914 during the First World War.

Petar Krstić (1877–1957), who studied in Vienna and succeeded Davorin Jenko as musical director of the National Theater, composed a whole series of "musical plays" in the style of the German *Singspiel*. The best ones were based on Serbian literary works, including *Ajša* of S. Ćorović (1905), *Koštana* of B. Stanković (1907), and *Dorćolska Posla* (Dorćol Affairs) of I. Stanojević (1908). Krstić brought Serbian orchestral compositions to new heights with such works as his Scherzo in D Minor (1902), *Pathetic* Overture (1903), and *Serbian Dances* (1904). The Belgrade School influenced later composers such as Miloje Milojević (1884–1946) and Stevan Hristić (1885–1958), both of whose early careers were interrupted by the First World War. By then a national school of Serbian music based on excellent Western training was already well established.

The advent of socialism brought something new to Serbian cultural life at the turn of the century—socialist singing groups. The first such group was founded in Belgrade in 1898 when the Society of Printing Workers organized a choir called "Djura Jakšić" and then "Jedinstvo" (Unity). This group initiated the move to raise a statue to the poet Jakšić in Kalemegdan Park. In the fall of 1905 representatives of various workers' clubs formed another choral and dramatic ensemble. It was named after the first proletarian poet of Serbia, Kosta Abrašević (1879–1898). This ensemble, which still exists, was devoted to "the singing and recitation of socialist poems and presentation of socialist dramas. . . ." Among its founders were Dimitrije Tucović and Jovan Skerlić, who was then still in his Marxist phase. The group was known for its ideological zeal and for its high artistic standards.

Outside of Belgrade, there was little musical life beyond folk music and the chants of the Serbian church. Generally there were choral societies, whose repertoire consisted largely of an ever increasing number of Serbian compositions. An exceptional figure in the musical life of the Serbian hinterland was the Czech Robert Tollinger (1859–1911), who came to Šabac from Vojvodina in 1902. He spent the last decade of his life as a gymnasium teacher of music in Šabac. Tollinger composed music based on Serbian texts, but he did not go to folk music for his themes; rather, he adhered to the classical European mode of expression. Moreover, he stressed instrumental, rather than choral, music.

Tollinger came to Šabac at a time when *La Prière d'une vierge* was considered the pinnacle of piano literature and popular tavern songs were the highest rung of sophistication. As a cellist and as a teacher and director of instrumental and vocal music, Tollinger did much to cultivate the musical tastes of his adopted city.

The National Theater of Belgrade flourished from 1900 to 1914 under the management of such luminaries as Branislav Nušić, Rista Odavić, Milan Grol, Dragomir Janković, and Milan Predić. The repertoire included a rich range of Serbian and foreign works, from the classics to the avant-garde products of symbolism and neoromanticism. Plays were usually directed by the most competent actors until 1911, when Grol and Predić engaged the Moscow director Aleksandr V. Andreev. In 1912 they also engaged a Serb, Milutin Čekić, who had been trained in Germany. These were the Belgrade theater's first professional directors. In 1909 Grol and Predić established the first Serbian school of acting, which produced a galaxy of native actors. At the same time, the National Theater encouraged foreign companies to visit, and these influenced the standards of Serbian theater. During the seasons of 1912–1913 and 1913–1914, in the atmosphere generated by the Balkan Wars, the stage became a platform for nationalist displays and patriotic tirades. The last play to be produced before the National Theater closed in 1914 because of the First World War was Jovan Dragašević's historical epic *Hajduk Veljko*. The theater then moved to Skopje, but was forced to close there too by mid-1915.

Outside of Belgrade professional theater was rare or nonexistent, except for stock companies that toured the provinces. Some of these, notably Dimitrije Ginić's troupe and Kosta Delini's troupe, were on a high artistic plane. The educational impact of their work is incalculable. These traveling companies were an important link between Serbian provincial life and the great world of European culture.

Serbian painting between 1903 and 1914, like the other Serbian arts, was much influenced by Paris, but in this case not so much directly as through central Europe. One reason for this was the influence of Djordje Krstić (1851–1907), outstanding Serbian artist and teacher, who was himself a product of the Munich School of Applied Art. Similarly, the other most influential teacher of art in Belgrade at the turn of the century, Kiril Kutlik, was a Czech who had received his training in Prague and Vienna. Munich was the chief focal point for young Serbian artists in those days. In 1894 the German school of impressionism led by Max Liebermann and Max Slevogt organized the Munich *Sezession* (Secession). It reached Vienna in 1897 and was a landmark in the history of the international art nouveau style.

The most distinguished Serbian artist of the early twentieth century was Nadežda Petrović (1873–1915), who studied with both Krstić and Kutlik in Belgrade and then went to Munich to work in the private school of the Slovene painter Anton Ažbè and in the studio of Julius Exter. Her first public exhibition, which took place in Belgrade in 1900, was so avant-garde for Serbian society that it was greeted with derision. Upon her permanent return to Serbia in 1903, she was active in writing reviews and articles on art for Serbian newspapers and magazines. She also helped found the first Serbian art society as well as a league of Yugoslav artists called *Lada*. In 1907 some of its distinguished members, including the later renowned Croatian sculptor Ivan Meštrović, put on a most significant exhibition in Belgrade which was a landmark in the development of the whole Yugoslav *moderne* movement. As a painter, Nadežda Petrović passed through various styles of avant-garde expression from impressionism to her own kind of fauvism. Her works include scenes of the Serbian landscape, peasants at work, and members of her family and circle of friends.

Another product of the Munich school of impressionism was Risto Vukanović (1873–1918). Though a Hercegovinian by birth, he was educated in Belgrade, from where he went to St. Petersburg and Munich, and it was to Belgrade that he returned with his German wife Beta, also a painter. There they opened a private school of painting and, like Nadežda Petrović, contributed much to the development and organization of art in Serbia. However, both he and his wife clung to the older style of Munich academic painting and chose to express themselves in realistic and monumental forms. Rista Vukanović died in Paris in 1918. Beta remained in Belgrade for many years.

Still another Serbian painter who studied in Munich was Leon Koen (1859–1934), whose second phase, from 1898 to 1905, reflected the Secessionist group of Franz Stuck. His themes were frequently Biblical, historical, and mythological. Another Belgrade Jew of the early twentieth century who studied in Munich and later in Paris was Moša Pijade (1890–1957). Best known as a leader of the Yugoslav communist movement, Pijade deserves to be remembered also as an excellent painter in his younger days. His three self-portraits, done between 1910 and the end of the First World War, are some of the best works of Serbian art in this period. Marko Murat (1864–1944), a Dalmatian Croat who came to Belgrade in 1894 to teach art, contributed much to the development of Serbian painting, especially with his *plein-air* style. Also a product of the Munich Academy of Art, he was especially well known in Serbia for his monumental picture "The Entry of Tsar Dušan into Dubrovnik," which won him the title of *officier d'Académie* in Paris in 1900. He exhibited his best works at the First Yugoslav Exhibition in Belgrade in 1904, after which his reputation was secure. Milan Milovanović (1876–1946) went to Munich in 1897 after working in Kiril Kutlik's school in Belgrade. He studied there with Anton Ažbè and in the Academy, and then went to Paris, to the Colarossi Academy and the École des Beaux-Arts. Returning to Belgrade in 1906, he made several tours of Old Serbia, Macedonia, and Mount Athos, and in 1908 exhibited his paintings of these regions in Belgrade. In 1912 he was made an instructor in the School of Art in Belgrade. Mališa Glišić (1885–1915), who studied with Risto Vukanović in Belgrade and spent the years 1908–1910 in Munich, served for a while as a painter for the National Theater in Belgrade. During the Balkan Wars he painted battlefield scenes, especially during the siege of Edirne (Adrianople), in which he participated. During the First World War he fought in the defense of Belgrade and also painted it. Transferred to Niš during the evacuation, he died in 1915 of typhus. Other Serbian painters of the time, all of whom studied in Munich among other places, include Miloš Golubović (1888–1961), Ljubomir Ivanović (1882–1945), Borivoje Stevanović (1878–   ), and Branko Popović (1882–1944).

The triumph of "modernism" over academic painting did not occur in Serbia until after the First World War. However, the painters of the early twentieth century made it possible for the latest trends in West European art to reach at least Belgrade if not the interior of Serbia.

Sculpture came late to Serbia, perhaps because, as in Russia, while the Orthodox Church encouraged painting, it forbade statues in the churches, just as the Muslim Turks had forbidden statuary throughout the centuries of their rule. Nevertheless, the Serbian government had need of public monuments. They, too, were a sign of Serbia's modernization. The first native of Serbia to elevate the art of Serbian sculpture to the standards of European art was Djordje Jovanović (1861–1953). After having studied art in Vienna, Munich, and Paris, he returned to Belgrade in 1892 to become a teacher. In 1905 he joined

Risto Vukanović and Marko Murat in founding an art school in Belgrade. He later was its director till 1921. He was commissioned to do some of Belgrade's best-known monuments and busts of Serbia's distinguished men.

Another Serbian sculptor of the period was Simeon Roksandić (1874–1943), a native of Croatia. After studying art in Budapest and Munich, in 1897 he made his home in Serbia, where he died during the Second World War. He was best known for his powerful sculptures of such classical themes as the "Boy with Turtle," "The Fisherman," and "Boy Plucking a Thorn from His Foot." He also made the monument at Čukur Fountain (Kükürt Çeşme) commemorating the incident in 1862 that led to the Turkish bombardment of Belgrade.

The Second Balkan Alliance System, 1908–1912

Austria-Hungary's annexation of Bosnia and Hercegovina was a major turning point, not just for Serbia but for the European Powers as well, on the road that was to lead to the First World War. The Dual Monarchy's overweening action widened the growing rift between the Central Powers and the Entente. Serbia benefited from the crisis in that it could no longer be ignored by the powers as a negligible quantity. Serbia was more determined than ever after 1908 to pursue its own ends in southeastern Europe before it was destroyed by Austria-Hungary.

The attainment of Serbia's goals in the Balkans required Great Power support and the solidarity of the Balkan peoples. During the crucial three years following the annexation crisis, these goals were entrusted largely to Foreign Minister Milovan Milovanović.

Among the Great Powers, Milovanović relied most heavily on Russia, which he hoped would play the same role in the unification of the Serbs that France had played in the unification of Italy. In this he did not enjoy the wholehearted support of his countrymen, for Russia's weakness in the annexation crisis had been most disappointing. Yet Milovanović correctly gauged Russia's position after 1908.

Russia had three traditional policies to choose from with respect to the Balkans: to dominate the Porte as its protector, to divide the Balkans with Austria, or to organize the Christian Balkan nations for their common purposes. The nationalistic Young Turk revolution made the first course impossible. The annexation crisis made the second choice impossible; Austria-Hungary's act had ended the Austro-Russian agreement of May 5, 1897, to maintain the status quo in the Balkans. Only a Balkan alliance was left. Izvolskii had made quite clear Russia's choice of this course in his speech of December 25, 1908, to the Duma, in which he openly advocated a league of Balkan states, including Turkey. Three days later Sir Edward Grey wired to Sir Arthur Nicolson, the British ambassador in St. Petersburg, "Izvolskii's speech seems to me to be very satisfactory. . . . I am glad he emphasized the need for community of feeling between the Balkan States and the combination of all three of them with Turkey for defense of common interests. I am quite in favor of this and will encourage it, whenever I can." To achieve his purpose, in 1909 Izvolskii sent to Belgrade the Russian minister in Teheran, Nikolai Hartwig, a zealous Panslavist.

From 1909, a Bulgarian alliance became the cornerstone of Milovanović's Balkan policy. His great fear was that Austria-Hungary would be able to win over Bulgaria for its purposes, thus placing Serbia in a vise. Bulgaria was the strongest state in the Balkans at the time, with the best army and greatest prestige. It was true that Bulgarian and Serbian interests clashed in Macedonia, but so did Bulgarian and Austro-Hungarian interests. Both had their eyes on Salonika and the Aegean. Having no common border with Austria-Hungary, Bulgaria was not nearly as exposed as Serbia was to the might of the Dual Monarchy.

In March 1909 Milovanović visited Sofia and was warmly received. Eager to enlist Bulgarian support against Austria-Hungary, Milovanović offered a partition of Macedonia between Serbia and Bulgaria. However, the Bulgarians insisted on the territorial integrity of all Macedonia; besides, they were unwilling to give up their very successful policy of maneuvering between the Russian and Habsburg empires. How far mistrust divided the Serbs and Bulgars may be seen from the fact that when the latter suggested, at the height of the annexation crisis, that Serbia occupy the Sancak of Novi Pazar, Milovanović feared that Austria-Hungary had put the Bulgars up to it in order to have an excuse to invade Serbia. Despite these mutual suspicions, Milovanović needed the Bulgars. Just one week after Serbia's ignominious recognition of the annexation of Bosnia and Hercegovina by Austria-Hungary, Milovanović invited Bulgarian Premier Malinov to consider an accord with Serbia. "Serbo-Bulgarian solidarity," Milovanović wrote him, "is the prime and most indispensable condition, not to be replaced by anything, for the independence of the Balkan Peninsula and the solution of the Balkan problem on the basis: the Balkans to the Balkan peoples." The Bulgarian premier's reply was restrained; he feared that the news of Milovanović's offer would reach the Porte while Milovanović feared that Malinov would use his offer in trading with Vienna.

The Russians undertook a concerted effort to carry out Izvolskii's plan of a Balkan alliance. In Istanbul, Russian Minister Charykov promoted the idea of a Balkan league that would include the Turks. Nothing came of it except a series of meetings in late 1909 and 1910, which brought many Balkan leaders face to face. Tsar Ferdinand visited Belgrade as well as St. Petersburg and Istanbul. King Peter journeyed to Sofia and the Russian capital. In Belgrade Russian Minister Hartwig arranged for *pourparlers* between Milovanović and Bulgarian Minister Toshev. In September 1909 the Bulgarian minister to Rome, D. Rizov, visited Belgrade after a reconnaissance of European Turkey. He made clear to Milovanović that Bulgaria wished to keep Macedonia intact, perhaps as an autonomous province. Rather, he suggested a division in which Serbia would take the Sancak of Novi Pazar, the Albanian littoral at the mouth of the Drin, and Old Serbia to the Šar Mountains, while Bulgaria would take Thrace, including Edirne. Like many other Serbian political leaders, Milovanović doubted that a separate Macedonia could long maintain its autonomy against Bulgaria but would merely add another unnecessary and complicating factor in Balkan politics.

Throughout the three years following the annexation of Bosnia and Hercegovina, all the Balkan states were engaged in seeking agreements with one another. What troubled Belgrade was that these arrangements bypassed Serbia. Tsar Ferdinand attempted to bring Bulgaria, Greece, and Montenegro together as a counterweight to Romanian-Turkish rapprochement. However, in March 1911 a new pro-Russian government was formed in Bulgaria. With Russian encouragement, the new Bulgarian Premier and Foreign Minister Geshov sought an accord with Serbia in order to put an end to Turkish punitive measures in Macedonia. Negotiations began just as the Italo-Turkish War broke out in September 1911. After five months of difficult negotiation, carefully watched over by the Russian ministers in Sofia and Belgrade, a Serbo-Bulgarian Treaty was finally concluded on March 13, 1912.

By this treaty the two states agreed not only to aid each other if either were attacked, but to take joint action against any power that tried to "annex, occupy, or even temporarily to invade with its armies" any Balkan territory under Turkish rule, even though only one of the signatories considered the attempt to be injurious to its interests. This article was obviously aimed at Austria-Hungary. Other articles provided that the two parties would not conclude peace except jointly, and that a third party could be admitted into the alliance with the agreement of both signatories. This last provision had especially Montenegro in view.

A crucial secret annex to the treaty provided, in the first article, that the two allies would confer with each other whenever the *status quo* in the Balkans was threatened and one of them concluded that military action was necessary. Any agreement was to be communicated to Russia for its consent, and any disagreement was to be submitted to Russia for arbitration. Despite this gesture toward Russia, the essence of this provision lay in the fact that Serbia and Bulgaria reserved the right to decide when it was most convenient for them to attack Turkey. Article 2 provided that all territories won from Turkey should be held in condominium until their repartition, within three months after the conclusion of peace. The annex stipulated three zones—one to go to Serbia, one to Bulgaria, while the third, claimed by both allies, was to be negotiated. The Serbian zone was to consist of the area north and west of the Šar Mountain range, that is, Old Serbia and the Sancak of Novi Pazar. The Bulgarian zone was to include the territory east of the Rhodope Mountains and the Struma River. The intermediate regions of Macedonia lying between the Šar Mountains and the Rhodope Mountains, the Archipelago, and Lake Ohrid were, if possible, to be formed into an autonomous province (as Bulgaria had long desired); however, if this were impossible, Bulgaria was to have the southern region, including Ohrid, Serbia was to be awarded the northern region, and the disposition of the rest was to be left up to the arbitration of the Russian tsar.

Finally, a separate military convention was concluded at Varna on May 29, 1912, by the two allies, with further agreements by their general staffs in June and August defining what help each ally was to supply the other in case of war.

This Serbo-Bulgarian alliance was followed by a Greco-Bulgarian alliance of June 12, 1912, which was purely defensive in character. It provided that if either of the signatories were attacked by Turkey, the other would come to its aid. A military convention between Bulgaria and Greece was signed in October 1912.

Serbia's relations with Montenegro were even more complicated than with Bulgaria. Though both states were Serbian ethnically, politically there had been a long dynastic rivalry between Prince Nicholas and both the Obrenović and Karadjordjević rulers of Serbia. Relations became particularly strained in October 1907 when a local plot against the life of Prince Nicholas—known in Montenegrin history as the "Bomb Affair"—was found to have connections with Belgrade. Austria-Hungary's annexation of Bosnia and Hercegovina momentarily brought the two states together again; both lodged protests against the annexation. Cetinje sent an emissary, Janko Vukotić, to Belgrade in October 1908. He was arrested on the way, in Zagreb, which increased his outrage against the Dual Monarchy. In Belgrade he and the Serbian government agreed to collaborate and to conclude a treaty and a military convention in the future.

This friendship cooled quickly because of another plot against Nicholas—the "Kolašin Affair" of 1910, which was put down with great severity. Cetinje blamed the Serbian government and King Peter for the outcry in the Serbian press against the manner in which the accused were tried and punished, as well as for harboring Montenegrin political émigrés. When the Serbian government expelled some of these émigrés, it only heightened the indignation of the Serbian press against Prince Nicholas and his government.

In 1910 another event took place that strained relations between Montenegro and Serbia. Prince Nicholas proclaimed himself king on the fiftieth anniversary of his reign. This was largely an act of vanity on the part of a despotic old ruler and not at all hailed by his people. The press of Serbia was unanimously opposed to it as being harmful to the cause of future Serbian unification. Belgrade's *Politika* wrote, "The whole tendency of the Cetinje celebrations is toward supremacy among the entire Serbian people. . . . Serbia is alone called upon to be the plenipotentiary representative and leader of all the other branches of the Serbian people." It is significant that while Serbia sent only Crown Prince George to the jubilee in Cetinje, Bulgaria was represented by Tsar Ferdinand himself as well as his son. Nicholas and Ferdinand took the occasion to conclude an entente in which they mutually agreed that "neither will undertake any action in the Balkans without previously informing the other." However, Serbian-Montenegrin relations were so cool that Montenegro was not even asked at the time to join the Serbo-Bulgarian alliance.

Instead, Russia concluded a secret military convention with Montenegro in late 1910 in which Russia assumed the obligation of providing the Montenegrin army with an annual subsidy, munitions, and military instructors. In exchange, article 3 stipulated, "The Royal Government [of Montenegro] assumes the obligations of placing all of the armed forces of the Kingdom at the disposal of H.I.M. [the Emperor of Russia] at his first call." The treaty also obliged Montenegro not to undertake any military action or conclude any military treaties with anyone else without previous Russian consent. In case of war, the Montenegrin general staff was to be headed by a Russian general. Thus Montenegro became, in fact, the military preserve of Russia.

In 1911 King Nicholas proposed to Serbia an agreement for common action against Turkey, which Serbia rejected at the time. However, in March 1912, during a state visit to Vienna, King Nicholas had talks with Bulgarian representatives which led him to propose to Bulgaria an offensive military alliance against Turkey in August 1912. Bulgaria accepted and also informed Serbia and Greece. Accordingly, on September 14, 1912, the representatives of Serbia and Montenegro, meeting in Lucerne, Switzerland, signed a similar treaty. About the same time (perhaps as early as June 1912) Montenegro also concluded a similar treaty with Greece. With these agreements the Balkan alliance system of the four Christian nations bordering on European Turkey was complete. All that remained was to find an auspicious occasion for war against the Turks.

Serbia and the Balkan Wars, 1912–1913

The year 1912 was an auspicious time to start a war against Turkey. The Turks were still engaged in their war with Italy over Tripoli. European Turkey was wracked by mutinies against the Young Turk regime. The Albanians were engaged in a full-scale national rebellion that wreaked havoc in Old Serbia and Macedonia as well. When pro-Bulgarian guerrillas in Macedonia threw bombs in the Turkish market of Kočani, and the Turks replied with a massacre of local Christians, a mass demonstration of protest took place in Sofia. Meanwhile border incidents between Turkey and its northern neighbors occurred almost constantly.

Once both sides began to mass troops along their borders, the European Powers sought to convince the Balkan states that they would not countenance a war. Instead of heeding these signals, the Balkan allies engaged in last-minute talks to coordinate their efforts. Turkey's attempt to put pressure on its would-be assailants by mobilizing its troops, especially near the Bulgarian border, under the guise of maneuvers backfired. The allies replied with an open mobilization of their own. On October 8, 1912, by previous arrangement with its allies, Montenegro declared war on Turkey.

Two days later Austria-Hungary and Russia sent a rather tardy note to Turkey calling for reforms in the spirit of article 23 of the Treaty of Berlin (1878). They also sent the Balkan allies a firm note informing them that in the event of any armed conflict, they would permit "no modification of the territorial *status quo*" in the Balkans. The three Balkan allies that were not yet at war with Turkey replied by listing their grievances against Turkey and stating that they would present their demands for reforms directly to the Porte. On October 13 they sent identical notes to the Porte in which they categorically demanded that basic reforms involving administrative autonomy, elections to regional assemblies, local militias, and free education be carried out within six months in European Turkey.

The Porte replied to this quasi ultimatum by recalling its envoys from Belgrade, Sofia, and Athens. Having all the excuse they needed, the three allies declared war on Turkey on October 17 and 18 in three separate acts. On the latter day Turkey ended its war with Italy, by the Treaty of Lausanne, in order to free itself for war in the Balkans. In so doing it gave up Tripoli.

There were three theaters of war: on the Turco-Bulgarian frontier in Thrace, in Macedonia and Old Serbia, and on the Greco-Turkish border. Four small countries whose total population numbered barely 10 million took on an empire of nearly 25 million inhabitants. However, the Balkan allies were able to put into the field a total of 725,000 men (of whom 553,000 were fighters); besides, the allies had the support of the Christian population of European Turkey. The Turks had 307,000 troops in the field, with another 104,000 Albanians; however, the Albanians would not fight outside their own ethnic territory. The Greek fleet prevented the Turks from moving their soldiers from North Africa to the Balkans.

All of the allies garnered great victories against the Turks and routed them on all fronts. The Bulgars defeated the Turks at Kirk Kilissa (Kirklareli) on October 24, and in less than a month Istanbul was within earshot of Bulgarian guns. The Serbs crossed the Macedonian border on October 19–20 and on October 24 inflicted a defeat on the Turks at Kumanovo and effected a meeting with Montenegrin forces in the Sancak of Novi Pazar. After 523 years the battlefield of Kosovo was again in Serbian hands, as well as the patriarchal church of Peć. Between November 15 and November 19 the Serbian First Army fought a decisive battle at Bitola (Monastir), in which the Turks lost half their men while the other half fled to Albania. The Greeks were equally victorious in Thessaly and quickly marched into Macedonia to take Salonika on November 9, one day ahead of the Bulgars. Even before that, on November 3, the Turks appealed to the powers for their intervention. Having nothing left to them in Europe except Ioannina, Shkodër (Scutari), and Edirne (Adrianople), the Turks chose to propose peace to the Bulgars, who had been stopped at Çatalca, about 20 miles west of Istanbul, thanks as much to cholera as to Turkish resistance. On December 3 Bulgaria, Serbia, and Montenegro signed an armistice with the Turks. The Greeks did not join them, for they still hoped to win the siege of Ioannina and thus to gain Epirus.

The peace conference opened in London on December 16, under the watchful eyes of the ambassadors of the powers and Sir Edward Grey. It was attended by the Greeks as well, even though they were still fighting. On January 23, 1913, just as an agreement was in sight, the Young Turks, who could not bear the loss of Edirne and the Aegean islands, overthrew the Turkish government and resumed fighting, with disastrous results. The Greeks took Ioannina on March 6, and the Bulgarians, aided by the Serbs, took Edirne on March 26. Five days later, at Turkey's insistence, the powers intervened, and another armistice was eventually concluded.

According to the peace treaty, which was signed in London on May 30, 1913, the Turks gave up all their European territory beyond the line between Enez (Enos) and Midye (Midia), except for Albania, which was only nominally theirs at the time. How this territory was to be divided was not left up to the belligerents but to the six powers of Europe.

The conference of ambassadors meeting in London under Grey's chairmanship was split into the two blocs of the day—the Entente and the Triple Alliance. No longer committed to their earlier insistence on no territorial modifications in the Balkans, the diplomats of the powers undertook to carve up the map even as the belligerents in the Balkans were carving up the actual territory. The problems that concerned the conference most were Albanian independence, Serbia's demand for a commercial outlet to the sea, and Montenegro's demand for Shkodër and northern Albania. All three issues were painfully related.

Austria-Hungary and Italy both regarded Albania as a natural field for the expansion of their influence and as a barrier to Serbia's expansion. On November 10, 1912, Austria-Hungary had formally informed the Serbian government that it was not to aspire to an Adriatic outlet through Albanian territory. A week later it also demanded that Montenegro abandon its claims to Shkodër. When the whole matter came before the London conference, Serbia and Greece were forced to give up their plans to partition Albania. The conference also refused to grant Serbia a corridor to the Adriatic coast. Instead, it decided that Serbia would have free access, by rail, to a neutral Albanian port. As for Albania, the conference settled on autonomy under Turkish suzerainty. Austria-Hungary tried to have as much territory as possible awarded to Albania—not only Shkodër but a good deal of Old Serbia and Macedonia, including Peć, Prizren, Djakovica, Debar, Ohrid, and Struga. Eventually only Shkodër was awarded to Albania, and even this was difficult, since the Montenegrin forces of occupation would not leave it until a naval blockade by the powers forced them to withdraw.

By the Treaty of London of May 30, 1913, the Turks were allowed to keep no European territory except for a small patch east of a line from Enez to Midye, and were forced to give up Crete. The status of Albania and the Aegean islands was left up to the decision of the powers. It was now left for the Balkan allies to divide up their own spoils. The attempt inevitably revived old hostilities and conflicting ambitions, especially between Serbia and Greece on the one hand and Bulgaria on the other.

Serbia was dissatisfied with its agreement of February 24, 1912, with Bulgaria, and in late January 1913 asked for a revision of the treaty.

In its notes of February 22 and May 5, 1913, it elaborated on its position. In brief, the Serbian argument was that it had concluded the agreement in the expectation of getting an outlet to the sea, which it regarded as vital to its economic development. Inasmuch as the powers blocked its egress to the Adriatic, Serbia was forced to ensure itself an outlet via Salonika, to be served by a railroad linking Skopje and Bitola with that port. To justify its demand, the Serbian government explained that while Serbia had had to forego an important acquisition with the creation of Albania, Bulgaria had received a sizable area in Thrace that had not been in the original agreement. Thus Serbia was allegedly entitled to additional compensation in Macedonia, not only in the middle zone disputed by Serbia and Bulgaria but also in the rest of Macedonia. To buttress its arguments, the Serbian government pointed to Bulgaria's failure to send troops to the Vardar front as envisaged by their agreement, whereas Serbia had sent troops to aid the Bulgars in Thrace. In short, the Serbs held that revision of the Serbo-Bulgarian agreement was necessary in that it did not really correspond to the scope and results of the actual military operations.

The Bulgarian government rejected Serbia's claims with arguments of its own. The Bulgars were not to blame if Serbia abandoned its claim to an Adriatic outlet without consulting Bulgaria; besides, Bulgaria had been forced by the powers to give up Silistria to Romania and to abandon certain positions along the Sea of Marmora. As for the disposition of Bulgarian troops during the war, their participation in the Vardar front had been agreed upon conditionally; the important thing was that it was the Bulgarian armies that broke the main military might of the Turks. With these and other arguments the Bulgarian government declined to see why any revision of the Serbo-Bulgarian agreement was necessary.

The Greeks had their own quarrel with the Bulgars, which became especially bitter after the Greeks occupied Salonika. On November 3, 1912, the Greek government presented the Bulgars with its proposals for determining the new boundary, which Sofia also rejected, as it did two subsequent Greek proposals.

The nationalistic press in all three countries raised a clamor that swept up the masses. Incidents flared up wherever the various forces of occupation met. Each country had its own war party and bellicose military clique. Inevitably, Serbia and Greece banded together and concluded an agreement, on May 1, 1913. The eleven-point treaty

provided for the following: a mutual guarantee of each other's possessions and mutual aid in case of attack; mutual support in their
territorial claims and the obligation to deal with Bulgaria jointly; a
joint effort to gain a common border west of the Vardar; recognition
of the principle that the Greco-Bulgarian and Serbo-Bulgarian borders
should be based on what each side actually occupied as well as on the
principle of equilibrium; disputes with Bulgaria were to be submitted
to the heads of the Triple Entente for arbitration, and if Bulgaria refused, Serbia and Greece were to aid one another; Serbia was to have
free use of the port of Salonika for fifty years, via a railway linking
with Skopje and Bitola. A military convention was signed on the same
day specifying what help Serbia and Greece were to give one another
in the event of an attack by Bulgaria or any other state.

Although Romania avoided joining this alliance, by June 10, 1913,
it was ready to inform the Great Powers that it could not remain
neutral if a new conflict in the Balkans should ensue. For its part, Bulgaria found a natural supporter in Austria-Hungary. Russia was
anxious to prevent any conflict and, employing the status of arbiter
that the Balkan agreements had given it, offered its arbitration. When
neither Serbia nor Bulgaria responded positively, the Russian government invited all four premiers of the Balkan states, on May 30, 1913, to
St. Petersburg.

While not refusing this summons, the Bulgarian war party, headed
by Tsar Ferdinand, decided to confront Russia with an accomplished
fact by winning a quick war against Serbia and Greece. On the night
of June 29–30, 1913, Bulgarian troops attacked the forces of both
countries without any declaration of war. Indeed, Tsar Ferdinand
neglected even to inform his own government. When it learned of the
attack, the horrified cabinet ordered General Savov, the Bulgarian commander, to halt the offensive. Premier Danev asked Belgrade and
Athens to order a cease-fire, but it was too late. The news of the attack
reached Belgrade just in time to interrupt a debate in the National
Assembly over the hotly contested issue of whether Premier Pašić
should accept the Russian invitation to St. Petersburg. The Serbian
war hawks were as pleased as their Bulgarian counterparts at the prospect of a war, and as confident of winning it. Romania declared war
on Bulgaria on July 10, while Turkey took advantage of the situation
by reoccupying eastern Thrace and Edirne.

The Second Balkan War was a disaster for Bulgaria. It faced not only a Serbian army of some 350,000 men, supported by 12,000 Montenegrins, and a Greek army of about 200,000, but also some 437,000 Romanian troops and 255,000 Turkish troops when these two countries joined the fray. The Serbs trounced the Bulgars at Bregalnica, in the Vardar valley, between June 30 and July 8. The nine-day battle was fought along a front of 75 kilometers, with great losses on both sides. The Serbs lost about 16,000 men, the Bulgars about 25,000. Many deaths were caused by cholera, which the Bulgarian troops brought with them from Thrace. Meanwhile, the Greeks overwhelmed the Bulgars and occupied Kavalla, Serrai, and Drama. On July 11 the Romanians occupied the Dobrudja quadrilateral without firing a shot. Throughout, Tsar Ferdinand urged Austria-Hungary to take the opportunity to crush Serbia, but Vienna preferred to choose its own time. Peace negotiations began in Bucharest on July 30, 1913. By August 10 the peace treaty was signed.

In general, the Treaty of Bucharest awarded the Serbs and the Greeks all of the Macedonian territory that their troops occupied at the time. Thus it marked a military defeat for Bulgaria as well as a diplomatic defeat for that country's new protector, Austria-Hungary. The Russians took a middle ground in supporting Serbia's expansion without diminishing Bulgarian gains too drastically. By the Treaty of Bucharest Serbia shared with Montenegro the Sancak of Novi Pazar, and it received the provinces of Kosovo, Metohija, and all of nothern and central Macedonia, known as Vardar Macedonia, which included not only the disputed middle zone to which the Serbo Bulgarian treaty of alliance had referred but also most of Bulgaria's undisputed share as well. The Kingdom of Serbia increased its territory from some 48,300 square kilometers to 87,300 square kilometers, or nearly double, and its population from around 2,912,000 to 4,444,000. In addition to the size and economic potential of these acquisitions, Serbia's victories in the Balkan Wars were of great historical moment. No more Serbs were left under Turkish rule. Kosovo had finally been avenged. Moreover, the Serbs of Serbia and the Serbs of Montenegro had at long last achieved a common border, and their political unification now seemed more possible than ever. Serbia also came to include many non-Serbs— Macedonian Slavs, Turks, Vlachs, Albanians, and others; however, the Serbian policy was to regard the Macedonian Slavs as so many Serbs and to look upon the rest as unwanted interlopers or material for eventual assimilation.

Bulgaria received only a small portion of eastern, or Pirin, Macedonia and a stretch between the Mesta and Maritsa rivers on the Aegean seaboard, with the second-rate port of Dede Agach (Alexandroupolis). Greece received southern, or Aegean, Macedonia and a portion of Thrace, including the ports of Salonika and Kavalla. A part of eastern Thrace with Edirne was restored to Turkey. Romania received the southern Dobrudja. Thus Bulgaria lost not only the better part of its gains but also some of its previous territory.

The boundaries between the allies were defined in special bilateral agreements. Serbia signed such an agreement with Greece on August 16, 1913, and with Montenegro on November 12, 1913. Turkey took advantage of the dissolution of the Balkan alliance and gained various economic and other concessions in separate peace treaties with Bulgaria (in Istanbul, September 24, 1913), Greece (in Athens, November 14, 1913), and Serbia (March 14, 1914).

With the end of the Second Balkan War, Serbia found itself in a new position in Balkan affairs. The Balkan alliance system was no more. The peninsula was divided into two blocs—Serbia, Greece, and Romania versus Bulgaria and Turkey. As the Great Powers exerted efforts to win over the various Balkan countries, the hostility between the Triple Entente and the Triple Alliance found expression in Balkan politics as well. For Serbia this meant an even greater fear of Austria-Hungary and dependence on Russia and the Entente.

Despite its severe losses in life and its material sacrifices, Serbia emerged from the Balkan Wars stronger than ever. Its economy was making rapid strides forward, partly in response to the challenge of the Tariff War with Austria-Hungary. Railway building received a fresh start, so that by 1914 Serbia had over 1,000 miles of railroads. State finances had improved. Impressive cultural advances had been made. Serbia's territory was practically doubled. Its prestige among the South Slavs was greater than ever, and though the Bulgarians were obviously no longer included in the grand design of South Slavic unification, the Yugoslav idea was stronger than ever, especially in the Habsburg lands. There was every reason for optimism, except one: Austria-Hungary remained an obstacle to the realization of the Yugoslav idea and a threat to Serbia's very existence.

Greater Serbia and the Yugoslav Idea

Out of the nationalism of the nineteenth century emerged three visions that moved Serbs: a Greater Serbia, a united Yugoslavia, and a Balkan Peninsula that belonged to the Balkan peoples. All three ideas came to a head in the early twentieth century.

The First Balkan War brought the last of these goals dramatically forward by driving the Turk almost entirely out of Europe. However, as the Second Balkan War demonstrated, once this goal was attained, the Balkan alliance system was broken up by rival ambitions. Serbia and the rest of the Balkan allies showed that their territorial aspirations far surpassed the limits of national self-determination, and that they were willing and eager to appropriate areas inhabited by other nationalities. After the Second Balkan War it was impossible to include the Bulgars in the Yugoslav confraternity even though, ethnically, they were no less "Yugoslavs," that is, South Slavs, than were the Serbs, Croats, or Slovenes. Aside from the conflict over Macedonia, the Balkan alliance would not have preserved its original *raison d'être* once the Ottoman lands of Europe had been liberated. After 1913 it was clear that to finish the task of liberation in the Balkans would require a confrontation with the Habsburg Empire. Bulgaria and Greece had no interest in this formidable task as neither had even common borders with the Dual Monarchy. On the contrary, Bulgaria thought it to her own interest to ally herself more closely with Austria-Hungary.

If the idea of Balkan unity was dead in 1913, Yugoslavism was not. Having waned for a while after the generation of Bishop Juraj Strossmayer (1815–1905) and Franjo Rački (1828–1894) left the scene, the Yugoslav idea grew strong again after the turn of the century, especially in the Habsburg lands, where the Croats, Serbs, and Slovenes had a more immediate interest in union than did the Serbs of an already independent Serbia. This resurgence of Yugoslavism found its strongest political expression in the Croato-Serbian Coalition, which was founded in Croatia on December 12, 1905, by a group of Croatian and Serbian political parties, and in the common indignation that seized all South Slavs over Austria-Hungary's annexation of Bosnia and Hercegovina.

Even in Serbia itself, where the idea of a Greater Serbia in which all Serbs were united had a more compelling attraction than union with other South Slavs, the Yugoslav idea was strong. Its chief proponents in Serbia were not the statesmen, who, until 1914, saw it as a distant dream rather than as a practical present goal. It was the Serbian intelligentsia who promoted Yugoslavism in Serbia in the early 1900s, just as they had in 1848, and as then, so now the government in Belgrade followed rather than led.

In 1904 a group of young intellectuals and students founded a society in Belgrade known as the *Slovenski Jug* (The Slavic South). Its program proclaimed the unity of the Serbs, Croats, Slovenes, and Bulgars. Among its activities this very popular organization presented "Yugoslav Soirées" at Kalemegdan Park, which was decked out with banners bearing the slogan "South Slavs—Unite!"

Though the Serbian government gave material support to these gatherings, it felt understandably restrained about flaunting political Yugoslavism in Vienna's face, especially after its ignominious promises to Austria-Hungary in its note of 1909 after the annexation of Bosnia and Hercegovina. However, it could at least have Belgrade play the role of the cultural Piedmont of the South Slavs. Thus when delegates from all the South Slavic lands came to the coronation of King Peter I in 1904, an exhibition of Yugoslav art was arranged for the occasion. In May 1904 Belgrade was host to some 200 Bulgarian students. In the same year it was host to the First Congress of Yugoslav Youth, a conference of South Slavic writers, and a congress of South Slavic physicians. The writers organized congresses in Belgrade in 1905 and in Sofia in 1906. At the outbreak of Serbia's Tariff War with Austria-Hungry in 1906, South Slavic students throughout the Habsburg dominions staged demonstrations in favor of Serbia. When the Austro-Hungarian government refused to permit forty members of a Zagreb youth choir to go to Belgrade, their Serbian hosts simply crossed the river into Zemun on the Austro-Hungarian side and held their celebration there. In August 1906 a congress of 800 teachers from Serbia, Macedonia, Bosnia and Hercegovina, Dalmatia, Vojvodina, Slavonia, Croatia, and Montenegro met in Belgrade and were received by King Peter. And so it went.

The Annexation Crisis of 1908, the great treason trial of fifty-three Serbs held by the Austro-Hungarian authorities in Zagreb, and the Friedjung Trial in Vienna in December 1909 only inflamed Yugoslav passions all the more. The youth in all the South Slavic land organized societies, staged demonstrations, and founded newspapers and journals that propagated Yugoslav unity. Serbia's successes in the Balkan Wars gave them more enthusiasm than ever. After 1913 there was an all-pervasive condition in the air that the final liberation of all Yugoslavs was at hand. This conviction was shared by Serbia's youth. The idea of Serbia acting as the binding center of a great union of nearly 12 million Yugoslavs was a powerful myth. In June 1903, when the newly elected King Peter had stopped in Vienna on his way to Belgrade, several hundred Serbian, Croatian, and Slovenian students had greeted him at the station with the cry "Long live the Yugoslav King!" Those words still had a mighty echo ten years later.

Nevertheless, in Serbia itself, while the Yugoslav ideology was nurtured with sincere enthusiasm, especially by the intelligentsia, the idea of the unification of all Serbs offered a more immediate attraction. Before the Balkan Wars Serbia's population was 2.9 million. After the Balkan Wars it was 4.4 million, including many Albanians, Turks, and Macedonian Slavs (whom Belgrade regarded as Serbs). In view of the fact that there were about 7 million Serbs in southeastern Europe, the task of Serbian unification was only half done by 1913. There was still the prospect of unification with Montenegro, with which Serbia now had a common border. But the greatest number of Serbs outside of Serbia lived in the Austro-Hungarian lands—especially in Vojvodina and Bosnia-Hercegovina, but also in Croatia, Slavonia, and Dalmatia. The fact that these Serbs lived in ethnically mixed areas in which they were a bare majority, a mere plurality, or even less than that did not dismay the proponents of a Greater Serbia. The Pan-Serbs were just as willing to incorporate the Croats as fellow citizens as some nationalists in Croatia were disposed to regard their Serbian neighbors as "Orthodox Croats." In any event, the proponents of a Greater Serbia were not all that bound to the doctrine of national self-determination anyway, but were led by geopolitical, economic, and military considerations as well as by the historic myth of resurrecting Tsar Dušan's empire, which was hardly exclusively Serbian in composition.

Again, as with the Yugoslav idea in Serbia, it was not the statesmen who upheld the goal of a Greater Serbia; they were restrained by their dealings with Austria-Hungary and the other Great Powers. Indeed, the most active proponents of the Greater Serbia idea, the military, regarded the statesmen as cowards and traitors to the cause. Ever since

1903 there existed a precarious balance between the civilian and the military authorities in Serbia; King Peter let the political parties rule, while the military conspirators who had murdered King Alexander had the final word in army matters. It was the military who were willing to risk a war over Bosnia and Hercegovina in 1908. When the Serbian government was forced instead to make a humiliating state ment in March 1909 in which it accepted Austria-Hungary's annexation of those provinces and promised to reduce the Serbian army and disband all volunteer groups, many Serbian army officers were disgusted, as were many civilians.

Out of this feeling of bitter disappointment came the formation of two patriotic organizations whose methods were quite different but whose aims were so similar as to cause others, notably the Austro-Hungarian government in 1914, to confuse them. They were the *Narodna odbrana* (The National Defense) and *Ujedinjenje ili smrt* (Unification or Death). Both organizations were for a Greater Serbia.

The National Defense was founded in December 1908, in the midst of the Annexation Crisis. A group of prominent citizens organized it to channel the indignation of the Serbian nation into practical measures such as the sending of volunteer units to Bosnia and Hercegovina to fight the Austro-Hungarian forces. It was precisely such action that the Serbian government was forced to disavow and suppress by its note of March 1909 in answer to Austria-Hungary's ultimatum. After that the National Defense was required to concentrate on cultural activities. However, it did maintain a network of confidential agents among the South Slavs of Austria-Hungary.

This was far from enough for some Serbs, especially army officers associated with the Conspiracy of 1903. In 1911 they formed the secret organization called *Ujedinjenje ili smrt*. Its enemies called it *Crna ruka* (The Black Hand). It was headed by Colonel Dragutin Dimitrijević, who was known by his pseudonym Apis (the sacred bull of the ancient Egyptians). One of the conspirators of 1903, Dimitrijević had been regarded as the real minister of war in Serbia, even though he actually held more modest positions. In addition to the hard core of military conspirators in the organization, there were also two groups of civilians involved. One was headed by Ljuba Jovanović, known as Čupa ("tousled hair"), a lawyer by training and an avid student of Western secret revolutionary societies by avocation. The other group was led by Bogdan Radenković, the president of the organization of Serbs in the Ottoman Empire, who epoused a pan-Serbianism with a strong strain of Orthodox clericalism. In 1910 he became an official of the Serbian ministry of foreign affairs, dealing with affairs in Macedonia and his own native Old Serbia.

The organization had both a public and a secret mission. The former was advanced by a daily newspaper called *Pijemont* (Piedmont), edited by Jovanović-Čupa. The secret aims of the society were defined in a constitution of 37 articles. The first three articles proclaimed the society's goals as follows:

Article 1: This organization is formed in order to achieve the ideal of the unification of Serbdom. . . .

Article 2: This organization chooses revolutionary action rather than cultural, and is, therefore, kept secret from the general public.

Article 3: The name of the organization is Unification or Death.

Article 4 described the operations of the society by stating that it would do the following:

1. in accordance with its essential nature, it will influence Serbia, at official levels and throughout all classes of society, to become a Piedmont;

2. undertake the organization of revolutionary activities in all territories inhabited by Serbs;

3. will fight with all the means available to it those outside the frontiers who are enemies of the ideal;

4. will maintain contact with all states, organizations and individuals who are friendly toward Serbia and the Serbs;

5. offer help to all peoples and organizations who are likewise struggling for liberation and unification.

Like the Italian Carbonari of the previous century, the society possessed a seal, engraved with a skull and crossbones, a dagger, a bomb, and a bottle of poison. It also had a blood-chilling initiation ceremony complete with an oath taken in a dark room lighted by a candle on a table draped in black cloth and bearing a cross, a dagger, and a revolver. The oath was administered by a hooded and masked figure in black. Each member belonged to a cell and had a conspiratorial pseudonym. Article 30 of the bylaws was reminiscent of the Russian Nechaev's *Revolutionary Catechism* and of the self-abnegation of the Russian terrorists of the late nineteenth century. "Each member must realize," it read, "that in becoming a member of this organization the individual loses his personality; he can expect no glory, no personal benefits, material or moral. Any member, therefore, who attempts to misuse the organization for his personal, class or party interests will be punished. If the organization suffers any damage because of him, he will be punished by death."

It is debatable to what extent the Unification or Death Society succeeded in penetrating and influencing Serbia's ruling circles. Colonel Dimitrijević-Apis was in a strategic position in 1913 as the newly appointed chief of intelligence of the Serbian general staff. Since his department made use of the National Defense Society's network of confidential agents in Bosnia and Hercegovina, the Unification or Death Society was able to use these same agents. Some members of Unification or Death had also joined the National Defense Society to operate as undercover agents within it. One of these, Captain Milan Vasić, was even one of the general secretaries of the National Defense; however, his death in 1913 during the Second Balkan War ended this link at the top. After that there were agents of Unification or Death only in some of the local units of the National Defense. The president of the National Defense, General Boža Janković, was a conservative who was strongly on the side of Premier Pašić, whereas Unification and Death was very much opposed to the Pašić government.

Colonel Dimitrijević-Apis and his military henchmen expressed a general aversion to the civilian government of Serbia, which they accused of being cowardly and unpatriotic. They were particularly against Pašić's Radical party, which *Pijemont* excoriated as "a gang of men without conscience, who are attacking not only the purse of the people and state funds, but also our army."

The climax of the conflict between Apis and Pašić came in the spring of 1914, over Macedonia and the so-called Priority Question. The issue was whether the civil or the military authorities were to have the upper hand in the territories acquired during the Balkan Wars. Macedonia and Old Serbia had not been placed under the Serbian constitution at the time of their annexation, and both the new civil and military officials there vied for power and precedence. The Pašić government was squarely behind civilian control, which enraged the conspirators among the military. The latter placed such pressure on King Peter, directly and through their ties with the opposition in the Assembly, that on June 2, 1914, Pašić resigned. However, the Independent Radicals and Progressives in the opposition were so divided that King Peter had to ask Pašić to withdraw his resignation. Pašić insisted on, and got, the dissolution of the obstreperous National Assembly on June 10.

The next day King Peter announced that his poor health no longer permitted him to carry out his duties as king. He designated his second son, Alexander, as regent and commander in chief of the army. (His first son, George, had been forced to abdicate his rights as heir apparent in 1909 after the riotous youth had killed his own manservant.) Elections for the new Assembly were scheduled for August 14, but they did not take place. On June 28, 1914, a young Bosnian student called Gavrilo Princip assassinated the Archduke Franz Ferdinand in Sarajevo. One month later Austria-Hungary declared war on Serbia.

XI

Serbia and the Creation of the Kingdom of the Serbs, Croats, and Slovenes, 1914-1918

Serbia Enters the First World War

Serbia was in the thick of a bitter political campaign on the eve of elections for a new National Assembly when the news reached Belgrade of the assassination of Archduke Franz Ferdinand, heir to the throne of Austria-Hungary, in Sarajevo on June 28, 1914. The murder took place on St. Vitus's Day (June 15 O.S.), the anniversary of the Battle of Kosovo, a day when Serbs everywhere commemorated the loss of their independence and hailed the exploits of their champions for freedom. The archduke, who had come to Bosnia to observe military maneuvers, was visiting the capital of a province whose largest ethnic group was Serbian. His assassin was a nineteen-year-old Bosnian Serb, Gavrilo Princip, who along with his equally young accomplices, had connections in Belgrade. The archduke's assassination was the sixth attempt on the life of an Austro-Hungarian official to be perpetrated by South Slavic subjects of the Dual Monarchy in four years, and the most serious.

The news immediately subdued partisan passions in Serbia, and a deep foreboding settled over the land. It was no secret that, especially since the annexation of Bosnia and Hercegovina, there were powerful men in Austria-Hungary who would welcome any excuse to destroy Serbia. For nearly a month anxiety reigned as everyone went about his business and the electoral campaign continued. Then on July 23, 1914, at 6:00 P.M., Baron Vladimir von Giesl, Austro-Hungarian envoy to Serbia, presented to the government a note that amounted to an ultimatum.

The note began with a reminder of what Serbia had promised in its declaration of March 31, 1909, after Austria-Hungary's annexation of Bosnia and Hercegovina, namely: to accept the annexation and to live as a good neighbor, and to suppress all acts within its borders that were hostile to Austria-Hungary. "It is clear from the statements and confessions of the criminal authors of the assassination of the twenty-eighth of June, that the murder at Sarajevo was conceived in Belgrade," the note charged, "that the murderers received the weapons and the bombs with which they were equipped from Serbian officers and officials who belonged to the *Narodna Odbrana*, and, finally, that the dispatch of the criminals and of their weapons to Bosnia was arranged and effected under a safe-conduct by Serbian frontier authorities." The note then presented the full text of a statement that the Serbian government was required to print on the first page of its official organ on July 26 (July 13 O.S.). This statement read as follows:

The Royal Serbian Government condemns the propaganda directed against Austria-Hungary, that is to say, the whole body of the efforts whose ultimate object it is to separate from the Austro-Hungarian Monarchy territories that belong to it, and it most sincerely regrets the dreadful consequences of these criminal transactions.

The Royal Serbian Government regrets that Serbian officers and officials should have taken part in the above-mentioned propaganda and thus have endangered the friendly and neighborly relations, to the cultivation of which the Royal Government had most solemnly pledged itself by its declaration of March 31, 1909.

The Royal Government, which disapproves and repels every idea and every attempt to interfere in the destinies of the population of whatever portion of Austria-Hungary, regards it as its duty most expressly to call the attention of the officers, officials, and the whole population of the Kingdom to the fact that for the future it will proceed with the utmost rigor against any persons who shall become guilty of any such activities, activities to prevent and to suppress which, the Government will bend every effort.

In addition, the Austro-Hungarian note required the Serbian government to pledge itself to the following:

1. To suppress every publication which shall incite to hatred and contempt of the Monarchy, and the general tendency of which shall be directed against the territorial integrity of the latter;

2. To proceed at once to the dissolution of the *Narodna Odbrana,* to confiscate all of its means of propaganda, and in the same manner to proceed against the other unions and associations in Serbia which occupy themselves with propaganda against Austria-Hungary; the Royal Government will take such measures as are necessary to make sure that the dissolved associations may not continue their activities under other names or in other forms;

3. To eliminate without delay from public instruction in Serbia, everything, whether connected with the teaching corps or with the methods of teaching, that serves or may serve to nourish the propaganda against Austria-Hungary;

4. To remove from the military and administrative service in general all officers and officials who have been guilty of carrying on the propaganda against Austria-Hungary, whose names the Imperial and Royal Government reserves the right to make known to the Royal Government when communicating the material evidence now in its possession;

5. To agree to the cooperation in Serbia of the organs of the Imperial and Royal Government in the suppression of the subversive movement directed against the integrity of the Monarchy;

6. To institute a judicial inquiry against every participant in the conspiracy of the twenty-eighth of June who may be found in Serbian territory; the organs of the Imperial and Royal Government delegated for this purpose will take part in the proceedings held for this purpose;

7. To undertake with all haste the arrest of Major Vojislav Tankosić and of one Milan Ciganović, a Serbian official, who have been compromised by the results of the inquiry;

8. By efficient measures to prevent the participation of Serbian authorities in the smuggling of weapons and explosives across the frontier; to dismiss from the service and to punish severely those members of the Frontier Service at Šabac and Loznica who assisted the authors of the crime of Sarajevo to cross the frontier;

9. To make explanations to the Imperial and Royal Government concerning the unjustifiable utterances of high Serbian functionaries in Serbia and abroad, who, without regard for their official position, have not hesitated to express themselves in a manner hostile toward Austria-Hungary since the assassination of the twenty-eighth of June;

10. To inform the Imperial and Royal Government without delay of the execution of the measures comprised in the foregoing points.

Finally, the note informed the Serbian government that Vienna expected a reply "by Saturday, the twenty-fifth instant, at 6 P.M. at the latest," that is, within forty-eight hours.

The note was accompanied by a five-point memorandum which summarized those findings of the criminal investigation in Sarajevo that concerned Serbia, namely: that the plot for the assassination of Archduke Ferdinand was hatched in Belgrade by Gavrilo Princip, Nedeljko Čabrinović, Milan Ciganović, and Trifko Grabež, with the help of Major Voja Tankosić; that Princip, Čabrinović, and Grabež—the three young Bosnian Serbs—were given six bombs and four Browning revolvers by Ciganović and Major Tankosić; that the bombs were hand grenades manufactured in Kragujevac, in Serbia; that Ciganović instructed the youths in the use of the grenades and put Princip and Grabež through shooting practice sessions at the Topčider range; and that Ciganović enabled the three Bosnians to cross the frontier secretly, and that a Captain Rade Popović and a customs official called Radivoje Grbić, along with other private persons, helped smuggle weapons across the frontier by way of Šabac and Loznica.

The Viennese government had sent copies of its note and accompanying material in advance to its envoys in Berlin, Rome, Paris, London, St. Petersburg, and Istanbul with instructions to make known its contents on July 24. The accompanying material included allegedly incriminating excerpts from Serbia's newspapers from August 1910 to May 1914, excerpts from a book entitled *Narodna Odbrana* (Belgrade, 1911), excerpts from a report on the activities of the "Dušan the Mighty" Society of Kragujevac for 1912–1913, and similar exhibits, including a description of a picture hanging in a room of the Serbian war ministry which portrayed the dawning of a new day over the Serbian lands and which bore the caption "The still unliberated lands of Bosnia, Hercegovina, Vojvodina, Srem, Dalmatia. . . ."

The Austro-Hungarian note had been received in Belgrade by Dr. Lazar Paču, who was acting for Pašić during the latter's absence from the capital. Pašić was electioneering in the southeast of Serbia. He was summoned back immediately and was telegraphed the contents of the Austro-Hungarian note piecemeal as his train made station stops along the way. Meanwhile Crown Prince Alexander, acting as regent for his father, King Peter, sent a telegram to Tsar Nicholas II explaining the situation. "We are prepared," he wrote, "to accept those Austro-Hungarian demands which are in keeping with the position of an independent country as well as those which Your Majesty might recommend. We shall severely punish all persons who can be proven to have participated in the assassination. Some of the demands cannot be carried out until the laws are changed, and this requires time. We have been left with too little time. . . . We may be attacked when the time is up, for the Austro-Hungarian army is massing on our border. It is impossible for us to defend ourselves, and therefore we beg Your Majesty to hasten to our aid as quickly as possible. . . ." What the Russian government thought about the situation may be seen from Foreign Minister Sazonov's warning to the German ambassador in St. Petersburg, Count Friedrich von Pourtalès, that if Austria attacked Serbia, Russia would declare war.

Following Russian advice, the Serbian government framed a reply which, as the foreign envoys in Belgrade were told in advance, "will be conciliatory, and we have accepted all the Austro-Hungarian demands that we could. Unless it wishes war at all costs, the Austro-Hungarian government will be able to be completely satisfied by the Serbian answer." The Serbian reply was delivered personally by Premier Pašić to the Austro-Hungarian minister in Belgrade just fifteen minutes before the expiration of the allotted forty-eight hours.

The tone of the Serbian reply was indeed one of appeasement, though it had dignity. It observed that Serbia had lived up to its promises of 1909, that it had not engaged in any movement to change the position of Bosnia and Hercegovina, and that it was not responsible for the writings of the Serbian press and the activities of patriotic societies. Even though not one citizen of Serbia was among those conspirators arrested by the Austro-Hungarian authorities, the Serbian note said, the Serbian government was willing to bring to justice any of its citizens for whom the Austro-Hungarian government could offer any evidence of complicity. The reply condemned all propaganda against the territorial integrity of the Austro-Hungarian lands and promised severe action against its perpetrators. Specifically, the Serbian reply agreed to comply completely with the first six demands of the Austro-Hungarian ultimatum. Namely, it was willing to amend the constitution and change the laws of Serbia in order to enforce the necessary censorship of the Serbian press; it was willing to suppress the *Narodna odbrana* and similar patriotic societies, even though no proof was given of their complicity; it was willing to purge its public instruction in the schools of any material that was objectionable to Austria-Hungary; it was willing to dismiss from the army and the administration all officers and officials who the Austro-Hungarian government could prove had acted against the territorial integrity of the

Dual Monarchy; while it professed not to understand the precise meaning of Austria-Hungary's fifth demand, the Serbian government expressed willingness to accept the cooperation of Austro-Hungarian agents on its own soil insofar as this did not contravene international law or Serbian judicial procedures; the Serbian government was further willing to undertake a judicial inquiry against all persons on Serbian territory who were suspected of complicity in the assassination; as for Major Tankosić and Milan Ciganović (who was an Austro-Hungarian citizen), the Serbian government ordered the immediate arrest of the former and was looking for the latter, who had disappeared; the Serbian government also promised to intensify measures against the smuggling of weapons and explosives into Austro-Hungary and to punish the border officials at Šabac and Loznica who had permitted the conspirators to cross the border; the Serbian government further agreed to make all necessary explanations for any untoward statements by its officials; and finally, it promised to keep the Austro-Hungarian government informed of all further steps that it was taking in compliance with its demands.

The Serbian reply ended with the following statement: "The Royal Government considers it to be in the interest of both parties not to hurry in deciding this matter, and therefore it is always prepared, in the event that the Imperial and Royal Government is not satisfied with this reply, either to bring this question before the International Court in The Hague or to have this done by the Great Powers which assisted in the formulation of the Serbian Government's declaration of March 18/31, 1909." In sum, Serbia was willing to accept all the Austro-Hungarian demands that did not violate its independence as a sovereign nation.

Just fifteen minutes after receiving the Serbian reply, Baron Giesl sent a letter to the Serbian government informing it that the reply was unsatisfactory and that he and his staff were leaving Belgrade forthwith, that he was turning over the Austro-Hungarian legation to the protection of the German minister, and that his letter was to be regarded as ending diplomatic relations between Austria-Hungary and Serbia.

The Serbian government responded by calling for an emergency meeting of the last elected National Assembly on July 27, in Niš. In a declaration to the people of Serbia informing them of the Austro-Hungarian action, the Serbian government stated, "We consider it our duty to call the people to the defense of the fatherland, in the belief that everyone will gladly respond to our call. If we are attacked, the army will do its duty, while citizens who are not called to the colors are advised to remain at home and to go about their business peacefully." The government then proceeded to Niš. Meanwhile the army was mobilized, and elections for a new Assembly were canceled.

The moderation of the Serbian reply made a deep impression on the European Powers. Even Emperor William II of Germany advised Vienna, on reading the Serbian reply, that there was no longer any reason for war and that Vienna should call off its mobilization. While the cabinets of the European Powers became momentarily engaged in various efforts to stave off a war, the Serbian government followed Russia's advice and slowly pulled back its forces into the comparative safety of Serbia's hinterland. Meanwhile Foreign Minister Count Leopold von Berchtold and the war party in Austria-Hungary did all they could to promote a war with Serbia. Berchtold even used a false report of a Serbian attack on the Austro-Hungarian army at Kovin to dispose the reluctant Emperor Francis Joseph I to sign a declaration of war. On July 28, 1914, at 1:20 P.M., the Serbian government, which was already in Niš, received by telegram Austria-Hungary's declaration of war. It was the first time in history that a war was declared by an open telegram. That same night Belgrade was subjected to a bombardment by Austro-Hungarian guns in Zemun and by gunboats on the Sava and the Danube.

The Question of Serbia's Guilt

The extent of Serbia's responsibility in the assassination of Archduke Ferdinand and the events that followed is a question that has been frequently debated. If certain aspects of the problem are still debatable, it is because the available evidence has gaps in it. Yet it is possible to reach certain conclusions.

The most important of these is that the Serbian government itself neither planned nor abetted the assassination of the archduke. Serbia was in no position to do anything that might provoke a war with Austria-Hungary. It was still physically weakened by the Balkan Wars. Internally it was divided by partisan struggles, especially the whole "Priorities Question," which set the military and the civilian administration at odds with one another in the newly annexed lands. Also, local Albanian and pro-Bulgarian raiders in those lands were a source of great trouble. Moreover, it was quite clear that in the event of war with Austria-Hungary, Bulgaria would attack Serbia from the east. Certainly Russia was in no position to provoke a war with Austria-Hungary, as its defeat by Japan in 1905 showed, and its counsels to Serbia throughout the Sarajevo crisis were those of caution and moderation. At no time, therefore, was Austria-Hungary able to implicate the Serbian government in the plot to murder the archduke.

Although the Austro-Hungarian ultimatum blamed the *Narodna odbrana* (National Defense), this charge was never proven. The Serbian organization that trained, armed, and dispatched the young Bosnian assassins was the Unification or Death society (*Ujedinjenje ili smrt*), better known as the Black Hand. This secret organization did not enjoy the support of the government; in fact, the government was actively hostile toward the group. This was amply shown when it brought the leader of the Black Hand, Colonel Dimitrijević-Apis, to trial in Salonika in April 1917 for allegedly planning to murder Crown Prince Alexander, and executed him.

On the other hand, it is also clear that the Pašić government knew something about an intended assassination of someone in Bosnia. Pašić received and annotated in his own hand a report that reached him through the intelligence network of the *Narodna Odbrana* to the effect that two Bosnian high school students had crossed from Serbia into Bosnia with six hand grenades and four revolvers. The name of their intended victim was not mentioned, but Pašić could have guessed that the incident might be connected with the Archduke Ferdinand's much publicized visit to Sarajevo. The question is, What measures did Pašić undertake to prevent an assassination? First, he brought the matter before the cabinet. Second, he ordered an investigation by civilian authorities at the border while the minister of the interior issued special orders to customs officials to be on the alert for any illicit traffic in weapons across the border. Third, he ordered an investigation of Colonel Dimitrijević-Apis by military authorities while the minister of war issued orders to border guards to prevent any armed men from crossing into Bosnia. Fourth, he took several measures to stop the conspirators who had already crossed the border. *Narodna Odbrana* warned its agents in Bosnia against giving aid to any assassins. Moreover, it actually refused to give asylum to its agent who had led Princip and Grabež to Bosnia because he had not been authorized to do so but had been used by the Black Hand; the man was sent back to Bosnia, where he was arrested and sentenced to death. Later this sentence was commuted to twenty years in prison. Pašić also tried to warn several Bosnian political leaders, through Belgrade's chief of police, against the possibility of an attempt on the archduke's life, but the warnings were not taken seriously; the Bosnian leaders believed that security measures in Sarajevo would be as strong as in 1910 when Emperor Francis Joseph visited the city.

The most important question is, Did the Serbian government warn the Austro-Hungarian government that armed men had crossed from Serbia into Bosnia? Various sources claim that it did. The Austro-Hungarian government twice claimed that it did not. The truth seems to be that the Serbian government did not officially inform Vienna of what it had learned about armed men crossing from Serbia into Bosnia. It would have been obviously embarrassing and awkward for the Serbian government to admit that it had permitted such a thing to happen. On the other hand, the Serbian minister to Vienna, Jovan Jovanović-Pižon, did visit Count Leon von Bilinski, the joint minister of finance and chief civilian authority for Bosnia and Hercegovina, prior to the assassination and expressed the fear that "among the Serb youths there [during the maneuvers] there might be one who will put a live cartridge in his rifle and he may fire it." It is not clear whether the Serbian envoy expressed such fears on his own initiative or on orders from Belgrade. An official in Bilinski's office claimed that Jovanović begged Bilinski not to consider his statement as an official communication or take it as either a direct or an indirect warning. Yet several Serbian sources have claimed that a warning was given to the Austro-Hungarian government. There is no evidence of any warning but that given by Jovanović to Count Bilinski, and that was so vague that it was dismissed. Had the Serbian envoy transmitted all the details known at the time in Belgrade, they may not have been ignored.

Granting the Serbian government's negligence in permitting a secret society that had infiltrated the army, government, and *Narodna Odbrana* to train and send armed men into Bosnia to commit a political murder and in not informing Vienna of it, there is still the question, Was this reason enough for Austria-Hungary to declare war on Serbia? However one answers, the fact is that the Serbian reply to the Austro-Hungarian ultimatum was so conciliatory that even Emperor William of Germany was persuaded that it removed any reason for declaring war. The Serbian government went as far in its appeasement as any nation could go without sacrificing its own sovereignty. Serbia had already once sacrificed this sovereignty to Austria-Hungary, in 1881. It was not willing to do so in 1914. If Vienna had not been intent on destroying Serbia's sovereignty, even at the cost of a war, that war would never have occurred. As for the question of responsibility for the First World War, it is clear that the crime at Sarajevo and the Austro-Serbian war that followed provided only the spark for the larger conflagration, of which Serbia was not a cause but a victim.

Serbia in the First World War

On August 1, 1914, Germany declared war on Russia, and two days later on France. On August 4 Germany declared war on Belgium, and Great Britain on Germany. On August 5 Montenegro declared war on Austria. On August 6 Austria declared war on Russia, and Serbia on Germany. On August 8 Montenegro declared war on Germany. On August 12 France and Great Britain declared war on Austria-Hungary. Thus within two weeks after being attacked, Serbia had allies everywhere and help from no one. It needed help badly, for the war had caught it unprepared militarily and financially.

Serbia bore the brunt of a full attack by three Austro-Hungarian armies which comprised some 250,000 men. The first enemy troops entered Serbia across the Drina and Sava rivers on August 12. The first big test of strength came during the night of August 15–16, when the contending armies met in a bloody four-day battle on the slopes of Cer Mountain in northwestern Serbia. They were fairly evenly matched, though the Austro-Hungarian forces had the advantage of making a united attack whereas the Serbian forces had to be brought up piecemeal. Nevertheless, the Serbs won a smashing victory and actually pushed the invaders back across the Drina and the Sava so that by August 24 not a single Austro-Hungarian soldier remained on Serbian soil. Morale was so high that, at the urging of the Allies, the Serbs undertook a counter offensive in Srem and Bosnia. The Russians were eager for a diversion to bring them relief on the Eastern Front. However, the Austro-Hungarian forces struck back with vigor, and the Serbs were forced to fall back for lack of supplies. Apart from a lack of munitions, many Serbian soldiers lacked even uniforms and boots and were forced to fight in their civilian clothing. Belgrade had to be abandoned by early December. The Serbian retreat was considerably hampered by the mass flight of the civilian population.

The arrival of munitions from the Allies via Salonika and of fresh recruits enabled the Serbs to begin a new counteroffensive on December 3. Within twelve days, they had another great victory, this time along the Kolubara River southwest of Belgrade. Serbia was again cleared of enemy soldiers, and Belgrade was taken back. The Battle of the Kolubara was Serbia's greatest victory in the First World War. This second failure of the Austro-Hungarian armies to "crush Serbia" cost them 50,000 soldiers and 200 cannon.

Frantic efforts were made on all sides to bring the other Balkan countries and Italy into the war. By the end of October Turkey, which was in the hands of the Germanophile Young Turks, chose to join the Central Powers. On November 2 Russia and Serbia declared war on Turkey, and three days later Great Britain and France followed suit. As for the other Balkan nations, Greek Premier Eleutherios Venizelos hoped for a new Balkan alliance against Austria-Hungary into which Bulgaria and Romania were to be enticed by territorial gains in Macedonia and Transylvania, respectively. The Serbs supported this venture but had little hope that it would succeed. Meanwhile the Turks attempted to form a Turkish-Bulgarian-Romanian alliance on the side of the Central Powers. It seemed to the Entente Powers that it was more important to win over Bulgaria and Romania than Greece, especially since Venizelos had neither his sovereign, King Constantine, nor the Greek army behind him. A period of bargaining with Bulgaria and Romania ensued, which demoralized the Serbs. At the expense of Serbia, the Russians offered Sofia all of the Macedonian territory it had hoped to get after the First Balkan War. However, the Bulgarian government held out for even better offers from the Central Powers. The Romanian government assured the Bulgarians that it would maintain benevolent neutrality in case of a Bulgarian attack on Serbia if the Bulgarians would renounce Dobrudja. While the Entente Powers found it difficult to force Serbia to make concessions to Bulgaria in Macedonia, the Central Powers had no difficulty in offering Bulgaria not only Macedonia but also eastern Serbia as well as Dobrudja and Kavalla if either Romania or Greece should join the Entente, and even a part of Turkish Thrace, as well as a substantial loan of 200 million francs.

On October 14, 1915, the Bulgarian government declared war on Serbia, even though the Bulgarian people had little desire for such a war. Romania and Greece remained neutral. Italy was enticed into the war on the side of the Entente in May 1915, after it had been promised the South Tyrol and Trentino, Gorizia, Gradisca, Trieste, Istria, all of Dalmatia with its most important islands, a part of Albania, and the Dodecanese Islands, as well as gains in Africa. The secret Treaty of London of April 26, 1915, which offered these prizes to Italy, was a severe blow to Serbia and to all the South Slavs, for it imposed the double loss of a substantial South Slavic population as well as a vitally important coastline.

After Austria-Hungary's defeat at the Battle of the Kolubara River (November 16–December 15, 1914), as well as at Przemyśl on the Russian Front (March 22, 1915), Germany took over the command of the Central Powers' Balkan operations especially after the French and the British made Salonika the base for their thrust north into the Balkan Peninsula in early October 1915. The Allies' move to Salonika caused a split in the Greek government between Venizelos and King Constantine, as a result of which Venizelos formed his own pro-Allied government in northern Greece while the King ruled the rest of Greece as a neutral. On October 6 General August von Mackensen began a great offensive in Serbia. Belgrade fell on October 9 and Smederevo two days later. Meanwhile the Bulgarians attacked Serbia on October 11, though it was not until three days later that the two countries declared war on each other. It was the intention of the Central Powers to drive through Serbia and make contact with their Turkish ally.

By this time Serbia was exhausted by war and disease. The Austro-Hungarian armies had left devastation in their wake. The war zones were covered with ruins and unburied corpses. In early 1915 a terrible epidemic of typhus swept over the land, cutting down 135,000 soldiers and civilians. Meanwhile, as Serbia faced a massive military threat from the north, Bulgarian and Albanian guerrilla raiders harassed the south in an effort to cut Serbia's lifeline to Salonika and the Allies. General Mackensen had under his command three German armies, three Austro-Hungarian armies, and two fresh Bugarian armies, with a total of around 600,000 soldiers. The armies of Serbia and Montenegro had less than half that number, and they were exhausted and lacked equipment. Mackensen's plan was to push through central

[623]

Serbia along the Morava River while the Bulgars cut across the Vardar River farther south to cut off Serbian communications with Salonika. Vastly outnumbered and overpowered, the Serbs retreated toward Kosovo, where they hoped to concentrate their troops and join the Montenegrins, who were also hard pressed by the Austro-Hungarians. After a month and a half of desperate fighting, the Serbian army reached a critical point. Acutely aware that the Allies in Salonika could send no reinforcements, the Serbian high command decided on a mass withdrawal via Montenegro and Albania to the Adriatic coast, where the Allies could help them.

There ensued, on November 28, 1915, one of the most horrible retreats in the history of human warfare. Three columns of soldiers and fleeing civilians—men, women, and children—set out from Peć and Prizren, over the mountains of Montenegro and Albania, in the hope of reaching Shkodër and Elbasan. Everything that could not be carried or pulled was burned, buried, or thrown into the river. Old King Peter went along, riding on a gun carriage. General Putnik, who was ill, had to be carried all across Albania in a makeshift enclosed sedan chair. The retreating forces were mercilessly cut down along the way by winter snows and freezing wind, hunger, and disease. Only about 150,000 soldiers reached the Albanian coast and Shkodër. Another 10,000 died there because the Italian command would offer them no help. Thus the terrible march continued south to Durrës and Vlonë, where, thanks to the plea of Tsar Nicholas II, the French fleet transported the survivors to Corfu (Kerkira). So many soldiers died on the nearby islet of Vido that the Serbs named it the Island of Death. Between January 23 and March 23, 1916, about 4,000 Serbian soldiers were buried on the little island; 7,000 more had to be buried in the surrounding sea for lack of space. Many of the 120,000 survivors were taken to North Africa to a camp at Bizerte, but many remained on Corfu and surrounding islands. The civilians were evacuated largely to France and its North African possessions.

Meanwhile, in early January 1916 the Austro-Hungarian forces struck Montenegro full force. By January 13 they were in the capital, Cetinje. King Nicholas and his government withdrew to Podgorica (Titograd), where they attempted to conclude a separate peace, but the terms offered were so humiliating that Nicholas and some members of his government left for Italy, where his daughter was queen, while the sick Prince Mirko remained behind, demobilized the army, and awaited the Austro-Hungarian occupation.

The situation in the Balkan Peninsula was desperately bad for the Allies in 1916. On May 26 a Bulgarian and German force took Fort Rupel in Greek Macedonia, which heightened the suspicion that King Constantine was secretly bound to the Central Powers. Finally, after much debate and hesitation, the Western Allies decided to open a new front at Salonika and to reinforce their troops with the remnants of the Serbian army in North Africa and Corfu. After being equipped and drilled, about 115,000 Serbian soldiers were brought to the Balkan Front and placed under the command of French General Maurice Sarrail, who headed all the Allied forces there. The Bulgarian and German forces tried to deprive the Allies of their beachhead but failed. In early September 1916 the Allies began their offensive. Once more the Serbian army demonstrated its will to fight by beating back the Bulgarian-German forces until it took Kajmakčalan Peak after a bloody battle. By November 19 Serbian and French troops entered Bitola together, thus freeing at least that small part of the Kingdom of Serbia. Later the Allies pushed forward as far as Lake Ohrid.

One of the reasons for this success was Romania's entry on the side of the Entente on August 27, 1916. Impressed by the success of a Russian offensive under General Brusilov, the Romanians decided finally to cast their lot with the Allies in the hope of obtaining the Austro-Hungarian provinces of Transylvania, Bukovina, and the Banat of Temesvár (Timişoara). Their advance into Transylvania momentarily diverted the forces of the Central Powers, though, in the end, the failures of the Romanian army were to make Romania more of a liability than a help.

While the Serbian army made an amazing recovery and the Allies enjoyed limited success on the Salonika Front, Serbia and Montenegro suffered greatly under enemy occupation. Serbia's thirteen western districts were occupied by Austria-Hungary. Serbia east of the Morava River and Macedonia were occupied by the Bulgarians. The forces of occupation imposed a reign of terror and plunder on their victims. Beatings, arrests, sequestration, and executions, of both women and men, were common occurrences. The Austro-Hungarian authorities alone interned some 150,000 persons, many of whom died in concentration camps. Factories were stripped of machines and tools, stores were looted, forests cut down, and mines recklessly exploited. Various administrative and punitive measures made it difficult, if not impossible, for people to procure food and other necessities, so hunger and disease were rampant. In the Bulgarian zone, hundreds of people were liquidated because they stubbornly affirmed their Serbian nationality. There were mass deportations and executions. In the town of Surdulica, for example, 3,000 Serbs perished. Bulgarian policy was so harsh that there were cases of mutiny by Bulgarian soldiers, and 3,000 inhabitants of Toplica were driven to a desperate uprising when Bulgarian officials attempted to impress local youths into their army. The uprising was cruelly suppressed; about 20,000 men, women, and children perished, 36 villages around Leskovac were completely destroyed, and the entire adult male population of Niš, about 4,000 men, were deported, most of them never to return. All of Serbia was in agony. The fear of further uprisings caused the Austro-Hungarian authorities to undertake the mass deportation of intellectuals as well as all males capable of bearing arms. By the end of October 1916, according to statistics gleaned by American Red Cross officials from Austrian officers, about 30,000 Serbs had been interned in Austrian camps or used as laborers in mines and farms.

The Serbian Government and the Yugoslav Committee

Throughout Serbia's trials during the war, the Serbian government continued to exist, though its existence was often precarious. The king, the prince-regent, the cabinet and other officials, the National Assembly, and the diplomatic corps moved from Belgrade to Niš as soon as war was declared. However, when Niš became endangered, the government decided to move farther south, to Bitola. Just as it was about to make this move, on October 16, the enemy cut railroad communications between Niš and Vranje. This caused the government to decide to move to Čačak instead, but enemy operations made even this impossible. Therefore, it retreated southward, via Raška and Kosovska Mitrovica. Throughout this withdrawal the Serbian government maintained constant telegraphic communication with its diplomats abroad and kept sending appeals to the Allies for help. When the Austro-Hungarian and Bulgarian forces threatened to capture the entire Serbian army and government, King Peter, Prince Alexander, the military command, the cabinet, members of the Assembly, various officials and clerks, and—by this time—a mass of civilian refugees moved to Priština and began the torturous march to Shkodër in northern Albania.

The Serbian government made every effort to obtain Allied help for the refugees when they arrived. The British responded generously by sending food to southern Italy, but the Italians would not transport it to the waiting Serbs until Tsar Nicholas and French President Poincaré interceded with the king of Italy, and then the food was dumped beyond reach in Durrës in order to avoid Austro-Hungarian naval and air attacks. Finding Shkodër too cramped and exposed to Austro-Hungarian naval attacks from Kotor, and receiving no help from the Italians, the Serbian government and army moved south to Corfu. There the government installed itself for most of the duration of the war. There, too, the Serbian National Assembly met and deliberated until the spring of 1918.

As the fortunes of war changed in favor of the Allies, the concerns of the Serbian government-in-exile turned from the immediate problem of sheer survival to the shape of things to come. The possible defeat of Bulgaria and the dissolution of the Dual Monarchy imposed the necessity of making plans and arrangements for Serbia's future.

Two large conceptions of the future figured in Serbian thoughts—a Greater Serbia and a Yugoslavia. Until the war it was the goal of a Greater Serbia that attracted most Serbs, both politicians and the citizenry, because it was more immediate and closer to Serbian hearts. It envisioned the piecemeal aggrandizement of Serbia by the annexation of surrounding provinces where there was a sizable Serbian population. After the Balkan Wars the main targets were Bosnia and Hercegovina, along with an outlet to the Adriatic Sea. However, there were hopes of gaining other provinces as well, notably Vojvodina. The whole idea of a Greater Serbia envisioned a centralized Serbian state, under the Karadjordjević dynasty, whose population would be very largely Serbian and Orthodox.

The ideal of a Yugoslav state was always more popular among the Croats, Serbs, and Slovenes of the Austro-Hungarian Monarchy than it was in Serbia. Though it excited several generations of Serbia's intellectuals and youth, the idea of a Yugoslav state presented pragmatic politicians with all kinds of problems. Even once the Bulgarians were no longer included in the Yugoslav idea, the fact was that the Serbs,

Croats, and Slovenes were not one people; they had never all been politically united, and there were cultural, historical, linguistic, and religious differences among them.

While the Dual Monarchy remained intact and the likelihood of realizing an independent Yugoslav state seemed remote, it was easy to minimize and gloss over these differences and not be too concerned with practical problems. However, once the dissolution of the Habsburg Empire became a real possibility and the Yugoslav movement within that empire became a political entity, Serbia's leaders had to confront the very real problems that the prospect of a Yugoslav union posed. What would be the role of Serbia in particular and of the Serbs in general in a Yugoslav state that they would have to share with others? How would such a state be organized—as a centralized state, a federation, or a confederation? What would be the role of the Kara-djordjević dynasty? Or of the Serbian Orthodox Church? How would Montenegro react to such an idea? How would the internal boundaries of such a political entity be determined? What would happen to the Serbian national ethos? How would the economy of a Yugoslav state be administered? Finally, of course, what would the three big Allies have to say about the creation of such a state? All these questions concerned Prince Alexander, Premier Pašić, and the Serbian government-in-exile on Corfu.

These questions also concerned the representatives of the Yugoslav movement in the Habsburg Empire, especially the Yugoslav Committee, which was formed abroad, in Italy, to act as the free voice on the movement. The Yugoslav Committee was conceived in Florence on November 22, 1914, when a group of Croatian exiles—notably Ante Trumbić, Frano Supilo, and the sculptor Ivan Meštrović—met with some Serbian politicians from Bosnia and Hercegovina and agreed to organize an agency that would make known to the Allied governments and peoples the wishes of the South Slavs in the Dual Monarchy. The founders of the Yugoslav Committee were particularly fearful that with the downfall of Austria-Hungary, Italy might benefit by annexing South Slavic provinces. They did not realize how justified their fears were until they learned of the secret Treaty of London in 1915.

The Yugoslav Committee set as its function to represent Yugoslav interests abroad as an information agency and to engage in certain political activities. One of these was to prepare and submit to the Serbian government plans concerning the political organization of Yugoslav territory in Austria-Hungary as it was liberated. Another was to organize the many thousands of South Slavic emigrants in North and South America to support the cause in money and fighting volunteers. In early 1915 the Yugoslav Committee began to sign up recruits for an "Adriatic Legion." In meetings held in Trieste on April 11 and April 18, 1915, the Yugoslav Committee received the political support of representatives of the Croatian Party of Rights (a nationalist party) and of the Slovenian National Progressive party. Though the chief South Slavic political parties in the Dual Monarchy—the Croat-Serbian Coalition and the Slovenian Popular party—remained officially reserved, privately they assured the Yugoslav Committee's chief spokesman, Ante Trumbić, that they approved of the committee's work. A tangible boost to the Yugoslav Committee's legitimacy to speak on behalf of the Croats, Serbs, and Slovenes of Austria-Hungary came in March 1915 when a congress of 563 Yugoslav emigrants to the United States met in Chicago and declared their support of the committee and its program.

It was the Yugoslav Committee that alerted the Serbian government to the danger that the Allies would promise Italy large Yugoslav territories. In response to the news that the Allied negotiations with Italy were reaching their conclusion, seventeen Croatian, Serbian, and Slovenian leaders, political émigrés, seven of whom were national deputies elected before the war, hastily met in Paris on April 30, 1915, and formally constituted themselves as the Yugoslav Committee. London was designated as its seat, and Trumbić was elected president. Though the memoranda of the committee had no effect on the outcome of the Treaty of London, they did make the Allies aware of the Yugoslav case as never before. Through its dealings, the Yugoslav Committee acquired the *de facto* stature, if not the official status, of a kind of government-in-exile for the South Slavs of the Dual Monarchy. Thanks to Yugoslav emigrants in North and South America, this quasi government had funds and military recruits. Thanks to the stature and experience of its leaders, it also had the ear of the Allied governments. As Austria-Hungary's dissolution grew more imminent, the political importance of the Yugoslav Committee grew correspondingly.

This was a troublesome matter for Nikola Pašić's government-in-exile on Corfu. The premier would have preferred to have the Serbian government be the only voice of the South Slavs in diplomatic negotiations and in the liberation of the South Slavic lands. This was not only a matter of efficiency or prestige. In actual fact, Pašić and his government were caught between two conceptions—a Greater Serbia and a Yugoslavia—which few people were willing to realize were not complementary but actually in conflict with each other.

On the one hand, the Serbian government declared repeatedly after the outbreak of the war that its aim was the liberation of all the South Slav lands. On August 4, 1914, in his proclamation to the Serbian army, Prince-Regent Alexander referred to "the groans of millions of our brethren which have reached us from Bosnia and Hercegovina, from the Banat and Bačka, from Croatia, Slavonia, Srem, and from our sea, rock-bound Dalmatia." While this reference may have been only to the Serbs living in those lands, there was nothing ambivalent about the declaration the Serbian government made to the National Assembly in Niš on December 7, 1914. It referred quite specifically to "the struggle for the liberation and unification of all our captive brethren Serbs, Croats, and Slovenes." This statement of Serbia's war aim was greeted by the Assembly with thundrous applause. On April 28, 1915, Pašić was asked before the National Assembly, still in Niš, to comment on Italian-Serbian relations in the light of rumors concerning Italy's entry into the war at the price of Yugoslav aspirations. The premier replied that Italy would have to reckon with the unity of "the Serbo-Croato-Slovenian people." On May 6, 1915, a "Yugoslav Congress" was held in Niš under the aegis of the Serbian government. It declared, "In these historic days of sacrifice and hope in justice and freedom, we declare in the first place the complete and indissoluble unity of the Serbs-Croats-Slovenes, not only as an unconditional prerequisite for a better future, but also as an ethnographic and genetic axiom that must be politically realized just as it has been morally and spiritually." Following a secret session, the Serbian National Assembly in Niš on August 10, 1915, solemnly reaffirmed its "determination to continue the struggle for the liberation and unification of the Serbo-Croato-Slovenian people." Upon his return from a tour of the Western Allied capitals, Prince-Regent Alexander declared in his statement of April 20, 1915, on Corfu, that the Allies were now willing "that we make Serbia Great to embrace all Serbs and Yugoslavs, that we make it into a mighty and powerful Yugoslavia. . . ."

From the start there was a difference between Pašić's conception and that of the Yugoslav Committee as to how the future Yugoslavia would be achieved. This divergence involved three large issues: which South

Slavic territories were to be liberated and united, and when; how their unification would take place; and how the future state would be organized.

It was the expectation of the Yugoslav Committee that all the Yugoslav lands would be liberated and joined into one state at the same time. Less optimistic, Pašić viewed Yugoslav unification as a gradual process, to be achieved like the unification of Italy in the nineteenth century, in stages, with Serbia as the South Slavic Piedmont. For the moment his biggest ambition was that Serbia acquire Bosnia and Hercegovina, that it unite with Montenegro, and that it acquire an outlet to the Adriatic Sea. Everything else was secondary and might have to wait.

What strengthened Pašić's hand in particular was the support the tsarist Russian government lent to the creation of a Greater Serbia. Russia was not at all interested in the creation of a large Yugoslav state. The official Russian attitude was rather brutally expressed by Foreign Minister Sazonov to two Serbian representatives in May 1915: "Concerning the Croats and the Slovenes, I can tell you nothing. They are fighting against us. If it were necessary for the Russian people to fight only half a day to liberate the Slovenes, I would not agree to it."

As to the manner of Yugoslav unification, the Yugoslav Committee saw this as the union of equals together creating a common state as partners. The Serbian government saw itself as the liberator and gatherer of captive brethren and their spokesman before the nations of the world. Serbia's leaders kept emphasizing Serbia's role as the liberator of the Yugoslav peoples. Serbia's assumption of this role made the Yugoslav Committee decidedly uncomfortable, for it put the Yugoslavs of Austria-Hungary in a morally and politically inferior position. With the complete collapse and occupation of Serbia by the enemy, Trumbić stated in an article of March 20, 1916, in *L'Écho de Paris* that misfortune had now united all the Yugoslavs, in other words, that both the Serbians and the other Yugoslavs were in need of liberation. However, Serbia salvaged its army, and Pašić was opposed to giving the Yugoslav Committee any control over an armed force of its own.

Pašić saw the union as the extension of an already existing political entity—Serbia. In the light of Serbia's history, it was natural for the Serbs of Serbia to envisage this as simply another in a whole series of territorial annexations by which Serbia had grown since 1804. As a statesman, Pašić found it more practical to build on an existing and internationally recognized state structure. Adhering to the time-honored devices of international diplomacy, he even used the argument of "compensation" to further the unification of the Yugoslav peoples of Austria-Hungary with Serbia, namely, in his reply of September 14, 1915, to a collective note by the Allies concerning Bulgaria's reward for joining the Allies; Pašić stated that in exchange for relinquishing the larger part of Serbian Macedonia to Bulgaria, his government sought not only what it previously desired—Bosnia, Hercegovina, and an Adriatic outlet—but also Croatia and the city and harbor of Fiume (Rijeka). None of the modes of Yugoslav unification envisaged by Pašić—either liberation and annexation by Serbia or "compensation" for Serbia's sacrifices—corresponded to the principles of equality, fraternity, and self-determination nurtured by the Yugoslav Committee.

As for the internal organization of the future state, the leaders of the Yugoslav Committee looked to a federal system, though under the Karadjordjević dynasty, whereas Pašić saw the new state system as an extension of Serbia's centralism. He saw no reason to sacrifice the hegemony of 7,200,000 Serbs in the new state over 3,500,000 Croats and Slovenes, both because of the Serbs' numerical preponderance and Serbia's central political position and prestige as the Piedmont of the South Slavs. Besides, he was not about to relinquish the leading role of his own Radical party. However, Pašić did not make a point of his views. On the contrary, he encouraged the idea that it was premature to discuss the internal organization of the new state while the war still held the fate of all Yugoslavs in the balance. He wished to avoid any squabbling among the Serbs, Croats, and Slovenes that might give the Italians, Bulgarians, Magyars, and others an opportunity to divide them.

Although the Serbian government and the Yugoslav Committee avoided a quarrel over their basic divergences, they were at serious odds over several specific issues which, in fact, reflected their larger differences.

One such basic conflict occurred over the Serbian government's lack of an energetic stance against Italy's ambitions in the eastern Adriatic. Basically, the members of the Yugoslav Committee feared, with reason, that the Serbian government, specifically Pašić, was not as interested in pursuing Yugoslav aims as in pursuing Serbian aims. On the one hand, during a tour of the Allied capitals that Prince-Regent Alexander and Premier Pašić made in March 1916, Alexander clearly affirmed that his ideal was "the unification into one homeland of all Serbs, Croats, and Slovenes, who are one people with the same traditions, the same language, and the same aspirations. . . ." On the other hand, in an interview by representatives of the Russian press, as reported in the *Corriere della Sera* of May 6, 1916, Pašić declared, "We Serbs cannot but recognize the indisputable right of Italy to hegemony on the shores of the Adriatic. We also wish to reach the sea, but . . . we only aspire to obtain an economic outlet." While this last was a fair statement of Serbia's long-standing aim in the Adriatic, it was certainly not the aim of the Yugoslav Committee, which was opposed to giving Italy one inch of the eastern Adriatic coast.

It would be wrong to assume that even Pašić, with his Pan-Serbian outlook, was eager to abandon any Yugoslav territories to others. However, a significant difference between the Yugoslav Committee and the Serbian government was that while the former could afford, as a non-political agency, to put forward the maximum program of the Yugoslav ideology, the Serbian government could not; as a political entity it was forced to deal with the hard realities of its own position and the vagaries of Allied diplomacy. The fact was that after the disastrous retreat of 1915–1916 Serbia was a totally defeated nation and that the Serbian government was engaged in a salvage operation. If Pašić showed deference to the Allied desire to entice Italy into the war on their side, even at the price of Yugoslav territory, he had already shown a similar deference to earlier Allied wishes in offering Serbian Macedonia to Bulgaria as payment for that country's help. Nevertheless, the Yugoslav Committee was most unhappy with the Pašić government over its inability to stave off Allied promises of Yugoslav territory to Italy in the secret Treaty of London.

Another such conflict came over the question of Yugoslav volunteers. The Yugoslav Committee zealously recruited volunteers, both among South Slavic refugees from the Dual Monarchy and emigrants in North and South America. This show of strength was politically important to give the Yugoslav Committee leverage in its would-be position as an equal and independent partner in the task of Yugoslav liberation. In its appeal in November 1916 for recruits, the Yugoslav Committee took the public stance that Serbia needed and deserved the help of all Yugoslavs to liberate itself. Moreover, the Yugoslav Committee made it known to the Serbian government that its volunteer units should have an identity of their own, though under the Serbian army, and that these units should be in the forefront as the Habsburg Yugo-slav lands were occupied and liberated.

Pašić's government and the Serbian military were suspicious of the idea and even hostile to it. It was contrary to the instincts of the mili-tary to have an army of disparate parts, and for this reason they would have preferred to absorb all volunteers into existing units of the Ser-bian army. More importantly, for political reasons Pašić disliked the idea of enhancing the prestige of the Yugoslav Committee in such a tangible way. The Serbian government was much happier recruiting its own Serbian volunteers from America and the Habsburg lands and taking them into the Serbian army. Thus the Serbian government in fact squelched the Yugoslav Committee's plans for an "Adriatic Le-gion."

The question of volunteer units arose again as thousands of Serbian, Croatian, and Slovenian soldiers in the Austro-Hungarian army in Russia were either taken prisoner or defected to the Russians. Many of them were languishing in camps and dying of cold and disease. Finally the Russian high command was persuaded to permit these men to join volunteer units to fight for the Allied cause. However, regard-less of their national origin, and sometimes against their will, these men were organized into a Serbian army under Serbian officers sent from Corfu. By June 1916 this volunteer division of four regiments numbered around 15,000 men. The Serbian government charged the officers with the task of "creating units imbued with Serbian ideas, and which will be willing to die for the liberation of the Serbian hearth and for the unification of Serbdom and the Yugoslavs."

The whole conflict between the Pan-Serbian and the Yugoslav con-ceptions found an arena in this volunteer division in Russia. The crudely chauvinistic attitude of the Serbian officers and their offensive treatment of the men alienated the non-Serbs among the volunteers. This conflict was exacerbated by the outbreak of the March Revolution in 1917. Under the impress of the new spirit of democracy and national self-determination that the revolution fostered, the dissident volunteers and some of their officers demanded that a special representative com-mittee be established to participate in the command of the corps. At one of several meetings held for this purpose, according to an official report of April 4, 1917 (dated March 21 O.S.), twelve officers of the Second Regiment demanded the following: that the unit be called the

Yugoslav Volunteer Corps, that it be operated in that spirit, with equality in pay and status between the Serbian and non-Serbian personnel, and that all Serbian flags and insignia be exchanged for Yugoslav ones; that the Croats and Slovenes be put into units of their own so as to minimize friction with the Serbs; that the corps not be regarded as part of the Serbian army, under Serbian officers, but as "a separate Yugoslav revolutionary army made up of revolutionaries from the Yugoslav provinces of the Austro-Hungarian Monarchy"; and that more volunteers be recruited from among the Yugoslav prisoners of war in Russia. The statement by these officers called for an end to any idea of hegemony by one Yugoslav people over another. "Everyone must realize," it read, "that there cannot exist either a Greater Serbia or a Greater Croatia and a Greater Slovenia."

The commandant of the corps, General Mihailo Živković, replied by expelling thirty-one dissident officers and returning them to their status as prisoners of war. On the basis of his recommendations, the Serbian government in Corfu decided to permit volunteer officers to adopt Serbian citizenship if they so desired, and to change the name of the unit, if necessary, to the Volunteer Corps of Serbs-Croats-Slovenes. "We shall not yet use the name Yugoslavia," the Serbian government's decision read, "because the Bulgars, who are Yugoslavs, are not with us." The government also permitted battalions and regiments within the corps to be designated as Croatian or Slovenian whenever the number of recruits justified this. At the time, only about ten percent of the corps consisted of Croats and Slovenes.

Instead of satisfying the dissidents, the new regulations caused many of them to leave. Some 149 officers left because they did not wish to accept Serbian citizenship. By the end of May, 12,735 soldiers had left, thus leaving only about 20,000 officers and men out of the previous total of around 30,000. General Živković attributed this defection to the influence of Austrian and Bulgarian agitators as well as to the followers of Supilo and various Croatian and Slovenian nationalists. "Their aim is clear," he warned the Serbian government, "the creation of a Yugoslavia as a federal republic with the complete equality of the Serbs, Croats, and Slovenes."

Matters became so serious that Pašić called on the Yugoslav Committee to help restore order in the Volunteer Corps. However, the Yugoslav Committee was hardly in a mood to comply inasmuch as it was engaged at the time in a sharp conflict over the Serbian government's reluctance to have it recruit Yugoslavs in South America. The Yugoslav Committee wished to organize a "Yugoslav Legion," which would be "the representative on the battlefield of the Yugoslav program and the will of the Serbian, Croatian, and Slovenian people in Austria-Hungary for liberation from it and unification with Serbia into a single state; that [would] fight for the liberation of the Yugoslav lands of Austria-Hungary." Pašić had no intention of allowing the Yugoslav Committee such a political advantage.

Meanwhile the hard-pressed Russians had no desire to let the much needed manpower of the Volunteer Corps go to waste in squabbling and inactivity. On March 26, 1917, the Russian high command asked that, if the corps refused to fight any longer on any front but its own, its men at least be used for agricultural work. This only hurried the Serbian government's decision to transfer the corps to the Balkan Front at Salonika as soon as possible.

Relations between the Yugoslav Committee and the Serbian government continued to be poor throughout the war. One of the founders and leading members of the Yugoslav Committee, Frano Supilo, resigned on June 5, 1916, because he could no longer work with the Serbian government. Matters were not helped any by Pašić's tendency to ignore the Yugoslav Committee in his dealings with others and to neglect to keep it informed. The Yugoslav Committee replied in kind, even to the extent of working behind Pašić's back and pursuing aims that were at variance with Serbia's policy. In time, under the pressure of the changing fortunes of war, it became clear that some accord between the Serbian government and the Yugoslav Committee was imperative. This realization led to their meeting on Corfu in July 1917.

The Corfu Declaration of July 20, 1917

During the first half of 1917, many important changes took place in the course of the war which complicated an already complex situation for Serbia. A general military stalemate between the leading belligerents in Europe, various cautious attempts by Austria-Hungary to explore the possibility of concluding a peace, the tenuous existence of the Balkan Front at Salonika, the March Revolution in Russia and the fall of the tsarist government, and the entry of the United States into the war in April all contributed to a swiftly changing situation.

Inasmuch as the tsarist regime had provided Serbia with its strongest support, its overthrow in March 1917 was of grave concern to the Pašić government. Various assurances by the leaders of the Russian Provisional Government indicated that the revolution would cause no change in the Russian official attitude toward Serbia. When a group of representatives of the Serbian Kingdom and of the Yugoslav Committee called on the new Russian premier, Prince Lvov, he assured them, "We love Serbia. It has suffered more than anyone else. It must be not only restored but greatly enlarged and united into a Greater Serbia. Transmit my greetings to all your people. Long live Greater Serbia." While this statement may have warmed the hearts of certain Serbs in the delegation, it must have rankled the feelings of Dr. Ante Mandić, the Croatian representative of the Yugoslav Committee.

Prince-Regent Alexander and the Pašić government were very suspicious of the new Russian Foreign Minister Pavel Miliukov, who was known for his pro-Bulgarian sympathies in the past. On March 24, 1917, Miliukov made a public announcement which, this time, gladdened Mandić and the Yugoslav Committee. "We wish the creation of a Yugoslavia, solidly organized," the Russian foreign minister declared. "We shall erect around glorious Serbia an impassable barrier against German ambitions in the Balkans. Liberated Russia can have no other ambition or other ideal than the liberation of nations, the victims of German imperialism." This statement was a coup for the Yugoslav Committee in that it was the first official recognition of the idea of Yugoslav unification ever made publicly by any responsible statesman of the Great Powers. Yet neither Premier Lvov's pro-Serbian statement nor Miliukov's pro-Yugoslav declaration was of much practical import. It was clear to interested observers, especially to Pašić as he read Minister Spalajković's dispatches from Petrograd, that the Provisional Government was very provisional indeed and on shaky legs. Miliukov's downfall in early May 1917 confirmed this assessment. As Pašić reported to Prince-Regent Alexander, "Russia has been thrown into an uncertain and revolutionary situation whose end it may not be possible to predict unless extreme elements are not suppressed in time and common sense prevails."

It was precisely in that uncertain time, in late April and early May, when there were fears that a further move to the left might cause Russia to leave the war and conclude a separate peace, that Pašić decided to hold a conference with the Yugoslav Committee.

The Serbian government faced not only an unsettling situation abroad but also internal problems and difficulties of its own.

Not the least of these was politics within its own ranks. The Pašić government was based on a coalition of the Radical party, the Independent Radicals, and the Progressives. The Radicals were in the driver's seat, with Pašić as premier and foreign minister, Momčilo Ninčić as finance minister (after Paču's death in October 1915), Marko Djuričić as minister of justice, and Ljubomir Jovanović as minister of the interior. The Independent Radicals were represented by Ljubomir Davidović as minister of education and Milorad Drašković as minister of public works. The Progressives had Vojislav Marinković as minister of the national economy and General Božidar Terzić as war minister.

On the whole, this coalition government on Corfu operated without the National Assembly which, after the fall of Serbia, was convened only once in 1915 and once in 1916, and only once more until the end of the war, from February to April 1918. This National Assembly consisted originally of 166 deputies, of whom 123 got out of Serbia. Of these, 85 gathered in Rome. When they were joined by 10 more from Athens, they organized a parliamentary club, which moved its seat to Nice. On their insistence, the Serbian government called them to Corfu for a meeting of the National Assembly, which lasted from September 10 to October 22, 1916. The Pašić government met with the hostility of many deputies, despite the fact that the majority were Radicals. The chief cause of their discontent was the government's inactive foreign policy and unclear program for the future. After the Assembly adjourned, the Pašić government might have relapsed into its rather comfortable life on balmy Corfu. However, it faced another, even more serious, source of dissension—the military.

The conflict between Pašić and the Black Hand, or Unification or Death, movement was of long standing. It came also to involve Prince-Regent Alexander. An ambitious man, Alexander had no intention of being the pawn of the Black Hand. To counter their influence, he organized his own clique of officers, the White Hand, and then proceeded to move against Colonel Dimitrijević-Apis and his group.

Alexander and his supporters trumped up charges that Apis and his henchmen were plotting a mutiny in the army and the assassination of the prince-regent. A treason trial was held in Salonika between April 2 and June 5, 1917. As a result of the court-martial, Apis and two colleagues were executed on June 26, 1917, after being forced to stand beside their graves for over two hours while their sentence was read. According to three eyewitness accounts, Apis's last words were "Long live Great Serbia! Long live Yugoslavia!" Alexander made every effort to give the impression that the chief reason for Apis's death was his involvement in the assassination of Archduke Franz Ferdinand in Sarajevo. It is possible that Alexander did so to clear the way for a separate peace with Austria-Hungary, though this has never been proven. At any rate, although he had found a convenient way of getting rid of his enemies, the affair left a bad impression and smacked of foul play.

Just before deciding to convene a conference with the Yugoslav Committee on Corfu, Pašić was confronted with another problem with which he was already familiar—the dissidence between the Serbs on the one hand and the Croats and Slovenes on the other in the Volunteers Corps in Odessa. This problem became so acute that the Russians decided to intervene. On May 3, 1916, the Russian chargé d'affaires on Corfu, Pelikhin, insisted on calling on Pašić, though the latter was sick in bed, and transmitted to him Miliukov's desire that the Serbian government establish harmony in the Volunteer Corps by instructing the commanders to end all intolerance.

Another problem that worried the Serbian government in 1916 and 1917 was the Montenegrin question. In Montenegro there were two camps at the time, those who supported King Nicholas against unification with Serbia and those who were for union. King Nicholas was not willing to sacrifice his throne to a union with Serbia; he even staked his claim to certain territories that Serbia hoped to annex. Prince-Regent Alexander regarded his Montenegrin royal uncle as a decided challenge to his own ambitions and was eager to rid himself of this threat. Pašić was in strong support of union with Montenegro. Accordingly the Serbian government accepted Pašić's proposal that the matter of union with Montenegro not wait until the end of the war. Pašić persuaded Montenegrin Premier Andrija Radović to submit to King Nicholas a memorandum, on August 19, 1916, in which he urged the old monarch to abdicate for the sake of union with Serbia and the creation of a larger union of Serbs, Croats, Slovenes, and—Radović hoped—perhaps eventually even Bulgars. The memorandum proposed that Prince-Regent Alexander be regarded as King Peter's successor, as he already was, but that King Nicholas's son Prince Danilo should succeed him, then Alexander's male heirs, and then the princes of both dynasties in turn. At first allegedly in favor of the idea, King Nicholas later opposed it, presumably after his stay in Italy, where his daughter was queen. The Italians preferred a small Montenegro which they could influence to a Greater Serbia which they could not.

After that relations grew worse between the Montenegrin and Serbian governments and also among the members of the Montenegrin government itself, which was divided between Separatists and Unionists. Pašić was able to secure the resignation of Radović's cabinet, which was quite a blow to Nicholas, and to organize a Montenegrin Committee abroad, headed by Radović, for furthering the cause of Montenegrin-Serbian union. When that committee wished to proclaim as its program "the unification of Montenegro with Serbia and the liberated Serbo-Croato-Slovenian lands," Pašić persuaded Radović to change this to "unification with Serbia and the other Serbian lands." Pašić explained that Serbian-Montenegrin unification had to take place first, whether there was to be a Yugoslavia or not. With the appearance of the first issue of the Montenegrin Committee's newspaper *Ujedinjenje* (Unification) in Paris on April 2, 1917, the plan of a Serbian-Montenegrin union came out into the open. Meanwhile Pašić made arrangements with the Serbian high command to make certain that the Serbian army would enter Montenegro before the return of the exiled King Nicholas. It is indicative of the Montenegrin Committee's dependence on Pašić that it never attempted to join forces with the Yugoslav Committee, though the two committees were on cordial terms.

Still another worry of the Serbian government on Corfu was the perennial Macedonian Question. Two aspects of this question made the Serbian government apprehensive. One was the fear that Bulgaria would offer the Allies a separate peace in exchange for that large part of Macedonia it had lost to Serbia in the Second Balkan War. Pašić feared that Miliukov's pro-Bulgarian sympathies might sway the Russian Provisional Government to support Bulgaria in such a move. To avert any such settlement of the Macedonian Question, Pašić proposed that the Serbian minister of education be given 300,000 francs to carry on a cultural campaign to counter Bulgarian influence in Macedonia, in the event that a plebiscite were held in Macedonia after the war.

The Macedonian Question also cast a shadow on the Serbian government's relations with the Yugoslav Committee. On the one hand, the Serbian government insisted that the Macedonian Slavs were Serbs; on the other, it had kept that province as occupied territory since 1912, without granting it the privileges of the Serbian constitution. This was hardly model treatment of a liberated brotherly people. At the same time, some Macedonian Slavic émigrés in Russia and Switzerland worked hard to convince the Allies that the best solution for them would be an autonomous Macedonia as part of a Balkan federation consisting of Serbia (within its borders of 1912), Montenegro, Dalmatia, a divided Vojvodina, Croatia, Albania, Bulgaria (minus the Pirin region), and Macedonia.

Just as the Serbian government had problems, so, too, the Yugoslav Committee had its own difficulties. One of the most serious was the political situation in Croatia and the other Yugoslav lands of the Habsburg Monarchy. Another was dissension within the membership of the committee itself.

The position of the Yugoslav Committee was inevitably compromised by the continued loyalty of the Croatian Diet to the House of Habsburg. This loyalty was solemnly affirmed on March 9, 1917, in an effusive address to Francis Joseph's successor, Charles IV. There were doubtless many people in the Yugoslav lands of the Dual Monarchy, especially among the Croats and the Slovenes, who favored an Austrian Empire in which the South Slavs would enjoy the same rights in a Triple Monarchy as the Magyars did in a Dual Monarchy. This attitude was strengthened by the expectation that the Habsburg Monarchy would survive, owing to the Austro-Hungarian government's note of December 12, 1916, indicating its readiness to negotiate a peace, and the new emperor's pledge in his accession speech to work for peace. On May 18–19, 1917, ten days before the opening of Parliament in Vienna, a group of Croatian and Slovenian politicians met in the Austrian capital and issued a declaration in which they affirmed their loyalty to the Habsburg crown. At the same time, they called for the immediate establishment of an autonomous Yugoslav territory within the empire, to consist of Croatia and Slovenia, which would be equal in rights with Hungary. The declaration made no mention of Serbs. Because of the subsequent urging of especially the Slovenes, thirty-three South Slavic deputies to Parliament formed a Yugoslav caucus on May 29. The next day their president, the Slovene Anton Korošec, read the following statement in Parliament:

The undersigned national deputies who are banded together in the Yugoslav Caucus declare that, on the basis of the national principle as well as of Croatian state rights, they demand the unification of all the lands of the Monarchy which are inhabited by Slovenes, Croats, and Serbs, into a single, autonomous political body, free from the rule of alien peoples and founded on a democratic basis, under the scepter of the Habsburg-Lotharingian Dynasty, and that they will bend all their efforts to the realization of this demand by their united people.

Whether or not the "May Declaration," as it came to be known, was encouraged by the court in Vienna is still an open question. However, there is no doubt that it momentarily won the support, whether sincere or tactical, of the leading political forces among the Habsburg South Slavs, including some prominent Serbs, notably Srdjan Budisavljević and Valerijan Pribićević.

In one respect the May Declaration advanced the Yugoslav cause. A united autonomous Yugoslav within the Habsburg Empire would have replaced the previous eleven administrative units and thirteen different codes of law of the South Slavs in that empire. Now even Ante Starčević's Croatian nationalist Party of Rights adopted the view that "the Slovenes, Serbs and Croats are a single people," even though it envisaged Yugoslavia as an extension of a Greater Croatia. On the other hand, the May Declaration was another blow to the prestige and moral authority of the Yugoslav Committee, which supported a Yugoslavia of a different sort under the scepter of the Karadjordjević dynasty. In fact, it shook many of its members in their conviction in the possibility of an independent Yugoslavia, a conviction that was already badly shaken by Supilo's defection from the committee. Mutual suspicions divided the committee as never before. The position of its Serbian members became especially awkward.

It was the difficulties that both the Serbian government and the Yugoslav Committee faced that forced them to realize the need for closer harmony between them. Previously accustomed to ignoring the committee, on March 30, 1917, Pašić sent Trumbić a cordial letter in which he proposed that, in view of poor communications between them, the Yugoslav Committee send at least four of its members to

Corfu to advise the Serbian government on matters relating to the Yugoslavs of Austria-Hungary. Despite some suspicion on the part of a few members that Pašić wished to weaken the Yugoslav Committee, his proposal was well received. In early May Pašić invited Trumbić to come with a Croat from Croatia Proper, a Serb from Bosnia, and a Slovene representative as well as Stojan Protić, Pašić's emissary to the Yugoslav Committee, to Corfu for an exchange of opinions "concerning all questions." Again despite some suspicions of Pašić's intentions, the Yugoslav Committee designated the following delegates: in addition to its president, Trumbić, who was a Dalmatian Croat, Bogumil Vošnjak, a Slovene; Hinko Hinković, a Croat from Croatia Proper; and Dušan Vasiljević, a Serb from Bosnia. Additional representatives included Dinko Trinajstić of Istria, who was the Yugoslav Committee's agent on Corfu; Stojan Protić, the Serbian government's agent on the Yugoslav Committee; and Franko Potočnjak, a Croat who, much to Trumbić's discomfort, was personally invited by Pašić, though he had left the Yugoslav Committee, largely for personal reasons. The representatives of the Serbian government included N. Pašić, M. Ninčić, V. Marinković, M. Drašković, and Lj. Davidović. No Montenegrin was present. Rather, the Montenegrin Committee was given an opportunity to ratify the work of the Corfu Conference later.

The conference lasted from June 15 to July 20, 1917. During those 36 days it met in 24 sessions. The main task of the conference was to agree on a declaration concerning the nature of the future Yugoslav state. It was apparent throughout that while Pašić stressed the unitary nature of that state, Trumbić dwelt on the individual nature of each constituent land and asked for what amounted to a federal structure, though he avoided calling it that. The final declaration was a compromise. The conference rejected Trumbić's proposal that each constituent territory maintain its own administrative and legislative bodies in addition to corresponding central bodies; however, the declaration did refer vaguely to a limited local autonomy. As for other questions of formal internal organization, for example, that the new state would be a constitutional and parliamentary monarchy based on a democratic system with universal manhood suffrage, and so on, the members of the conference were in easy agreement. The really thorny questions involved agrarian reform and the provisional administration of the newly liberated territories. These questions were not included in the declaration.

The Corfu Declaration, which was signed by Pašić and Trumbić on July 20, 1917, consisted of a preamble and fourteen articles.

The preamble enunciated "again and most decidedly" that the Serbs, Croats, and Slovenes were "the same by blood, by language, both spoken and written, by the feelings of their unity, by the continuity and integrity of the territory which they inhabit undividedly, and by the common vital interests of their national survival and the manifold development of their moral and material life." After expressing homage to France, England, the United States, and "new, free, and democratic Russia" for proclaiming the principles of national freedom and self-determination, the declaration proceeded to list the "modern and democratic principles" on which the future Yugoslav state would be based. The fourteen points that followed form the most important document in the history of the Yugoslav movement up to that time.

1. The Kingdom of the Serbs, Croats, and Slovenes, known also under the name of South Slavs or Yugoslavs, shall be a free, independent Kingdom with a single territory and single citizenship. It shall be a constitutional, democratic, and parliamentary monarchy headed by the Karadjordjević dynasty, which has given proof that it is not separated from the people in its ideas and feelings and that it places the freedom and will of the people above all else.

2. This State shall be called: the Kingdom of the Serbs, Croats, and Slovenes, and its ruler: the King of the Serbs, Croats, and Slovenes.

3. It shall have a single coat of arms, a single state flag, and a single crown. These state emblems shall be composed of our present individual emblems. The integrity of the state shall be designated by the state coat of arms and the state flag.

The state flag, as the symbol of unity, will be exhibited on all of the official institutions of the Kingdom.

4. The individual Serbian, Croatian, and Slovenian flags are equal and may be exhibited and freely used on all occasions. The individual coats of arms may also be used freely and on all occasions.

5. All three national names: Serbs, Croats, and Slovenes, are completely equal on the entire territory of the Kingdom, and everyone may use them freely on all public occasions and in all official agencies.

6. Both alphabets, the Cyrillic and the Latin, are also completely equal and everyone may freely use them on the entire territory of the Kingdom. All state and autonomous authorities are obliged and have the right to use both the one alphabet and the other, in conformity with the wishes of the citizenry.

7. All recognized religions may be exercised freely and publicly. The Orthodox, the Roman Catholic, and the Mohammedan religions, which are the

strongest among our people by the number of their adherents, shall be equal before the state and have the same rights.

On the basis of these principles the legislative authority shall take care to preserve and maintain religious peace, which conforms to the spirit and the past of our entire people.

8. The calendar should be coordinated as soon as possible.

9. The territory of the Kingdom of the Serbs, Croats, and Slovenes embraces that entire territory which is inhabited by our three-named people in a compact and unbroken mass, and it cannot be reduced without damaging the vital interests of the whole.

Our people ask for nothing alien: they ask only for what is their very own, and they desire to be freed and united completely, as a single whole. Therefore, consciously and deliberately, they reject every partial solution of their national liberation and unification. Our people pose as an indivisible whole the problem of their liberation from Austria-Hungary and their unification with Serbia and Montenegro in a single state.

According to the principle of free national self-determination no one part of this whole can be rightfully separated and joined to any other state without the agreement of the people themselves.

10. In the interest of the freedom and equal rights of all nations, the Adriatic Sea shall be free and open to one and all.

11. All citizens on the entire territory are equal and have the same rights before the state and before the law.

12. Electoral rights in the election of national deputies to the National Representative Body as well as to communes and other administrative units are equal and universal, and shall be carried out by direct and secret suffrage in the communes

13. A Constitution, which shall be promulgated by a Constitutional Assembly elected on the basis of universal and equal, direct and secret suffrage, shall be the basis for the entire life of the state, the source and the point of departure for all authority and rights, and it shall determine the entire life of the state.

14. The Constitution shall also give the people the opportunity to develop their individual energies in autonomous units as defined by natural, social, and economic circumstances.

The Constitution is to be accepted in its entirety by a numerically qualified majority of the Constitutional Assembly.

Both the Constitution and other laws which shall be promulgated by the Constitutional Assembly shall go into force when the King sanctions them.

It should be noted that the whole Corfu Declaration was based on the proposition that the Serbs, Croats, and Slovenes were, in fact, one people; hence the awkward expression "the three-named people" (*troimeni narod*). However dubious this claim was from an ethnographic standpoint, it represented the prevailing conception of the Yugoslav ideology at the time. It was a view, however, that had been far more prevalent in the Yugoslav Committee than among the leaders of Serbia. Nevertheless, Pašić, Prince Alexander, and other Serbian leaders also used the formula in their public pronouncements. The question is, Why did both the Serbian government and the Yugoslav Committee not only accept such a definition but even stretch the truth to make it fit such a conception? For example, the Corfu Declaration claimed that the Serbs, Croats, and Slovenes spoke the same language, whereas in actual fact Slovenian is a quite distinct language. In addition to the excessive enthusiasm of romantic nationalism, the chief answer probably lies in the burning desire of both the Serbian government and the Yugoslav Committee to present a solidly united front to the Allies. President Wilson had already enunciated the principle of national self-determination, as had the Russian Provisional Government, Lloyd George, and other Allied leaders. It was also necessary for the Yugoslavs to appear united in the face of Italian pretensions to the eastern Adriatic coast. On the other hand, as soon as men such as Trumbić discussed the *internal* organization of the new state, they necessarily pleaded their case for local autonomy by pointing to the differences among the Serbs, Croats, and Slovenes. It should be added that it occurred to none of the delegates at the Corfu Conference to regard either the Macedonian Slavs or the Montenegrins as distinct nationalities, even though the former were by no means Serbs ethnographically, whereas the latter, though Serbs, had a long separate political existence of their own.

While the conference somewhat reluctantly agreed to accept the name *Yugoslav* as being *equivalent* to "Serbs, Croats, and Slovenes," it would not agree on the name *Yugoslavia* for the new state, although the entire session of June 29 was spent on the problem. No one advanced the argument, as in times past, that the name *Yugoslavia* (that is, literally *South-Slavia*) was inappropriate as long as the Bulgars were not included. Rather, it was the consensus that the name *Yugoslavia* was somewhat artificial, that it was not equally familiar to all, and that one could not, and should not, ask the Serbs, Croats, and Slovenes to abandon their own names for one that was strange to so many of them.

The toughest question that confronted the conference concerned the internal organization of the future state. It required more discussion than any other question. While Pašić stood for a centralized system such as Serbia already had, Trumbić announced that although he was for state unity, he was not for a united state. "This is not a fine point," he assured the rest, "but a conception." He pointed out that Croatia, for example, already possessed a tradition of autonomy and its own legislation concerning internal affairs, religion, education, and justice, and that the other lands, especially Dalmatia, Istria, Slovenia, and, to a lesser extent, Bosnia and Hercegovina, had a similar sense of their own autonomy. He might have included Montenegro, which was, after all, an independent kingdom. Thus, while he professed agreement with the principle of state unity and stated that he opposed a federal system, both because of economic considerations and because it would be too difficult to draw the boundaries of the constituent units, Trumbić nevertheless asked the conference to leave open the opportunity for some local autonomy. He specifically warned that while the Serbian constitution might well suit a country as compact and homogeneous as Serbia, its provisions would hardly suit the much larger and diversified Kingdom of the Serbs, Croats, and Slovenes.

It is not surprising that Trumbić had no support from the Serbian members of the conference, not even those representing the Yugoslav Committee. However, he was not supported by his Croatian and Slovenian colleagues either. The Croats Hinković and Potočnjak came out strongly for centralism. The Slovene Vošnjak came closer to Trumbić's conception by asking for a centralized state but with some local autonomy; however, he specifically rejected federalism as being too "complicated" for the South Slavs. Vošnjak picturesquely described the central government as the father and local governments as the children, whereas in a federal system, he warned, they were all fathers.

Countering Trumbić's vague, even contradictory, proposal, Pašić and his Serbian colleagues unabashedly called for a purely centralized system. Pašić even warned that, in view of the strength of their feelings, the Serbs would opt for a Greater Serbia rather than for a federal Yugoslavia. He dismissed the existing autonomies of the various Habsburg South Slavic lands as mere vestiges of the struggle against an alien rule: there would be no need for this in a state of one's own. Jovanović and Marinković stressed that economic considerations and a united foreign policy required a unitary state. Davidović was candid enough to observe, "Our people are easily won over by ideas of decentralization, and the greater part of their energies would be wasted on this. It would be difficult to apportion the burden. Everybody will think that he is carrying most of the burden. So, too, with the benefits, everyone will think that the other one is getting more."

After the long discussion was over, Trumbić was so completely put on the defensive that he ended up by declaring that his aim, too, was a single state with a single legislature and a single executive power. He even specified those aspects of the new state that he conceded had to be unified: one political territory, one ruling house, one citizenship, one foreign ministry, one customs border with no internal customs, one merchant marine, one army, one currency and financial system, one system of state property, one postal and telegraph system, one system of roads and railroads, and one budget. Still hoping to preserve some measure of local autonomy, he suggested that it would be politically undesirable to incorporate the centralized solution in the declaration in such absolute terms. Rather, he urged, let the people themselves decide in a future constitutional assembly.

This led to an even livelier debate as to the nature of the constitutional assembly and, specifically, the kind of vote that would be needed to accept the new constitution. A subcommittee of the conference proposed that a "qualified majority" be required, for, as Marinković pointed out, "If a third of the people do not wish a union, then it is better not to have it." Nearly all the conference members agreed, however, that the vote should not be along ethnic lines, but that a purely numerical "qualified" majority should decide. Pašić advised that the majority be defined as three-fifths of the votes, and this recommendation was duly recorded in the minutes. Again Trumbić cautiously sought a compromise by suggesting some combination of a numerically and ethnically qualified majority, but he was outvoted. Thus the numerically superior Serbs were left with a decided advantage.

It is obvious that in all these and still other confrontations at the Corfu Conference the Yugoslav Committee gave in substantially to the Serbian government. This was inevitable in view of the fact that the Yugoslav Committee was divided and Trumbić had little support from his own colleagues. If Trumbić surrendered so easily, it was, as he later put it in his memoirs, because it was more important to be united on the territorial question vis-à-vis Italy than to quarrel over questions of internal organization that would have to be settled later anyway by a constitutional assembly.

The Corfu Declaration was merely declaratory and carried no legal force. Whatever its moral claims were to represent the South Slavs of Austria-Hungary, the Yugoslav Committee had no legal right to do so. Moreover, it was obvious that the real outcome would depend on the course of the war and, as ever before, on the wishes of the Great Powers. The Corfu Declaration did not, in fact, settle anything. Trumbić and others may have regarded it as the Magna Charta of Yugoslav unification. For Pašić it was a tactical move in response to a given political situation. On the international level, he had to count on the weakening of Russia's support as a result of the March Revolution. In the Corfu Declaration, which he regarded as being more declaratory than legally binding, he had a token of Yugoslav unity with which he could impress the Allies and counter both Italian ambitions along the eastern Adriatic coast and the consequences of the May Declaration by the Yugoslav caucus in Vienna. He also reduced the Yugoslav Committee to a compromise in which he got the advantage, and had their signed acceptance of the Karadjordjević dynasty. Neither Pašić nor the Yugoslav Committee were very happy over the Corfu Declaration. Pašić was not willing to use it any more than he had to, and especially once the Bolshevik Revolution eliminated Russian support entirely, he reverted easily to his original policy of assuring Serbia's enlargement first. As for the Yugoslav Committee, it adhered loyally to the Corfu Declaration until it became clear that Pašić had no intention of treating the committee as an equal partner and representative of the Habsburg South Slavs even though he had signed a declaration with its president. Relations between the Serbian government and the Yugoslav Committee were more strained than ever as they entered the last year of the war.

From the Corfu Declaration to the Liberation of Serbia, November 1, 1918

Pašić's first step after releasing the Corfu Declaration was to go to Paris to attend an Allied conference concerning the fate of the Balkan Front at Salonika. He arrived on July 25, 1917, just in time to learn that the British were asking to withdraw a part of their troops to the Middle East, where they were hard pressed in Palestine and Mesopotamia. During the conference the news arrived of a collapse on the

Russian Front, which made any Russian support for Serbia's cause all the more impossible.

Pašić thereupon went to London, on July 30, to see if he could do anything to persuade the British not to pull out of the Balkan Front. He failed in this, much to the disappointment of the Serbs, since the Serbian army, which was strung along a line fifty-eight kilometers long, was exhausted to the point of near collapse. However, Lloyd George did, on two public occasions in Pašić's honor, affirm his government's support of a liberated and renewed Serbia, and Balfour declared in Commons that Serbia would assume an honored place at the peace conference and that it would be compensated for its sacrifices. Though vague, such declarations were comforting to the Serbs inasmuch as none of the Allies had ever made a formal commitment to any gains for Serbia.

From London Pašić returned to Paris, where he met with French War Minister Paul Painlevé to inform him of the desperate condition of the Serbian army. Most of all, Pašić was worried by a report from Prince-Regent Alexander saying that when Alexander asked General Sarrail, the Allied commander of the Balkan Front, to shorten the Serbian line, Sarrail threatened to give up Bitola and all of Serbia's territory. Painlevé assured Pašić that this would not occur.

As British troops continued to leave the Balkan Front and anticipated Greek reinforcements failed to arrive, the Serbian government and high command turned in desperation to the United States, which, though at war with Germany since April, had not yet declared war on Austria-Hungary. In early August the Serbs asked the United States to send a contingent of troops primarily of Yugoslav origin, trained and equipped by the United States. The American military representative in Salonika explained that the United States could hardly do such a thing as long as it was not at war with Austria-Hungary; besides it was against American policy to organize army units along ethnic lines. The Serbian envoy in Washington, Ljuba Mihajlović, assured the Serbian government that it was quite enough to expect the United States government to close its eyes to the recruiting that Serbia and the Yugoslav Committee had been doing on their own among Yugoslav immigrants there. Pašić worked so desperately to get any Allied reinforcements for the Serbian army that he even asked about the possibility of having Japan send soldiers.

From Paris Pašić went to Rome, on September 6. He had tried to mollify Italian public reaction to the Corfu Declaration by various statements in advance of his trip. For example, he told a London *Times* reporter that the principles on which the new Serbo-Croato-Slovenian state would be founded were identical with those on which Italy had built her greatness, and that he was confident that this state and Italy could join forces and together contribute to the Allied cause. In Rome Pašić tried to reach an agreement with the Italian government concerning Istria, Dalmatia, and the islands. The Italians promised that they would not hinder the unification of the Yugoslavs.

Following Pašić's return to Corfu on September 12, many changes took place on the international scene that affected Serbia's position greatly. The most disruptive of these was the Bolshevik Revolution in November and the formal withdrawal of Russia from the war with the Treaty of Brest-Litovsk. On the other hand, the fact that the United States had entered the war, though not yet against Austria-Hungary, raised Serbian hopes that the United States might enter the breach left by Russia and help Serbia. The Serbian government desired material aid and political support from the United States. It was more immediately successful in the former aim than the latter. Barely a month after the American declaration of war, the Serbian government took steps to obtain financial aid and military supplies. In mid-June the United States government approved a loan of 3 million dollars, largely for aid to Serbian soldiers, their indigent families, wounded veterans, and prisoners of war. It could not accede to the latter's request for troop reinforcements in the Balkan Front, not even after it had declared war on Austria-Hungary on December 7, 1917.

As for political support, the Serbian government sent a mission to Washington under Dr. Milenko Vesnić, Serbia's envoy to Paris. The five-man mission remained in the United States from December 20, 1917, to mid-February 1918. On being introduced to President Wilson by Secretary of State Robert Lansing, Vesnić handed the president a personal letter from Prince-Regent Alexander thanking him and the American people for their aid and expressing the hope that "the American people and their chief will continue to show their kindness by giving their material assistance to the Serbian nation in its struggle for justice and the liberation of its brothers, who are impatiently awaiting the day when they will be in a position to proclaim loudly their decision to unite with it in a free Serbia." There was no mention of Yugoslav unification. Similarly, when Vesnić addressed the United

States Senate on January 5, 1918, he said nothing about the Corfu Declaration and its aspirations for Yugoslav unification, which caused the Yugoslav Committee in London to lodge a protest with Prince-Regent Alexander and the Serbian government on Corfu.

However, while Vesnić ignored the Yugoslav Question publicly, he did speak of it privately. On December 27 Vesnić had a conference with Lansing and other state department officials about Serbia's war aims which brought the Italian envoy di Cellere to the state department to denounce the "absurd Jugo-Slav aims and complaints against Italy." On January 5 Vesnić had a similar conversation with President Wilson's confidant and personal representative Colonel Edward M. House.

The Serbian Mission may have had several reasons for not bringing the Yugoslav Question into the open. The Yugoslavs in America were badly disunited, and certain elements among them were actively hostile to the Serbian mission. The American public knew nothing about the Yugoslav Question. As for the American government, Vesnić felt that Washington was not interested in Yugoslav unification at the time and that it would be impolitic to raise the issue publicly, especially after President Wilson had stated in his speech of December 4, 1917, before Congress that though he wished Congress to declare war on Austria-Hungary, he had no wish to cause the dissolution of the Habsburg Empire.

On January 5, 1918, Lloyd George addressed the British trade union representatives concerning Britain's war aims. Among these aims, he mentioned the restoration of Serbia and Montenegro, but instead of saying anything about a future Yugoslav state, he declared his agreement with Wilson that the destruction of the Dual Monarchy was not a war aim of the Allies. Rather, he was for granting the peoples of that empire true autonomy.

That very day Colonel House invited Vesnić to a private talk. On President Wilson's orders, Colonel House showed Vesnić an advance text of the president's famous Fourteen Points and asked for the Serbian envoy's opinion. Vesnić wrote on the margin of the draft his objection to point 11: As long as the Austro-Hungarian Empire continued to exist, its subject nationalities would oppose it. Three days later President Wilson delivered his Fourteen Points speech before Congress. Apparently Vesnić's objection caused no change in the text.

Points 10 and 11, which touched on Serbia and the Yugoslav Question, read as follows:

10. The peoples of Austria-Hungary, whose place among the nations we wish to see safeguarded and assured, should be accorded the freest opportunity of autonomous development.

11. Romania, Serbia and Montenegro should be evacuated; occupied territories restored; Serbia accorded free and secure access to the sea; and the relations of the several Balkan States to one another determined by friendly counsel along historically established lines of allegiance and nationality; and international guarantees of the political and economic independence and territorial integrity of the several Balkan States should be entered upon.

The similarity between Lloyd George's view and Woodrow Wilson's is obvious. Both speeches caused consternation in the Yugoslav Committee and in Yugoslav émigré circles in general. They also troubled the Serbian government. As the American special diplomatic agent to the Serbian government at Corfu, H. Percival Dodge, cabled Washington on January 16, 1918, "there is depression among the Serbians here . . . at the passage in the recent speeches of the President . . . and the British Premier relating to Austro-Hungarian Empire which are interpreted as meaning that Serbia will not have support of the Allies in securing union with her of the Yugoslavs." Pašić wrote to the Yugoslav Committee on January 18 that he believed these speeches to be but the first intimations of a general reorientation of the Allied policy as a result of Russia's withdrawal from the war. "England and America," he warned, "hold that they might attain peace more easily and quickly if they abandon the demands that the peoples of the Austro-Hungarian Monarchy be given the complete right of self-determination, but that they be assured an internal and autonomous part. This concession and retreat from the pure principle that every nation shall have the right of self-determination proves that our Allies do not wish to fight till a final victory, even though they make declarations that they will not give up until they defeat the enemy."

Nothing illustrates more sharply the difference between Pašić and the Yugoslav Committee than the opposite ways in which they reacted to a common misfortune. Ever the practical politician whose immediate ambition was Serbia's gain, Pašić accommodated himself to the new situation; officially he sent stern notes to the Allies demanding an explanation, but more quietly he intimated that, though Serbia continued to favor the dissolution of the Habsburg Empire and the realization of the Corfu Declaration, he was willing to bargain. His minimum demand was Bosnia and Hercegovina. Characteristically he justified this demand not by the principle of national self-determination but by a legalistic argument. As the Serbian minister in Washington, Mihajlović, explained it to Secretary of State Robert Lansing on January 22, since the Allies proposed to redress the wrong done Belgium by Germany's violation of its neutrality, guaranteed by international treaties in 1870, they should also compensate Serbia for Austria-Hungary's annexation of Bosnia-Hercegovina in violation of the Treaty of Berlin of 1878. Pašić cautioned Mihajlović in his instructions against revealing his change of policy to Croats and Slovenes in the United States, "because our brethren may be angry when they hear that Bosnia and Hercegovina may be liberated from Austrian bondage while they must still remain under Austria." He expressed his attitude in very paternalistic terms: "Our brethren now stand on this demand: all or nothing. They do not act as a good father would who, when unable to free all his children, frees those that he can, and as for the rest, he watches for the right time when he will be able to free them as well." When Mihajlović demurred against this repudiation of the Corfu Declaration, Pašić replied that he had been misunderstood: he was still for the declaration, but the Yugoslav union was not the decisive issue at the moment. This was in keeping with Pašić's whole attitude that Yugoslav unification was a process that would have to be carried out in stages. He sent similar instructions to the Serbian envoys in Paris and London. All three were so dismayed that they failed to carry out their instructions and suffered the consequences by being either transferred or pensioned. Worst of all, the matter did not remain a secret but came to the attention of the Yugoslav Committee in London, which reopened the quarrel between it and the Serbian government.

Instead of being as diplomatically discreet as the Serbian government, the Yugoslav Committee registered energetic protests against the Allied policy toward Austria-Hungary, beginning with a polite but firm statement by Dr. Trumbić in the London *Times* of January 11, 1918. The Yugoslav Committee also requested Pašić to convene a grand conclave in France to be attended by all the deputies of the Serbian National Assembly, the Yugoslav Committee and the Montenegrin Committee in their entirety, representatives of Yugoslav organizations in North and South America, and representatives of youth organizations, of the military and volunteer units, and of the trades and industry. It was suggested that the prince-regent preside as King Peter's representative. A similar request came from the chiefs of the Serbian parliamentary opposition.

Pašić chose to misunderstand their requests and called instead a meeting of just the Serbian National Assembly, on Corfu. This led to a rash of correspondence between the London Committee and the Serbian government in which Pašić insisted that the National Assembly should meet on Corfu, the seat of the Serbian government, and that it would be unconstitutional for persons other than the deputies to take part in the work of the Assembly. The Serbian premier was, as always, adamantly opposed to lending the Yugoslav Committee or any other organization even the suggestion of a legal status as the spokesman of the Yugoslavs; this role he reserved for Serbia.

The Serbian National Assembly met on Corfu on February 25, 1918. It consisted of 110 deputies. Before it convened, Pašić attempted to appease the opposition leaders by offering a coalition government, but the offer was rejected. Instead, the opposition demanded that the Assembly first be convened, that Pašić then resign, and that negotiations take place to form a new government. Apparently Pašić's opponents desired the opportunity to present their complaints against him and Minister of the Interior Ljubomir Jovanović, who was regarded as the chief architect of the notorious Salonika court-martial of Apis and his followers in the Black Hand. The Pašić government underwent a test of strength in a vote for a new president of the Assembly to replace the ailing Andra Nikolić. When only 54 deputies voted for the government's candidate and 50 for the opposition candidate, Pašić and his government resigned.

Negotiations for a new government took almost a month, from February 25 to March 23. The opposition exacted a heavy price: Pašić was to declare a coalition government indispensable; he could be premier but not foreign minister; on no account was Ljubomir Jovanović to be a member of the government; the trial of Apis and the Black Hand was to be investigated; the government's relations with the high command were to be reviewed, and so on. Pašić's reaction was that a coalition government was necessary but not indispensable; that he could not sacrifice Jovanović over a trial for which the whole government of that time, including the Independent Radicals and Progressives, shared responsibility; and that he could not abandon the conduct of Serbia's foreign policy, since no one else was capable of replacing him. Accordingly, on March 27 Pašić simply reconstituted his previous cabinet, and four days later the Assembly resumed its work.

On March 31 Pašić delivered a report to the Assembly concerning his government's foreign policy. While the Assembly found the general lines of that policy acceptable, the opposition decried the government's alleged lack of energy and initiative in pursuing it. It is interesting that Pašić made no reference in his report to the Corfu Declaration, purportedly in order not to give Italy offense. Such caution only lent credence to the opposition's charges. However, the sharpest attacks were reserved for Pašić's domestic policy. He was accused of heading a nonparliamentary, autocratic government of usurpers who acted on their own. Some deputies also complained of a harmful personality cult and political fetishism with which the Radical party surrounded Pašić. Far from seeing him as the grand old man whose long white whiskers suggested an all-wise fatherly deity, some of his enemies saw him as "the demon of the Serbian nation," in the phrase of one deputy. After fifteen days of discussion concerning the government's reports, the Assembly took up the matter of the government's request for authorization to obtain war credits of 250 million dinars. Following an acrimonious debate, all 42 of the opposition members walked out in protest, leaving only 53 pro-government deputies to vote for the appropriation.

The opposition bloc insisted that Pašić be ousted. They even sought the prince-regent's intervention, presenting him on May 20 with a bill of particulars of Pašić's alleged misdeeds. It cited his disregard for the law, his reprisals against political opponents, and his favoritism toward his supporters. At the same time, in wishing to persuade the prince-regent to appoint a new government himself, the opposition was itself guilty of seeking an unparliamentary act. The prince-regent refused to reply to the opposition's demarche. To prevent any further maneuvers, Pašić in fact dissolved the Assembly, simply by letting the Radical deputies know that they could leave. While this did indeed end the affair, the whole session of the Assembly, the last to be held on Corfu, left a bad impression on everyone. Pašić's high-handed treatment only seemed to confirm the opposition's charges.

The partisan feuding reverberated even at the Salonika Front, where it further demoralized the troops. And certainly the Assembly did not even remotely satisfy the Yugoslav Committee, which wanted a meeting of quite a different sort.

Relations between the Yugoslav Committee and the Serbian government became progressively worse. Never pleased with the Corfu Declaration, and now particularly displeased with both Pašić's actions and his inaction after the speeches by Lloyd George and Woodrow Wilson, Trumbić decided to work actively for something he had wanted for a long time, namely, Allied recognition of the Yugoslav Committee as the representative of the Dual Monarchy's South Slavs. This became the most crucial issue between the Yugoslav Committee and the Serbian government in mid-1918. At the same time, the Yugoslav Committee worked energetically to persuade the Allies with various memoranda that they must not sacrifice the subject nationalities of Austria-Hungary. The émigré groups of other nationalities—Czechs, Slovaks, Poles, and Romanians—were similarly engaged.

This effort coincided with the successful attempts of Great Britain's two leading experts on central European affairs—Henry Wickham Steed of the London *Times* and the "Enemy Propaganda Department" of the Foreign Office, and historian Robert W. Seton-Watson—to bring about a change in British policy. In a memorandum to the Foreign Office, Steed described the failure of Britain's Austrophile policy and suggested another approach, namely: "To try to break the power of Austria-Hungary, as the weakest link in the chain of enemy States, by supporting and encouraging all anti-German and pro-Ally peoples and tendencies." Or as Arthur H. Frazier, American representative at the Supreme War Council, quoted Steed in a dispatch to Washington, "We have 31 million friends in Austria-Hungary and 20 million enemies. Why not help our friends?" This proposal became especially attractive after the German army began a concentrated effort to break through the British sector of the Western Front. As the Allies began to withdraw from their earlier position of maintaining the territorial integrity of the Habsburg Empire, both the Serbian government and the Yugoslav Committee were presented with a situation that was increasingly favorable to the Yugoslav cause.

The Yugoslav Committee greatly advanced its position in this period, owing to two related acts. Steed and Seton-Watson facilitated a meeting between the Yugoslav Committee and certain liberal Italians, notably former Senator Andrea Torre and G. A. Borgese, who deplored the now no longer secret Treaty of London and who wished to identify their country with liberal nationalism rather than with imperialism. While these Italians acted as purely private individuals, certainly without the approval of their foreign minister, Baron Sidney Sonnino, they did have the unofficial blessing of Premier Vittorio Orlando. In his amiable meeting with the Italians, Trumbić made quite clear that the Yugoslav Committee would not surrender an inch of Yugoslav territory, and the Italians explained that they had no power to repudiate the Treaty of London as such. However, they did reach an accord, recorded in the Torre-Trumbić Agreement of March 7, 1918, in which the Italians supported Yugoslav unification and both parties called for a free Adriatic Sea and a division of their liberated territories in Austria on the basis of the principle of national self-determination. Though this agreement had no legal status, it in fact gave the *coup de grâce* to the Treaty of London. Thus the Yugoslav Committee made a substantial contribution to the cause of Yugoslav unification and greatly added to its own prestige.

A second and related project of the Yugoslav Committee was its participation in the Congress of Oppressed Nationalities of Austria-Hungary, which met in Rome on April 10, 1918. Here Czech and Slovak, Polish, Romanian, and Yugoslav representatives proclaimed the right of their peoples to self-determination, denounced the Austro-Hungarian Empire as a hindrance to their free development, and called for a common struggle for its downfall.

On April 21 the Italian government recognized the Czechoslovak National Council as a *de facto* government, a step whose import was not lost on the Yugoslav Committee. By May 29 Secretary of State Lansing declared his government's sympathy for the Czechoslovak and Yugoslav cause. On June 3 all the Allies made similar declarations. At last the cause of Yugoslav unification received open and official recognition.

It was only natural for the Yugoslav Committee to want recognition as the official spokesman for the Yugoslavs of Austria-Hungary. To this Pašić was stubbornly opposed. As he explained in his note of August 5 (July 23 O.S.), 1918, "Serbia, which together with its Allies is waging war for the liberation of the Serbs, Croats, and Slovenes and for their unification with the Kingdom of Serbia and Montenegro, represents our triune Serbo-Croato-Slovenian people abroad and speaks in its name in international relations. Therefore, there would be a certain dualism if our Allies were to appoint their representatives to the Yugoslav Committee." Pašić argued that Serbia played the same role toward the Yugoslavs that Italy did toward the Italians of Austria, or that Romania did toward the Romanians of Hungary as long as it was in the war. As for the Czecho-Slovaks and the Poles, their case was different, Pašić observed, because they had no existing free country of their own. Similarly, when the Serbian minister in London, Jovan Jovanović, asked for instructions concerning the Serbian government's attitude toward possible Allied official recognition of the Yugoslav Committee, Pašić reminded him in a dispatch of July 12 (June 29 O.S.), 1918, that the Corfu Declaration allowed for no dualism but proclaimed the principle of unity. "Serbia is thus the Yugoslav State, its army is the Yugoslav army, and to it as an independent state belongs the right officially to represent our national problems," Pašić declared. "The Yugoslav Committee should be the expression of the will of our people under Austria-Hungary to be liberated and united with Serbia. Its duty is to assist the Serbian Government, and as for all who wish to fight with gun in hand, their place is in our army." It is obvious that Pašić, who had but a short time ago preferred to be silent about the Corfu Declaration and not to exert himsef to advance the Yugoslav cause as distinct from Serbia's more immediate aspirations, was apparently prepared to champion the Yugoslav cause now that it had Allied approval. This was a position he was not willing to share with the Yugoslav Committee.

At this point even Steed and Seton-Watson decided to intervene. On August 8, 1918, they telegraphed a note to Prince-Regent Alexander asking him to take the matter into his own hands and bring about an understanding between the Serbian government and the Yugoslav Committee, especially inasmuch as the Allies had already recognized the Czechoslovak National Council. Ignoring the whole matter of the official recognition of the Yugoslav Committee, which was the main point, Alexander replied simply that he knew of no differences in principle between the Serbian government and the Yugoslav Committee, and that the patriotism of both sides would smooth out any disagreements.

Dissatisfied with this, Seton-Watson decided to try to shame Pašić publicly into acceding to the viewpoint of the Yugoslav Committee. He published a sensational article entitled "Serbia's Choice" in the

August 22, 1918, issue of his review *New Europe*. "Only a knave or a fool," he wrote of Pašić, "would call his patriotism in question; but his outlook and standards are those of a vanishing era, and he is too old to shake off altogether the semi-Turkish traditions of his youth." Seton-Watson accused Pašić of ruling by illegal methods, of bypassing the National Assembly, of suppressing all political opposition, and of undermining the cause of Yugoslav unification. He asked that Pašić form a coalition cabinet and devote all his energies to supporting the national cause. He insisted that Allied recognition could go only to the two signatories of the Corfu Declaration, the Serbian government and the Yugoslav Committee, and that these two bodies should act as equal factors in complete harmony. Whichever Serbian politician fails to understand this, the article ended, was a traitor to the best interests of his people and not worthy of support. By his violent article Seton-Watson accomplished little except to widen the breach between Pašić, his Serbian opposition, and the Yugoslav Committee. Perhaps as an object lesson, it was at this very time that Pašić dismissed the Serbian minister to Washington, Ljuba Mihajlović, for insubordination. He was quite within his rights, for the envoy had disobeyed instructions and acted independently on several occasions; but Mihajlović was known for his pro-Yugoslav zeal, and his dismissal rankled feelings even more. In early September Wickham Steed telegraphed Prince-Regent Alexander again, putting forward as the Yugoslav Committee's opinion the need for a Serbian coalition government. He also tried to persuade the prince-regent to come personally to the West to receive Allied recognition of the whole Yugoslav people as an ally.

In a long letter to Pašić, sent from Paris in late September, Trumbić made clear the Yugoslav Committee's stand. Again affirming his committee's recognition of Serbia as the Piedmont of the Yugoslavs and their representative in international affairs, Trumbić objected to Pašić's stand that Serbia should be their *exclusive* representative. On the other hand, he disclaimed any idea that the Yugoslav Committee desired to act as a government to which the Allies would send their representatives. What Trumbić wanted was to have the presumably willing Allies recognize the Yugoslavs of Austria-Hungary as allies and the Yugoslav Committee as their representative. This was all the more necessary in view of the Congress of Central European Nations Allied with the Entente, which was to be held in Paris on October 15. To be

on a par with the Poles and Czechoslovaks at that congress, the Yugoslavs of Austria-Hungary had to be represented by the Yugoslav Committee. To deny that committee recognition as their representative,
Trumbić warned, was to disavow it. Finally, Trumbić was forced to
remind Pašić that Serbia constituted only about a third of the total
Yugoslav population. He also insisted that any analogy between Serbia's
position and that of Italy and Romania was false, since the latter two
countries entered the war on the basis of an agreement with the Allies
that they would have the right to annex certain territories. This was
not the case with Serbia. "Our lands in A-H [Austria-Hungary]," he
warned bluntly, "will not give themselves over to Serbia or Montenegro to be annexed, but they will give to the people in them the
freedom to choose of their own will to enter into a single state with
Serbia and Montenegro."

While the Serbian government and the Yugoslav Committtee argued back and forth, the Yugoslavs and other subject nationalities
in Austria-Hungary were attending to their own destinies. On October 6, 1918, a National Council of Slovenes, Croats, and Serbs was
organized in Zagreb. It was joined two days later by the popular
Croato-Serbian Coalition. This council declared itself to be "the political representative body for all Slovenes, Croats, and Serbs who
live in Croatia-Slavonia with Rijeka [Fiume], Dalmatia, Bosnia-
Hercegovina, Istria, Trieste, Carniola, Gorica, Styria, Carinthia,
Bačka, Banat, Baranja, Medjumurje and the other regions of south-
western Hungary." Its avowed program was "the unification of all
Slovenes, Croats, and Serbs, in a national free and independent state
of Slovenes, Croats, and Serbs, established on democratic principles."
The National Council constituted itself as a kind of *de facto* government of the Yugoslavs in the quickly dissolving Austro-Hungarian
Empire. On October 19 it announced the election by its central committee of Dr. Anton Korošec, a Slovenian Roman Catholic priest, as
president; the Croat Dr. Ante Pavelić (not the later Ustaša leader)
and the Serb Svetozar Pribićević as vice-presidents; and the Serb Dr.
Srdjan Budisavljević, the Dalmatian Croat Dr. Mate Drinković, and
the Croat Dr. Ivan Lorković as secretaries.

Convinced that any delay would be ruinous and that all existing
differences between the Yugoslav Committee and the Serbian government had to be resolved, Trumbić asked Pašić to convene a meeting
of his government, the Yugoslav Committee, all Serbian parties, and

the Montenegrin Committee, to be held preferably in Paris and by October 25. Pašić refused.

On October 29, six days before Austria signed the armistice, the Croatian Diet in Zagreb solemnly proclaimed Croatia's independence and its entry into a sovereign state of the Slovenes, Croats, and Serbs headed by the National Council of the Slovenes, Croats, and Serbs. Two days later Emperor Charles recognized this act and even agreed to transfer the Austro-Hungarian Adriatic fleet to the new state, hoping thus to keep it out of Allied hands.

Meanwhile, another serious change took place that was of even more immediate import to Serbia: the September offensive by the Allies on the Balkan Front, under the command of French General Franchet d'Esperey, succeeded in pushing the enemy back. Thanks to the arrival of American troops on the Western Front and the failure of the last German offensive there, reinforcements could be sent to the Salonika Front. Moreover, the abdication of King Constantine and Venizelos's triumph in Greece finally made possible the arrival of Greek reinforcements as well. Thus the Serbian part of the front was reduced to some thirty-three kilometers. However, it was precisely there that the main thrust of the Allied offensive was concentrated. Hopeful that the liberation of their homeland was imminent, the Serbian army fought with special valor. They advanced almost forty miles in a single week. By the last week in September one town after another in Serbian Macedonia fell to the Allied forces, including Skopje itself. By the end of the month Bulgaria sued for peace and signed an armistice in Salonika. According to its terms, the Bulgarian army was to be immediately demobilized and all its equipment turned over to the Allies, it was to evacuate all Serbian and Greek territory, and the territory and transport system of Bulgaria was to be made available for Allied operations. Tsar Ferdinand abdicated on October 4. The Serbian army continued its advance from Macedonia into Serbia, freeing Vranje on October 5, Niš on October 11, and Belgrade on November 1. Not stopping there, it crossed into the Banat, two days before the conclusion of an armistice between the Allied Powers and Austria-Hungary.

Serbia was at last liberated, after a terrible war that had caused it to lose a quarter of its people, including 62.5 percent of its male population between the ages of fifteen and fifty-five. Whole cities and regions had been decimated. Šabac, which had 14,000 inhabitants in 1914, had only 6,000 in 1919 and was economically dead. A similar fate had befallen Kragujevac, Kruševac, Niš, and other economic centers. The Serbian landscape was pocked with ruined villages, gutted factories, fallen bridges, torn-up railroad tracks, demolished schools and hospitals, and empty fields, but Serbia was free once again.

While Serbia was being liberated, the German and Austro-Hungarian forces of occupation in Old Serbia and Montenegro were pushed back, thanks especially to guerrilla action under Kosta Pećanac, who had been flown into that territory from the Salonika Front. His successful cutting of lines of communication created panic in the ranks of the enemy and caused mass surrenders. This coincided with a general uprising against the forces of occupation in western Serbia, the Sancak of Novi Pazar, Hercegovina, and Montenegro, which permitted the entry of Serbian troops. These were welcomed everywhere, including Montenegro. Meanwhile, the French government refused King Nicholas, who was in exile in Bordeaux, permission to return to Montenegro, with the excuse that military operations were still in progress there. In Montenegro a whole rash of committees and councils were hastily formed, all claiming the right to act in the name of the people of Montenegro for their unification with Serbia.

Serbia and the Unification of the Serbs, Croats, and Slovenes

The State of the Slovenes, Croats, and Serbs, which proclaimed its independence in Zagreb on October 29, 1918, was a new factor in the Yugoslav Question that neither Pašić nor the Yugoslav Committee in London could ignore. Its existence gladdened the hearts of the Yugoslav Committee, but it troubled Pašić greatly. Here was a Yugoslav state that had declared its own freedom without the benefit of liberation by the Serbian army. In fact, its declaration of independence was proclaimed even before Serbia itself was entirely liberated, for Belgrade was not in Serbian hands until November 1, and the last enemy soldiers did not leave Serbia until November 3. The government of the State of the Slovenes, Croats, and Serbs, the National Council, enjoyed a double legitimacy, being based on the principle of national self-determination as proclaimed by the Allies as well as on the recognition of Emperor Charles IV of Austria-Hungary. On October 31 this government sent a note to the governments of the Allies which declared:

The State of the Slovenes, Croats, and Serbs which has been constituted on the territory of the South Slavs that has previously been a part of the former Austro-Hungarian Monarchy, and which is ready to join in a common state with Serbia and Montenegro, formally announces that it is not in a state of war with the Allied states. It is happy to be able to declare that it regards the Allied states as friendly states, and that it expects that they will extend their powerful support, at an international Congress and in accord with their declared principles, in guaranteeing the sovereignty of the united state of all the Slovenes, Croats, and Serbs.

The note also informed the Allies that the former Austro-Hungarian navy was now in the hands of the National Council and under the Croatian flag. On November 1 the National Council telegraphed the Yugoslav Committee in London its decision, which was also transmitted to the Allies, to authorize the Yugoslav Committee to represent the State of the Slovenes, Croats, and Serbs in its international relations. On October 31 the Slovenes formally selected their own government and placed it under the authority of the National Council in Zagreb. On November 2 Bosnia and Hercegovina followed suit. On November 3 an armistice was concluded between the Allied Powers and Austria-Hungary.

Far from facilitating relations between the Allies and the still unrecognized Yugoslav government in Zagreb, the armistice put the Yugoslavs in a very bad position. By the terms of the armistice with Austria-Hungary, the Allies reserved the right to enter the territory of the Dual Monarchy, to take over the transportation system and all military objects, and to maintain order. These provisions gave Italy the opportunity to occupy all those territories on the Yugoslav coast that it had been promised by the Entente Powers in the Treaty of London. What particularly hurt the Yugoslav Committee was its inability to attend the deliberations of the Allied Supreme War Council in Versailles; but the Yugoslavs of Austria-Hungary, unlike the Czechoslovaks or the Poles, did not enjoy official recognition. Serbia was their spokesman, and Serbian Minister Vesnić, who did attend the conference, not only failed to do anything for the Yugoslavs but did not even protest decisions made at their expense, for instance, that the Italians occupy the eastern Adriatic coast or that the Yugo-slavs surrender the former Austro-Hungarian navy to the Allies.

Meanwhile the National Council in Zagreb directed two missions to establish contact with the Serbian government. One left Zagreb on November 4 and was received in Belgrade four days later after a hazardous trip. This mission's task was to get the Serbian government to send troops into Vojvodina, Croatia, and Slovenia to help the National Council maintain order, and to send food and supplies to the Dalmatian coast. The Serbian high command was not in a position to do this on any significant scale, both for lack of the necessary means and because it was still under the orders of the Allied command in the Balkans. Nevertheless, small Serbian detachments did go into the territory under the National Council, including Fiume and other Dalmatian towns except for Zara (Zadar), which was already in Italian hands. The Serbian troops were ordered to avoid any conflict with the Italians.

The second mission, headed by President Anton Korošec himself and including Melko Čingrija and Gregor Žerjav, all members of the Yugoslav caucus in Vienna, grew out of a mandate by the caucus to go to Switzerland to establish contact with the Yugoslav Committee and to learn what they could of the general situation. While this mission was in progress, the National Council was established in Zagreb and Korošec was made president of the new state. When the mission arrived in Geneva on November 1, they learned of the desperate situation in which the Yugoslav Committee found itself vis-à-vis the Serbian government and the Allies. It was clear to them that a meeting of all interested Yugoslav parties with Pašić was imperative in order to settle their problems. The most pressing of these problems for the Yugoslavs was the Italian occupation of the eastern Adriatic coast, over which the National Council in Zagreb sent a barrage of protests and pleas for support to the Allied Powers and to Serbia.

On November 3 Korošec sent a note to the governments of France, Great Britain, Italy, and the United States asking them this time to recognize the National Council of the Slovenes, Croats, and Serbs in Zagreb as the government of the Yugoslav people inhabiting the territory of the former Austro-Hungarian Monarchy. On November 5 Pašić sent a note to the Allied Powers supporting this request. By that time he had already agreed to a meeting in Geneva with the

Korošec mission. Pašić, who was sick in bed in Paris in early November, was under pressure from all sides. In addition to the Yugoslav Committee and its British friends, Pašić had to deal with the Serbian parliamentary opposition, whose chief leaders were Milorad Drašković and Marko Trifković. As Pašić informed Prince-Regent Alexander on November 1, these two men came to him to insist on the formation of a coalition government and the recognition of the Yugoslav Committee as a recognized spokesman for the Yugoslavs of former Austria-Hungary. If their demands were not met immediately, they threatened to form a committee of their own which would work against the Serbian government and for the Yugoslav Committee. On Corfu Pašić could deal with the opposition as he chose, but in a newly liberated Serbia things looked different. Besides, alone the Yugoslav Committee could be dealt with easily, but once it became the designated spokesman of a *de facto* government of Yugoslavs that was seeking recognition on its own, this too was a different matter. Pašić decided to go to Geneva to parley with the Yugoslavs.

The Geneva Conference lasted from November 6 to November 9, 1918. The Serbian government was represented by Pašić, while Drašković, Trifković, and Voja Marinković represented parliamentary groups in the Serbian National Assembly. The National Council of the Slovenes, Croats, and Serbs was represented by Korošec, Čingrija, and Žerjav. The Yugoslav Committee sent Trumbić, Gustav Gregorin, Jovan Banjanin, Dušan Vasiljević, and Nikola Stojanović. The Montenegrin Committee was not represented. The chief items on the agenda were: recognition of the National Council in Zagreb as the representative and government of the State of the Slovenes, Croats, and Serbs; the question of the organization of the future common state; a joint protest against the Italian occupation of Yugoslav territory; and relations with Montenegro.

At the start of the first meeting, held on November 6 in the Hôtel National, Pašić pointed out that in view of the existence of the National Council in Zagreb, the Yugoslav Committee ceased to play a role and should be excluded as a party to the negotiations. Korošec disagreed and pointed out that the Yugoslav Committee had the mandate of the National Council to act as its representative in foreign affairs. Pašić thereupon withdrew his objection. After all, he was also forced to endure the presence of his own Serbian parliamentary opposition. Apparently he thought that the purpose of this meeting was solely to manifest Yugoslav unity, and as he expected no tangible result to come from it, he was disposed to overlook procedural technicalities.

The other participants of the conference had greater expectations for it. The real work of the meeting commenced with a proposal by Milorad Drašković that ran directly counter to his own premier's policy. He asked for the formation of a joint government consisting of the representatives of both sides, which would take over from both the Serbian government and the National Council, thus in effect accomplishing the unification until it was made formal by a constituent assembly. Since this was the last thing that Pašić wanted, he proposed instead the creation of a political and military committee consisting of four members from the Serbian side and three from the National Council, which would conduct the foreign affairs of both sides while the Serbian government and the National Council continued to administer the internal affairs of their respective jurisdictions until a constituent assembly determined otherwise. This proposal was a decided departure from Pašić's previous stand. Apparently it was aimed at obtaining a united front in foreign affairs without interfering with the power of his own party in Serbia itself until the future union became a reality.

Trumbić's proposal was based on the idea that the government in Zagreb should first establish itself and become recognized as an independent sovereign state, and then it and Serbia should agree on a union as equals. However, Pašić assailed the idea for two main reasons: it violated the principle of unity contained in the Corfu Declaration and established a duality, and it threatened to separate the Serbs of the former Austro-Hungarian Monarchy from their long awaited union with Serbia. Trumbić denied both arguments but observed that neither the Serbs nor the Croats were ready for a radical change and that a more familiar arrangement would be useful as a transition. Trumbić's proposal found favor with the other participants and put Pašić in a very awkward position; the Serbian premier could not accept even a temporary dual arrangement that would continue to separate the Serbs, and yet he could not afford to break with the National Council, for that would also separate the Serbs. To make his situation worse, on November 8, in the midst of the proceedings, he received a telegram from French President Raymond Poincaré conveying to him his urgent desire that all the Yugoslav people join in one united front free of even the slightest division. France was already interested in establishing a strong line of friendly states in eastern Europe against Communist Russia.

In view of this development, Pašić sent Korošec a formal note in which he finally officially recognized the National Council in Zagreb as "the lawful Government of the Serbs, Croats, and Slovenes" (the order of the enumeration was his). At the same time he urged the Allied Powers to do the same.

That same day, Trumbić brought in a more detailed elaboration of his proposal. On November 9 all twelve participants of the conference signed a statement that came to be known as the Geneva Declaration. This historic document, which was supposed to supersede the Corfu Declaration, began with the following words:

By the joint efforts of the Allied nations and the United States of North America, by the strength of the Serbian, Croatian and Slovenian people, all forcible obstacles to their unification have been shattered on the field of battle and on the sea. The representatives of the Government of the Kingdom of Serbia and parliamentary political groups, the representatives of the National Council in Zagreb, the representatives of the Yugoslav Committee in London, gathered in Geneva, the city of liberty, are happy to be able to declare unanimously, solemnly and before the entire world their unification in a state of Serbs, Croats and Slovenes. The people of Montenegro, to whom our fraternal embrace is open, will doubtlessly hasten to greet this act, which was ever their greatest ideal, and to join us.

On this day and by this act a new state appears and manifests itself as an indivisible integral state and member of the society of free peoples. The borders which used to divide us are no longer.

The declaration then briefly laid down the fundamental lines along which the new state was to be organized. These were more fully described in the minutes of the Geneva Conference, which were signed by Pašić, Korošec, and Trumbić. The minutes were arranged in four sections.

The first section included Serbia's recognition of the National Council as a lawful government. It also stipulated that both the Serbian government and the National Council would administer their own territories until a constituent assembly, elected by universal, equal, direct, and secret suffrage, established a constitution. The international borders of the new state were to be drawn, it was hoped, on the basis of the right of national self-determination.

The second section established a joint cabinet of ministers whose task it was to conduct the affairs of the new state until a constituent assembly met. Without interfering with the existing administrative systems on both sides, the joint ministers as a body were to have charge of foreign affairs; military matters affecting the whole; the navy and merchant fleet; the preparations for a constituent assembly; the coordination of a joint system of transportation and communication; the feeding of the population and reconstruction of the war-devastated economy; and the return and rehabilitation of prisoners, orphans and widows, wounded veterans, refugees, and deportees. The joint cabinet, which was to have its seat in Paris as well as in the homeland, was to consist of members divided equally between the representatives of the Serbian government and the National Council "without prejudice for the future." The number of ministers was established at twelve; they were to deliberate on all matters jointly rather than to have charge of individual portfolios, with six being named immediately and six after further consultation. When Montenegro joined, its participation in the cabinet would be subject to negotiation. The three ministers on Serbia's side were Ljuba Davidović, Mihailo Gavrilović, and Dragoljub Pavlović. Both Davidović and Pavlović were members of the opposition. Gavrilović was assistant foreign minister. The National Council designated Janko Brejc, Melko Čingrija, and Dušan Vasiljević—a Slovene, a Croat, and a Serb.

The third section of the minutes simply declared the signatories' intention to have the National Council send a note of protest to the Allied Powers, which the Serbian foreign minister would support in a similar note.

The fourth section was devoted entirely to Montenegro. It declared that country to be an integral part of the Serbs, Croats, and Slovenes. It also announced as its program that Montenegro be included in the new state and promised to conduct appropriate negotiations with Montenegrin Minister Milo Vujović, whom the signatories recognized as the official representative of the Montenegrin government.

Thus the Geneva Declaration had two main accomplishments: it founded a common Yugoslav state, and it left the form of that state to a future constituent assembly. It also rested on the assumption that the people of the Yugoslav lands were ethnically one, and that their political union was based on the joining of three states: the Kingdom of Serbia, the Kingdom of Montenegro, and the State of the Slovenes, Croats, and Serbs.

The Geneva Declaration was a political defeat for Pašić. One eyewitness, Franko Potočnjak, said that Pašić signed the document which tears in his eyes. A sick man of seventy-three, Pašić described his action in Geneva thus to his colleague Protić: "In the hardest moment of my life, when the question of unification was being solved, I steeled my heart, accepted Serbia's humiliation and my own, and sacrificed them to national unification, in the firm conviction that our people, who are just judges, would quickly mend the injustice and grant recognition to the Kingdom of Serbia, which had given proof of sacrificing everything for unity. . . ."

Pašić was not the only leader in Serbia who disliked the Geneva Declaration. Prince-Regent Alexander was opposed to it, among other reasons because it made no mention of the Karadjordjević dynasty. Unlike the Corfu Declaration, it left the question of the form of government completely open, to be decided by a constituent assembly. When Stojan Protić, vice-premier and ranking cabinet member in Pašić's absence, received the news of the Geneva decisions, he wrote back to Pašić from Corfu, "Let us hope that our brother Serbs, Croats, and Slovenes in deceased Austria-Hungary will become convinced that such a solution is not useful for the proper and organic development of our nation. Let us hope that deceased Austria-Hungary will soon cease to darken the paths of our national unity with its morbid shade." Protić was alluding to a thought that increasingly troubled the minds of Pašić's followers, namely, that the Yugoslavs of the Dual Monarchy, particularly the Croats, were thoroughly imbued with an Austro-Hungarian mentality and with political instincts acquired under Habsburg domination that seemed quite inappropriate when dealing with one's brethren. In a later telegram to Pašić, sent on November 11, Protić specified certain objections to the Geneva decisions. He noted that it was wrong to have the ministers of the joint cabinet take their oath to "both the King and to the National Council rather than to the King alone." He disliked the idea of having a collegial ministry instead of separate joint ministers for each portfolio. He also registered the Serbian cabinet's disapproval of Pašić's designating the Serbian members of the joint ministry without their prior approval. However, it is safe to assume that the particular objections that Protić raised to the Geneva Declaration were not the main reasons for its rejection by the Serbian government. To get rid of the agreement as a whole, Protić submitted to Pašić the resignation of the entire Serbian cabinet, and he urged Pašić to resign as well. In a personal note to Pašić, which he wrote as a fellow Radical, Protić castigated the work of the Geneva Conference as being worse than useless. He was especially bitter about "that vampire Austro-German delegation that you call the central ministry, which has its seat abroad, as well as in the fatherland." Protić's suggestion was that if the crown agreed, the Serbian government would go to the people of Serbia and then act in accord with the results of the election; otherwise let the crown and the opposition find their own solution.

Pašić returned to Paris on November 10 and was soon followed by the other participants of the conference. There he informed them of the Serbian government's unwillingness to accept the Geneva decisions and of its intent to resign. He also informed them that he was returning to Serbia. The Serbian rejection shocked all the participants. Pašić assured them that the prince-regent and the Serbian government were still willing to work for the realization of the Corfu Declaration.

Pašić offered his resignation to the crown, but it was not received. Alexander took Pašić's view that he had been reluctantly forced into a bad agreement because of the expectation of the Allies. Instead, the prince-regent gave him a mandate to form another government. Pašić nominated a new Serbian cabinet on November 16 while still in Paris. The main changes in the government were that Pašić divested himself of the portfolio of foreign affairs and gave it to his former assistant Mihailo Gavrilović, and he included members of the opposition in the cabinet, notably Marko Trifković, who was made minister of the interior. Pašić asked the crown's permission to increase the number of cabinet posts to include candidates whom the National Council in Zagreb would nominate in agreement with Ljubljana and Sarajevo. He suggested that the Croats nominate three men, one each for Croatia Proper, Slavonia, and Dalmatia; that the council for Bosnia and Hercegovina pick two men, a Serb and a Muslim; that the Slovenes also pick two; and Vojvodina one. Such an enlarged cabinet, Pašić hoped, could represent all the Serbs, Croats, and Slovenes but would still be subject to the Serbian crown. Obviously this was his alternative to the joint ministry that the Serbian government had rejected so resolutely.

Pašić's new cabinet was temporarily sworn in on November 18 in Paris. If the opposition thought they were going to put through their own program in the coalition cabinet, they were mistaken. Pašić sped off to London, partly in order to begin the organization of the enlarged cabinet that he proposed. Besides, the newly formed cabinet quickly spun into a crisis when the opposition learned that at no point had the Serbian *crown* rejected the Geneva Declaration, as Pašić had purported. In fact, Živojin Balugdžić, minister of the court, assured them that Prince-Regent Alexander, who was in Belgrade with the army while the government was still in Corfu, had never been informed of the declaration in its entirety. For a variety of reasons, which went beyond poor communications, the National Council in Zagreb was completely uninformed about the events in Geneva or the debacle that followed until November 14, when Lt. Col. Dušan Simović, a representative of the Serbian high command, brought it the news. It was in such circumstances that Prince-Regent Alexander took the political initiative and provided the channel by which Yugoslav unification was finally achieved.

Prince Alexander Karadjordjević, heir to the throne and regent of Serbia, was an ambitious man of thirty in 1918. The first step in the consolidation of his power was to gain control over the army whose commander in chief he was. To accomplish this he did not hesitate to get rid of Colonel Dimitrijević-Apis and to break the power of the Black Hand, even though it meant the death of falsely accused men. Alexander was able to carry out his design owing to the cooperation of Pašić and the Radical party. Although he left the government and foreign policy in Pašić's hands, Alexander was not a mere bystander. He and Pašić together toured the Allied capitals during the war to bolster Serbia's cause. He also stood by Pašić's decisions and avoided interfering with his premier, even though he was urged by various quarters to intervene. However, Alexander's confidence in Pašić was severely shaken by the Geneva Conference. If the unification of Yugoslavia was a necessity that the allies encouraged, then Prince Alexander was determined to be the center of that unification when it occurred.

It so happened that most of the other important protagonists in the rapidly unfolding drama also came to the conclusion, each for his own reasons, that Prince Alexander was the best hope and most effective channel for unification. It was because of this development, in the face of the deteriorated and chaotic situation among the various Serbian and Yugoslav representatives in Switzerland, France, and England, that the center of gravity of the Yugoslav Question moved back to where it belonged, to Belgrade, Zagreb, and the other capitals of the Yugoslav lands.

The first contact between the National Council in Zagreb and Prince-Regent Alexander in Belgrade took place on November 8, 1918, when the former's mission was received first by General Petar Bojović, commandant of the First Serbian Army, and then by the newly arrived prince-regent. The mission also met with Momčilo Ninčić, the first minister of the government to arrive in liberated Belgrade. As a result of the mission, the Serbian high command dispatched some troops into the Yugoslav lands of former Austria-Hungary and sent a special emissary to the National Council in Zagreb, Lt. Col. Dušan Simović. His chief task was to act as a military liaison and commander of the Serbian troops in the State of the Slovenes, Croats, and Serbs. However, Simović also acted as a political envoy. Arriving in Zagreb on November 13, the next day he supplied the National Council with its first report of the Geneva Conference. The same day, he sent a report to Belgrade on the political situation in Croatia. "All the Serbs without exception," he wrote, "are for the Karadjordjević dynasty. That is the view of all the Dalmatian Croats, the greater part of the Croats of Bosnia-Hercegovina, nearly all the Croats of the Littoral, and all the younger Croatian intelligentsia. The same view is also shared by the Slovenes, except for the Clericalists. These people represent the majority of the Serbo-Croato-Slovenian people." He described Zagreb as being "intoxicated with the idea of Yugoslav solidarity." Simović assured Belgrade that "the majority of the National Council and the Government stand on the proposition of an indissoluble and indivisible state of the Serbs, Croats, and Slovenes under our dynasty." Such a report was certainly at variance with the guidelines contained in the Geneva Declaration. Simović ended his report with the reminder that the Serbian government had not yet responded to the National Council's desire, expressed in its note of October 31, 1918, to unite the Yugoslav lands with Serbia.

Two days later, on November 16, 1918, Minister Ninčić sent a message to Svetozar Pribićević, Serbian vice-president of the National Council and one of its leading members. As a leader of the most powerful political force in Croatia, the Croato-Serbian Coalition,

Pribićević had declared, on July 9, 1918, that between the Croats and the Serbs "there can be no harmony but only unity." On the other hand, he was even more eager to achieve the complete unification of the Habsburg Serbs with Serbia. Therefore, he was deeply disturbed when he received a message from Minister Ninčić in Belgrade warning him against the decision taken in Geneva, especially against its dualistic arrangement. "We in Belgrade," Ninčić wrote, "are increasingly gaining the impression that certain Croatian circles have as their plan to separate Serbia and Montenegro from the rest of our provinces, and in this manner: instead of a unitary state in which they fear that the Serbs might have the main say, to create a purely Austrian combination. It even lacks any originality but simply copies the relation between Austria and Hungary." Ninčić suggested that most Croats in Croatia would accept the idea of an indivisible state of Serbs, Croats, and Slovenes under the Karadjordjević dynasty if it were clearly shown to them that if they did not accept this, all the Serbs in the former Habsburg lands would join Serbia.

Pribićević agreed with Ninčić's assessment of the Geneva Declaration and openly proclaimed the idea of dualism in a Yugoslav union with Serbia "a perilous and ruinous element." As acting president of the National Council, he threatened to leave it and let the Croats have their "Croatian republic" if they wished. Just as the members of the Serbian cabinet chided Pašić for acting without their authorization in Geneva, so Pribićević charged Korošec with having gone beyond his mandate in concluding the Geneva agreement. Thus Pribićević dedicated himself to the annulment of the Geneva Declaration at the same time that the Serbian government repudiated it.

Pribićević's efforts were greatly bolstered by Simović's presence in Zagreb. On the occasion of the presentation of Simović's credentials to the National Council, when one of its members raised the question of Serbia's recognition of an independent State of Slovenes, Croats, and Serbs, Simović replied that he had no authority to speak on that subject; however, he assured the Council as a soldier and an officer that Serbia, which had sacrificed a million and a half casualties for the liberation and unification of its brethren on the other side of the Danube, the Sava, and the Drina, could never accept the establishment of a new state that would continue to separate the Serbs. He also warned that in such an event Serbia would certainly keep the territory that was occupied by its troops and included in the armistice with Hungary.

Political opinion in Zagreb in those days became divided between two poles—the centralists and the federalists. The centralists, led by Svetozar Pribićević and the Croato-Serbian Coalition, urged immediate union with Serbia and Montenegro under the Karadjordjević dynasty and in a unitary state. They were joined by a group of Ante Starčević's Croatian "Party of Rights"; the Social Democrats; the younger Yugo-slav-oriented intelligentsia; many Croats in Dalmatia, the Littoral, and Bosnia-Hercegovina; and all the Serbs, who were a sizable minor-ity in Croatia. The federalists were less numerous and less certain of their goals. What united them was a fear of Serbian hegemony. Their main strength consisted of the People's Peasant party of Stjepan Radić; the majority of Starčević's "Rightists"; the Croatian nationalist "Frankists" (named after their deceased leader, Josip Frank); and the greater part of the Croatian middle class in Croatia Proper. Their general aim was to preserve a maximum of autonomy and territory for Croatia, and their preference was for a republic rather than a monarchy, especially a Serbian one.

Under more normal circumstances, it is possible that the centralists might have succeeded, at least for a time, with their counsels of caution and delay. However, many pressures militated against them. There was much chaos and disorder throughout the land in the wake of a dissolved Austro-Hungarian Monarchy. In addition to general looting amid the pell-mell of demobilized soldiers straggling to their homes, thousands of armed deserters were organized in bands called "Green Cadres," whose chief occupation became plundering. The government in Zagreb was also worried by various signs, both real and imagined, of "Bolshevism" in various quarters, under the influence of the October Revolution in Russia. Meanwhile the Italians, in occupying the coast, were going beyond their line of demarcation. Throughout all of this, the National Council was deprived of any reliable news concerning the work of its representatives in western Europe and desperately in need of help. It could hardly get this help from the Allies when it was not even recognized by them. It became increasingly clear to many that the quickest way out of the situation was immediate union with Serbia.

The first major move toward such a solution was made by those

Croats who were closest to the Italian occupation, the National Council for Dalmatia, in Split. At its meeting of November 14, 1918, this body resolved that "the Presidium of the government of the National Council of S.C.S. in Zagreb must establish contact as soon as possible with the Serbian government in Belgrade regarding the formation of a common government for the entire sovereign state of S.C.S." The resolution was formally transmitted to the National Council in Zagreb on November 16. This was followed on November 19 by a resolution at a mass meeting in Zagreb of Croatians from the Adriatic coast calling on the National Council to begin immediate negotiations with the Serbian government for the formation of a united state. On that same day the National Council in Zagreb heard of a similar request from the National Council of Bosnia and Hercegovina in Sarajevo. On November 22 the National Council in Zagreb received a note from two ministers of the Serbian government in Belgrade, Ljubomir Jovanović and Momčilo Ninčić, saying that, in the absence of the other ministers who had not yet reached Belgrade, they were happy to receive the reports of the National Council's decision of October 19 and the Croatian Diet's decision of October 29 to join in a common state with Serbia and Montenegro. "The Serbian government," the ministers announced rather belatedly, "desires to undertake negotiations with the National Council as soon as possible for the final solution of the question concerning the formation of a single state for the ethnographic territory of the Serbs, Croats, and Slovenes." The next day, November 23, the Central Committee of the National Council in Zagreb met to consider the whole question of union with Serbia. The debate over how and when to effect such a union lasted two days. Many proposals were advanced. Finally Dr. Josip Smodlaka of Split delivered a moving plea in favor of immediate union and urged the appointment of a committee of seven members to formulate a single proposal from the many that had been made and to submit it to a secret vote of the National Council. This was done. That committee, which included various elements, from Pribićević to Radić and the Social Democrats, came back with the recommendation that the National Council send a delegation of twenty-eight members to Belgrade to effect an immediate union with Serbia and Montenegro.

The instructions to this delegation included the following points: (1) The final organization of the new state could be determined only by a general popular constituent assembly of the Serbs, Croats, and

Slovenes, by a two-thirds majority. This assembly was to meet within six months after peace was concluded. (2) Until such time, the government of the country was to be conducted by a Council of State consisting of all of the members of the National Council in Zagreb plus five members of the Yugoslav Committee in London; a corresponding number of representatives of the Kingdom of Serbia, to be chosen by the National Assembly in consultation with the various political parties; and a corresponding number of Montenegrin representatives to be chosen by the Montenegrin National Assembly. (3) This Council of State was to designate a provisional state flag and naval ensign at its first meeting. (4) The King of Serbia, i.e., Prince-Regent Alexander, was to rule as Regent of the State of the Serbs, Croats, and Slovenes until the constituent assembly met. He was to take an oath to the Council of State. He was to rule in accord with parliamentary principles. He had the right to initiate legislation and had the veto power. (5) The provisional seat of the government and of the State Council was to be determined by common agreement. (6) The Council of State was to carry out elections for the constituent assembly, on the basis of universal (male), equal, proportional, and secret suffrage with representation for minorities. (7) A State Cabinet, responsible to the Council of State, was to consist of a premier and several ministers as well as seven State Secretaries with full voting rights—one each for Serbia, Croatia and Slavonia, Bosnia and Hercegovina, Slovenia, Dalmatia, Montenegro, and Bačka-Banat-Baranja. (8) Foreign affairs, the armed forces, the merchant fleet, state finance, and post and telegraph were in the sole jurisdiction of the central government. All other matters were in the jurisdiction of the provincial governments, though under the supervision of the central government. (9) The provincial governments would be under the supervision of provisional councils representing local parties. The head of the Croatian government was to be a *Ban* appointed by the ruler on the nomination of the provincial government. (10) The provincial governments were to receive their funds from the State Cabinet within a budget to be approved by the Council of State. (11) All existing laws and other regulations were to remain in force, as well as the organization of the judicial and administrative systems.

These instructions were based in the main on the provisions of the Corfu Declaration, but with changes in the direction of a greater federalism. On November 27, 1918, all of the designated delegates—except

Stjepan Radić, leader of the Peasant party, who was disqualified by a majority of the Central Committee because of his "agitation" —left by special train for Belgrade. They arrived the next day, after being taken across the river from Zemun by boats, since the bridge had been destroyed in the war. The citizens of Belgrade gave them a warm reception.

Meanwhile other regions were also voting their unification with Serbia. The first of these was Vojvodina. On November 25, an assembly in Novi Sad consisting of 757 delegates from 211 communes, including 578 Serbs, 89 Croats, 62 Slovaks, 21 Ukrainians, 6 Germans, and 1 Magyar, unilaterally declared their union with Serbia. The Serbian government accepted immediately.

In Montenegro a National Council was organized in Cetinje with the direct encouragement of Lt. Col. Dušan Simović. Its first act, on November 8, was to declare its intention to unite Montenegro with Serbia. At the same time another body, the Provisional Central Committee, established itself in Andrijevica. It carried out elections for a Great National Assembly of 176 representatives. The struggle was between the centralists, who were for unconditional union with Serbia, and the federalists, who wished to preserve as much autonomy for Montenegro as possible. The two parties were called the "Whites" and the "Greens" because of the color of the paper on which their leaflets were printed. The Greens were accused of being separatists because of their attachment to King Nicholas, who was forced to remain abroad. They suffered a complete defeat in the elections. On November 24 the Great National Assembly met in Podgorica (today Titograd) and, two days later, declared that "the Serbian people in Montenegro are of one blood, one language and one aspiration, one religion and custom with the people that lives in Serbia and in other Serbian regions" and voted for the following measures:

1. That King Nicholas I Petrović Njegoš and his dynasty be dethroned;

2. That Montenegro unite with brotherly Serbia in one state under the Karadjordjević dynasty, and thus united that it enter the common fatherland of our triune people the Serbs, Croats, and Slovenes;

3. That an Executive Committee of five members be elected to administer affairs until the unification of Serbia and Montenegro is concluded; and

4. That the former king of Montenegro Nicholas Petrović, the Government of the Kingdom of Serbia, the friendly Entente Powers, and all neutral states be informed of the decision of this assembly.

This decision was signed by 163 representatives. Five did not sign, pleading illness. The Assembly appointed a delegation of twelve members to go to Belgrade forthwith. It was led by Archbishop Gabriel Dožić, metropolitan of the Montenegrin Orthodox Church.

There remained only the unification of the State of the Slovenes, Croats, and Serbs with Serbia. The delegation of the National Council in Zagreb was bound by some specific guidelines on the basis of which it was to conclude a union with Serbia. However, the National Council had already declared its intention to join Serbia, and it made no provision for what course of action its delegation in Belgrade should follow in case its proposals were not accepted by the Serbian government. Such an eventuality seemed unthinkable. On the other hand, the Geneva Declaration had lost all validity after its repudiation by the Serbian government, and the Corfu Declaration, which had always been very vague about the particulars of unification, now seemed rather outdated. As for the Serbian side, there was a significant lack of responsible leaders to carry on negotiations. Premier Pašić and most of the cabinet were either out of the country or still straggling to Belgrade. Of the Radical party leaders, only three were in Belgrade at the time—Stojan Protić, Ljubomir Jovanović, and Momčilo Ninčić—and of these only the first was in the new enlarged cabinet. Thus Protić represented the Serbian government vis-à-vis the delegation from Zagreb. However, as he was known to be Pašić's alter ego, it was Jovanović's task to be at his side and keep a watchful eye for the prince-regent. Ninčić was useful as a link between Alexander and Svetozar Pribičević. In view of Pašić's very convenient absence, Prince-Regent Alexander was undoubtedly the central figure. Old King Peter played no role whatever. He was not even in Belgrade at the time, and when he did arrive, without any fanfare whatever, his people did not recognize him in the street because of his beard. He did not play even a symbolic role in the proceedings that led to the unification. Also, there was no possibility of convening the Serbian National Assembly at the time, since the vast majority of its members were scattered across the Balkans and the breadth of Europe.

It was made apparent to the Zagreb delegation from the start that the business of unification was to be accomplished quickly; during their reception, Prince-Regent Alexander announced that he intended to leave Belgrade in two or three days to go to Sarajevo to meet the enlarged cabinet there on its way to Belgrade, and then to Paris. At its first meeting, in the Belgrade District Court House on November 29, the delegation selected a three-man committee to meet with the three Serbian ministers in order to agree on what procedure to follow. The visitors' initial thought was that the Serbian National Assembly should pick a delegation that would proclaim the act of unification jointly with the delegation from Zagreb. However, the absence of the National Assembly made that impossible, and no one wished to postpone the proceedings. Thus it was for the prince-regent to accept the terms of unification, to be presented in the form of an Address to the Throne. In the discussion of what was to be in the address, the delegation found itself torn between Ante Pavelić's insistence on the inclusion of various specific demands and Svetozar Pribićević's proposal of the unconditional acceptance of immediate unification.

On the afternoon of November 30, the delegation was joined by Protić and Jovanović, who came to transmit the gist of the prince-regent's intended reply to their address. Ante Pavelić informed them of the eleven conditions contained in the National Council's instructions to its delegation. Protić took exception especially to the first, which seemed to leave the question of the monarchy open. He was assured that the other conditions made clear the National Council's acceptance of the monarchy, and that this would be stressed in the address.

After that it seemed best to proceed with framing a suitable Address to the Throne. Pavelić hesitated, however, and asked that the delegation wait until it received word from Trumbić in reply to a telegram. At that point Pribićević suggested that the delegation hear from Dr. Rudolf Giunio, Trumbić's authorized emissary, who had just arrived. Giunio transmitted the opinion of the Yugoslav Committee and of Trumbić himself that the quickest possible unification with Serbia was an urgent national necessity and that it should take place along the lines indicated by the Corfu Declaration. That same day the delegation received a telegram from the Yugoslav Committee in Zurich which described in desperate terms the poor position of the unrecognized Yugoslavs at the coming Peace Conference and urged quick unification with Serbia as the only way "to successfully protect the integrity of our borders which are threatened from all sides." The delegation's task was clearly indicated. It worked far into the night to complete its Address to the Throne.

The presentation by the National Council's delegation of its Address

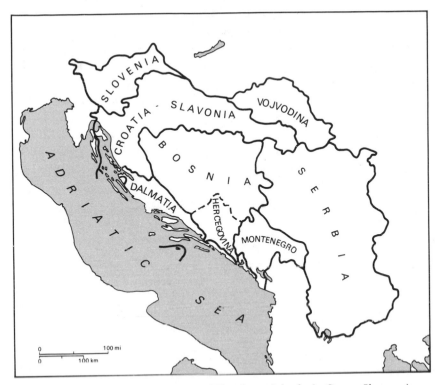

Formation of the Yugoslav State (Kingdom of the Serbs-Croats-Slovenes)
after the First World War

to the Throne and its formal acceptance by Prince-Regent Alexander,
the act that marks the final unification of the Serbs, Croats, and
Slovenes, took place on December 1, 1918, at 8:00 P.M. The delegation
was received in the Royal Palace by the prince-regent, in the company
of General Živojin Mišić and four ministers of the Serbian government.

The Address to the Throne was read by Dr. Ante Pavelić. After an
introduction which referred to the decisions of October 19 and November 24 of the National Council of the Slovenes, Croats, and Serbs to
unite with Serbia and Montenegro, Pavelić described the main terms
of the union as understood by the National Council, namely: that the
ruler of the new state of the Serbs, Croats, and Slovenes was King
Peter, that is, his regent and heir, Prince Alexander; that a parliamentary government be established with a single national representative
body until a constituent assembly was convened; that already existing
local autonomous administrative bodies continue to function until

such time, under the supervision of the central government; and that a constituent assembly be elected on the basis of universal, equal, direct, and proportional male suffrage within six months after the conclusion of peace. The longest single passage of the address, which came as the climax, was devoted to a complaint against the Italian occupation of the eastern Adriatic coast. The address ended with the hope that the prince and the entire nation would work to assure the just determination of the new state's borders "in accordance with our ethnographic borders and by the application of the principle of national self-determination, proclaimed by the President of the American States [sic] Wilson and all the Powers of the Entente."

In his reply, Prince-Regent Alexander expressed his joy at the decision of the National Council, and then declared:

In accepting this announcement, I am convinced that by this act I am fulfilling my duty as a ruler, for I am thereby only at last carrying out that for which the best sons of our blood, of all three religions, all three names, on both sides of the Danube, Sava, and Drina, began to work even during the reign of my grandfather of blessed memory Prince Alexander I and of Prince Michael, that which corresponds to the desires and views of my people, and so in the name of His Majesty King Peter I, I proclaim the unification of Serbia with the lands of the independent State of Slovenes, Croats, and Serbs in a single Kingdom of the Serbs, Croats, and Slovenes.

He "completely accepted" the views contained in the Address to the Throne and promised to be true to democratic parliamentary principles and to bend every effort to obtain just frontiers for the Kingdom of the Serbs, Croats, and Slovenes despite the provisions of the Treaty of London.

With this exchange Serbia ceased to exist as a separate and independent entity. In its long political existence it had been many things: in medieval times a grand *županate,* a kingdom, an empire; then a despotate and an Ottoman *paşalık* in early modern times; and finally an autonomous vassal principality within the Ottoman Empire, then a free and independent principality and kingdom. As of December 1, 1918, Serbia was a part, and by no means the larger part, of a Kingdom of the Serbs, Croats, and Slovenes. But just as Serbia did not cease to exist under any of its previous transformations, even under Ottoman overlordship, so it did not cease to exist after 1918 as a cultural and spiritual community that continued to be deeply aware of its historical heritage. That Serbia still lives.

GENEALOGICAL CHARTS

NAMES, TERMS, AND DATES

SERBIA'S CURRENCY

BIBLIOGRAPHY

GLOSSARY

INDEX

The Obrenović Dynasty

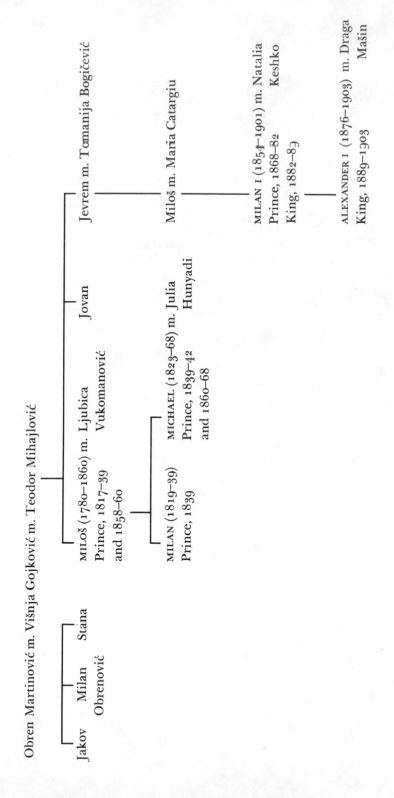

Obren Martinović m. Višnja Gojković m. Teodor Mihajlović

Jakov   Milan   Stana
        Obrenović

MILOŠ (1780–1860) m. Ljubica   Jovan   Jevrem m. Tomanija Bogičević
Prince, 1817–39   Vukomanović
and 1858–60

MILAN (1819–39)   MICHAEL (1823–68) m. Julia
Prince, 1839   Prince, 1839–42   Hunyadi
                     and 1860–68

Miloš m. Maria Catargiu

MILAN I (1854–1901) m. Natalia
Prince, 1868–82   Keshko
King, 1882–89

ALEXANDER I (1876–1903) m. Draga
King, 1889–1903   Mašin

The Karadjordjević Dynasty

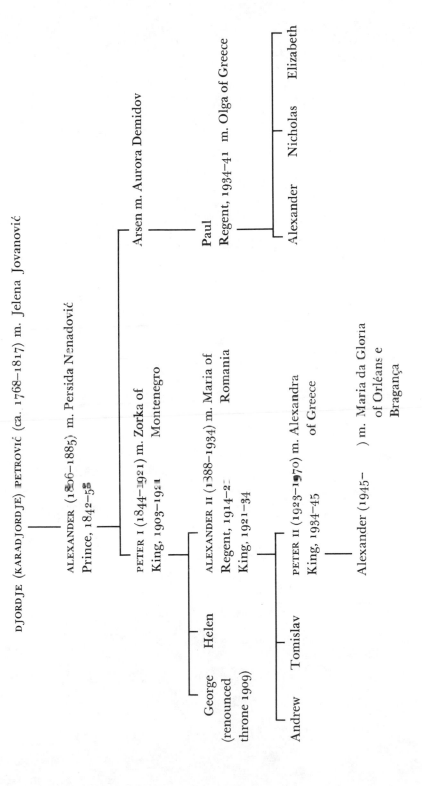

DJORDJE (KARADJORDJE) PETROVIĆ (ca. 1768–1817) m. Jelena Jovanović

ALEXANDER (1806–1885) m. Persida Nenadović
Prince, 1842–58

PETER I (1844–1921) m. Zorka of
King, 1903–1921   Montenegro

Arsen m. Aurora Demidov

Paul
Regent, 1934–41   m. Olga of Greece

Alexander   Nicholas   Elizabeth

George
(renounced
throne 1909)

Helen

ALEXANDER II (1888–1934) m. Maria of
Regent, 1914–21   Romania
King, 1921–34

Andrew

Tomislav

PETER II (1923–1970) m. Alexandra
King, 1934–45   of Greece

Alexander (1945–   ) m. Maria da Gloria
of Orléans e
Bragança

Names, Terms, and Dates

Except for certain accepted Anglicized forms—*Belgrade, Serbia,* rather than *Beograd, Srbija*—proper names have been rendered in their original language. Thus, for example, *Hercegovina* and not *Herzegovina,* which is neither Serbo-Croatian nor English. The author has chosen to omit English definite articles before place names; if one writes *the Vojvodina,* then one should also write *the Hercegovina,* and nobody does that even though both names mean "the duchy." Unlike Serbo-Croatian, the English language does not distinguish between *Srbi* (Serbs everywhere) and *Srbijanci* (the Serbs of Serbia); there are times when the distinction is an important one. The author was tempted to inaugurate a distinction between *Serb* and *Serbian* for this purpose but abandoned the idea, especially since the English adjectival form for both would still be the same *Serbian.*

Personal names have been rendered in their original form, with the exception of rulers and prelates with names of Biblical, Greek, or Roman origin with common Western forms. Thus Prince *Miloš* is called by his Serbian name, but his successor is called *Michael* rather than *Mihailo.* Metropolitan *Leontius* of Belgrade is not called *Leontije,* his Serbian name, particularly because he was not a Serb but a Greek. Metropolitan *Peter* is not called *Petar.* However, I balked at calling St. Sava, Serbia's greatest national saint, by his Greek monastic name of *Sabbas,* and at calling Djordje Petrović *Karageorge* rather than *Karadjordje.* Apparently my Serbian blood is thicker than ink or water. Many Turkish personal names have a title of rank or honor affixed to them—Paşa, Efendi, or Bey. In any alphabetical listing, such as the index of this book, these titles should not determine the place of the name.

Readers who accept French accent marks and German umlauts should not reject Serbo-Croatian or Turkish diacritic marks. There is a distinct advantage to using these signs since they permit both Serbo-

Croatian and Turkish to be phonetically regular; thus one should have a minimum of trouble in pronouncing them correctly if one learns the function of a few marks. Below is a pronunciation guide for both languages.

Serbo-Croatian

c = *ts* in *cats*
ć = between *t* in *tune* (*tyoon*) and *ch* in *church*
č = *ch* in *church*
dj = between *d* in *dew* (*dyoo*) and *j* in *John*
dž = *g* in *germ*
h = between *h* in *human* and *ch* in the German *Ich*
j = *y* in *you*
lj = *li* in *million*
nj = *ni* in *opinion*
š = *s* in *sure*
ž = *s* in *measure*

Turkish

c = *g* in *germ*
ç = *ch* in *church*
ğ = soft guttural g, like the *y* sound of *gh* in *eight*
ı = *i* in *sir*
j = *s* in *measure*
ö = German *ö*, or French *eu* as in *peu*
ş = *s* in *sure*
ü = *ü* in German *über*, or French *u* in *tu*
â = *a* in *bad*

Since Serbian is written in the Cyrillic alphabet, which is akin to the Russian, Ukrainian, or Bulgarian, Serbian names are written here in the Latin alphabet as used in writing Croatian, in accordance with the Library of Congress system. Russian and Bulgarian names in this work also conform to the Library of Congress system for those languages.

It is the custom of Yugoslav writers to render Turkish terms in their domesticated Serbo-Croatian forms: thus *dahija* for *dayı, spahija* for *sipahi,* and so on. I have rendered Ottoman terms in their original Turkish form. Since both Serbo-Croatian and Turkish plurals have a variety of forms, I have chosen to use the English *s* (or *es*) for the plural; thus *uskoks* rather than *uskoci,* and *timars* rather than *timarlar.*

In dealing with Serbian history, it is impossible to avoid the use of certain specific native and Ottoman terms. Many of these terms, especially those used more than once have been defined in a glossary for the reader's convenience.

Place names in southeastern Europe often have several forms, which reflect the ethnic complexities and political vagaries of the region. For example, the chief city of Yugoslav Macedonia is called *Skopje* by the Macedonian Slavs, *Skoplje* by the Serbs, and *Üsküb* by the

Turks. Western diplomatic historians have compounded the confusion by using their own forms, usually Germanic or Gallic, so that their readers could hardly guess that the treatics of Passarowitz, Sistova, and Jassy were concluded in Požarevac (Serbia), Svishtov (Bulgaria), and Iaşi (Romania). In general, I have used *Webster's Geographical Dictionary* whenever it suited my historical purposes, which was most of the time. Every effort has been made to preserve historical and ethnic integrity.

Unless otherwise stated, all dates in this work are according to our Gregorian calendar. However, as readers are aware, both the Serbs and the Ottoman Empire had calendars of their own, as did the French for a while in the period covered by this account. The Serbian state, like the Russian Empire, clung to the Julian calendar until the latter part of the second decade of the twentieth century. It took the Bolshevik Revolution of 1917 to accomplish this modernization in Russia. In Serbia the Gregorian calendar was adopted by a decree of January 23, 1919. The Serbian Orthodox Church still adheres to the old Julian calendar. The Gregorian calendar was introduced in Catholic Europe in 1582, at which time the calendar was advanced by nine days. In the eighteenth century the discrepancy between the Julian and Gregorian calendars amounted to eleven days, in the nineteenth century to twelve days, and in the twentieth century to thirteen days. Thus while Saint Sava, in the thirteenth century, celebrated Christmas on December 25, young Karadjordje celebrated it on January 5, and on January 6 as leader of the First Serbian Insurrection in 1804, while Serbs today celebrate Christmas on January 7 (New Style).

Though Muslims, the Ottoman Turks adopted the Julian calendar in 1677 A.D., or 1088 Anno Hegirae, but continued, like the Arabs, to number years since the Hegira (*Hijra*), Mohammed's migration from Mecca to Medina in 622 A.D.

It is no comfort to the historian who deals in dated documents that when it was March 24, 1804, for the Serbs, it was 24 Zilhicce 1182 for the Ottoman pasha of Belgrade, and April 5, 1804, for the Austrian General Simbschen on the other side of the Danube, not to speak of Napoleon's agents in the Balkans, for whom it was 15 Germinal XII according to the French revolutionary calendar! Readers who know that the "Great October Revolution" of 1917 in Russia really took place in November will not be surprised to learn that Serbia's "Constitution of 1888" was promulgated in 1889, or that when the Serbian press refers to "the events of May 29," it means the assassination of King Alexander Obrenović and Queen Draga on June 11, 1903. If all this seems terribly strange and complicated to American and British readers, as it well might, they should remember that Protestant Britain and the American Colonies did not change from the Julian to the Gregorian calendar until 1751, some 169 years after Pope Gregory proclaimed the new calendar, and that while George Washington's birthday is celebrated on February 22 (or on the nearest Monday, since 1971!), his birth certificate clearly records that he was born on February 11.

Occasionally it has seemed necessary in the present work to give both the Julian and the Gregorian dates—as in the case of dated documents or proclamations, or of events tied to church holidays such as the "Presentation Constitution" or the "St. Andrew Assembly." To distinguish Julian from Gregorian dates, the accepted abbreviations *O.S.* (Old Style) and *N.S.* (New Style) are used.

Serbia's Currency

Modern Serbia did not have a monetary system of its own until the establishment of the dinar in 1873. The most common currency was the Ottoman piaster, which the Serbians and other South Slavs called the *groš* (from the popular Turkish name *guruş* or *kuruş*, which is related to the Latin *grossus* and the German *Groschen*). It was divided into forty *paras*. However, the currency of other countries, notably of the Austrian Empire, also circulated in Serbia. At the time of the Austro-Turkish War of 1788–1791, the Ottoman piaster and the Austrian silver florin (or *forinta*, as the Serbs called it) were held to be of equal value. However, as Ottoman coinage suffered increasing debasement, the Serbians preferred the "imperial" (*cesarski*) money of the Habsburg Empire as well as the currency of Russia and other lands. Paper money of any origin was long a rarity in nineteenth-century Serbia, in good part because of an economically undeveloped society's distrust of anything so flimsy. Metal coins were not only more durable, but their gold or silver content gave them an intrinsic value.

By the time of Prince Miloš Obrenović, Serbia had in circulation as many as forty-three denominations of various origins—10 in gold coins, 28 in silver, and 5 in copper—each with its own name and value. To bring some order into this chaos, Miloš established in 1819 a formal exchange rate based on the *groš* as the unit. After Serbia gained its autonomy in 1829–1830, to protect the state income from the decreased value of the debased Ottoman piaster, Prince Miloš decreed in 1833 that in Serbia, especially for tax purposes, the *groš* would equal two piasters. This also became the regular commercial rate in Serbia, though Miloš insisted on paying tribute to the Ottoman Porte at the rate of 1:1, thus cutting Serbia's obligation to the sultan in half.

In Serbia the piaster or *groš* was based on the Austrian gold ducat, which was fixed in metallic content and had been generally stable in exchange value since the early nineteenth century. Before Miloš's decree of 1833, the value of the Ottoman piaster or *groš* relative to the Austrian gold ducat varied as follows:

Date	1 Austrian gold ducat =
1801–05	8 piasters
1809–11	10 piasters
1813–16	12 piasters
1817–19	14 piasters
1820	15 piasters
1826–33	24 piasters

After Miloš's decree, the value of the piaster or *groš* in Serbia in relation to the Austrian gold ducat, French franc, and American dollar was as follows:

Date	1 Austrian gold ducat =	1 Serbian groš in francs	1 Serbian groš in dollars
1833–54	48 piasters	.25	.05
1855–65	54 piasters	.22	.04½
1866–73	60 piasters	.20	.04

In 1868 Prince Michael forbade the importation of any foreign copper coins, especially since so many of these were damaged or were no longer in circulation in their country of origin. Instead, he had new copper coins minted, in Vienna, in denominations of 1, 5, and 10 tax *paras,* with his own likeness on the coins.

In 1873 Serbia followed the Greek and Romanian example and became a member of the Latin Monetary Union (founded in 1865 by France, Italy, Belgium, and Switzerland) after establishing a new national currency, the *dinar,* which was divided into 100 *paras.* From 1873 to the First World War, 1 dinar was equal to 1 French franc, or $0.193. Between 1878 and 1883, the Serbian government introduced gold, silver, and nickel coins; in 1885 the National Bank of Serbia issued paper notes, all of which drove various foreign denominations from general circulation.

Bibliography

The following list of books is intended for readers who wish to consult works in English and other major Western languages that deal with Serbian history. While much has been published in these languages on Serbian history, many works are now outdated and hard to find, and a large number of them were never meant to be scholarly. The following selection has generally given preference to works that are recent, accessible, scholarly, standard, or unique in their coverage. This is not to say that they are all of equal merit. Readers who desire a more complete listing of books, in both the Yugoslav and non-Yugoslav languages, may profitably consult the following bibliographies:

A. Bibliographies

Académie bulgare des sciences. *Bibliographie d'études balkaniques.* Sofia: Institut d'études balkaniques, 1966–.

Akademiia nauk SSSR, Institut slavianovedeniia. *Istoriia Iugoslavii.* Iu.V. Bromlei et al., editors. Moscow: Izdatel'stvo Akademii nauk SSSR, 1963. Vol. II, pp. 333–389.

American Historical Association. *A Guide to Historical Literature.* Edited by George Matthew Dutcher et al. New York: Peter Smith, 1949.

––––––. *The American Historical Association's Guide to Historical Literature.* Edited by George Frederick Howe et al. New York: Macmillan, 1961.

Djordjević, Dimitrije V. *Istoria tēs Servias 1800–1918.* Thessaloniki: Institute for Balkan Studies, 1970. Pp. 419–458.

Horecky, Paul L., editor. *Southeastern Europe: A Guide to Basic Publications.* Chicago and London: The University of Chicago Press, 1969. Part Six, Yugoslavia, Chapter 47, by Charles and Barbara Jelavich. Pp. 501–515.

Kerner, Robert Joseph. *Slavic Europe: A Selected Bibliography in the Western European Languages.* Cambridge, Mass.: Harvard University Press, 1918.

Petrovich, Michael B. *Yugoslavia: A Bibliographic Guide.* For the Slavic and Central European Division, Library of Congress. Washington: U.S. Government Printing Office, 1974. Especially pp. 25–40, "Serbian History."

Savadjian, Léon. *Bibliographie balkanique, 1920–1938.* Paris: Société générale d'imprimerie & d'édition [etc.] 1931–1939. 8 vols.

Stavriano, Leften S. *The Balkans since 1453.* New York: Rinehart. 1958. Bibliography, pp. 873–946.

Südost-Institut München. *Südosteuropa-Bibliographie.* Munich: R. Oldenbourg, 1945–

Savez društava istoričara Jugoslavije. *Historiographie yougoslave, 1955–1965.* Jorjo Tadić, editor. Belgrade: Fédération des Sociétés historiques de Yougoslavie, 1965.

Yugoslav National Committee for Historical Studies. *Ten Years of Yugoslav Historiography, 1945–1955.* Jorjo Tadić, editor. Belgrade: "Jugoslavija," 1955.

B. General Surveys

Akademiia nauk SSSR, Institut slavianovedeniia. *Istoriia Iugoslavii.* Edited by Iu.V. Bromlei and others. Moscow: Izdatel'stvo Akademii nauk SSSR, 1963. 2 vols. See especially vol. I.

Denis, Ernest. *La grande Serbie.* Paris: Delagrave, 1915. Also translated into Czech by Jindřich Vančurd, *Velké Srbsko.* Prague: Šolc and Šimáček, n.d.

Devas, Georges Y. [pseudonym for Djurdje Jelenić]. *La nouvelle Serbie; origines et bases sociales et politiques, renaissance de l'état et son développement historique, dynastie nationale et revendications libératrices.* Paris, 1918.

Djordjević, Dimitrije V. *Istoria tēs Servias 1800–1918.* Thessaloniki: Institute for Balkan Studies, 1970.

Haumant, Émile. *La formation de la Yougoslavie (XVe–XXe siècles).* Paris: Bossard, 1930. Institut d'études slaves de l'Université de Paris. Collection historique, 5.

Jireček, Konstantin. *Geschichte der Serben. Vol. I* (to 1371). Gotha, 1911. Vol. II (1371–1537). Gotha, 1918. Allgemeine staatengeschichte, 1.

Kállay, Béni. *Geschichte der Serben von den ältesten Zeiten bis 1815.* Translated from the Hungarian by J. H. Schwicker. Budapest, Vienna and Leipzig: W. Lauffer, 1878. The Hungarian original is *A szerbek története.* Budapest, 1877.

Kanitz, Feliz P. *Das Königreich Serbien und das Serbenvolk, von der Römerzeit bis zur Gegenwart.* Leipzig: B. Meyer, 1909–1914. 3 vols.

Lazarovich-Hrebelianovich, Stephan L. E., prince, and Eleanor Calhoun Lazarovich-Hrebelianovich. *The Servian People, Their Past Glory and Their Destiny.* New York: C. Scribner's Sons, 1910. 2 vols.

Mijatovics [Mijatović], Elodie Lawton. *The History of Modern Serbia.* London: W. Tweedie, 1872.

Pogodin, A. L. *Istoriia Serbii*. St. Petersburg, 1910.

Ranke, Leopold von. *Serbien und die Türkei im neunzehnten Jahrhundert*. Leipzig: Dunker & Humbolt, 1879. Sammtliche Werke, 2. The earlier editions (Hamburg, 1829, and Berlin, 1844) are entitled *Die serbische Revolution; aus serbischen Papieren und Mittheilungen*.

Temperley, Harold W. V. *History of Serbia*. London: G. Bell, 1917.

C. Special Studies in Modern Serbian History

Avakumović, I. "Literature on the First Serbian Insurrection (1804–1813)," *Journal of Central European Affairs*, XIII (October, 1953), 256–260.

Bilimek-Waissolm, H. von. *Der bulgarisch-serbische Krieg 1885*. Vienna, 1886.

Bogičević, Miloš, ed. *Die auswärtige Politik Serbiens, 1903–1914*. Berlin: Brückenverlag, 1928–1931. 3 vols.

Boppe, A. *Documents inédits sur les relations de la Serbie avec Napoléon I, 1807–1814*. Belgrade, 1888.

Bresnitz, P. F. *Die Geschichte Serbiens vom Jahre 1868 bis auf den heutigen Tag unter den Königen Milan und Alexander*. Berlin and Leipzig, 1895–1898. 3 vols.

Castellan, Georges. *La Serbie à l'époque du Prince Miloš*. Paris, 1966.

Castellan, Yvonne. *La culture serbe au seuil de l'indépendance 1800–1840*. Paris, 1967.

Cunibert, Barthélemy S. *Essai historique sur les révolutions et l'indépendance de la Serbie depuis 1804 jusqu'à 1850*. Leipzig: F. A. Brockhaus, 1855. 2 vols.

Dragnich, Alex N. *The Development of Parliamentary Government in Serbia, 1869–1889*. Berkeley: Unpublished dissertation, University of California, 1945.

———. *Serbia, Nikola Pašić and Yugoslavia*. New Brunswick, N.J.: Rutgers University Press, 1974.

Djordjević, Dimitrije. *Révolutions nationales des peuples balkaniques 1804–1914*. Belgrade: Institut d'histoire, 1965.

Djordjević, Vladan. *Das Ende der Obrenovitch; Beiträge zur Geschichte Serbiens, 1897–1900*. Leipzig: S. Hirzel, 1905.

———. [V. Georgévitch]. *La Serbie au congrès de Berlin*. Paris, 1891. Published the same year in *Revue d'histoire diplomatique*.

Feuerlicht, R. S. *The Desperate Act: The Assassination of Franz Ferdinand at Sarajevo*. New York: McGraw-Hill, 1968.

Gopčević, Spiridion. *Serbien und die Serben*. Leipzig: B. Elischer, 1888.

Hadrovics, László. *Le peuple serbe et son église sous la domination turque*. Paris: Presses universitaires de France, 1947.

Harding, Bertita. *Royal Purple: The Story of Alexander and Draga of Serbia.* Indianapolis: Bobbs-Merrill, 1935.

Helmreich, Ernest C. *The Diplomacy of the Balkan Wars, 1912–1913.* Cambridge, Mass.: Harvard University Press; London: H. Milford, Oxford University Press, 1938. Harvard Historical Studies, V.

Jakšić, Grgur [Grégoire Yakchitch]. *L'Europe et la résurrection de la Serbie (1804–1834).* Paris: Hachette, 1907.

Jelavich, Charles. *Tsarist Russia and Balkan Nationalism: Russian Influence in the Internal Affairs of Bulgaria and Serbia, 1879–1886.* Berkeley and Los Angeles: University of California Press, 1958.

Kállay, Béni [Benjamin von]. *Die Geschichte des serbischen Aufstandes, 1807–1810: Aus dem Handschriftennachlass herausgegeben von Ludwig von Thallóczy.* Translated from the Hungarian by Stephen Beigel. Vienna: A. Holzhausen, 1910.

Lascaris [Laskares], M. *Hellenes kai Serboi kata tous apeleutherikous ton agonas, 1804–1830.* Athens, 1936.

Lončarević, Dušan A. *Jugoslaviens Entstehung.* Zürich: Amalthea-Verlag, 1929.

MacKenzie, David. *The Serbs and Russian Pan-Slavism, 1875–1878.* Ithaca, N.Y.: Cornell University Press, 1967.

Markov, Walter M. *Serbien zwischen Österreich und Russland, 1897–1908.* Stuttgart: W. Kohlhammer, 1934.

Marković, Svetozar. *Izbrannye sochineniia.* Moscow: Gosudarstvennoe izdatel'stvo politicheskoi literatury, 1956.

McClellan, Woodford D. *Svetozar Marković and the Origins of Balkan Socialism.* Princeton, N.J.: Princeton University Press, 1964.

Mijatović, Čedomilj. *A Royal Tragedy: Being the Story of the Assassination of King Alexander and Queen Draga of Serbia.* London: E. Nash, 1906.

———. *The Memoirs of a Balkan Diplomatist.* London, 1917.

Morison, Walter A., translator. *The Revolt of the Serbs against the Turks (1804–1813): Translations from the Serbian National Ballads of the Period.* Cambridge: The University Press, 1942.

Mousset, Jean. *La Serbie et son église (1830–1904).* Paris: Droz, 1938.

Nenadović, Matija. *The Memoirs of Prota Matija Nenadović.* Edited and translated from the Serbian by Lovett F. Edwards. Oxford: Clarendon Press, 1969.

Nickels, S. *Assassination at Sarajevo: A Collection of Contemporary Documents.* London: Cape, 1966.

Ninčić, Momčilo [Momtchilo Nintchitch]. *La crise bosniaque (1908–1909) et les puissances européennes.* Paris: A. Costes, 1937. 2 vols.

Novaković, Stojan. *Die Wiedergeburt des serbischen staates (1804–1813).* Translated from the Serbian by G. Grassl. Sarajevo, 1912.

Pavlowitch, Stevan K. *Anglo-Russian Rivalry in Serbia, 1837–1839: The Mission of Colonel Hodges.* Paris: Mouton, 1961.

Paxton, R. V. *Russia and the First Serbian Revolution: A Diplomatic and Political Study. The Initial Phase, 1804–1807.* Stanford University, Unpublished dissertation.

Popov, Nil. *Rossiia i Serbiia. Istoricheskii ocherk russkogo pokrovitel'stva Serbii s 1806 po 1856 god.* Moscow: Izdatel'stvo K. Soldatenkova, 1869. 2 vols.

———. *Serbiia posle Parizhskogo mira. I. Sviato-Andreevskaia skupshchina (1858–1859).* Moscow: Tipografiia A. I. Mamontova, 1871.

———. *Vtorichnoe pravlenie Milosha Obrenovicha (1859–1860).* Moscow, 1880.

Pribram, A. F. *The Secret Treaties of Austria-Hungary 1879–1914.* Edited and translated by A. C. Coolidge and others from the German. Cambridge, Mass., 1920–1921. 2 vols.

Schmitt, Bernadotte E. *The Annexation of Bosnia, 1908–1909.* Cambridge, England: The University Press, 1937.

Sforza, Carlo. *Pachitch et l'union des Yougoslaves.* Paris: Gallimard, 1938.

Taillandier, René G. F. *La Serbie au XIXᵉ siècle: Kara-Georges et Miloch.* Paris, 1872. 2nd ed., Paris: Didier, 1875.

Tomasevich, Jozo. *Peasants, Politics, and Economic Change in Yugoslavia.* Stanford: Stanford University Press, 1955.

Übersberger, Hans. *Österreich zwischen Russland und Serbien. Zur südslawischen Frage und der Entstehung des ersten Weltkrieges.* Köln-Graz: Böhlau, 1958.

Vucinich, Wayne S. *Serbia between East and West: The Events of 1903–1908.* Stanford: Stanford University Press, 1954. Stanford University Publications. University Series. History, Economics, and Political Science, vol. 9. 2nd edition. New York: AMS Press, 1968.

Wendel, Herman. *Der Kampf der Südslawen um Freiheit und Einheit.* Frankfurt-am-Main: Frankfurther Societätsdruckerei, 1925.

West, Rebecca [pseudonym]. *Black Lamb and Grey Falcon: A Journey through Yugoslavia.* New York: Viking Press, 1941. 2 vols.

Wilson, Mrs. N. [Flora Ames]. *Belgrade, the White City of Death: Being the History of King Alexander and of Queen Draga.* London, 1903.

Glossary

(S-C. = Serbo-Croatian; T. = Turkish; Gr. = Greek)

ağa (T.) – Title of Ottoman military commanders; also a title of respect often added to the bearer's name.

alaybeyi (T.) – The head or marshal of the Ottoman landlords (*sipahis*) of a district (*sancak*).

archimandrite (from Gr.) – An Eastern Orthdox church dignitary ranking just below a bishop; usually the head of a monastery, like a Western abbot.

armatoloi (Gr.) – The plural of the Greek *armatolós,* member of a local body of armed guards used by the Ottoman Empire to protect border areas and mountain passes.

ban (S-C.) – Governor or viceroy, from which the name of the region in Vojvodina known as Banat.

bašknez (S-C.), *başknez* (T.) – Chief *knez* (*q.v.*), from the Turkish word *baş,* meaning head.

beg (S-C.) – Serbo-Croatian form of the Turkish *bey,* generally a title indicating nobility or rank; more specifically the commander of a district (*sancak*).

berat (T.) – An imperial decree, patent, warrant, usually a decree awarding a title, position, or land.

beylerbeyi (T.) – Supreme military commander and governor of an Ottoman province.

beylerbeylık (T.) – The Ottoman region governed by a *beylerbeyi* (*q.v.*).

bezirgânbaşı (T.) – The spokesman and leader of the merchants in a locale.

binbaşı (T.) – A camp commander in the Ottoman army, literally "the head of a thousand."

bölükbaşı (T.) – A Janissary commander of a company, usually of a hundred men.

buyrultu (T.) – An order or decree, usually appointing an Ottoman official.

čaršija (S-C.) – The Serbo-Croatian form of the Turkish word *çarşi,* meaning market; also refers to the merchant class in general.

četnik (S-C.) – The member of a guerrilla band or army troop (*četa*).

çiflik (T.) – An Ottoman feudal estate or farm.

çiftlik sahibi (T.) – The owner of a *çiftlik* or farm, a large landowner in the Ottoman system of land tenure.

cihad (T.) – From the Arabic, a holy war against non-Muslims.

cizye (T.) – Tribute, poll tax.

dayı (T.), *dahija* (S-C.) – Literally an uncle, hence also a title of respect or rank; more specifically a Janissary commander.

derhentci (T.) – The guard of a highway, especially at mountain passes or canyons.

despot (from G.) – Originally a ruler, master; in medieval times a feudal lord or magnate, and more recently an Orthodox bishop.

devşirme (T.) – Historically, the selection of Christian boys taken from their families to be trained as Janissaries; sometimes called the "blood tribute."

esnaf (T.) – In Serbo-Croatian the word *esnaf* is used in the singular to denote a guild or organization of artisans; the Turkish word *esnaf* is the plural of *sınıf*, meaning a class or category.

ferman (T.) – An edict or decree of the sultan.

gâvur (T.) – A non-Muslim, infidel; usually an uncomplimentary term.

guslar (S-C.) – the player of a *gusle* (q.v.), a bard, chanter of epic poetry.

gusle (S-C.) – A South Slavic folk musical instrument consisting of a strand or strands of horsehair played by a bow; among the Serbs used exclusively to accompany the chanting of epic poetry.

haci (T.), *hadži* (S-C.) – Among Muslims, one who has made the pilgrimage to Mecca; among Christians, one who has made the pilgrimage to the Holy Land. In both cases the title is affixed to the bearer's name.

hajduk (S-C.), *haydut* or *haydud* (T.) – The original Turkish meaning is brigand or highway robber. Among the South Slavs the terms assumed a complimentary meaning when used for outlaws who opposed the Ottoman system.

hancı (T.) – Turkish innkeeper and, in Serbia, thus a representative of the Ottoman presence in the Christian countryside.

haraç or *harac* (T.) – Tax, tribute, more specifically the poll tax paid by non-Muslims in the Ottoman Empire in lieu of military service.

harambaşı (T.) —The leader of an outlaw band.

hatti şerif (T.) – An edict of the sultan to his grand *vezir* (q.v.), or chief minister; hence a solemn decree with the force of a constitutional provision.

herceg (S-C.) – From the German *Herzog*, meaning duke; hence the name of the province Hercegovina, "the Duchy (of St. Sava)."

Janissaries (from T.) – See *Yeni çeri*.

kadı (T.) – A Muslim judge.

kadılık (T.) – The jurisdiction of a *kadı*, or Muslim judge, an Ottoman administrative unit comprising part of a *sancak* (q.v.).

katun (S-C.) – Originally a *Vlach* (*q.v.*) term for a mountain pasture region or village (*cf*. Romanian *câtun*, Albanian *katund*, or Swiss *canton*, all from the Latin); a territorial unit, a district.

kaymakan (T.) – The representative or deputy of an Ottoman governor (*vezir* or *vali*) in a given territorial unit or in the execution of a given function; a district chief.

kırcali (T.) – Armed mounted units of irregular Ottoman troops, often the unruly mercenaries of Ottoman lords who opposed the central government.

kırserdarı (T.) – Commander of irregular army troops in the Ottoman Empire, charged with guarding roads and suppressing banditry.

kmet (S-C.) – In Serbia, a village elder; sometimes also called *knez* (*q.v.*), but of a village.

knez (S-C.) – In medieval Serbia, a prince; in Ottoman Serbia, the peasant leader, usually by popular election or consent, of the Christians of a district known as the *knežina* (*q.v.*), whose chief duties were tax gathering and keeping the peace.

knežina (S-C.) – In Ottoman Serbia, a territorial unit comprising a group of Christian villages and having an assembly of village representatives.

kulluk (T.) – Literally slave labor; labor without pay exacted by the state for public projects, especially the building and maintenance of roads. *Cf*. the French *corvée*.

martoloz (T.) – Turkish form of the Greek *armatolós*, member of a local body of armed guards used by the Ottoman Empire to protect especially border areas and mountain passes.

metropolitan (from Gr.) – In the Eastern Orthodox Church, the chief bishop of an ecclesiastical province, ranking just below a patriarch. *Cf*. the Western archbishop.

millet (T.) – In the Ottoman Empire, a nation or a people united by a common religion and therefore given some measure of autonomy.

müsellim (T.) – In the Ottoman Empire, the chief executive of a district (*nahiye*).

nahiye (T.) – In the Ottoman Empire, an administrative unit, part of a *kadılık* (*q.v.*).

oborknez (S-C.) – In Serbia, the chief *knez* (*q.v.*) of a *knežina* (*q.v.*), from the German word *ober* ("over, above").

okka (T.) – An oke, an Ottoman measure of weight. A Turkish *okka* $= 400$ dirhems $= 2.8$ pounds $= 1.283$ kilograms.

okrug (S-C.) – In modern Serbia, the largest administrative subdivision, literally a circuit (*krug* = circle). The Serbian Constitution of 1888 divided the country into fifteen *okrugs*.

opština (S-C.) – Literally a commune (*opšte* = common); in modern Serbia, the lowest administrative unit.

pandur (S-C.) – Word borrowed from Hungary, from the Latin *banderium,* to denote the local militiaman or policeman in Serbia.

paşa (T.) – In its Anglicized form, pasha, the title of high Ottoman dignitaries, both civil and military. The title is affixed to the bearer's first name.

paşalık (T.) – The territory governed by a governor with the title of pasha.

patriarch (from Gr.) – In the Eastern Orthodox Church, the chief bishop of an autocephalous or independent church, such as the patriarchs of Constantinople, Antioch, Alexandria, Jerusalem, or some of the national churches, such as Russia, Serbia, etc.

prečani (S-C.) – The term used for Serbs outside of Serbia, especially those in the Austro-Hungarian lands across (*preko*) the Danube and Sava rivers.

predstavnik (S-C.) – Literally a representative; specifically, in mid-nineteenth-century Serbia, the prince's chief minister and especially foreign minister.

râya (T.) – Collective noun denoting subjects, particularly the non-Muslim subjects of the Ottoman Empire.

sancak (T.) – Administrative region in the Ottoman Empire, a subdivision of a *vilâyet* (*q.v.*); from the word for flag or standard.

sancakbeyi (T.) – The governor of a *sancak* (*q.v.*).

serhat, or *serhad* (T.) – A frontier, border zone or province.

sipahi (T.) – From the Persian word for soldier, originally a cavalry soldier in the Ottoman Empire; specifically the feudal owner of an estate granted for military service in the Ottoman cavalry.

skupština (S-C.) – An assembly.

soviet (Russian) – The Russian or Church Slavonic word for a council. This form was used in Serbia during the First Insurrection (1804–1813) for the Governing Council (*Pravitel'stvuiushchii Soviet*). The later Serbian form is *savet*.

srez (S-C.) – In the Principality and Kingdom of Serbia, a district or county consisting of a number of communes.

subaşı (T.) – A steward or overseer of an Ottoman estate; also a local police officer.

tımar (T.) – An Ottoman fief or feudal estate granted to a *sipahi* (*q.v.*) in exchange for military service and offering an annual income of up to 20,000 aspers.

Tsintsars (in Serbo-Croatian *Cincari*). – Aromanians or Vlachs (*q.v.*), originally —and in some places still—a Romance-speaking people in northern Greece, Albania, Yugoslavia and elsewhere in the Balkan Peninsula, associated with mountain regions and the herding of sheep. Some Aromanians were Hellenized and lived in cities, where they were known as enterprising merchants.

uskok (S-C.) – A Serbian or Croatian refugee from the Ottoman Empire, especially in the sixteenth and seventeenth centuries, who fled to Venetian Dalmatia or the Habsburg lands. The *uskoks* were used by Venice and Austria as irregulars, raiders, and even pirates, against the Turks.

vezir (T.) – The highest rank in Ottoman officialdom, usually a minister or governor of a province. The grand vezir was the sultan's chief minister.

vilâyet (T.) – The term for an Ottoman province, governed by a *vali,* or governor.

Vlach, or *vlach* (in Serbo-Croatian *Vlah*) – As an ethnic designation, applied to Romance-speaking groups in the Balkan Peninsula (note the name Walachia for a part of Romania), especially the Aromanians under their various names. In medieval Serbia the name became synonymous with shepherd. The Turkish word for Vlachs is *Eflakar.*

vojvoda (S-C.) – In medieval Serbia, Bosnia, and other South Slav lands, a duke; hence the name of the province of Vojvodina (Duchy). In modern times a military commander or, especially in Montenegro, a clan leader.

voynuk (T.) – Christian military retainers (from the South Slavic *vojnik* = soldier) in the Ottoman army who served special functions such as grooms.

yatağan (T.) – A heavy curved knife, used as a sword.

Yeni çeri (T.) – Janissaries; literally "new army," branch of the Ottoman military service founded in 1328 by Sultan Orhan and long consisting of Christian converts to Islam who were taken as boys from their parents. By the nineteenth century this corps had deteriorated and become unruly, and was finally abolished in 1826.

zadruga (S-C.) – Extended family group of as many as fifty or more members comprising a South Slavic household (from *za druga* = for one another) and an economic unit. More recently any cooperative organization.

zeamet (T.) – A large Ottoman fief or feudal estate granted to a *sipahi* (*q.v.*) in exchange for military service and offering an annual income of over 20,000 aspers; larger than a *timar* (*q.v.*).

župan (S-C.) – Historically, the head of a South Slavic medieval tribal state.

Index

Note: For large topics, readers are advised to consult the chapter subheadings in the Table of Contents for each volume. Specific terms may be found in the Glossary.